# MARTYRED BUT NOT TAMED

*Thank you for choosing a SAGE product! If you have any comment, observation or feedback, I would like to personally hear from you. Please write to me at* contactceo@sagepub.in

—Vivek Mehra, Managing Director and CEO,
SAGE Publications India Pvt Ltd, New Delhi

**Bulk Sales**

SAGE India offers special discounts for purchase of books in bulk. We also make available special imprints and excerpts from our books on demand.

For orders and enquiries, write to us at

*Marketing Department*
*SAGE Publications India Pvt Ltd*
*B1/I-1, Mohan Cooperative Industrial Area*
*Mathura Road, Post Bag 7*
*New Delhi 110044, India*
E-mail us at marketing@sagepub.in

*Get to know more about SAGE, be invited to SAGE events, get on our mailing list. Write today to* marketing@sagepub.in

This book is also available as an e-book.

# MARTYRED BUT NOT TAMED

*The Politics of Resistance
in the Middle East*

## RAM NARAYAN KUMAR

www.sagepublications.com
Los Angeles • London • New Delhi • Singapore • Washington DC

*First published in 2012 by*

**SAGE Publications India Pvt Ltd**
B1/I-1 Mohan Cooperative Industrial Area
Mathura Road, New Delhi 110 044, India
*www.sagepub.in*

**SAGE Publications Inc**
2455 Teller Road
Thousand Oaks, California 91320, USA

**SAGE Publications Ltd**
1 Oliver's Yard, 55 City Road
London EC1Y 1SP, United Kingdom

**SAGE Publications Asia-Pacific Pte Ltd**
33 Pekin Street
#02-01 Far East Square
Singapore 048763

Published by Vivek Mehra for SAGE Publications India Pvt Ltd, typeset in 10/13 Berkeley by Tantla Composition Pvt Ltd, Chandigarh, and printed at G.H. Prints Pvt. Ltd, New Delhi.

**Library of Congress Cataloging-in-Publication Data**
Kumar, Ram Narayan, 1956–2009
    Martyred but not tamed: the politics of resistance in the Middle East/Ram Narayan Kumar.
        p. cm.
    Includes bibliographical references and index.
        1.   Government, Resistance to—Middle East—Case studies.   2.   Nationalism—Middle East—Case studies.   I.   Title.

DS63.1.K845          956—dc23          2012          2012033763

**ISBN:** 978-81-321-0960-0 (PB)

**The SAGE Team:** Rudra Narayan, Pranab Jyoti Sarma, Nand Kumar Jha
and Dally Verghese

# Contents

Ram Narayan Kumar
1956–2009

# Acknowledgements

All thanks to Gerti, Ram Narayan Kumar's wife of 25 years, for taking care of our friend's posthumous papers and authorising the release of the present 'Middle East' volume, which is based on his last manuscript. But of course it is first and foremost as Ram's life companion, prop and comforter that Gerti deserves the lasting gratitude of all those who cherish Ram's memory. Ram, it is true, almost never complained, and few of us ever saw him outwardly despondent. Yet, given his life circumstances and the odds he was up against, he would not have been human had he not known moments of lassitude or despair. There is comfort, therefore, in the thought that when work-weary, doubt-plagued or tempest-tossed, Ram could always rely on ready counsel and assured support, all grounded in that unique quality of wifely affection which need not exclude judgmental distance (without an element of that, any human relationship becomes sapless) but where criticism always comes enfolded in love, suffused with it, lit up from the inside by it. All those who feel grateful that there walked a Ram in their midst, must by the same token be thankful that there stood a Gerti by his side, living out in full the betrothal vow of the ancient Romans: *ubi tu Gaius, ibi ego Gaia.*

Special thanks are also due to Ananya Roy. Though a daughter of Bengal, she spent the better part of her youth in Lebanon, which she came to regard almost as home. She showed Ram around in Beirut and Damascus, shared with him her intimate knowledge of the region, and supplied him with nearly all the contacts—so judiciously selected—whose interviews are recorded here. After Ram's sudden demise, her interest in the book project did not flag: I always found her responsive, generous with her time and encouragements, forthcoming with pertinent advice and gaffe-averting tips. So—*onek onek dhanyobad, Ananya Debi! Apnar prabase chira-shanti bajai thakuk, ebong manobadhikar bishoye Ramer Bharat-Arab jugmo prochesta sapholya mandito houk!*

Tapan Bose, he too a son of Bengal, deserves special mention for being one of Ram's earliest and closest associates (since the days of the Bhopal tragedy down to the SAFHR phase), and special credit for introducing Ram to what became one of his main fields of activity: Kashmir. Nor is Tapan a complete stranger to *Martyred but Not Tamed*. He contributed some inputs to an earlier monograph by Ram on the Iraq war, which remained unpublished but sections of which were lifted into the present book. *Tapon Babu, apni sustho hoye uthun ebong Kashmir o annyna jaigai apnar dirgha diner aklanta karma-jibon phala-prasu houk!*

Words cannot convey what Ram's brother Gopal and sister Sita meant to him, and he to them. Nor can words begin to do justice to his close guard of friends and collaborators, the ones who have stood by him through thick and thin, some of them since the darkest days of the 1975–77 Emergency: Satish Jain, Ashok Agrwaal, Jothilingam, Harsh Mander, Nitya Ramakrishnan, Priya Jain, Navsharan Singh—plus the countless others whom I never met nor heard of, but who I know are there, and who must forgive me for leaving them unmentioned. To them all: *Hamare mitr ki pavitr mahatvakankshaen, jo jivanparyant nirantar apurn rahin, maranottar saphalta ko prapt hon! Hamko vah sabhi prayas karne chahiye jisse unke dvara prajvalit jyoti prakashman rahe!*

Last not least: many well-deserved kudos to Gopal and Evelyn Ram for undertaking to search for a publisher; then persisting, insisting, pressing on, and eventually succeeding! And our heart-felt gratitude to SAGE India for taking up the wager of publication, and accepting to deliver the present book into the hands of its future judges—the Indian public.

Jean Ecalle

# Foreword

*We are not permitted to choose the frame of our destiny. But what we put into it is ours. He who wills adventure will experience it—according to the measure of his courage. He who wills sacrifice will be sacrificed—according to the measure of his purity of heart.*

—Dag Hammarskjöld, *Markings.*

*In our age, the road to holiness necessarily passes through the world of action.*

—Dag Hammarskjöld, as quoted by W. H. Auden.

## The Last Station

In the summer of 2007 the author of the present book, Ram Narayan Kumar, was able to realise a long-held, long-cherished project: to visit the Middle East, see things for himself, and listen to some of the actors at the heart of the intertwined dramas unfolding there.

He was fortunate in that he could rely on the guidance of a well-connected Indian academic, Mrs Ananya Roy, who was raised in Lebanon, speaks fluent Arabic, and indeed regards the region as home. She briefed Kumar on the devilish complexities of recent Middle East history, and introduced him to some of the key contacts he was to make during his two months there.

The immediate occasion for the trip was a conference on human rights that took place in Damascus in September 2007. But Syria was only an interlude, preceded and followed by two fruitful sojourns in Beirut. Nor were Kumar's contacts limited to Lebanese or Syrian nationals; they crucially included Iraqi politicians and academics, as well as veterans of the Palestinian struggle.

From the start, it was Kumar's intention to produce a report of some sort, though he may not have made it clear to all his interlocutors. In the event, the material harvested over this short period—field-notes, tape-recorded interviews—proved so rich that he decided to turn it into a full-fledged book. He knew only too well that by so doing he was inviting the charge of presumptuousness—after all, it takes some cheek to write and opine, no matter how self-effacedly, about the politics of a place where you have spent a bare couple of months, especially when the politics are as arcane as Lebanon's and the actors as proud. Yet he brushed the objection aside, so keen was he to correct the current perceptions that Indians have about the rights and wrongs in the Middle East conflicts. He also hoped that his book might lay the basis for joint Indo-Arab initiatives at volunteer level.

Actually, this talk of Kumar penning a book based on a one-off, two-month immersion in the Middle East is misleading. He had long been following events in the region, out of legitimate curiosity and also because he felt that the interests at stake and the forces clashing there, as well the competing narratives that are an integral part of the clash—this whole drumming-up of the terrorist threat and the 'war' against it—were highly relevant to the sort of struggles he had been engaged in, for the better part of his militant life, in his native India. Moreover, in the preceding year (2006), Kumar had done an impressive amount of background reading on the Middle East and devoted a full six months to investigating the Iraq war and its causes. He even wrote a book-length essay on the subject but eventually gave up trying to get it published because he felt that the piece smacked too much of a compilation and did not reflect enough first-hand knowledge.

After his 2007 Middle East summer, Kumar returned to the rough and tumble of human rights activism in India. This meant he had to struggle to snatch away enough moments of leisure to put his notes in order and start working on his manuscript. To make matters worse, his health began to give way. His once phenomenal stamina had already been undermined by years of hectic work, incessant travels, three jail terms and the nerve-racking, soul-wrenching stress of factional struggles. Then in the early months of 2009 his health took a sudden plunge. When in the spring of that year he returned to Austria, where his beloved wife, a practicing physician, has her livelihood, he was quickly diagnosed with a severe form of diabetes. Not one to spare himself, Kumar devoted his weeks in hospital to the manuscript. He even managed to complete a provisional draft, which he sent to a dozen or so acquaintances to elicit some feed-back. Then in mid-June he returned to Kathmandu, where SAFHR, the human rights organisation he was most closely associated with, has its headquarters. But no sooner had he landed there than he got again sucked into the all too familiar vortex of hectic work, tensions and deadlines. To cap everything, some of his earlier associations came back to haunt him, threatening blackmail, or worse. On 30 June 2009 he was found dead on the floor of his Kathmandu flat. To all appearances, he had been felled by a massive heart attack, at the age of 53.

This account would remain incomplete were I not to evoke the pall of gloom and dereliction that must have enveloped Kumar's last months. By itself, the diabetes diagnosis didn't carry an immediate death sentence, but it meant that his years, perhaps his days, were numbered. That at any rate is how he understood it. It meant therefore that a lifetime of toiling and struggling was about to end, not of course without some solid, tangible accomplishments, yet without results even remotely proportionate to the goals he had set himself or to the effort expended. To make the loss more poignant, Kumar was then about to conclude, together with the SAFHR team, a three-year programme about 'Impunity and accountability in India'—a programme which, maybe for the first time in his life, held the promise of a wide mobilisation, but which he clearly foresaw would founder, with him gone. Add to that the indifference or incomprehension of some of the companions that had been closest to him. In these last years and months *'he would get criticised for everything he did or didn't do'*. Even the tepid response to his last manuscript must have stung: of the scores of people who received a copy, only two read it and responded—one of them being Ananya, his *cicerone* in Beirut and Damascus. This about sums up the level of support that Kumar was receiving on the eve of leaving this world.

## The Flame Within

Although this is not the place to sketch Kumar's life,[1] the reader is entitled to some information about the sort of man he was and the inner fire that kept him going.

To say that he was *driven* would be to understate the case. Right from his adolescent years, without anyone prodding him, without ever looking back, without thought of risk, without rest, breaks or intermissions, he plunged headlong into grass-roots work, public campaigns, and defiance of authority—which over and over again put him in trouble's way, like during the 1975–77 state of Emergency when, barely 20, he was jailed and tortured.

Over the years his struggles would assume many forms, and take him through strange alleys and by-ways, but the one constant through it all was a raw sense of justice that knew no rest, and brooked no compromise.

This inevitably brought him into closer and closer contact with India's leftist and Marxist scene, but it is essential, especially when prefacing this last book of his, which is a foray into the Middle East imbroglio, to state as clearly as possible where he agreed with Marxism and where that agreement ended. Though Kumar was reluctant to discuss his metaphysics and we too, sensing his priorities, refrained from querying him on these matters, that much is certain: he didn't share the philosophical premises of Marxism.

For one thing, 'conscience' to him was neither derivative nor peripheral, but the exact opposite: primary and central. It was the one compass through life's moral dilemmas, never to be abdicated before, or superseded by, supposedly 'objective laws' of history. He held that such abdication of the autonomous moral imperative was responsible for the deviations, too recurrent to be accidental and too serious to be forgivable, that the Marxist project—ostensibly a project for justice—underwent whenever and wherever it was 'realised'.

Another essential point where Kumar parted ways with Marxism was in his attitude towards the great myths or Utopias (of whatever hue: religious–millenarian, national–revivalist, secular–revolutionary, etc.) that inspire men to great collective endeavours. While acknowledging their 'illusoriness' in an ultimate sense, he would add that these illusions (and the need for them) are so deep-rooted as to be structurally inseparable from life. They are almost on a par with our own self-perception as separate egos. Like hope, they spring eternal, in some form or other, and like hope, they are the vector of history's great leaps forward. The issue with them, therefore, is not their illusoriness, which is a given,[2] but their *quality* as life-shaping forces, which varies from case to case and demands a discerning approach. In one word, Kumar tended to look on these thought or faith systems like a benign Buddhist would, not like a contemptuous Marxist. We often forget that when it comes to consequent negation or the systematic unmasking of illusion, Marxists (and we moderns in general) are truly wimps and weaklings compared with Vedantists or Buddhists. Nor do Marxists realise that with the narrow focus of their critique and their undiscerning, metaphysically immature animus against 'superstructures', they upset life's essential equilibria. All these points must be borne in mind if we are to appreciate Kumar's attitude (puzzling at first sight, in its combination of aloofness and silent sympathy) towards those of his Arab interlocutors that profess adherence to the Shia world view.

So much for the side of Kumar that was untouched by Marxism. Now to the part of him that was shaped and coloured by it. Right from the start, as a human rights worker and participant in scores of mass campaigns (beginning with the Right-to-Work campaign of his youth and the agitation on behalf of the coal-miners of Jharkhand) Kumar would find, time and again, that the most eager, sincere, committed helpers and co-workers came from the communist rank and file or from members or ex-members of sundry revolutionary movements. His lifelong friend and collaborator Tapan Bose, who drew him into the Bhopal campaign and later introduced him to Kashmir, was originally close to Naxalism. Psychologically, this comradeship in arms and all these years of shared struggle inevitably rubbed off on Kumar.

There is yet another sense in which Kumar became indebted to Marxism. As a student of society and wide-ranging reader, he came to appreciate Marxist methodology, the habit, which is second nature to nearly all Marxist authors, of sober, painstaking socio-economic analysis, and their wholesome (if often crude and one-sided) way of exposing the economic interests that underpin so much of collective life but hide under deceptive disguises. Kumar's masterly second chapter ('The Discovery of Oil and the Geography of Imperial Conquest') shows him putting his Marxist schooling to impressive use. Conversely, while broadly appreciative of such Middle East specialists as Robert Fisk, Kumar would lament their fixation on the colourful or the anecdotal at the expense of the socio-economic aspects.

But basically, Kumar, for all his analytical acumen, grasp of facts and attention to current events, was not in the business of describing, much less of predicting, but in that of *willing* and *acting*. And whereas his thinking was nuanced, his acting seldom was. Or rather, it betrayed none of the half-heartedness and hesitancy which tend to plague those who delight in the endless ambiguities of life to eternally postpone the moment of commitment. When facing conflictual situations (and given that he assiduously sought them out, that was his default mode) Kumar's typical approach was to take stock carefully; weigh both sides dispassionately; and come down, wholly and passionately, on *one* side. He would then re-calibrate his whole discourse accordingly. A re-appraisal might take place somewhere down the road if he saw reasons for it, but it would usually be fairly abrupt as well.

There are of course huge problems with this philosophy of action, especially for the temperamental ditherers, the sticklers with formal consistency, or the hankerers after the balanced, all-round picture. But one thing at least must be said in its favour: *it is true to life*. What is indeed the 'definitive, balanced, all-round truth' about a historical sequence (say, the 1857 'Mutiny') or a historical figure (say, J. Nehru or Churchill) other than a lifeless, ghost-like construct—something that may elude even an archive rat or defeat a biographer of Nehru/Churchill after decades of painstaking research? Even if we assume the ideal existence of this objective, integral, summative truth, we are driven to the strange conclusion that this 'truth' is never *operative,* at any moment or in the least degree, for the simple reason that none of those who ever met, followed or fought Nehru or Churchill ever had this ethereal object in front of their mind's eye. What they saw instead, and responded to, was one of the many facets of the man, which existed in an unstable superposition and successively manifested in the course of his career. This is not to imply, mind you, that all these facets had equal weight or significance. This is simply to say that it is the singular facets, at least the dominant ones, that really matter, not their futile and near unachievable 'averaging'.

Kumar approached the Middle East conflict(s) in exactly this spirit. His looking was patient and attentive, but once he had done with looking, his choosing was decisive and incisive—it was a *cutting through*. As a result the present book, which at first sight may seem a perceptive yet biased account, is in fact something rather different: it is the fruit of Kumar's attempt to find the *truest* of the many warring viewpoints; to place himself right at its centre; and then to describe how things appear and feel when viewed from that centre.

## Why the Middle East?

Way back in July 2009, on the day after Kumar's cremation ceremony, while on the bus that was taking us to the *samyag* where the ash scattering was to take place, I heard one of our company snap: *'What business did Kumar have to involve himself with the Middle East mess—a conflict raging half a world away, of no concern to him or his work!'*
What business indeed did he have?

The short answer is that Kumar, as already mentioned, wanted to pave the way for joint Arab–Indian initiatives. On the home front, in India, he hoped to correct a number of entrenched misperceptions. He also wanted to counteract the current Indo-Israeli rapprochement—in diplomacy, intelligence sharing, military co-operation,[3] also in the co-ordination of propaganda drives and anti-terror discourse.

Kumar also had a long history of working in defence of India's Moslems—in Kashmir with Tapan Bose[4] and Ashok Agrwaal,[5] and in Gujarat with Harsh Mander.[6] Given the fact of transnational Moslem solidarity and fellow-feeling, which has its mirror image in a transnational suspicion of them, it was but a natural step for Kumar to zero in on the area where the clash is at its most intractable—i.e., the Middle East.

But the deeper reason was the pivotal nature of the battles that are being joined there. By temperament and 'avocation'—or let us say, in the light of what he regarded to be his mission in life—Kumar was an enemy of stasis and inertia. He was always scanning the horizon for causes that combine

1. clear injustices crying for redress
2. a sufficient potential for militancy
3. a measure of 'exemplariness', i.e., the promise, however faint, that victory, if and when it comes, will take society one notch higher, bring a qualitative betterment in the fabric of human life, rather than effecting a simple change-of-shift among the oppressors and exploiters

Kumar felt that the Middle East conflict had a textbook quality in that respect. It pits a slowly but steadily declining West against an aspiring, re-awakening Levantine culture heavy with unclear potentialities and still groping its way towards the future. There is also the third actor, Israel, which is but the latest shape of an enigma that flickers down the ages, as stubborn in its defiance of decipherment as in its refusal to go away. That said, the present book has many layers, and its vital parts may not be those that meet the eye.

The first thesis of the book is that by going down the road it has chosen, Israel can only bring further degradation upon itself and visit more misery on the region. It merely articulates a prime truth that is dazzlingly obvious to practically every earthling—apart from the brain-washed variety that inhabits the USA and the guilt-ridden sort that lives in Europe.

The second thesis is that the West is bound to receive its comeuppance for two centuries of greedy, cynical interference in the destinies of the defenceless. Either it will have to disengage from Moslem lands or slowly haemorrhage. There is hardly any need to press the point. Abroad as indeed at home, the West seems headed for relative decline, maybe slow and undramatic, but impossible to avert. You can almost feel its power go.

The third thesis or hope implicit in the book is that the people of the Levant, as indeed the wider Arab circle and the still wider Moslem world, are bound sooner or later to regain their rightful place. This would be but the local manifestation of a trend that we can see at work worldwide. All the great culture areas that had fallen behind over the last few centuries are in the process of regaining a position roughly equivalent to their natural *weight,* as measured by their past historic achievements and contributions to civilisation. The Arab world may still be lagging behind but its re-awakening can only be a matter of time. In that sense, it would seem that some form of Arab renaissance is definitely on the cards: it is as good as *maktoub.*

But the real concern at the heart of this book, the hub round which it entirely revolves, is neither a diagnosis nor a set of cheap predictions but a genuine interrogation, the answer to which is entirely open: will the momentous changes in the making be *worth it?*

This is the *real* question, the one that pulsates through nearly all the dialogues and in turn generates a host of sub-questions, such as: How thorough is the soul- searching currently underway among Arabs? How are they going to negotiate the tough choices between reform and tradition? How can Arabs keep battling their external enemies—a clear duty, but one that diverts a disproportionate share of their energies into aggression—while cultivating, on the domestic front, the virtues of tolerance and mutual accommodation which their fractured societies so badly need? Will the Islamic societies permit the emergence of a sufficient secular space in civilian life? Which of the competing interpretations of the much-vaunted *Guardianship-of-the-Jurist* doctrine is going to prevail among Shias? Will it be that of ayatollah Khomeini of Iran or that, almost diametrically opposed, of the recently deceased ayatollah Fadlallah of Lebanon?

## About the Present Shape of the Book

When death overtook Kumar, he was still planning to devote one or two months to his manuscript. After his funeral, all his associates concurred on the need to complete the book and release it in the form and medium most likely to ensure a decent circulation. Since I had already co-authored a few things with Kumar in the past and was familiar with his way of thinking, and since I happened to share many of his views on the Middle East question (which we had frequently discussed), I gladly accepted overall responsibility for seeing the manuscript through to publication.

The pivotal Chapter 2 (on 'Oil') practically stood in finished form but the other parts had been written in haste and required some editing. The main difficulties, however, were these:

First, Kumar had intended his book to serve, not primarily as a testimony, but rather as a catalyst for joint Arab–Indian programmes and initiatives. As a consequence, he didn't face his Arab interlocutors as a cold-eyed reporter, but addressed them almost as one addresses future friends, with all the restraint and consideration that the hoped-for relationship implies.[7] With Kumar gone, the perspective alas stood reversed, and it was the book's value as testimony that took precedence. This called for a slight shift in perspective, the addition of short critical footnotes,[8] some end-of-chapter comments, and a few updates.

Second, Kumar had been planning to append a carefully crafted afterword, to confer unity and direction on what was, in essence, a kaleidoscope of often divergent opinions and *pro domo* pleadings. In the absence of any written notes left by him, I had to rely on my recollections of our numerous exchanges, or (as sparingly as possible) second-guess what he might have said, or again (even more sparingly) supply a few comments of my own. Throughout, I tried to keep the two strands separate.

One last caveat: whereas the end-of-chapter notes strive to give a fair hearing to the competing viewpoints and to reflect the many-sidedness of things, the afterword had to be ruthlessly *ekagra*, i.e., one-pointed and unwavering in its focus on the essential.

As a matter of authorial decency, the most sensitive interview transcripts—or should we say, *interview elaborations*—were submitted, as e-files and in paper form, to the interviewees. Their reactions, I regret to say, were sometimes disappointing. Some disowned their contribution and demanded not to be identified by name, which of course we respected. Others vouchsafed no answer, despite repeated reminders. Altogether, this inconclusive back-and-forth added to the delays.

By now, our readers should be clear under what adverse circumstances, and impelled by what sense of urgency, Kumar wrote the present book, which became his parting message. They should therefore show leniency for its various inaccuracies or shortcomings, to which this editor may unwittingly have contributed his share. *Fecimus quod potuimus; feciant meliora potentes.*

**Jean Ecalle**
Orsay, France
17 July 2010

## Notes

1. For that, we refer to his mid-life autobiography *Confronting the Hindu Sphinx*, Ajanta Publ., New Delhi, 1991.
2. Their illusoriness, if truth be told, has little in common with what 'illusion' suggests in common parlance. He who wishes to reason sanely on these matters should avoid the crude binary *illusory/real* and argue in terms of *degrees* of illusoriness. By that token, the systems in question are among the most solid forces that shape history.

3. Just one example from many: Mossad agents are passing on their expertise in the dark arts of counter-insurgency, most specifically in the tecnique of *targeted assassinations,* to the Indian paramilitary forces battling various Naxalite insurrections, especially in the Gond tribal territory. See the Afterword, also Arundhati Roy's recent piece in *Outlook.*

4. Director of SAFHR (South Asian Forum for Human Rights).

5. An advocate specialising in human rights litigation. Author of *In search of Vanished Blood,* which documents cases of death in, or disappearance from, custody.

6. A social activist, writer, and noted Gandhian. Has been working for communal harmony, notably in Gujarat after the 2002 riots.

7. He may have committed a few *faux pas,* though. As was his wont, Kumar didn't shy away from recording the spontaneous reactions of his interlocutors—their hesitations, nervousness, fidgetiness, even their occasional bursts of irritation or anger. In a culture as face conscious as that of the Arabs, such portrayal is considered very bad form and can easily cause great offence. We hope it won't, because it was entirely well-meant on Kumar's part: dismissal of formality was his way of signalling sympathy, even spiritual intimacy.

8. Wherever the distinction matters, Kumar's footnotes are marked *A.N. (Author's Note)* whereas ours end with *E.N. (Editor's Note).*

# 1

# Imagining war:
# Anticipations and outcomes

*I shall give a propagandist reason for starting the war—never mind whether it is plausible or not. The victor will not be asked afterward whether he told the truth or not. In starting and waging a war it is not right that matters, but victory.*
— Adolf Hitler, 22 August 1939[1]

*This is the world's fight. This is civilisation's fight. This is the fight of all who believe in progress and pluralism, tolerance and freedom.*
— President George W. Bush, 20 September 2001, in an address to a joint session of Congress and to the nation

'*A*re you a Shia?' I asked, turning to one of my four Arab interlocutors. The man, a young Iraqi professor I had met in Beirut in the second week of September 2007, was teaching international humanitarian law at Kufa University in Iraq. He was also a member of the Iraqi Council of Representatives.[2] The five of us were sitting in a stylish coffee shop in the western, predominantly Sunni part of the city, chatting over thick, sweet Arabic coffee and drawing from an apple-flavoured *nargileh*.[3] In the background, the large television screen was transmitting an interview with Nabih Berri, the Shia Speaker of the Lebanese Parliament. He was discussing the political stalemate that had followed the re-election of

President Émile Lahoud, a Maronite Christian considered close to Syria. It was a highly contentious issue that had precipitated the assassination of several high-profile, pro-Western politicians, including former Prime Minister Rafiq Hariri. This latter murder, commonly blamed on the Syrian secret service, was now under investigation by a UN-backed international tribunal. The interview was deflecting the attention of my interlocutors, but I was patient. It was *ramadan*. We had met at 8 p.m., after the ritual breaking of the fast, and my interlocutors were a bit tired and languid after finishing their first evening meal. The meeting had been arranged, at my request, by a professor of international law at the Lebanese American University.

The professor was a sympathiser of Hizbullah, the armed resistance group and Lebanon's ascendant political force. His friends, it seemed, had come to Beirut for professional and political counsel. Sitting there in the coffee shop were two Iraqis, one Jordanian teacher from Amman, the Lebanese professor, and myself. Clearly, Beirut, despite its sectarian divisions, the frequency of lethal blasts, and the threat of Israeli aerial bombings (those of July and August 1986 had set a record for savagery), was an open and welcoming place, where the beleaguered members of sundry Arab resistance movements, including those of occupied Iraq and Palestine, liked to relax and recoup their energies. Not for nothing was tiny Lebanon known as the kaleidoscope of the Middle East.

The Iraqi professor from Najaf—let me call him Ahmed—seemed a bit uneasy with my question.

*Yes, I am indeed a Shia. But I wonder why you should ask. When the Western media and Middle East pundits talk about the rise of Shia influence in Iraq, it is mostly as a subtext for their reprobation of Iran and Hizbullah. They seldom see this Shia resurgence as the harbinger of a democratic future for Iraq, which Western meddling, since World War I, has done its best to thwart. You see, the Shia, despite being the majority population in Iraq, have throughout history also been among the most disadvantaged. These Shia of Iraq, traditionally at the receiving end of injustice, discrimination and persecution, are now trying to undo the inequities of history, and that too despite the current war. I wished you would realise this.*

Ahmed had a rather sombre mien. He was taking long, bubbly pulls at his **nargileh**, churning up the smoke-filtering water at the base. I wondered if I had been tactless in raising this question so early in our conversation. We were after all in Lebanon where the rise of Shia power in the form of Hizbullah was the clearest, if unintended, outcome of past Israeli aggression.

The brutal invasion of Lebanon, launched by Israel in 1982, had one avowed purpose: to decapitate the Palestinian guerrilla movement that had been operating from Lebanese soil since the early 1970s. The main outcome of the invasion and subsequent occupation, however, was the birth of Hizbullah. With support from Iran and Syria, it has since become the main torch-bearer of Arab resistance to Israel's hegemonic designs. But then wars, especially wars of choice, have a way of confounding the calculations of those who launch them.

Professor Ahmed, after pulling and puffing his aromatic smoke for what seemed to me an inordinately long time, gradually assumed a more benign countenance and, at last, responded to my questioning gaze.

*The United States launched its war on Iraq after trumpeting this ficti-tious threat of weapons of mass destruction, when the real motives were strategic and economic. The intention was to set up a friendly regime there, with help from sectarian forces if necessary, as had been done in the other oil-rich countries of the region. Everyone, including the Americans, knew that it was not a war for democracy or nation building. Nor was it about ending corruption or the tyranny of Saddam Hussein. Everyone knew that America and its European allies never had serious problems with authoritarianism, religious fanaticism and corruption as long as the regimes concerned accommodated US and Israeli interests. Everyone knew that with the world's second largest oil reserves and a population of just over 25 million people, mastery over Iraq could enable the United States to achieve overall control over the oil resources, or at least to lessen its uncomfortable dependence on Saudi Arabia. It was common knowledge that the reconstruction effort in Iraq, after the colossal destruction of the 1991 war and the decade-long sanctions, would be paid for from repatri-ated Iraqi funds and oil revenues, rather than from international aid, let alone compensations or reparations. Many American analysts and po-litical pundits have themselves suggested that the neo-conservative cabal ensconced in the White House had colluded with Israel in pushing for war. Israel of course had its own reasons for wishing Iraq invaded and Saddam toppled.*[4]

*In my view, the war was fought not only to secure Israel but also to establish a US friendly regime in the heart of the Middle East, thus countering Syrian and Iranian intransigence. The primary aim was to obtain a long-term alternative to Saudi Arabian oil. But let me not tax you with my theories on the whys of the American war at this stage. The simple fact is that it was not a war driven by altruism, or concern for the welfare and human rights of Iraqis. Nor was it a war to secure the world against terrorism or weapons of mass destruction. It was founded on lies and justified by lies—plain, threadbare, preposterous lies. But then, this has always been the hallmark of Western interference in our region. When the British went about carving out Iraq and recasting the map of the Levant in the 1920s, they would talk endlessly about the principles of self-determination, the need to end 'corrupt Oriental despotism' and to promote democratic development. All along, their true motives were military dominance, strategic control, and the grabbing of petroleum resources. But let us talk about the legacies of past imperialist wars a bit later. The point I wish to make here is that the war has not gone the way the US and its allies had imagined and planned for. The war, contrary to all calculations, has become a catalyst for the mobilisation of the dispossessed and the deprived, in Iraq and beyond. For aught we know, it may one day be remembered as an epochal turning point—the start of a new era of popular resistance, of a new militancy that may ultimately become the nemesis of Western imperialist hubris.*

I felt confused. That the military interventions in Afghanistan and now in Iraq—the former ostensibly reactive, the latter allegedly pre-emptive—in reality sprang from a murky mix of fear and self-interest, cleverly exploited by the neo-conservatives, and couched in the language of national security, was clear enough. That these types of ventures were ultimately doomed to failure could also be taken for granted. Their immorality aside, history, especially colonial history, suggests that those who unleash unilateral aggression soon enough find themselves unable to manage the resulting chaos. Brute military force may topple a regime, it may lay waste a country, but the notion that it may radically transform a nation's internal political conditions, not to speak of its civic ethos—that notion has about it a touch of the insane. Such aggression can only lead to a cycle of random slaughter, all-consuming devastation, and enduring agony for all involved—without even the few redeeming features that issue-driven, fate-deciding civil wars may possess. In the present instance, the results are plain for all to see. Iraq and Afghanistan are now writhing in such an agony of violence, chaos and moral anarchy that the interventionists have not only had to renounce their earlier posture about instilling clean governance, respect for human rights, etc., but have even found themselves compelled to collaborate with the very forces they had previously identified as 'evil' and had vowed to remove.[5]

Today, the leaders in Kabul are entering into parleys with some of the deposed leaders of the Taliban. The catchphrase is no longer eradication, but 'give and take'! Likewise, the US-led coalition in Iraq is seeking allies among Ba'athist elements and Sunni fundamentalists, the better to counter 'Iran's meddling' in the country's affairs, even if that means arresting the evolution towards democratic rule and kissing goodbye to the prior promises of ending tyranny and restoring freedom. But try as they may, one thing is clear: these clumsy attempts at a partial return to the *status quo ante* won't avail. Beyond that, it is really hard to visualise what may eventually emerge from this state of violence and anarchy. Maybe the aggressors will tire in the end and withdraw unilaterally. As for their being brought to account, that possibility simply does not exist for the simple reason that in this unipolar world order of ours the aggressor countries control all the international mechanisms of law enforcement.

To be sure, the American establishment is aware of the seething anger that its war crimes evoke in the Arab world. But it does not seem to care. In the aftermath of the 1991 Gulf War, Martin Indyk, then Executive Director of the Washington Institute for Near East Policy, told the US House of Representatives, 'What matters is not whether they hate us or love us—for the most part, they hate us. They did before. But whether they are going to respect our power.'

This being the position, how and on what basis can we talk about the 'coming retribution' or 'fantasise about the "nemesis of imperialist hegemony"'?

Take Iraq. The popular resistance against occupation has already become mired in sectarian violence, with the Sunni and Shia at each others' throats. The Shia, despite constituting between 60 to 65 per cent of the population, have long remained excluded from the political power structure. Naturally enough, they are seeking democratic power. Just as naturally, the Sunni diehards of Iraq, the leaders of most Arab countries, and of course the United States, all wish to block them for fear that Iran would gain undue influence in the Middle East. Thus, Iraq has been slowly sliding down the road of sectarian strife and civil war, and the turmoil threatens to engulf the neighbouring countries, perhaps even the entire region.

Professor Ahmed's Iraqi companion—let me call him Mohammed Ghazi—who had so far been following the conversation with silent attention, now gulped down his cup of coffee, cleared his throat, and asked if I was acquainted with the political context and pre-history of the Shia effervescence in Iraq. That was too good an opportunity—I requested him for an exposé.

*The Shia of the Arab world have for long been the underdogs. Perhaps only 15 per cent of Muslims worldwide, the Shia constitute a majority in only four countries of the Middle East: Iran, Iraq, Lebanon and Bahrain. Only 13 per cent of the population in Syria is Shia. But the Ba'ath Party, the party in power in Syria, has been fairly secular, especially since the 1970 takeover by Hafiz al-Assad, an Alawi Shia. It has been more respectful of the rights of the minorities, including a number of Christian denominations, than most Arab countries in the region. Once known as Greater Syria, the east Mediterranean area, which Europeans used to call 'the Levant', emerged from Ottoman rule after Turkey's defeat in World War I. Then, following a 1920 decision by the League of Nations, it came either under British or French mandate.*

*T. E. Lawrence and Gertrude Bell are the two most celebrated and romanticised figures among the British covert agents active in Arabia before and during the war. After graduating from Oxford with a thesis on the influence of crusaders on the medieval architecture in Palestine, Lawrence joined the British army as a map officer in Cairo in 1914. After the outbreak of the war, Lawrence first worked with Colonel Leachman as an intelligence analyst, then as a field operative with a mission to incite Arab chiefs against the Ottoman Empire. Gertrude Bell, a female mole and fixer with high connections in the British Empire, was to assist him in his historical task. She shared Lawrence's Oxford background and interest in Mesopotamian history. She travelled to India to persuade the British Viceroy to put up money and men to shore up the Arab uprising. Lawrence and Bell typified that class of glamorous, state-sponsored nomads who combined an essential allegiance to the British Empire with a fascination for the never-ending, oblivion-giving deserts and their visual complement, the nomadic Arabs.*

*The complex empathy which they brought to their work (and writings) put an ennobling varnish on their main activities: the harvesting of political intelligence and carrying out of covert actions. This helped the British to spread a camouflage of mystique over their calculations of cold self-interest.*

*Lawrence and Bell, who together were to conceive the future kingdom of Iraq, with its boundaries and its king, had no patience with the Shia. They loathed their doleful religious practices, were wary of their seditious political tempers, and held them responsible for the frequent uprisings in the region. True, the Shias were the numerical majority in Iraq, but what of that! The friends of Lawrence and Bell were all Sunni, and Sunnis were to become the country's rulers and keep the Shia down. The British partnership with the Sunni minority was also motivated by tactical considerations. It was convenient to have a minority government in Baghdad—should that government ever try to assert its independence, popular opposition could be stirred up at short notice to make it see reason. The Shia Arabs, for their part, never accepted the notion of British mandate. Ayatollah Mohammed Taqi Shirazi, from his seat in Karbala, actually issued a fatwa (a religious proclamation having force of law to the faithful) which de-legitimised the foreign rule. The declaration came with a call to jihad. The ensuing uprising was eventually put down, but military reinforcements had to be called in from South Asia, and the costs were high—2000 British Indian causalities. No count was made of the Shia Muslims killed. To the imperialist mind, they were not worth a count.*

*Eventually the British left, but their example had set the standards for the successor regimes. There was a brief intermission in Sunni minority rule after 1958 when Brigadier Abdul-Karim Qassem, incensed by the brazenly pro-American policies of Prime Minister Nouri al-Said (an erstwhile officer of Ottoman Turkey whom Lawrence had recruited during World War I), staged a successful coup. Qassem had the last of the Hashemite kings, Faisal II, killed, and went on to rule Iraq for a brief five years, until he lost power in February 1963 after yet another coup, organised by the Ba'ath Party. Abdul Salam Aref led the new Ba'ath government and appointed Ahmed Hassan al-Bakr, Saddam Hussein's cousin, as prime minister. Saddam Hussein himself, armed with lists of communist party members and sympathisers, mostly Shia, supervised their arrest, torture and execution under the direction of the CIA. This was later confirmed by King Hussein of Jordan in the course of an interview he gave to Mohammed Heykal, the celebrated editor of Cairo's Al-Ahram newspaper.*[6] *In July 1968, Ahmed Hassan al-Bakr deposed Aref in a bloodless coup and appointed his cousin Saddam Hussein as Vice-President of Iraq. The new government signed an agreement with the Shah of Iran, brokered by US Secretary of State Henry Kissinger, which temporarily resolved Iraq's long-standing border dispute with Iran. The contentious area was in the South, where the waterways of the Tigris and Euphrates rivers meet to form the Shatt-al-Arab delta, before flowing into the Persian Gulf. The US-inspired pact, signed in 1975 and known as Algiers Agreement, recognised 'the median line of the main navigable channel' as the boundary between Iraq and Iran. It conferred equal access and equal share of the waterways to both sides.*

*Al-Bakr's eleven years in government came to a sudden and mysterious end in July 1979. Citing health problems, Al-Bakr announced his decision to step down from the presidency and handed over the reins of government to Saddam Hussein. The facts behind the transfer of power remain unknown. But it is widely acknowledged that Saddam Hussein's road to power opened after he returned from his Cairo exile, following Qassem's assassination in February 1963, with his CIA-supplied lists of Iraqi communist activists and went on to supervise their liquidation. Saddam Hussein then took over the Ba'ath Party's internal security agency, the Jihaz al-Haneen, and used that key position to become the central figure of authority throughout Ahmed Hassan al-Bakr's years as President. Saddam Hussein was only 42 years old when he in his turn became President, with all the main attributions of power merged in his office: besides being President of the Republic, he was also Chairman of the Revolutionary Command Council, Secretary-General of the Ba'ath Party, Prime Minister and Commander-in-Chief of the Armed Forces. He also took the title of Field Marshal. The purges that followed, the totalitarian State model he imposed, his systematic reliance on family loyalists, also his history of CIA connections going back to the days of his Cairo exile—all these aspects are well-known and well-documented, and we needn't dwell on them. What bears repeating, however, is that Saddam Hussein, like Iraq's earlier tyrant rulers, was merciless in his suppression of Shia aspirations. A Shia political party, the Dawa Islamiya, established under the auspices of Ayatollah Mohsen Hakim, the pre-eminent Najaf cleric, had already been banned before Saddam Hussein assumed absolute power. Now, it so happened that Ruhollah Khomeini, the Iranian ayatollah and fierce Shah opponent, had also sought refuge in Najaf in 1964 and had been operating from there ever since. Under pressure from the United States, Saddam had him expelled in 1978. Two years later, Saddam ordered the execution of Ayatollah Mohammed Baqir al-Sadr, a widely respected scholar and former associate of Khomeini.*

*Saddam Hussein's rise to absolute power in Iraq, coinciding as it did with the Islamic Revolution in Iran, suited the United States just right, because of Saddam's known hostility towards Ayatollah Khomeini. A distinct change in the American attitude to Iraq soon became noticeable. Thus, in September 1980, Zbigniew Brzezinski, National Security Advisor to President Jimmy Carter, declared: 'We see no fundamental incompatibility of interests between the United States and Iraq... We do not feel that American–Iraqi relations need to remain frozen in antagonism.'[7] The United States, enraged against Ayatollah Khomeini and reeling under the humiliation of the capture of its Tehran Embassy, the detention of its entire staff, and its incapacity to free them, prodded Saddam Hussein to abrogate the 1975 Algiers Agreement with Iran and to launch against the neighbour state what was to become a decade-long war, that cost the two countries one million human lives and about \$1 trillion in expenses.*

*The war finally ended in 1988, under a UN-sponsored ceasefire. Iraq also had to borrow approximately \$500 billion from Saudi Arabia, Kuwait and the United Arab Emirates. The Americans had their work cut out for them: Khomeini's call for an Islamic Revolution in all Arab countries, and Iran's renewed (if tentative) support for Kurdish Iraqi separatists made it easy for the US to fan the flames of hatred and incite hostilities between the two countries. Thus, coaxed by the United States, Kuwait and Saudi Arabia, Saddam became the Arab shield against the threat of a region-wide Islamic revolution.*

*In 1982, Iraq was removed from the American list of state-sponsors of terrorism. This cleared the way for the Western arms industry to supply military hardware and support systems to Iraq. Over the years, the US Department of Commerce approved export consignments to Iraq, worth millions of dollars, from its official arms suppliers and a variety of other agencies. The consignments included agents of biological and chemical warfare, although both the US and Iraq had signed the 1972 Biological and Toxin Weapons Convention (BTWC) that prohibited their use. The Convention had been in force since 1975 and the US administration possessed detailed knowledge of Iraq's use of chemical weapons against Iranian* *troops and later against Kurdish insurgents. Under US wheedling, Iraq also received lethal weaponry from America's strategic partners across the globe. The money for the purchases was loaned mainly by Kuwait and Saudi Arabia. By the time of the 1988 ceasefire, Iraq had come under a staggering debt of $100 billion.*

*In March 1984, the United States established full diplomatic relations with Iraq. Donald Rumsfeld visited Baghdad as President Reagan's emissary, just after the United Nations had formally released a report about Iraq's use of chemical weapons. The White House wedged in to stop a Congressional initiative that sought to impose sanctions on the Iraqi regime, brazenly citing its strategic and commercial interests. Later on, shortly after the Iraqi air force had used chemical weapons to put down the Kurdish uprising at the village of Halabja in March 1988, killing upwards of 5,000 civilians, the American navy directly attacked Iranian vessels threatening Iraq. As a former officer of the US Defense Intelligence Agency later clarified, 'The use of gas on the battlefield by the Iraqis was not a matter of deep strategic concern to us'.*

*The Congressional investigations into the Iran-Contra affair have since established that the US involvement in that long, merciless war was a thoroughly cynical business. It followed a strategic decision by the White House to feed the war until both Iran and Iraq had physically and psychologically exhausted themselves. It is now known that while formally supporting Iraq, the United States secretly facilitated the sale of weapons to the Iranian government, especially between August 1985 and 1986. The Congressional investigations proved that President Reagan had instructed the CIA to carry out these arms sales with utmost secrecy, hiding all operations even from the US Congress. The Congress was notified only in November 1986, after a Lebanese newspaper let the cat out of the bag by publicising the undercover sales.*

I interrupted Mohammed Ghazi to ask why America's retaliation to Saddam Hussein's invasion of Kuwait was so ferocious, if Saddam had all along been a creation and tool of US interests, as he was implying. The following is a summary of his long and detailed answer.[8]

*First of all, you should bear in mind that by the time the Iran–Iraq war ended, the United States was globally on the ascendancy. Not only were Iran and Iraq completely exhausted, but the Soviet Union, too, had conceded defeat in Afghanistan—it had signed a UN-sponsored accord in April 1988 under which it agreed to withdraw all its troops before the end of February 1989. Arguably, the Geneva Accord (1988) on Afghanistan can be seen as the beginning of the end for the Soviet Union, which eventually dissolved in December 1991. Within months of signing the Geneva Accord, in December 1988, Mikhail Gorbachev addressed the United Nations' General Assembly: not only did he announce that the Soviet Union would henceforth renounce class war as the basis of its foreign policy, but also that it was to unilaterally withdraw its troops from Eastern Europe. Soon after George Bush became the 41st US President in January 1989, the Soviet Union withdrew its troops from Czechoslovakia. In April 1989, the Soviet forces left Hungary, which opened its borders with Austria. Lithuania, Estonia and Latvia became sovereign over the next months. In Poland, the Solidarity movement swept the elections in June 1989. That same month, Gorbachev went to West Germany to announce that the Berlin Wall 'was not eternal'. He also told the Warsaw Pact countries that they were free to choose their own roads to socialism or democracy. In September, East Germans began to flee to capitalist Europe across Hungary, while Gorbachev advised Erich Honecker to go in for reforms. Then, on 9 November 1989, the Berlin Wall was torn down. By the time George Bush and Mikhail Gorbachev met in Malta on 2 December 1989, it was clear that a new era of American ascendancy, fraught with unpredictable possibilities, had begun.*

*After the war with Iran, Saddam Hussein had to shift focus to Iraq's internal problems. The long war had nullified the significant economic achievements of the 1970s. Iraq's agriculture, dependent on fresh water supplies from Iran and Turkey, was in the doldrums. Turkey took advantage of Iraq's weakness to frequently interrupt the southward flow of the Euphrates, ostensibly to fill up a massive reservoir behind the newly completed Ataturk Dam. Turkey had also gained considerable leverage from Iraq's compulsion to route much of its oil exports northward through Anatolia. As for Iraq's relations with Iran, they were irreparably damaged. Even Iraq's southern Arab neighbours—Kuwait, Saudi Arabia and the United Arab Emirates—countries that had used Iraq as a shield against the threat of Iranian expansion, quickly turned their backs. Its industry devastated, Iraq had to face skyrocketing imports. With the war over, it also needed to demobilise its mammoth military. For the hundreds of thousands who were dismissed from the armed forces, there were few openings in the job market, because a large number of women had joined the industrial* workforce during the war years. Iraq was also under pressure to repay the huge debts it had accumulated. On top of that, the lowering of oil prices, due to overproduction by Kuwait and other Gulf countries, had diminished the country's internal revenues. The OPEC-set price of $18 a barrel had fallen to $14. This meant a huge loss. Kuwait was also stealing Iraqi oil by drilling sideways across the border.

Outwardly, the United States still behaved as if it was keen to uphold its friendship with Iraq. The US National Security Directive, issued on 26 October 1989, stated that 'normal relations between the United States and Iraq would serve our longer-term interests and promote stability in both the Gulf and the Middle East'. Saddam Hussein himself reciprocated by indicating his readiness to end the long era of socialist economy. On 4 June 1989, he even hosted a large meeting of business representatives from big corporations like Amoco, Mobile, Westinghouse, Occidental, Bell Textron, General Motors, and Xerox. Alan Stoga, a senior associate of Henry Kissinger's New York-based consulting firm, personally met with Saddam Hussein to discuss Iraq's options for rescheduling the national debt.

Saddam Hussein had every reason to be worried about the colossal debts and other financial liabilities that his country had accumulated. Some 500,000 Iraqi soldiers had died and the country was under a debt of $100 billion, the main creditors being Saudi Arabia, Kuwait and the United Arab Emirates. Saddam Hussein wanted these countries to show gratitude for Iraq's sacrifices, by waiving their loans and contributing to the reconstruction of Iraq's economy. That wasn't to be. Kuwait, in particular, behaved with aggressive surliness. Not content with pressing Iraq to repay its debts, Kuwait openly flouted the OPEC-set limits on oil production, driving oil prices down to the detriment of Iraq's fiscal balance. Overall, sustained overproduction by Kuwait and the United Arab Emirates was costing Iraq billions of dollars a year in lost revenue. In addition, as already pointed out, Kuwait was stealing oil from Iraq's Rumaila oil fields, just across the border, with the help of US-supplied slant drilling technology.

At first, Saddam Hussein tried to resolve his differences with Kuwait diplomatically, using the good offices of such countries as Egypt and Jordan. But Kuwait retorted arrogantly, flatly refusing to negotiate. Jordan's King Hussein didn't conceal his astonishment over Kuwaiti intransigence. To a visiting American journalist, he confided: 'He [Saddam Hussein] told me how anxious he was to ensure that the situation be resolved as soon as *possible. So, he initiated contacts with the Kuwaitis... this didn't work from the beginning. There were meetings but nothing happened [....] To my way of thinking, this was really puzzling. It was in the Kuwaitis' interest to solve the problem. I know how there wasn't a definite border, how there was a feeling that Kuwait was part of Iraq.'[9] Why then was Kuwait behaving in such a puzzling way?* Milton Viorst, America's Middle East expert, quoted a prominent Kuwaiti businessman as saying, 'I think that if the Americans had not been pushing in this direction, the royal family would never have taken the steps it took to provoke Saddam.' Kuwaiti Foreign Minister Sheikh Salem al-Sabah himself told Viorst that General Schwarzkopf regularly visited him to discuss military cooperation, and that Kuwait was confident of US support.[10] General H. Norman Schwarzkopf, the Supreme Commander of the US troops during the Gulf war, had been the 1st Battalion commander of the American Infantry Division in Vietnam—the very Division whose units earned infamy in the My Lai slaughter. He was also the son of Norman Schwarzkopf Senior who, together with the CIA and Britain's MI6, had worked to depose the Iranian government of Prime Minister Mohammed Mossadeq and to bring the Shah back from exile in 1951.

On 3 May 1990, Saddam Hussein told an Arab summit in Baghdad, 'We have reached a point where we can no longer withstand pressure.' Saddam Hussein tried to gauge the American position, but received mixed signals. On 12 April 1990, he met with five American senators in Baghdad. They were Robert Dole, Alan Simpson, Howard Mezerbaum, James McClure and Frank Murkowski. Ambassador April Glaspie was also present. Upon returning, the senators praised Saddam as a man of strength and intelligence.

Saddam Hussein was still hoping that Kuwait would step down from its high horse and negotiate a reasonable settlement. He persuaded King Hussein of Jordan and King Fahd of Saudi Arabia to convene a summit at Jeddah on 31 July 1990. The Sheikh of Kuwait did not attend but sent his Prime Minister with instructions to be 'unwavering', adding 'we are stronger than they think'. A day before the Jeddah meeting, Al-Sabah told King Hussein of Jordan, 'If they don't like it, let them occupy our territory [...] we are going to bring in the Americans.'

Before the Jeddah summit, Iraqi troops had already taken positions across the Kuwait border. On 24 July 1990 the US State Department spokesperson Margaret Tutwiler publicly announced that the United States did not have 'any defence treaties with Kuwait and there [were] no special defence or security commitments to Kuwait'. *Saddam Hussein, keen to understand the American position, met with Ambassador April Glaspie on 25 July 1990 and asked for a clarification. Saddam Hussein told her, 'I assure you, had the Iranians overrun the region, the American troops would not have stopped them, except by the use of nuclear weapons [....] Yours is a society which cannot accept 10,000 dead in one battle. You well know that if Iran agreed to the ceasefire, it wasn't because the United States bombed one of their oil platforms after the liberation of the Fao. So I ask: Is this Iraq's reward for its role in securing the stability of the region and for protecting it from an unknown flood? Is it reasonable to ask our people to bleed rivers of blood for eight years and then tell them, "Now you have to accept aggression from Kuwait, the United Arab Emirates, the US, or Israel [...]". We do not place America among the enemies. We place it where we want our friends to be and we try to be friends.'*[11]

In her reply, US Ambassador Glaspie told Saddam Hussein: *'I admire your extraordinary efforts to rebuild your country. I know you need funds. We understand that, and our opinion is that you should have the opportunity to rebuild your country. But we have no opinion on Arab–Arab conflicts like your border disagreement with Kuwait [....] James Baker [Secretary of State] has directed our official spokesmen to emphasise this instruction.'* She was merely reiterating the policy that had been communicated to her through a cable from the State Department a day before the meeting.[12] It has also been suggested that the reason why strong warnings were not issued to Saddam Hussein was that Egypt, Saudi Arabia and Kuwait maintained that Iraq was only bluffing to extort concessions, and also that the United States was so busy re-defining its relations with the Soviet Union that it had little attention left for trifling matters.[13] Whether intentionally or not, the fact remains that Saddam was misled. Richard Murphy,[14] for one, spoke admiringly of his statesmanship.

On the other hand, it is certainly true that the United States was busy managing the momentous changes that were taking place in Europe, and rejoicing over the melting away of the Soviet Union. Since the beginning of the year, Secretary of State James Baker had been urging Moscow to accept his plan for German reunification and NATO membership, which occurred in the middle of July 1990. Lithuania declared its independence in March of that year and Latvia followed suit in May. In June, the Russian parliament under Yeltsin abrogated the laws of the USSR, and declared the *formation of a Russian Republic. Then, in July, Ukraine and Belarus became independent. As a matter of fact, on the very day that Iraq invaded Kuwait, i.e., on 2 August 1990, James Baker was in Moscow to discuss Russia's new economic policies and, together with his Russian counterpart Shevardnadze, he issued a joint statement condemning the invasion.*

*The disintegration process came to a head one year later, in August 1991, after an abortive coup by Soviet hardliners to depose Gorbachev. The USSR effectively collapsed over the next month, with Central Asia seeing the birth of five new independent republics in quick succession: Turkmenistan, Armenia, Tajikistan, Kazakhstan and Kyrgyzstan. The formal dissolution came in December 1991, with the Soviet Union officially breaking up into fifteen successor states.*

*Things were not as advanced in that summer 1990, when the Kuwait crisis erupted, but there was no mistaking the trends. The sweeping transformations in the making, especially the inevitable emergence of a cluster of Central Asian republics in the Caspian after the foreseeable breakup of the USSR, called for a strategic rethinking of American policies in the Middle East—that 'debatable middle strip'. Under Soviet rule, these Republics had suffered 70 years of suppression, and at times outright oppression. Their populations are either Persian or Turkish speaking. They have their own historical memories and nostalgia, revolving around places like Samarkand and Bukhara, which were centres of power when Islam was in its heyday and Russia was groaning under Tatar rule. With such linguistic, cultural, and historical legacy, these Central Asian republics carried the potential of complicating the political equations in the region. This forced the United States to keep a watchful eye on developments there.*

*There was also an uncanny similarity between the economic potential and political problems of the new Central Asian republics and those of the Middle East countries. All of them possessed non-renewable petrochemical resources. A 1921 Treaty between Iran and the Soviet Union referred to the inland Caspian Sea as belonging to Russia and Persia. So Iran might press its legally recognised claim to demand a common strategy for the development and sharing of the Caspian Sea resources.[15] All these issues required careful tactical thinking on the part of the US, and the development of a military power base in the region, should the new republics attempt to link up with some of the more restive Middle East countries to assert their economic clout, and form an anti-Western, anti-Northern front. Such considerations may explain why the United States abandoned its initial support for a Russian proposal to convene a Middle East conference for a peaceful resolution of Iraq's invasion of Kuwait and a reactivation of the Arab–Israeli peace process. The end of the Warsaw Pact had the immediate consequence of freeing the American forces stationed in Europe for military operations in the Gulf. The end of the Cold War also made it tempting for the United States to test the limits of Russian cooperation in resolving a conundrum like Iraq's occupation of Kuwait. Russia had no choice but to pass the loyalty test, although it should be noted that its foreign minister Shevardnadze resigned soon after the UN Security Council adopted its Resolution 678 on Kuwait, authorising 'all necessary measures'.*

It is possible that the American ambassador in Baghdad was not thinking of the larger scenario when she talked with Saddam Hussein on 25 July 1990 and that he misinterpreted her polite and nuanced statements as America's 'green signal' for him to deal militarily with Kuwait. However that may be, Saddam Hussein cannot be accused of lying about his plans. When the US ambassador specifically asked what he hoped to achieve at the impending Jeddah meeting (on 31 July), Saddam said candidly that the outcome of the Kuwaiti–Iraqi meeting about the border dispute and the level of oil production would be decisive. He said: 'If upon meeting we see that there is hope, then nothing will happen. But if we are unable to find a solution, then it will be natural that Iraq will not accept death.' In the event, the Jeddah meeting ended in acrimony, with Sheikh Saad al-Sabah, the Kuwaiti crown prince, and Izzat Ibrahim, Iraq's second-in-command, trading insults. The die was cast, and Kuwait's invasion followed.

The military invasion of Kuwait, a sovereign state and UN member, created a situation in which the United States could swiftly mobilise the Security Council and form a worldwide coalition against Iraq. In November 1990, the US got the UN Security Council Resolution 678 passed, which authorised the use of 'all necessary means' to end the occupation of Kuwait. The Secretary of State James Baker told the Iraqi Foreign Minister Tariq Aziz that unless his country unconditionally withdrew its troops from Kuwait, the United States would not only destroy its regime but also render Iraq 'weak and backward'.

Saddam, with unimpeachable logic, offered to withdraw from Kuwait if Israel too could be pressured to withdraw from the occupied Palestinian territories. The United States reacted with the sort of theatrical outrage that *betrays a guilty conscience. All subsequent diplomatic efforts by the USSR, Europe and various Arab countries to get Iraq to withdraw from Kuwait were finally scotched when President George Bush Sr took the inflexible position that there would be 'no negotiations, no compromises, no attempts at face saving, and no rewards for aggression'.*

I interrupted Mohammed Ghazi's masterly narrative to ask why on earth the United States should have risked a protracted conflict, with unpredictable consequences for the region, if all it cared for was a smooth flow of oil. Saddam Hussein, who had been an American protégé, surely would have ensured that.

It was now the turn of the professor at the Lebanese American University, the facilitator of this meeting, who had so far been riveted to the television interview with Nabih Berri, to intervene. Let me refer to him as Professor Hassan Jerardi. He turned out to be as proficient with the world of oil as he was versed in international law and politics.

*President Bush Senior's uncompromising attitude, his unswerving resolve to punish Iraq, were less foolhardy than may appear at first sight. The decision was backed by the clear knowledge that the coming war, even if protracted, would not result in a cessation of oil supplies to the West. The years of OPEC* (Organization of Petroleum Exporting Countries) *power, the cartel's capacity to dictate oil prices (as it did during the oil embargo of the 1970s to bolster the Arab position after the October 1973 Arab–Israeli war) were long gone. To overcome this humiliating vulnerability, Western oil companies had been prospecting hard for new oil sources outside the Middle East. Huge reserves had already been discovered in the Gulf of Mexico, also in the North Sea at a depth of 10,000 feet under the sea-bed, and were becoming accessible thanks to recent advances in the technology of offshore drilling. Inland, an estimated 10 billion barrels of recoverable reserves had been discovered in Alaska. These findings had the potential of altering the global politics of oil. The discoveries themselves predated the 1973 embargo, which merely gave a new impetus to their development. Technological impediments were overcome, ecological concerns overridden. By 1980, the Mexican offshore production had crossed the mark of 2 million barrels a day. By the mid-1980s, an 800 mile-long, cross-tundra pipeline, leading all the way from the Alaskan North Slope to the port of Valdez, was in full operation, carrying 2.2 million barrels a day. The long and the short of it is that in the early 1990s, even as Iraq was developing its case against Kuwait, the Western world was feeling quite comfortable with its oil situation. The United States had upwards of a trillion barrels in strategic oil reserves, and could use them to flood the market in case of a shortage. In the event, these reserves were never used during the Gulf war. Oil prices did go up when the war began, as a mercurial market reaction, but almost immediately fell back to their normal level. Saddam Hussein and his advisors had forgotten that the vast oil reserves within the former Soviet Union were now freely available to the markets in Western Europe and North America.*

Professor Hassan Jerardi paused to take a few sips of coffee and a long pull at his *nargileh*, raising a cloud of fragrant smoke. But his knowing smile suggested that he had not concluded yet. Everyone waited expectantly for him to pick up the thread, which he soon did.

*There is something Yasser Arafat once said, something very significant, which I wish to mention. People outside the Arab world either paid no attention to that remark he made, or dismissed it as casual rhetoric. Arafat declared that Israel was the chief inciter behind America's [first] Iraq war. To understand the significance of Arafat's point, one must recall the vigour of Hizbullah's resistance to the Israeli occupation of south Lebanon and the morale-boosting impact Hizbullah's example was having on Hamas and the Palestinian resistance, in their own fight against Israeli occupation and rampant settlement policy, in Gaza and the West Bank. Hamas had taken the lead in organising the Intifada, the popular Palestinian uprising that began in December 1987, even as tens of thousands of Jewish immigrants from the former USSR were flowing into occupied Palestine. Many of these immigrants chose to settle, or rather were encouraged to settle, in the West Bank. Hamas (an acronym for 'Islamic Resistance Movement') was born as a Palestinian offshoot of the Muslim Brotherhood. Like Hizbullah, it values in its members purity of intent and conduct, religious devotion, and willingness for self-sacrifice as preconditions for the liberation of Palestine. It should also be borne in mind that at that stage, Hamas was largely identified with the Intifada movement—with all these TV visuals being beamed to the world, of unarmed Palestinian men, women and children defying Israeli tanks and pelting stones on heavily armed soldiers. Let me point out that Hamas, then, had not yet adopted its 'martyrdom missions', or 'suicide bombings' as the West prefers to call them. Hamas espoused this method only after Baruch Goldstein, an American-Jewish settler in the West*

*Bank, killed 29 Muslims during a prayer meeting at the Ibrahimi Mosque on February 1994.*[16] *It is also important to recall that in Lebanon itself the Taif Agreement, brokered by Saudi Arabia in 1989 to end the civil war, was being increasingly contested.*[17] *General Michel Aoun, the army chief of staff during the presidency of Amin Gemayel, who was widely regarded as an Israeli nominee, had spurned the Taif Agreement and was trying to set himself up as the head of a parallel government. René Moawad, the first elected President under the Taif Agreement and a Maronite Christian, had only just been assassinated in a massive explosion which had torn his armoured car to shreds. General Aoun was the suspected mastermind. He was, at the time, against Syria, so he turned to Iraq for support, which Saddam Hussein willingly extended. Israel for its part feared Iraq and its military capabilities. Hizbullah was already taking a heavy toll on Israeli occupiers in south Lebanon. By invading Kuwait, Saddam was setting a worrisome precedent from Israel's point of view. He was showing his contempt for the skewed political mapping of the Middle East, which had been arbitrarily drawn under foreign rule. Now, when it comes to mappings and borders, those of Israel are a permanent eyesore to all Arabs. If therefore Saddam Hussein was left off the hook after his Kuwait poker, he could become the Arabs' hero and spearhead a new campaign against Israel. It is in this context that we must read Arafat's statement about 'Israel being the first inciter of the American war in Iraq'. Israel wanted the entrenchment of the US army to in the region. The United States, of course, wasn't oblivious of its own long term interests, strategic and economic. Saudi Arabia, too, was in a state of panic and granted the American forces permission to station on its land—the holy land of Mecca and Medina—little thinking of the consequences which this act of folly might engender.*

The discussion was getting really stimulating, and opened unexpected vistas. But I was returning, in thought, to the Shias of Iraq, and the mixed feelings they must have harboured at the time. Given the history of tyranny, persecution, violence and never-ending wars which all Iraqis, but none more so than the Shias, had endured under Saddam Hussein, shouldn't they have welcomed the foreign intervention—never mind who led it—as a once-in-a-lifetime chance of getting rid of a hated regime? Shouldn't they have seized the chance to rise in revolt? That would have spared them the punitive sanctions which were to wreck their lives for 12 interminable years. Why did none of this happen? My questions must have sounded very stupid: Jerardi gawked at me with wide eyes, the corners of his lips curved in contempt, as I waited for a response. He then turned toward the television set, either in embarrassment or perhaps because Nabih Berri was making an interesting point. Mohammed Ghazi, who had been looking at me more kindly, began to explain, with as much patience as he could muster:

You must understand that the American game plan ruled out any democratic regime change. As Professor Jerardi explained, the United States wanted to restore Kuwait to the Al-Sabah family; militarily defang Iraq, so that it could no longer stand up to Israel; and force Saddam to fall in line with the main American demands, especially regarding oil politics. The United States and its allies knew that a truly democratic Iraq would immediately baulk at the foreign yoke and try to shake it off. They knew too that it would never reconcile itself to Israeli hegemony. Only corrupt, autocratic rulers can do that. Then you must remember that Kuwait, just like Iraq, had been intolerant and oppressive towards its Shia population, arresting and torturing members of the Dawa Party. As for the house of Saud, which combines political and military dependence on America with Wahhabi fundamentalism at home, it is a politically decadent and morally depraved establishment. Kuwait spent $30 billion to underwrite the Gulf War in 1991 alone, and has since been buying American F-15XP fighter jets and British Tornadoes worth billions and billions, without even possessing qualified pilots to fly them. Or think of this: in October 1990, the Israeli police killed 19 Palestinian demonstrators, who were taking part in a non-violent Intifada protest outside Jerusalem's Al-Aqsa mosque, the third holiest Muslim shrine after Mecca and Medina. Well, despite seeing all this, and understanding full well that the Israeli occupation of Palestine crucially depended on US collusion, Saudi Arabia, home to Mecca and Medina, felt no qualms about inviting a massive American military build-up on its soil! This is what the Americans want from Arab rulers. Iraq would never have fought Iran on America's behalf, dissipating its human and material resources for nearly ten years, if it had been a democracy. But Saddam, who had begun his career as America's man, had now become recalcitrant. He therefore had to be chastised, no matter at what cost to the Iraqi people, who count for nothing— just cockroaches to be trampled on, as Marine Lieutenant Colonel Dick White actually said. Either Saddam became subservient again, and might be forgiven; or he remained defiant, and the United States would find another autocrat to do its bidding.

The stark truth is that America's agenda of hegemony and remote control is fundamentally incompatible with any idea of democracy in the region. And that in the end is what rendered the 1991 war inevitable, and made it so bloody.

Iraq was bombed for 40 days on end, before Saddam's troops turned tail from Kuwait. Some 80,000 tons of explosives, including 15,000 pounds worth of 'daisy cutter' bombs, were showered on the country. Apart from the military installations, they devastated Iraq's entire civilian infrastructure: power stations, water purification plants, hospitals, oil refineries. The scale of the destruction was unprecedented. The Americans never provided the figures of Iraqi casualties, military or civilian. But Colonel Jean-Louis Dufour of France suggested that some 150,000 Iraqi soldiers were killed, in the most brutal fashion, while fleeing from Kuwait.

There has been much talk of the cruelties of the war and the deaths of unnumbered Iraqis—millions perhaps—under the subsequent economic sanctions. But there is a particularly sordid episode which, to this day, remains largely unknown—namely, the story of how the American-led coalition not only did not prevent, but actually supported the brutal military suppression by Saddam Hussein of the popular uprisings that broke out in the Shia dominated areas of Southern Iraq, in the immediate aftermath of the Iraqi withdrawal from Kuwait, and which led to the massacre of Shia civilians in their hundreds of thousands.

The outside world knows about the uprising in the Kurdish areas of northern Iraq, its attempted suppression by Saddam, and the creation of safe havens there under American auspices. But much less is known about the mass extermination of the Shia with American complicity.[18] That is why so few outsiders understand the nature of the on-going resistance in Iraq and its unrelenting fierceness.

Immediately after the ceasefire, Iraqi officials loyal to Saddam approached General Schwarzkopf for his permission to fly their military helicopters to southern and northern Iraq. Schwarzkopf enthusiastically replied: 'Absolutely no problem!' The General, as also his superior Colin Powell and their political bosses, knew perfectly well what the Iraqi military mission in the south and north of the country was all about. The CIA-run radio stations, transmitting from Saudi Arabia on Iraqi State radio *frequencies, and the Arabic service of the Voice of America, had for weeks been exhorting the people of Iraq to rise in rebellion against the tyrannical regime, telling them that it was the decisive moment in their lives: they had to act quickly and boldly, without fear, for the allied forces would come to their rescue against any attempted counteroffensive by Saddam. Thousands of people in Basra, Nasiriyah, Najaf, Amara, Samana, Karbala and other towns south of Baghdad, led by Shia revolutionary committees, responded to the call and took to the streets, tearing down posters of Saddam, storming the offices of the local administration and setting up street barricades. The Iraqi army, demoralised as it was after its rout in Kuwait, took no action at first. But then the American army let the Republican Guards, led by Hussein Kamal, a son-in-law of Saddam,*[19] *take the road to Basra and clamp down on the Shia revolutionaries. Heavily armed infantry, backed by tanks, crashed through the barricades, shooting into crowds, tanks rolling over the wounded, corpses hanging down from their barrels. The Republican Guards rounded up people more or less at random, lined them up by the road-side, and shot them dead. Thousands were taken out in trucks to the desert, killed and buried in mass graves. The guards entered hospitals, killed all the injured along with their doctors, and had their bodies dumped in mass graves. Many Western reporters who wrote about the uprising half-condoned the repression by harping on the threat of an Iranian-type Islamic revolution. The leaders of the revolutionary committees and prominent Shia clerics gathered in Beirut in the second week of March 1991 and beseeched the coalition leaders to be true to their word, and to intervene as promised. Ayatollah Mohammed Baqir al-Hakim promised that, were a new government to be set up in Iraq, it would not imitate the Iranian state model, but would follow democratic principles and guarantee equal rights to all Iraqis, whether Shia, Sunni or non-Moslem. But it would not have foreign troops stationed on Iraqi soil. That was too much for the American officials present at the Beirut conclave: they walked out. Coincidentally or not, Baqir al-Hakim, who was the first cousin of Sayyid Mohammed Hussein Fadlallah, an inspirer of Hizbullah, was later killed in a bomb explosion in Najaf in 2003, after the second American invasion of Iraq. Ayatollah Taqi al-Modaressi openly said that the American establishment seemed to prefer a defanged Saddam over a new government representing the deprived and the persecuted. He wondered why the CIA had to incite the people to rebel if all the US government wanted was to see the uprising drowned in blood.*[20] *The Americans knew what was happening. They had the full information. They later intervened to provide relief to the Kurds. But the Shias were sacrificed, because they were suspected of political sympathies for Iran. The American and British leaders remained brazenly impenitent. They even mocked the leaders of the uprising. British Premier John Major joked that 'he did not remember asking the Shia to mount this particular revolution'. Colin Powell said that it was a problem internal to Iraq and that he could not interfere. President Bush, who had previously supported the CIA's call for an uprising, talked about America's fears of getting involved in an urban guerrilla war. His national security adviser, Brent Scowcroft, assured Saddam that 'we are not going to intervene, as we have said before, in a civil war'. It was an act of crass betrayal that the Iraqis would never forget nor forgive.*

I asked Mohammed Ghazi why the Shia dissident leaders and clerics from Iraq had gathered in Beirut in March 1991. He had mentioned the bonds between the Hizbullah and the Dawa party of Iraq. Were these just informal connections, based on mere religious sympathies, or was there coordination at the organisational level? Did Iran patronise and facilitate these relations?

*You must know that all the Shia communities of the Middle East are spiritually rooted in Karbala, where Imam Hussein, the grandson of the Prophet Mohammed, attained martyrdom in the year AD 680 while fighting the army of Yazid I. Yazid I was the son of Muawiyah and the founder of the Umayyad dynasty, which ruled from Damascus. After proclaiming himself Caliph, Yazid I coerced all prominent Muslims and tribal chiefs to acknowledge his leadership. Imam Hussein refused. His refusal had to do with very basic principles of Islamic society that require the ruler to respect the* umma *(the community of the faithful) and to defer to its wisdom in conducting public affairs. Yazid I and his father Muawiyah had other views. They were usurpers of power who had established their dynasty through murder, deceit and ill-gotten wealth. You have here the starting point of the Shia movement—the Shia dream, yet unfulfilled, of a revolution against worldly tyranny. As we understand it, the road to this revolution goes through the pursuit of knowledge, law, justice, morality, and also, crucially, through the cultivation of a spirit of self-sacrifice. The Najaf seminaries, a venerable institution of learning overseen by four Grand Ayatollahs, and the Karbala seminaries, another major centre of Islamic theology, have been the main sources of inspiration for the Shia*

*revolutionary movements all over the Middle East. The function of these
institutions is to evolve, through discussions among scholars and jurists,
correct and binding doctrines on all important issues of life, sacral or
secular. It is to the seminaries of Najaf that all prospective revolutionary
cadres from Iran, Iraq, Lebanon and elsewhere come to study, and it is
there that they strike lifelong friendships.*

*The present generation of Iraqi Ayatollahs has had to function under se-
vere restrictions, police surveillance, and threats of imprisonment or murder.
Ayatollah al-Sayyid Ali al-Sistani, who is based in Najaf, was prohibited
under Saddam Hussein from leading prayers and holding lectures. After a
failed attempt on his life, in November 1996, which resulted in the death of
one of his followers, he lived under virtual house arrest. Sistani, Mohammed
Ishaq Fayyad and Bashir Hussein al-Najafi, are three highly respected figures. In 1991, the Iraqi government arrested Grand Ayatollah Abu Gharib
al-Qassem al-Khoei, who was then 95, along with all members of his family
and entourage, and hundreds of other clerics. He died under house arrest
the following year. His son Sayyid Mohammed Taqi al-Khoei was killed
in July 1994 in a stage-managed car accident. Ayatollah Hussein Bahr
al-Alum was arrested in June 2001 and then got 'disappeared'. Ayatollah
Shaykah Murtada al-Burujerdi was killed in April 1998. The authorities
had instructed him to stop leading prayers at the Karbala shrine. He had
refused. Grand Ayatollah Shaykh Mirza Ali al-Gharawi, along with his son-
in-law and other companions, were killed in June 1998. Grand Ayatollah
Mohammed al-Sadr, the father of Muqtada al-Sadr, was killed along with
two of his sons and three of his followers in February 1999.*

*Many of the Shia spiritual leaders who had been betrayed by the United
States and compelled to live in exile, returned to Iraq after the regime
change. Of those who returned, many, like Ayatollah Mohammed Baqir al-
Hakim and Ayatollah Abdul Majid al-Khoei, got assassinated. Mohammed
Baqir al-Hakim, the leader of the Supreme Council for Islamic Revolution
in Iraq (SCIRI), was killed in August 2003. He was the nephew of Grand
Ayatollah Mohammed Sayyid al-Hakim whose cousin Grand Ayatollah
Muhsin al-Hakim had been the mentor of Ayatollah Ruhollah Khomeini,
the founder of the Islamic Republic of Iran. Baqir al-Hakim, the leader of
SCIRI, who had lived in Iran since the early 1980s, also returned to Iraq
in 2003. A strong opponent of the American occupation, Baqir al-Hakim
perished in a bomb explosion, in August 2003.*

*That will do for the present picture.* But to really understand the strength, depth and resilience of the connections and sympathies that weld together all these Shia revolutionary movements across Iraq, Iran and Lebanon, we must go back a few centuries.

The first point to grasp is the pivotal role which Shia Arab scholars from southern Lebanon played in the religious consolidation of Safavid Iran between 1501 and 1722. This was the period when Iran became predominantly, and officially, Shia. The Safavid dynasty adopted Shiism as the state religion and invited a large number of clerics and scholars from south Lebanon, then known as Jabal Amil, to prop up the new religious order. These clerics and scholars, for their part, responded with enthusiasm—not only to escape the political pressure imposed by Ottoman Turkey on Lebanon's Shia religious institutions, but also because of the sheer opportunities and challenges which the rise of a Shia state presented. So, these scholars went on to teach several generations of Iranian Shia students, and to dominate Iran's main religious offices for well over a hundred years after the establishment of the Safavid Empire. Most of them eventually settled in Iran. Others got official appointments as clerics in Iraqi centres such as Najaf, Kufa and Karbala.

The cultural and social bond between the migrant scholars and the host population endured. The ancestors of Muqtada al-Sadr and his uncle, Ayatollah Mohammed Baqir al-Sadr, for example, were among those Lebanese who had migrated to Iran during the Safavid period. The strength of the bonds formed between the migrant scholars and the native population is borne out by the fact that in the late 1950s, the leaders of the Shia community in south Lebanon requested Sayyid Musa al-Sadr, a cleric descended from those early migrant scholars who had settled in Qom,[21] to return to Lebanon and work for their upliftment.

Born in 1928, Musa al-Sadr held a degree in law and political economy from the University of Tehran. He had also studied Islamic jurisprudence at both Qom and Najaf under Ayatollah Mohsin al-Hakim, the patron of Ayatollah Khomeini. The two of them—Musa al-Sadr and Khomeini— became acquainted. Iran was then under the Shah and most religious clerics, with some exceptions, had either been bought over by the regime or rendered silent. Sadr returned to south Lebanon, taught at various schools, and later set up his own schools. He also set up orphanages, technical institutes and hospitals and persuaded wealthy Shia merchants to make liberal donations *to help him organise the Shia youth. Musa al-Sadr played a major role in awakening and mobilising the Shia of Lebanon, and in preparing them for a greater role in the country's politics, which hitherto were the preserve of Maronite Christians and to a lesser extent of Sunni Muslims. In less than a decade, Sadr established himself as a popular leader of Lebanon's Shia community. He also opened his facilities in the south to members of Iran's Islamic opposition and later to the People's Mojahedin of Iran (PMOI) for them to get military training. He also facilitated contacts between the PMOI and the PLO.*

*Ayatollah Khomeini was then leading the militant Islamic opposition from Najaf, with the help of underground networks set up by Ayatollah Beheshti, Ayatollah Mottahari, Abol-Hassan Bani-Sadr, Ayatollah Taleqani and several others. Yasser Arafat himself once went to Najaf to meet with Ayatollah Khomeini. So you see the connections! Later, after becoming openly critical of the Shah of Iran, Musa al-Sadr disappeared in August 1978, while on his way to Libya over Rome. Many suspect Libya's Muammar Ghaddafi of personally arranging his disappearance. But no one really knows what happened. My own hunch is that the Shah of Iran and Israel were involved. Ayatollah Khomeini personally appealed to Ghaddafi for an investigation, but the case has remained a mystery. In any case, Musa al-Sadr's work in Lebanon had by then become irreversible. The movement he founded there, known as Amal, meaning 'hope', is now a major political force. When Israel invaded Lebanon in 1982, the radical elements within Amal, appalled at the PLO's failure to oppose the invasion, organised them-selves into a militia, which later came to be known as Hizbullah ('God's party'). It has since gone from strength to strength, becoming the formidable force responsible for driving the Israelis out of their 20-mile wide buffer zone in the south of the country. It is also a political party with substantial representation in the Lebanese parliament.*

*You see, there are all manner of connections, based on spiritual and historical affinities, which bind distinct revolutionary movements, loosely yet effectively, and act as powerful morale boosters. These connections, however, do not rest on organisational dictates or controls. They are founded on shared principles and a commonalty of goals: resistance to tyranny, imperial occupation, outside interference. That said, the exact course of the struggle differs from country to country and can only be decided through local initiatives and democratic mobilisation. Thus the people of Iraq, while ultimately responsible for their own political initiatives, may count on the counsel and supportive networking of like-minded organisations elsewhere. Those who depict the revolutionary networks in the region as an 'axis of evil' simply do not understand the spirit, substance and modus operandi of the alliance.*

At this point, I asked Mohammed Ghazi for clarifications about the two main Shia political formations in Iraq—namely the Supreme Council for Islamic Revolution in Iraq (SCIRI) and Hizb al-Dawa al-Islamiyya, or Dawa for short. What were their ideological orientations? Did they differ in their political agendas?

*It is difficult to give an exact account of their genesis, because these movements had perforce to develop clandestinely, under the sequence of tyrannical regimes that controlled Iraq ever since the British and the French sliced up the Levant. Broadly speaking, all these organisations originated in the anti-British revolts which took place in southern Iraq from 1918 onwards, and in simultaneous initiatives by enlightened ulemas and revolutionary-minded clerics to reform the religious institutions of their community. As already pointed out, Mohammed Baqir al-Sadr, father-in-law to Muqtada al-Sadr, played an important part in organising Dawa, with the help and guidance of other senior ulemas. Baqir al-Sadr was himself a cousin of Musa al-Sadr, the one who led the political awakening of the Shia community in Lebanon. Under severe persecution, Dawa managed to enrol the educated middle class as well as elements of the working class, mainly in impoverished, breadline areas like eastern Baghdad (now known as Medina al-Sadr), which previously housed pockets of Communist party followers. Dawa also organised women sections, giving a distinctively progressive orientation to what had begun as a religious reform. The advent of the Ba'ath party in the late 1960s brought new persecutions on an unprecedented scale. Shia publications like Risal al-Islam were banned; their religious institutions were closed; public celebrations of religious functions were forbidden; charismatic clerics were arrested or murdered. Leaders and active members of Dawa were imprisoned and executed.*

*Not only did Dawa survive this wave of persecution and terror; it openly defied the state in 1977, by organising an Intifada that saw the participation of thousands of people despite shootings, crackdowns, arrests, custodial torture and executions. Later on, inspired by the Iranian Revolution of 1979, Dawa organised its own military wing, despite the fact that membership of the party was an offense punishable with death. The Saddam regime portrayed the Shia as Iranian puppets or collaborators. In fact, proportionally, more Shias than Sunnis died in the meaningless war which Saddam waged against Iran under US instigation. Yet the Shia remained objects of execration. Government agents arrested and executed both Mohammed Baqir al-Sadr and his sister Bint al-Huda. Many Dawa leaders had to flee Iraq. Others went underground and organised clandestine cells to ensure the survival of the revolutionary struggle.*

*Throughout these tribulations, the democratic and progressive orientation of the movement remained unaffected. It even acquired sharper focus. Dawa's political vision, as articulated by al-Sadr, revolved around three main tenets: 'absolute sovereignty belongs to God'; 'the legislative and executive functions of the state are subordinated to Islamic injunctions'; and most significantly, 'the head of the state is to be directly elected by the people'. Dawa clarified its position on the role of Islamic jurists in a 2002 publication authored by Abdul-Halim al-Rahimi, which stated that 'delegating decision making to the jurisprudent does not mean that he can monopolise it without consulting qualified people and experts [....] Devolving governance to the jurisprudent in no way means that he will be the actual ruler or president of the republic. He may assign the execution of policies to whoever is elected by the community while assuming the role of a supervisor and guide. Thus, practical convergence is achieved between the two notions of shura (consultative body) and wilayat al-faqih (council of experts)'. Dawa also institutionalised a non-clerical technocratic leadership.*

*Today, the original Dawa has splintered, but the United Iraqi Alliance, which holds 128 seats in the Council of Representatives (out of a total of 275) represents most of the original Dawa. Ibrahim al-Jaafari, who headed the transitional government as Prime Minister from February to December 2005, and the current Prime Minister Nouri al-Maliki, both come from Dawa.*

*The Supreme Council for the Islamic Revolution in Iraq (SCIRI) also began as an offshoot of Dawa. Mohammed Baqir al-Hakim, the leader of the breakaway faction, was more in sympathy with Khomeini's vision of an Islamic republic. Yet the leaders of Dawa and SCIRI retained a good personal relationship, despite substantial differences on the question of leadership (is Ayatollah Khomeini's authority supreme?) and the attitude towards Iran (how binding is the Iranian model to us Iraqis?). Both Dawa and SCIRI incorporate a wide spectrum of views and strategic options, though all their members are unanimous in their firm rejection of outside hegemony.*

*One issue that generates much confusion and heated debate is this: should an Islamist government, elected by the people, cede power to a non-Islamist formation if defeated at the polls at a later date? Such differences have their legitimate place in the internal discourse within political Islam. At the level of practical politics, both Dawa and SCIRI are committed to the rules of democracy. Their larger regional perspectives overlap. A number of Dawa and SCIRI members supported the establishment of Hizbullah in the wake of the 1982 Israeli invasion of Lebanon. Of the two, Dawa is organisationally stronger within Iraq, because it represents, by and large, those elements of the resistance who remained in the country and bore the brunt of persecution under Saddam Hussein. Its leaders, mostly lay Shias, are keener to assert the independence of Iraq's nationalist movement vis-à-vis Iran. They were also the ones who most vigorously opposed such shadowy, pseudo-Shia groupings as Ahmed Chalabi's Iraqi National Congress and Iyad Allawi's Iraqi National Accord, both of which are sponsored by the CIA and the Pentagon. Muqtada al-Sadr, who has maintained his distance from both Dawa and SCIRI, stands for an even more radical rejection of foreign interference, and may yet become a key player if and when the Americans quit for good. He commands a several thousand strong militia called Jaysh al-Mahdi, which has successfully defied the coalition forces on more than one occasion. His popularity should be evident from the fact that despite his mercurial temper, which led him to boycott the elections in January 2005, his followers captured nearly 30 seats in the December 2005 elections.*

Mohammed Ghazi had drawn a fairly comprehensive yet clear enough picture of the Shia formations in Iraq, with their historical lineage and international ramifications. But what about the other contenders? What was the real weight of the Sunni groups in favour of a democratic reconciliation and a common front against the coalition forces? What about the unredeemed Ba'athists and their attempts to regain influence? What about the sectarian polarisation pitting Sunnis against Shias? What about the future of the more fanatical militias such as Al-Qaida, those that operate locally but with the backing of international state and non-state sponsors within the conservative Arab world?

I looked expectantly at Professor Jerardi and Professor Ahmed as I mumbled my questions. Nabih Berri's television interview had been over for quite some time, and Hassan Jerardi was now listening approvingly to Mohammed Ghazi, his eyes wide with excitement, thoughtful furrows on his forehead, and a smart twirl over his lips. It was now his turn to speak up.

*The imperialist invasion and occupation of Iraq, given its nature, motivations, and sheer brutality, has inevitably triggered a very complex mix of political processes; its violence shouldn't surprise anyone. It is difficult to foretell their eventual outcome in anything like precise terms, even if we are able to identify the political forces at work—formations, groups, or individuals. One thing is fairly clear, though: the genie is out of the bottle. The American aggression has sparked off myriad mutinies which cannot be contained within the geo-political order foisted on the Middle East by the Western powers.*

*A significant development to emerge from the apparent anarchy is that the Arab resistance can no longer limit its objectives to an unconditional withdrawal of the aggressors, whether they be the US-led coalition in Iraq or the Israeli occupation forces in Palestine. Nor is an imperialist disengagement likely in the near future. The aggressors may be forced to prolong their presence (even under constant harassment by decentralised and therefore uncontrollable guerrillas) because, as the old 'domino argument' goes, their exit would precipitate a crumbling of the current geo-political order. Its ideological underpinnings would collapse. Its indigenous representatives would be swept away. So the imperialist aggression may drag on, and the resistance to it may have to continue, until the conditions mature for a radical restructuring of the Middle East, through a double process: a progressive re-vitalisation of the Arab world, forged and tempered in the smithy of resistance, and an accelerating depletion of the material and moral resources of Western hegemony. The way we see it, the war coalition in Iraq is trapped in a feedback loop: the occupation kindles resistance, which they try to defeat by sending more troops, which generates more resistance.*

*The fact is that military occupation, as it always does, is now boomeranging on the aggressors, putting paid to all their calculations. The deluge of refugees, who are fleeing the country to escape anarchy and death, is taking anti-American sentiments to all parts of the Middle East, just as the expulsion of Palestinians by Israel has spread hatred of Israel far and wide. The*

American people may now be war-weary, and their leaders may be wishing for a scenario under which their troops could withdraw without losing face; but their economic interests (real enough), their strategic security imperatives (mostly misconceived), and above all the hubris of power stand in the way. Then there is America's misguided backing of Israel, which not only compounds the misery of Palestinians but breeds insecurity for Israel itself. The latest case in point was the US decision to isolate the newly elected Palestinian authority under Hamas. Hamas had won at the polls fair and square. But Hamas is anathema to Israel and therefore to the US, because it stands for armed resistance—conveniently re-labelled as 'terrorism'. Far from isolating Hamas, the move only strengthened its prestige and earned the movement new sympathies throughout the Middle East.

Similarly, all US attempts to impose a pro-Western, pro-Israeli government in Lebanon only legitimise Hizbullah and help it expand its cross-sectarian appeal. Previously, the US used to pursue its interests by relying on corrupt and authoritarian regimes. But lately, impelled by neo-con stupidity and prodded by Israel, it has taken to more direct interference, without shying away from military intervention against 'terrorist states'. The consequence, as in Iraq, is a revivification of the resistance.

In Palestine, these policies contributed to the electoral success of Hamas. That movement is not only an eyesore to Israel. It is also a living reproach to such supine states as Jordan, Egypt, Saudi Arabia and Kuwait, which always cave in to American pressure and, unlike Hamas, have yet to adopt a democratic mode of functioning.

Or take those US threats to attack Iran to prevent it from acquiring nuclear deterrence. All this swagger and sabre-rattling can achieve only one thing—reinforce the Iranian resolve to acquire such deterrence, and make it appear perfectly legitimate. Here you have the feedback loop at its finest!

As for the trump argument of 'civilisational superiority', which in former days apologists of Western expansion used to justify their colonial ventures, it now sounds rather hollow, given the record of the 'anti-terror warriors': wanton aggression against arbitrarily designated target nations; human rights atrocities galore; and the 'privatisation of war', that is, the deployment of mercenary forces let loose with license to kill with impunity.

Whether the West likes it or not, the ongoing wars cannot end without far-reaching changes: there will have to be a thorough recalibration of the *power equations, in the Middle East and beyond, and above all a redefinition of the organising principles of politics. The argument may sound far-fetched to those skeptical by nature of revolutionary visions, or to the silent admirers of the status quo. But I do maintain that the evidence on the ground, confusing as it may appear, supports my view.*

*Anyone who cares to study the recent history of the region will be struck by the potency of such motives as offended honour, or justice denied, to drive Arabs to rebellion. Our rebelliousness may lack discipline, our militancy may at times seem hopelessly fragmented, but we more than make up for it by our staying power and sheer daring.*

*The Ba'athists are probably the most discredited of all elements active in the Iraqi resistance, because of their record of tyranny. But their regime is gone for good, and there is nothing that can be done to put it back together, even if, on balance, the US might prefer a restoration of the status quo ante to the uncertainties ahead. Therefore, the sounder elements among the Ba'athists will have to undergo a serious self-appraisal and acknowledge their past errors.*

*The same holds true for the Sunni sectarian forces. Whatever the allure of Al-Qaida, with its fanatical violence, the Sunnis will eventually see it for what it is: a path to nowhere. Those Sunnis who live in the Gulf states will come to understand what a stiff price they were made to pay, in terms of cultural alienation, spiritual torpor and moral degeneration, for the illicit relationship which their dumb and corrupt leaders have contracted with their overseas lords, selling their oil for unwholesome wealth, and their souls for a seat at the table of the foreign masters. The Sunnis of Iraq, for their part, must overcome their sense of entitlement, and reach out to their long-suffering, long-despised Shia brothers. And all Arabs must come to see that the present arrangement cries to heaven: while the bulk of the Arab nation either vegetate below subsistence level or, in the case of the Palestinians, lead the lives of hunted animals, a minority wallows in fabulous wealth, in enclaves like Kuwait, Saudi Arabia and UAE, ruled over by comic strip characters. This era of subjugation and shame must come to an end. As for inter-Arab relations, the culture of dialogue and accommodation must once again prevail, as it had in the days of our vigour, over dogmatic inflexibility, sectarian violence, tribal exclusivism. It must even prevail over the artificial barriers between our nations. It is those divisions, not some pre-ordained fate, that turn us into helpless playthings of foreign forces. These divisions, besides, are completely at variance with the spirit of permeability and plural harmony, which Islam once spread among the component nations of the* Umma.

*The prospect of such an awakening is not so remote if you appraise the working model of resistance and inter-Arab solidarity that has already been developed by Hizbullah in Lebanon, by Hamas in Palestine, and by the Muslim Brotherhood in Egypt, Jordan and elsewhere. This model of resistance and solidarity is truly Islamic in the precise sense that while it enjoins on all people to combat aggression and occupation as a matter of religious duty, it also obliges them, again as a matter of religious duty, to eschew violence, coercion, and totalitarianism as ways of resolving their internal disputes.*

*This model of resistance and solidarity, we firmly believe, must eventually succeed in throwing off the yoke of dependence, overt occupation and covert manipulation, under which the Middle East has been labouring for too long. God willing, it may also pave the way for a new political arrangement, federal or confederal, for the whole region. It might even, on the spiritual front, usher in a new era of self-discovery. If all this comes to pass, the new model, with its theo-juristic logic transcending sectarian barriers and state demarcations, will be a fitting answer not only to the long chapter of Western hegemony, but also to the futile violence of Al-Qaida and the sectarian arrogance of the Wahhabi fanatics.*

Here was indeed an enthralling vision—but alas for the moment only a vision! Returning to the present, I wanted Professor Ahmed (the member of Iraq's Transitional National Assembly from Najaf) to explain the many competing insurgencies currently underway in Iraq. By all accounts, the conditions of life in the country are simply hellish. The Iraqi government remains fully 'transitional', even after the December 2005 vote. Ensconced in Baghdad's so-called 'Green Zone', it exists only by the mercy of American troops and private mercenaries, and its writ hardly extends beyond the Green Zone. Nearly 200,000 civilians have been killed since the start of the American invasion in 2003. About half a million people had already died between 1991 and 2003, under the impact of the UN-backed sanctions. Healthcare, education, electricity, water and sanitation facilities remain in an appalling state. Hundreds of thousands die premature deaths because of malnutrition or lack of medical care. Oil production isn't likely to return to its pre-war level under the present anarchy. Unemployment and underemployment are chronic. The total number of displaced Iraqis, counting both the internal refugees and those seeking shelter beyond the borders, is said to exceed three million. Of these, two million, mostly Sunnis, are reported to have fled to Syria, a country pilloried for its anti-Western stance and already under great internal strain. The presence of so many aggrieved Iraqi Sunnis could strain to breaking point Syria's policy of equal respect for all religious denominations. There are reports that influential Ba'athist elements sheltered in Syria are busy hatching plots to regain power in Iraq. The Kurds of northern Iraq, with their de- facto quasi-autonomy, are also a matter of grave concern to the governments of Syria, Turkey and even Iran, which have to contend with their own Kurdish minorities. Professor Ahmed and Professor Jerardi had talked about the war in Iraq becoming a catalyst for the mobilisation of the dispossessed, and eventually precipitating the end of Western hegemony. How could this vision take shape, if for the moment the most tangible consequence of the anarchy in Iraq was a general destabilisation of the region, which imperilled not just the regimes of the neighbouring countries but also the internal cohesion of their societies?

Professor Ahmed drew a long breath, and began once again.

*Let us discuss the human disaster in Iraq, which is an American legacy, a bit later. For the moment, let us talk about the myriad insurgencies and their likely impact.*

*First, we have the Kurds. Their nationalist struggle has a long and tragic history. It is easy to understand the Kurds' agony over the fact that, despite being the largest compact nationality in the Middle East, they have so far been denied the umbrella of an independent state. The responsibility for this and so much else squarely rests with those who drew the national borders in the region. The Kurds, however, have had their bitter experiences with struggle and repression, and are today, I daresay, wise enough to recognise that an independent state would inevitably mean a lot of bloodshed, and might not be the only way of securing their national survival. There are federal and confederal alternatives. They require time, patient dialogue, and the progressive consolidation of people-oriented institutions that will be transnational in character but won't threaten the existing states. Of course, there is no way to make definite predictions about what may eventually happen, but the evidence from the ground is that Iraq's Kurds have become a good deal wiser. Rather than aspiring to secession, they are now intent on consolidating their gains within a federal framework.*

*They have two disciplined militias, known as* Peshmerga *('those who face death'), each controlled by a solid political formation. The Kurdistan Democratic Party (KDP), currently led by Massoud Barzani, the son of the legendary Mustafa Barzani, is dominant in the western parts of Kurdistan. The Patriotic Union of Kurdistan (PUK), led by Jalal Talabani, is influential in the east. At the moment, Barzani is heading the provincial government and Talabani is President of Iraq. Their mutual animosity, once fierce, has abated somewhat, but there remain subtle differences in their visions of Kurdish national autonomy. There also exist other groups, with more radical perspectives on independence and close links to the Kurdish Workers Party (PKK) that operates from Turkish Kurdistan.*

*The US-led coalition in Iraq, desperate as it was for political, military and intelligence partners in the country, had little option but to appease the Kurdish groups by permitting them to keep their arms and remain virtually autonomous (but stopping short of full secession). In the past, American blandishments and promises of support may have succeeded in misleading some sections of the Kurds. At present, however, the momentum of resistance against the occupation is such that it binds, psychologically at least, all groups and factions in Iraq. All serious political formations also recognise the importance of dialogue with the people of the region, and the folly of entering tactical alliances with our conquerors for narrow factional, or even national, advantage. We have indeed our memories, and we know what these promises by foreigners are worth.*

*The US, under President Wilson, and its British ally, while fighting the Ottoman Empire, had promised to support an independent Kurdistan and an independent Armenia. Instead of that the conquerors washed their hands of the first modern genocide, that of Anatolia's Armenians—and forgot their promises to the Kurds, when the economic interests and strategic equations changed after World War I. In 1975, the United States pressured Iraq and Iran to resolve their border differences, leading to the Algiers Agreement, and encouraged both governments to join forces in suppressing the Kurdish nationalist struggle. The Shah of Iran and Saddam of Iraq were game. Again, as the two rivals for the Kurdish leadership, Talabani and Barzani, very well remember, the United States exploited their factional differences, in 1995, to frustrate Kurdish aspirations, and preferred to strike a deal with*

*Saddam Hussein. The Kurdish people and their leaders, like the Palestinians, and indeed all the struggling peoples of the region, are increasingly coming to the realisation that there are no solutions to their ordeals within the framework of the existing regional order, itself a reflection of the prevailing world order. We must all come together, and together defeat our common enemy. None of us will find redemption on his own, without first ending the injustices visited on us all. I think this realisation is beginning to dawn. How else do we explain, for instance, that the violence between Kurds and Sunnis in Kirkuk and Mosul, so intense in 2004–2005, is now abating?*

*The Sunni of Iraq, no matter what their numbers or area of residence, require protection and must have their rights safeguarded. There is, for instance, this large Sunni community which was grafted onto Kirkuk and Mosul during the Ba'athist rule to guard the oil resources against the Kurdish insurgents. The Kurds, naturally, resented and still resent their presence. These perverse legacies of our history must be resolved through negotiations and constitutional arrangements between the local actors solely, without outside interference.*

*To make a more general point, it is no exaggeration to say that the states of the post-colonial Middle East haven't had anything like a real history, I mean a history of their own and all their own. Our states were fashioned by the whims of the imperial powers, after World War I down to 1948, and ever since our governments have basically continued to serve the interests of these powers. As a result, they have failed—in many instances, they haven't even tried—to weld their motley collection of people, shuffled and shoved behind arbitrary borders, into political communities cohesive enough to accommodate all their ethnic, cultural and sectarian differences within an overarching historical project. This is evident in all our turmoil-torn societies, from Lebanon down to Kuwait.*

*In Lebanon, for example, Hizbullah is trying hard to create a new working model for dealing with the country's wounded, splintered society. To that end, it has been leading the armed resistance to Israeli occupation as an inclusive, all-Lebanese campaign. On the internal front, they have been pressing for new constitutional arrangements that would ensure the fair and just representation of the whole sectarian spectrum. On the face of it, it would have been logical, or should we say tempting, for Hizbullah to insist on a government elected through universal adult franchise (as some academics in their ivory towers actually demanded). After all, Lebanon is a Shia majority country. But Hizbullah holds that compromise is of the essence if we are to maintain social unity in our artificially divided societies. Naturally, it is impossible to achieve a perfect system while we live, survive and fight foreign aggression on a daily basis, to say nothing of the more insidious forms of outside interference. But there is no alternative to plural dialogue and compromise if we don't want to remain mired in the crippling divisions of the past.*

*The same applies to the Ba'athist elements, inside Iraq and elsewhere. They have erred against the principle of respect for the* umma, *the community, which is central to the Islamic concept of governance. They often did so under dictatorial pressure, but also out of sectarian arrogance or sheer thoughtless ignorance. However, these previous errors of hubris cannot justify their permanent political isolation. On the contrary, they need effective safeguards and protection as a minority, and we should grant these ungrudgingly, under a democratic dispensation. In return, the Ba'athist elements should display a spirit of contrition, and spurn all attempts by the occupiers of our land to co-opt them. They should also keep at arm's length the sectarian fanatics, who only deal in death, devastation and anarchy—and for the most part only kill fellow Muslims. Most of them are unwitting stooges of those outsiders they claim to fight. Look at the Afghans' fight against the Soviet invasion. Outwardly, it achieved its purpose, but because it relied so heavily on foreign 'helpers' with agendas of their own—on US military assistance, Saudi money, Wahhabi missionary zeal—what the victors inherited was little more than an empty shell, and today the Afghans' aspiration for independence appears no nearer fulfilment than in the darkest hours of the 1980s. Similarly, the misguided zealots who in present-day Iraq kill and maim their own people with drunken abandon should recognise that even if they were to succeed in driving the invaders away by such tactics, the fruits of their 'victory' would prove completely hollow.*

*There are signs that the people of Iraq are beginning to recognise this. Look at the December 2005 elections to the National Assembly. After some initial wariness and various boycott calls, the Iraqi Accord Front, a cartel of various Sunni nationalist groups, decided to take part, and eventually secured 44 seats out of 275. Another formation, the so-called Iraqi National Dialogue Front, led by non-sectarian Sunnis who prioritise national reconstruction and the end of foreign occupation, also took part and won 11 seats. Of course, substantial differences of opinion, factionalism and ego clashes continue to plague our emergent democracy. But there is no reason to despair. Efficient Sunni organisations such as the CMU (the Committee of the Muslim Ulemas, established in 2003 under the leadership of the Iraqi Muslim Brotherhood) and the HIC ('Higher Ifta Council', led by Abdul Qadir Alani) are sparing no efforts to isolate the fanatics and anarchists. There are also encouraging initiatives of Shia–Sunni rapprochement, much to the chagrin of the aggressors, who have been ranting against the new-found friendship between Muqtada al-Sadr, the Shia firebrand, and noted Sunni ulema Mohammed al-Kubaisi. Both of them have spoken out against sectarian violence and condemned all incitation to internecine conflict.*

I had been taking in Professor Ahmed's bold explanations, and was finding myself, to my surprise, rather taken in by them. I was struck by his focus on the big picture—the 'world order' with its injustice, then the formula of solidarity and resistance as an antidote to that 'evil order'. But his views were also uncomfortably akin—even if in antithesis, as a mirror image as it were—to America's obsession with the 'global': global economy, global trade, global war on terror. I was curious: how do the advocates of Arab resistance analyse this world order they are so critical of? By what exactly would they like to see it replaced? I asked Professor Jerardi for his views.

Professor Jerardi seemed to be struggling with his thoughts, even as he began speaking—slowly at first, even haltingly.

*This war for or against the Pax Americana is indeed global, on both sides of the divide, and there is a lot more to it than the assertion of American ambitions or our wish to frustrate these ambitions. This war springs from a collision of historical experiences. At some level, you might even say that it is a clash between incompatible conceptions of mankind's future. The outcome of this war will decide whether aggression and hegemony will be the organising principles of the world-to-be, or whether the instruments of political and military power, industrial production, scientific and technological development, the global resources, their marketing and accessibility to state and non-state actors—the whole infrastructure of collective life, in short—must remain subject to the jurisdiction of a moral law that is founded on a non-abdicable view of human worth. In that sense, a victory over the Pax Americana will also be a victory for all those Americans who* do not subscribe to aggression and hegemony as instruments of historical progress.

Tactical considerations aside (like lost scope for diplomatic manoeuvring in playing one world power against the other), the people of the Middle East had no reasons to lament the disintegration of the second superpower, the Soviet Union, or to regret the Cold War logic with its equilibrium of lethal force. In fact, the first post-Cold War years appeared to bode well for the new millennium. They brought the German re-unification, the re-organisation of Russia as a new federation within more realistic borders, and the emancipation of six Central Asian republics. Despite all the attendant ordeals, these developments suggested a move towards greater geopolitical legitimacy. At the very least, they marked a welcome departure from the mapping of the world under what we might call the 'Northern Empires'. Some of us even thought that the long chapter of Israeli hegemony would slowly come to an end. In any case, there were other encouraging developments: the unexpected (if short-lived!) detention of Pinochet of Chile in the United Kingdom; the constitution of the Hague Tribunal to judge war crimes; the adoption by the European states of the Rome Treaty; or again the Oslo and Madrid processes for peace in the Middle East. But those of us naive enough to expect a spontaneous moral restructuring of the world order after the disintegration of the USSR were overlooking the fact that the Cold War had not given way to 'peace'. The prize of world domination had simply been clinched by one of the two contenders. That victorious superpower, the US, had for the most part been using the language of human rights, democracy and global justice as convenient propaganda tools, without any earnest commitment to these values. Having broken free from the Cold War constraints by eliminating its global rival, how could the US resist the temptation of overwhelming the world with the show of its power, its economic, political, military primacy—its so-called 'full-spectrum dominance'? How could it resist slipping into the role of the world hegemon? Our delusions about impending global reforms were soon shattered. The juggernaut of the sole remaining superpower, driven by a cupidity much in excess of its discernment but equipped with irresistible means of coercion, lost no time in entering the strategic space previously guarded by the Soviet Union. Thus was the scene set for the first Gulf war.

The US military project in the Gulf region quickly morphed from a UN- mandated mission to undo Iraq's occupation of Kuwait, into a punitive venture—*a war to chastise and devastate a defiant country and then, twelve years on, to overrun and occupy it fully. There was no military power in the world that could have stopped the United States and its coalition. The capitalist Empire quickly shed the mask of liberalism and human rights that it had been wearing to fool the world about the real stakes of the Cold War rivalry, and swiftly resurrected the old imperial habits of conquest as an instrument of political and economic domination.*

In the past, imperial conquests used to be justified in the name of the West's 'civilisational mission'. Such a justification was no longer required. Nor was it convenient to let pesky notions of human rights, accountability, respect for the Geneva conventions and the like, shackle one's latitude in the methods of war waging. New rhetoric was called for. Soon enough, the strategic discourse within the new world order began to revolve round the conveniently extensible notion of 'terror', with its ill-defined but shudder-inducing dangers, its shadowy perpetrators and sponsors. 'Terrorists', as distinct from 'enemy combatants', would not qualify for the legal guarantees, exemption from torture, etcetera, that were extended to war prisoners under the bipolar world order, nor could there be any dialogue between those who stand for 'civilisation' and the dark hosts lurking beyond the frontiers of 'civilisation', in the shadowy realms of violence and terror. Within the old world order, militaries were required to be capable of meeting a potential challenge from a well-identified enemy. Under the new US doctrine—and practice—militaries are free to strike pre-emptively to thwart ubiquitous, unknowable 'terror threats'.

The rhetoric has been flourishing. William Shawcross, a British aristo-crat, writer, journalist and broadcaster, maintains that 'American power is often the only thing that stands between civility and genocide, order and mayhem.... It is a vital force for progress, in the Islamic world as much as anywhere else.' Michael Ignatieff, the Canadian-born US ideologue,[22] is eloquent and upfront. He writes that 'empire' is the appropriate word to describe the 'awesome' reality of the American power 'that polices the world through five global military commands; maintains more than a million men and women at arms on four continents; deploys carrier battle groups on watch in every ocean; guarantees the survival of countries from Israel to South Korea; drives the wheels of global trade and commerce; and fills the hearts and minds of an entire planet with its dreams and desires'. According to Ignatieff, 'it is an empire without consciousness of itself as such, *constantly shocked that its good intentions arouse resentment abroad. But that does not make it any less of an empire, with a conviction that it alone, in Herman Melville's words, bears "the ark of the liberties of the world".*[23] *Thus was the new rhetoric of the Pax Americana assembled.*

*The weakness of the global community and the supineness of the United Nations were put to the test in the Balkans. The NATO intervention in Kosovo in 1999 was never submitted to the UNSC for review and endorsement (as required under Articles 2(4) and 51 of the UN Charter). The Kosovo war trod rough-shod over the principle of state sovereignty.*[24]

*Bowing to force, the UN silently acquiesced in the violation. When the International Criminal Court (ICC) re-affirmed its position that 'the people of each state is the referent of its sovereignty', the United States withdrew from the ICC. The earlier laws of war and legal restrictions on its conduct (under the principles of proportionality, humanitarian respect and international accountability) were deemed no longer relevant by the US. Its propagandists and hired pens began to describe the United Nations, once advertised as the big hope for global peace in the early Cold War decades, as 'a lazy dog', dozing 'before the fire, happy to ignore Saddam, until an American President seized it by the scruff of the neck and made it bark'. This again is Ignatieff.*

*But then, the UN, like its predecessor, the League of Nations, had already shown long ago how toothless it was in the face of real emergencies, how ill-equipped to uphold a reasonable balance between force and law in international relations. And what else, in the end, could be expected of a body that lacks a standing army of its own and an independent financial basis? A body, furthermore, that is wholly dependent for its survival on the goodwill of the world's dominant power, which may alternately use it for its own ends or discard it as useless? Had not Cicero asked: 'What can be done against force without force?'*

*The brood of Frankenstein monsters which the United States had reared in the mountain ranges of Afghanistan came of age and multiplied. They helped both the United States and post-Soviet Russia in raising the spectre of 'global terror'. In 1999, Vladimir Putin, an undistinguished KGB man, had just been drawn from obscurity by President Boris Yeltsin and made Prime Minister, when a series of unclaimed bombings rocked Moscow and killed 300 people in apartment blocks.*[25] *Putin immediately blamed the atrocities on Chechen terrorists and sent his military to re-occupy the* breakaway republic. *Touting the threat of terrorism and posing as Russia's providential strongman, he went on to win the next presidential elections by a landslide, after which he could reclaim, unchallenged, something of the fullness of totalitarian powers enjoyed by earlier Soviet rulers.*

*The attacks on 11 September 2001 rendered much the same service to the United States, only on a far grander scale. Addressing both Chambers, President Bush Junior read out this ringing piece of oratory prepared by his speech-writers:*

> Our war on terror begins with Al Qaida, but it does not end there. It will not end until every terrorist group of global reach has been found, stopped and defeated.... They are the heirs of all the murderous ideologies of the 20th century. By sacrificing human life to serve their radical visions, by abandoning every value except the will to power, they follow in the path of fascism, Marxism and totalitarianism. And they will follow that path all the way to where it ends in history's unmarked grave of discarded lies.... We will direct every resource at our command—every means of diplomacy, every tool of intelligence, every instrument of law enforcement, every financial influence, and every necessary weapon of war—to the destruction and to the defeat of the global terror network.... Our response involves far more than instant retaliation and isolated strikes. Americans should not expect one battle, but a lengthy campaign unlike any other we have ever seen. It may include dramatic strikes visible on TV and covert operations secret even in success.... Every nation in every region now has a decision to make: either you are with us, or you are with the terrorists.

*The message couldn't be clearer: any state that refused to align itself with the United States would henceforth be regarded as hostile, and would have to reckon with US military might.*

*Thus, a simple Presidential proclamation of 'global war on terror' established the supremacy of American sovereignty. The sovereignty of other states became conditional on the decrees of the American imperium or the dictatorial whims of its dim-witted imperator.*

*In his West Point address on 3 June 2002, the President clarified the new doctrine: 'America has, and intends to keep, military strengths beyond challenges' and a 'readiness to strike at a moment's notice in any dark corner of the world'. Terror cells would be uncovered and gone after 'in 60 or more countries, using every tool of finance, intelligence and law enforcement'. The President pointed out: 'Some nations need military training to fight terror, and we will provide it. Other nations oppose terror, but tolerate*

*the hatred that leads to terror—and that must change.... All nations that decide for aggression and terror will pay a price.... We will lift this dark threat from our country and from the world.'*
This is a clear agenda of trans-hemispheric hegemony. A hegemonic project of such dimensions is, of course, bound to be met with aversion and inspire resistance, both of the peaceful and armed sort, just as the colonial conquests of an earlier age had done, or the American interventions in Korea, Vietnam and elsewhere, or the Soviet adventure in Afghanistan. The declared objective of the war—to take out terror cells in '60 or more countries'—is also rather a tall order to implement. What covert operations will the US mount in pursuit of this goal? What limits will it set itself? What will be its legal framework?

Consider this precedent. In August 1998, the US National Security Advisor Samuel Berger justified the cruise missiles attack on Sudan and Afghanistan with reference to the Anti-Terrorism and Effective Death Penalty Act of 1966, which authorises the President to 'use all necessary means, including covert action and military force, to disrupt, dismantle, and destroy international infrastructure used by international terrorists, including overseas terrorist training facilities and safe havens....'

Well and good. But on this occasion the cruise missiles attacks, which were launched in retaliation for the terrorist bombing of the US embassies in Nairobi and Dar es Salaam, targeted a factory in Khartum, Sudan, which was claimed to serve as a facility for producing VX nerve gas for use by Al-Qaida. The targeted factory turned out to be a major pharmaceutical plant whose destruction created a critical shortage of essential medicines in the country. The United States neither apologised nor offered restitution even after credible, independent reports showed that faulty intelligence had resulted in misdirected strikes. The world and the UN silently acquiesced. When, five years and a president later, the United States showed similar high-handedness, only on a scale 1,000 times larger, by invading Iraq in brazen defiance of world opinion, the UN once again acquiesced.

The stark truth is that no effective opposition to the project of global empire can come from within the established world order. But I do believe, as I told you before, that it can come from the Middle East. I do believe that the Middle East can and will become the West's nemesis. Not only will the United States and its international allies be forced to turn tail, not only will their regional side-kicks be humbled, but by the time these things *come to pass, the present world order, based on aggression, occupation and hegemony, will have been dismantled!*

I wanted to change the subject and take the discussion back to more mundane matters. So I asked Professor Ahmed about petro-imperialism: what in his view had been the role of oil in American calculations? Was the desire to control the Middle East oil resources, said to produce around 70 per cent of the world reserves, one of their reasons for going to war in Iraq? Professor Ahmed shook his head in irritation at the apparent naivety of my question.

*From the very start, oil has been at the root of the imperialist project in the Middle East. Oil is paramount. Oil is the umbilical cord of industry, armament, global finance, international trade. Jimmy Carter, worshipped by many as a peacenik, said in 1980, ten years before Saddam invaded Kuwait, that any attempt, by any 'outside' force to gain control of the Persian Gulf would be repelled by any means necessary, including military force. Nothing new there: all along, this gamekeeper mentality had informed the policies of the imperial powers, first Britain and then America, ever since they discovered oil in the region. But let us dwell a moment on this misleading expression—'outside'—used by Carter. This implied opposition between 'outsiders' (i.e., the oil-hungry counties which have to import our oil but might be tempted to snatch it) and 'insiders' (the rightful owners of the oil fields, i.e., the states of the region) obscures the fact that our formal ownership of the resources is of rather limited significance. It enriches a few; it gives us some leverage on the international scene; but when it comes to the crunch, the imperial powers let the mask slip: they resort to military reprisals, regime change, or occupation. That is how it has always been.*

*Surely, you recall what happened to Mohammed Mossadeq, the Prime Minister of Iran, after he nationalised the Anglo–Iranian oil company against the wishes of the Shah Mohammed Reza Pahlavi and the United States in 1951. The United States under President Eisenhower and Britain under Winston Churchill (who had just returned as Prime Minister) together mounted 'Operation Ajax'. The set of characters involved is interesting: leading the operation was Kermit Roosevelt, a CIA officer, and grandson of Theodore Roosevelt. He was assisted by Norman Schwarzkopf, the father of General Schwarzkopf who was to lead the first Gulf War against Iraq, and by C.M. Woodhouse of Britain's MI6. Mossadeq was deposed and placed under arrest. The Shah returned from his self-imposed exile. A grand consortium, including Jersey, Socony, Texaco and Standard, Shell and Anglo–Iranian, took over the oil operations in Iran.*

*Then there came the Suez Crisis, in 1956, following the nationalisation of the canal by Egypt under Nasser. The UK and France persuaded the Israelis to launch an invasion of the Sinai Peninsula. Then they intervened directly from their air-force bases in Cyprus and Malta, and took over the canal. The United States, which was in the middle of a diplomatic row with the Soviet Union over the latter's military intervention in Hungary, maintained a posture of neutrality, but forced the United Nations to create an Emergency Force to keep the canal open and enforce the cease-fire. The crisis indirectly precipitated the secret transfer of nuclear technology from France to Israel.*

*So Carter, with his famous 1980 statement, was merely reiterating a time-hallowed principle of imperial control. Too bad that after Khomeini's Islamic Revolution of 1979 the US had just lost its grip on Iran. Fortunately, there was remedy: Iraq was goaded into invading Iran. Bush Senior cajoled Saudi Arabia into increasing its oil production. The output from Alaska, the North Sea, Mexico and Venezuela was also used to kick oil prices down. Saudi Arabia possesses the largest reserves worldwide, estimated at 262 billion barrels. Iraq comes second with proven reserves of 113 billion. Saudi Arabia, despite its Islamic pretensions, has always existed by America's grace. But Iraq has never been an easy stooge because Iraqis, for all their sectarian divisions, do not accept imperial control; hence the temptation to foist on it docile leaders such as the Hashemite king.*

*But there were problems with Saudi Arabia, too. After the 9/11 attacks, it surfaced that 15 out of the 19 hijackers were from that country. Bin-Laden had made no secret of his wish to replace the effete Persian Gulf monarchies with real Islamist regimes. So the United States began to look for an alternative to the Saudi kingdom. The neo-cons, in cahoots with the oil corporations and the Zionist lobby, were able to sell the idea of military intervention and regime change in Iraq.*

*In 2001, Raad al-Kadiri, a senior analyst at the Petroleum Finance Company in Washington, said that Iraq was the ultimate prize because only 15 out of its 70 oil fields, capable of covering US needs for the next 100 years, were in full production, the rest were still being developed. That should explain why former oilman Dick Cheney, Pentagon boss Rumsfeld and other ringleaders of the neo-conservative lobby viewed the war on*

*Iraq as a worthy investment. This also explains why Paul Wolfowitz and his fellow lobbyists*[26] *had written an insistent letter to President Clinton, as early as January 1998, urging him to establish a strong US military presence in the region, to defend 'America's vital interests' and, if necessary, to remove Saddam from power. The current US ambassador to Iraq, Zalmay Khalilzad, in his earlier capacity as senior consultant for Unocal Corporation, had tried to win over the Taliban regime in Afghanistan for a pipeline project that would have allowed the United States to transport the Caspian oil across Afghanistan to Pakistani ports. The Taliban became evil only after they rejected the proposal. So, you see, there is absolutely no doubt that the control of the oil resources is central to American strategic thinking in the Middle East.*

*With extraction costs of approximately $5 a barrel, the lowest in the world, the producers and the corporations can pocket most of the profits, which then go into the armament, trade and banking sectors. The West's armament industries sell their products back to the oil sheikhs. Just three countries, Kuwait, Saudi Arabia and the UAE, between themselves purchased approximately $70 billion worth of weaponry, for which they have no real use. Their total population is not even 30 million.*

*That's the evil empire for you—the evil empire at work! It talks about human rights, democracy and development. Never mind that democracy in the Middle East means Hamas and Hizbullah, or the Muslim Brotherhood, or Iran. Yet all of them are treated as pariahs.*

*The plan for Iraq was to quickly topple Saddam; install Chalabis and Allawis as surrogate rulers; privatise the economy, mainly the oil sector; embrace Israel; and go on to crush what resistance there remained in the region. Well, things didn't go quite that way. So now Bechtel, Exxon and Halliburton must bide their time. Meanwhile, Americans can go on burning daily on their roads one out of every seven barrels of oil consumed worldwide. They can do so by arm-twisting Saudi Arabia and OPEC to push oil production up and keep oil prices down, against opposition from countries like Algeria and Venezuela. One thing they cannot do, though—develop Iraq's oil resources as they had planned. That much we achieved. And we mean to keep our oil underground until it can serve better purposes....*

I wondered what evidence there was of oil serving 'better purposes' in the Gulf countries.... Mohammed Ghazi had just talked about their 'unwholesome wealth' that bred 'a materialism and spiritual torpor completely at variance with the values of Islam'. Well, a resentful Saddam Hussein had tried to take over Kuwait. When compelled to retreat before the unstoppable American onslaught, his army attempted to destroy the Kuwaiti oil fields. Television viewers across the globe were fed pictures of the burning of Kuwait's oil-wells by the retreating Iraqi soldiers. Experts calculated that it amounted to the destruction of six million barrels of oil a day, worth $120 million, over a period of several weeks. Iraq was forced to compensate Kuwait for these losses and to pay back all the damages resulting from its six month-long occupation. The Kuwait Oil Company, a subsidiary of the Kuwait Petroleum Corporation, claimed $952 million in compensation, only for the cost of extinguishing the wellhead fires. Since then, Iraq's own oil infrastructure has suffered substantial damage, during the first Gulf War, then under the sanctions, then again during the 2003 invasion. No compensations there.

'Don't you fear that Iraq's oil industry might be damaged beyond repair if the war against the occupiers drags on, or if the sectarian conflicts among Iraqis are not swiftly resolved?', I asked Professor Ahmed.

The good professor was looking weary and pooped. He and his companions had been fasting the entire day, as they would for the whole month. Unless I let them go more or less immediately, they would have less than four hours of sleep before getting up for a quick pre-dawn snack. All the clients of the coffee shop had already left, and I couldn't help noticing how both Hassan Jerardi and Mohammed Ghazi were looking at their wrist-watches. I promised myself to raise no more questions. Professor Ahmed sounded angry.

*Wars are born from the commitment to conquer and to destroy what cannot be conquered. Most war heroes of legend, the sap of war stories, are cast in this mould. Saddam Hussein, dragged out of his hole by the American army, went to the gallows unrepentant, his self-respect apparently intact. Erwin Rommel, the legendary general and ace of tank warfare in World War II, also embraced death with honour. The superior petroleum resources of the British proved his undoing; they brought him defeat at the battle of El Alamein, in December 1942. The fallen hero also fell from grace— suspected of plotting a German surrender, he would soon be compelled by Hitler to take poison and die. This very same man, while retreating from the El Alamein battlefield, had written to his wife: 'Shortage of petrol! It is enough to make one weep!'*

True, Saddam's soldiers tried to destroy Kuwait's oil fields when it became clear that they would have to abandon the '19th province of Iraq'. Most of them never made it back. They were to be killed on their retreat. So they plundered and set the Kuwaiti oil wells on fire. They were not doing anything new. That is what war is all about—you conquer and, if thwarted, you destroy. That is how it has always been and, I fear, will continue to be, until maybe such a hypothetical day when access to the natural resources will be vested in the people rather than in their rulers. Even then I wouldn't bet on eternal peace. But back to the real world and its war practices. Let me recall three historical episodes:

1.  the destruction of Romania's oil fields and refineries during World War I in November 1916;
2.  the destruction of Borneo's Balikapan oil fields during World War II in January 1942; and
3.  the deposition of Reza Shah Pahlavi in Iran during World War II in January 1941 and the simultaneous preparations to destroy the oil wells of Iran, Saudi Arabia, Iraq and Kuwait in case the Germans managed to capture the region.

In August 1916, Romania, then Europe's largest oil producer, declared war on the Hapsburg Empire, thereby putting itself at war also with Germany. By October 1916, it had become clear that the German troops were poised to overrun Romania and take over its oil fields and refineries. On 31October 1916, the British Cabinet War Committee in London met to discuss the situation. It decided that 'no efforts should be spared to ensure, in case of necessity, the destruction of the supplies of grain and oil, as well as that of the oil wells.'

The British government entrusted the task to Colonel John Norton-Griffiths, an engineering contractor and parliamentary back-bencher known as 'Empire Jack' for his strong imperialist views. John Norton-Griffiths reached Bucharest on 18th November. The German troops had already overrun the Romanian defence columns and were fast approaching the town of Ploesti, which had the highest concentration of producing oil fields and refineries. Empire Jack's incendiary team went to work. First they set the oil fields on fire. The refineries came next. They were blown up with explosives, turning the petroleum stores into viscous lakes of fire. The Romanian sky *went dark with asphyxiating smoke, while walls of red flames rose from the burning oil derricks. It was as if the planet were on fire.* The German government later estimated the loss at 800,000 tons of oil. There was absolutely no production for the next five months. The Reparation Commission created under Part VIII of the Treaty of Versailles merely affirmed 'the responsibility of Germany and her allies for causing all the loss and damage to which the Allied and Associated Governments and their nationals have been subjected as a consequence of the war.'

The victors lost no sleep over the question of compensating Romania for its losses. As for John Norton-Griffiths, he was to commit suicide in September 1930—not from remorse, God forbid, but because the Egyptian authorities supervising the construction of the Aswan Dam, in which he was involved, had threatened to sue him for fraud.

The oil fields of Balikapan in Borneo were the prized possessions of the Royal Dutch Shell consortium. Even before the attack on Pearl Harbour, an American naval squadron had mined the harbour and trained the oil men there on how to destroy the installations in anticipation of the imminent Japanese invasion. This is what they did, elaborately, to the accompaniment of much fury and fire, in January 1942. The burnt oil fields of Borneo fell to Japan in January 1942. The Allied, of course, had carried out their sweeping destructions without any thought or concern for the rights of those who actually owned the oil resources.

One objective of the North African campaign of the Axis powers, led by General Erwin Rommel, was to complete the encirclement of West Asia's oil-rich areas. Rommel hoped to take Egypt, Palestine, Iraq and Iran before heading for Baku, to link up with the German military columns from the Soviet Union and then jointly capture the oil fields of the Caucasus. In this he failed, but the final collapse of his North African campaign, at the battle of El Alamein, 60 miles short of Cairo, was largely due a German failure of mobility caused by critical petrol shortages. But the British had not been taking any chances with the oil resources of the Middle East. There was this Reza Shah in Persia, former commander of a Cossack brigade, who had got himself crowned as emperor and dreamed of founding a new dynasty (the Pahlavi dynasty). He was a nationalist who believed in modernising his country on the strength of the newly discovered oil resources. In 1933, he had forced the Anglo–Persian Oil Company, controlled by the British government with a majority share of 51 per cent of the stock, to improve the terms of the concession. The British weren't happy but there wasn't much they could do about it then. In 1941, however, even as the German forces were making rapid advances from Russia towards the Caucasus and from North Africa towards the Middle East, the Allied forces, led by the British, quickly deposed Reza Shah, sent him off into exile, and had his 21-year-old son Mohammed Pahlavi installed in his place. Mohammed had had little exposure to life in Iran. As a child he had been brought up by a French nanny, had later attended a Swiss school, and was thoroughly westernised. This suited the British just right. Later, it would suit the Americans. But back then, during World War II, the Anglo–American oil men in the Middle East, their military advisers and political patrons, had other priorities on their minds. They were busy making preparations for destroying the oil wells, should the Germans enter the region.[27]

You see, historical memory is a highly selective affair, fashioned by cultural constraints and political loyalties. It is the realities of power that shape international law and dictate the working of its enforcement mechanisms. In April 1991, the UN Security Council adopted resolution 687 which held Iraq liable 'under international law for any direct loss, damage, including environmental damage and the depletion of natural resources, or injury to foreign governments, nationals and corporations, as a result of Iraq's unlawful invasion and occupation of Kuwait'. The resolution resulted in the formation of the United Nations Compensation Commission, on 20 May 1991.[28]

The Commission first dealt with the claims of individual victims of Iraq's invasion and occupation of Kuwait. By October 1997, the Commission completed the processing of these claims—2,587,938 in all—which it placed in three main categories A, B, and C of decreasing degree of importance. By the end of 2003, the Commission had awarded $8.22 billion to 1,494,487 individuals.

The remaining 60,814 claims, under 11 categories, ranged from business losses, claims from corporations, public sector enterprises, payment of relief, evacuation costs, etc. Several governments claimed compensation for damage sustained by their embassy buildings in Kuwait city or even in Baghdad; the termination of payments to their employees after closure of these embassies; and damages to personal properties supposedly incurred by their diplomats in occupied Kuwait. Although many of these claims were not supported by any evidence that Iraq was actually responsible, the

*Commission ruled that 'the breakdown of civil order in Kuwait and Iraq'*
*during the occupation, was sufficient to establish a causal link between the*
*losses in question and Iraq's presence in Kuwait. One government claimed*
*compensation for the costs of evacuating its nationals and diplomats from*
*Kuwait to Baghdad in cars, flying them out of Iraq, and leaving the cars*
*behind in Baghdad. The claims also included the costs of later recover-*
*ing and repairing the cars. The Commission ruled that the claims were*
*legitimate. The Commission also compensated the governments that chose*
*to evacuate their citizens from neighbouring countries, including Saudi*
*Arabia and Israel, on the ground that the 'threat of military action' by Iraq*
*justified the moves.*

*By March 2004, the Commission had resolved all but 3,374 cases,*
*awarding a total of $9,954,238,244 in 12,887 cases. Kuwait Oil alone, a*
*subsidiary of the state-owned Kuwait Petroleum Corporation, received $610*
*million for the costs of extinguishing the wellhead fires, sealing the wells,*
*and carrying out the necessary repairs. As already mentioned, the funds for*
*the payment of much of these reparations came from especially mandated*
*Iraqi oil imports—the infamous Oil-for-Food program, which lasted until*
*the final 'decapitation' of the Saddam regime in April 2003. Even then, the*
*UNCC continued to implement resolution 687, although at the same time*
*governments and international donor agencies, including those vehemently*
*opposed to the invasion of Iraq, were pressured into paying billions of*
*dollars for the 'reconstruction of Iraq'.*

*By now, all the pretexts used to justify the invasion of Iraq have been*
*exposed as bogus. But is there anyone asking the United Nations to scruti-*
*nise the war and its consequences? Or to impose upon the coalition forces*
*standards of reparations consistent with those that had been imposed on*
*Iraq, a decade earlier, for its invasion of Kuwait?*[29]

*Why doesn't the UN as much as attempt to enforce accountability on*
*the US, now that the American action against Iraq has been exposed as*
*naked, cynical aggression? This is of course a rhetorical question, which*
*Cicero answered long ago. I think I already quoted him a moment ago, but*
*the quote bears repeating: 'What can be done against force without force?'*

*Not content with caving in to American pressure and failing to condemn*
*the war, the UN actually contributed to the destruction of human lives and*
*to the denial of human rights in Iraq, by imposing and ruthlessly uphold-*
*ing a regime of sanctions whose inhumanity was deplored by several UN*

institutions themselves.[30] Thus the UN, this guardian body of the Universal Declaration of Human Rights, this organisation set up to prevent the scourge of war, actively connived in the crime of inflicting death on at least half a million children under the age of 5 (according to an official UNICEF estimate) simply to placate a vengeful United States.

'Reforming the United Nations' has long been a pet topic for those who hang around in its corridors but fail to gain privileged access. Their notions of reform lack teeth and amounts to little more than tickling a purring cat. All these crimes of omission and commission by the UN, its transformation from guardian of world peace and promoter of human rights to provider of foot-soldiers for the World Cop; all this shameful self-abasement calls for a much more searching scrutiny.

The real question is: how can a world organisation, led by a handful of powerful States in control of the Security Council, be trusted to act in accordance with the lofty principles of its Charter, when it is not bound by any human rights treaty or convention? What justification is there for the prerogatives of the Security Council, its legislative fiats and resolutions, which routinely overrule the proposals emanating from the General Assembly? Isn't the functioning of Security Council, with its permanent members unrepresentative of the world at large, shockingly undemocratic? And what about the General Assembly itself, with its voting procedure that gives equal weight to all members, from huge to minuscule? Aren't we here in front of two symmetric, mutually reinforcing absurdities? What national or international court is there, that has the jurisdiction and power to scrutinise, question, and if necessary rescind the Security Council decisions on grounds of illegality? The UN is not a state. It is an organisation of states. As such, it lacks any juridical authority over the sovereign states that are its members. Yet its rulings are supposed to be binding. Or again: all UN members are constitutional states that are sworn to respect the international laws and treaties, but the UN Charter itself carries no such provision.

It is meaningless, therefore, to talk about reforming the UN without first clarifying its 'legal' and 'political' personality, in addition to all the questions connected with its actual functioning. But why waste time on such issues? There are no listeners and there won't be, until we succeed in shaking up this confounded world order with its injustices. Then maybe people will pay attention, go inward, reflect. Then maybe we can build up a sustained public pressure for real reforms—reforms worth the name.

*This is a tall order but, believe me, this is what the resistance movements across the Middle East are actually trying to achieve, what their affiliates are struggling and dying for. This is, beneath all the confusion and chaos, their true, if still dimly conscious, goal.*

## Notes

1. Quoted in William L. Shirer, *The Rise and Fall of the Third Reich* (Simon and Schuster, 1960), p. 530.
2. With 275 seats, elected in December 2005.
3. Much like the South Asian hookah, it consists of a vase with an elongated pipe, and it filters the tobacco smoke through a water container.
4. I remember many who directly and indirectly suggested this: Patrick Buchanan in *American Conservative;* Chris Matthews on MSNBC's *Hardball,* former Democratic presidential candidate Gary Hart; General Anthony Zinni, former Commander of the US Central Command; Steve Kroft of the CBS and several others including Democratic Senator Ernest 'Fritz' Hollings and even Richard Clarke who very clearly said that 'behind the US decision to go to war against Saddam Hussein was President Bush's policy to secure Israel'. Nicholas Kristof of the *New York Times* quoted General Zinni as saying that the main advisors of President Bush wanted to help Israel to obtain honourable peace made urgent by its debacle in Lebanon because 'the road to Jerusalem leads through Baghdad'. I also remember a May 2004 issue of *Newsweek* that referred to the assurance given by Ahmed Chalabi, the favourite Iraqi dissident of Saddam Hussein's regime, nurtured and empowered by the Pentagon for his usefulness as a war-monger, that a post-Saddam Iraq 'would be an Arab country friendly to Israel.' *A.N.*
5. For example, in a news column titled 'Bring Back Hussein, the Lesser Evil', *Los Angeles Times*, 26 November 2006, the hawkish ideologue and Bush supporter Jonathan Chait floated a 'serious' proposal: 'Let us consider putting Saddam Hussein back in power; given his track record of maintaining stability, that may be the simplest way of stopping Iraq's descent into chaos.' Other neocon thinkers were musing aloud about 'Iraq needing a Pinochet'. *E.N.*
6. The interview appeared in the Egyptian daily *Al-Ahram* on 27 September 1963 and was quoted by Tariq Ali in his *Bush in Babylon* (Verso Books: London, 2003).
7. Sandra Mackey quotes the statement in her WoW book *The Reckoning: Iraq and the Legacy of Saddam Hussein* (W. W. Norton, 2002).
8. While summarising in places, I have also supplemented references and relevant information whenever required. *A.N.*

9. The interview was reported by Michael Emery in *San Francisco Chronicle*, 13 March 1991.
10. Milton Viorst's report on his discoveries appeared in *The New Yorker*, 30 September 1991.
11. These remarks are taken from the well-known *Glaspie Transcript*, and have been quoted and referred to in numerous books and articles on the subject.
12. This conversation is also drawn from the *Glaspie Transcript*.
13. Tom Mathews emphasised this point in an article that appeared in the 28 January 1991 issue of *Newsweek*.
14. A former US Assistant Secretary of State for Near Eastern Affairs.
15. Which at the time tended to be grossly over-estimated. *E.N.*
16. On 25 February to be exact, i.e., on the Jewish holiday of Purim which celebrates the Biblical episode—most probably mythical—about how queen Esther and her cousin Mordechai dealt with the wicked Haman. Goldstein had felt he was honouring the command in the Book of Esther, which says: "The Jews smote all their enemies with the sword, slaughtering and destroying them, and did as they pleased to those who hated them' (*Esther 9:5*).
17. That agreement perpetuates the Maronite Christian monopoly over the Presidency while making small concessions to the Sunni confessional block.
18. Actually, the Shia uprisings and their bloody suppression were widely covered in the Western press. The distortion, or deception, regards the role of the coalition forces, which were portrayed as helpless bystanders, wishing to intervene but agonising over what to do and ending up doing nothing. *E.N.*
19. Who years later fled to Jordan and defected to the CIA.
20. We too may wonder why. Gratuitous sadism, or simple strategic incoherence? Probably the latter. Services like the CIA routinely engage in destabilising enemy regimes and fomenting insurrections, 'just in case', without necessarily coordinating with the other state agencies or giving much thought to the consequences. *E.N.*
21. Qom is Iran's second most sacred Islamic city after Mashad. In the Ottoman period, it became a sanctuary where Shia clerics and scholars from Najaf, Kufa and Karbala would seek refuge from persecution.
22. Michael Ignatieff is Director of the Carr Center at the Kennedy School of Government, Harvard University. Because of his personable appearance and high media exposure, he has been nicknamed *the thinking girl's pin-up ideologue*. Towards the end of the second Bush term, Ignatieff recanted—sort of—and gave a half-hearted apology for supporting the Iraq invasion. He then repaired to his native Canada, where he tried, without much success, to revive the fortunes of the Liberal Party. *E.N.*
23. This amazing fustian is taken from a piece which Ignatieff wrote for the *N. Y. Times*, titled *The American Empire: The Burden* and published on 5 January 2003.
24. Which had been the accepted norm for 359 years since the Treaty of Westphalia in 1648.

25. These attacks were so effective in boosting Putin's popularity that they gave rise to all sorts of conspiracy theories. While it is most unlikely that Putin himself stood behind the bombings, Russia's opposition media did produce circumstantial evidence that he may have had advance warnings of a Chechen plot and that, sensing a godsend, he decided to let things take their course. E.N.
26. They had got together on the platform of the *New American Century,* a lobby group formed in 1997. They also spawned a number of other think tanks.
27. Their story is recounted in a book by Philip O. McConnell, *The Hundred Men,* published in 1985.
28. It comprised a Governing Council, a panel of Commissioners and a secretariat under the authority of the Security Council. It was to be financed by especially mandated imports of Iraqi oil. That was the so-called 'oil-for-food" programme, in force from December 1996 onwards.
29. For those interested in the niceties of international law, here are some excerpts from the UN charter about the rules of military self-defence.

Article 2(3) says: 'All members shall settle their international disputes by peaceful means in such a manner that international peace and security, and justice, are not endangered.' Article 2(4) says: 'All members shall refrain in their international relations from the threat or use of force against the territorial integrity or political independence of any state, or in any manner inconsistent with the purposes of the United Nations.' So much for offence, now about defence.

Here is what Article 51 has to say about the right to military self- defence:

Nothing in the present Charter shall impair the inherent right of individual or collective self-defence if an armed attack occurs against a member of the United Nations, until the Security Council has taken the measures necessary to maintain international peace and security. Measures taken by members in the exercise of this right of self-defence shall be immediately reported to the Security Council and shall not in any way affect the authority and responsibility of the Security Council under the present Charter to take at any time such actions as it deems necessary in order to maintain or restore international peace and security.

The law of military action in self-defence was the subject of a 1986 decision by the International Court of Justice in *Nicaragua vs US,* 1986 ICJ 14 [June 27]. In this decision, the court not only held the US support to the Contra rebels against Nicaragua's Sandinista regime to be in breach of international law, but also explained that the right to self-defence—individual and collective—came into force only when armed raids and attacks against one's territory 'occur on a significant scale'. The attacks must be intense, sustained, and 'leave no choice of means and no moment for deliberation'. There has to be 'no alternative means of protecting the essential rights of the State'. The danger has to be both serious and imminent. Even then self-defence has to follow the framework of 'reasonableness', remain proportional to the existing danger and—a very significant point that—it must not become punitive. The mere presence of a danger cannot be used to justify the use of aggressive force. In June 1981, the UNSC endorsed this view when Israeli aircrafts destroyed Iraq's Osirak nuclear reactor, in alleged self-defence. The UNSC condemned the attack as an act of aggression and ruled that 'Iraq was entitled to appropriate redress for the destruction it had suffered'.

30   The Sub-Commission on the Promotion and Protection of Human Rights, in its working paper, called the Iraqi sanctions *unequivocally illegal under existing international humanitarian law and human rights law.* Article 54 of Protocol I expressly prohibits the starvation of populations. Its Article 14 requires the warring parties to ensure free passage for all consignments of essential foodstuffs, medical necessities and other commodities or services essential for human survival. The Fourth Geneva Convention, under Article 23(1), requires the contracting parties to allow the free passage of all consignments of medicines, essential foodstuffs, clothing, tonics intended for children under fifteen, expectant mothers and maternity wards. Collective penalties are explicitly proscribed by Article 33(1) of the Fourth Geneva Convention. Article 50 of the Regulations to the Fourth Hague Convention also forbids general punishments and Article 3(2)(f) disallows *any deliberate deprivation of access to necessary food, drinking water and medicine.*

# 2

# The discovery of oil and the geography of imperial conquest

Mohammed Ghazi, one of my Iraqi interlocutors, had used the term *debatable middle strip* to describe how the Middle East appeared to Western strategic thinking at the end of the Cold War: it was *debatable* not only in the sense of being a coveted prize but also a potential trouble spot, an area of ill-defined contours and uncertain future. The term was not new. It had been coined a good century earlier by an American Admiral Alfred Thayer Mahan,[1] in the waning days of the Ottoman Empire, after fresh oil discoveries had turned the Middle East[2] into a geopolitical hotspot. The term is still appropriate to describe a region whose land, resources, ethnic texture and state borders have remained fiercely contested ever since the European powers, at the end of the First World War, acquired the League of Nations' mandate to 'guide its people towards self-rule'.

Back then, knowledge about the region's petroleum resources was still fragmentary. The illuminating and lubricating properties of what was initially known as *rock oil* were first brought to the attention of the western world by Benjamin Silliman, a professor of chemistry at Yale, who in April 1855 published his research on a viscous black liquid gathered from bubbling springs and salt wells around northwestern Pennsylvania. Drilling derricks had already been used in China for more than 1500 years to bore for salt, and the same technique, with minor adaptations, now lay behind the first gushing oil wells of Pennsylvania. Quick progress was made in the technique of oil extraction from asphalt. A new substance named kerosene (from Greek *keros* for wax) fulfilled the growing demand for a safe and low-priced illuminant. By 1859 the United States was producing $5 million worth of the stuff. Kerosene production rose to 3 million barrels in 1862. The Civil War gave a further boost to the industry. In 1866, John F. Rockefeller, who used to deal in wheat, salt and pork, established Standard Oil, soon to become the first—and long to remain the biggest—multinational corporation in the world.

'Rock oil' as an illuminating agent had long been in use, albeit very sporadically, in parts of Eastern Europe and Central Asia. Marco Polo mentions a spring-oil in Baku that produced oil 'fit to burn'. Burning oil was easy to come by in parts of Eastern Europe, especially around Romania, where peasants would dig ducts to trap oil from oozy springs. It led to the development of the famous 'Vienna lamp', the pride of the Hapsburg Empire, a variant of which was later adopted in the United States. In fact, Eastern Europe's and Central Asia's fitful familiarity with oil and its uses may go back to much older, partially lost Babylonian knowledge.

The development of the oil industry over the next decades is a fascinating and complex story, which inextricably combines advances in science, technology, military power and global markets. We can attempt no more here than to give a cursory review.

The invention of a heat-resistant incandescent light bulb by Edison in 1882 quickly ended the use of kerosene as lighting agent. But the appearance of the automobile, with its internal combustion engine, was soon to give an unstoppable momentum to the oil industry, which immediately recovered from Edison's invention. Henry Ford's gasoline-powered car proved its usefulness and reliability when San Francisco was rocked by a major earthquake in 1906. By 1912, the United States had already 902,000 registered automobiles, and gasoline had found a new, ever expanding market. Then there came aviation. The Wright brothers made their first flight at Kitty Hawk in 1903. In 1911 the Italian army pioneered the use of fighter planes in battle, successfully scattering the Turkish forces at Tripoli. In the 1870s, Russia became the first country to convert its shipping from coal to oil. The railroad industry, in Russia and elsewhere, and several branches of heavy industry soon followed suit. The opening of the Suez Canal in 1869 and the spread of telegraphic connections gave Britain easy access to the huge markets of South and East Asia. The oil resources were essential to sustain these developments. Industry, transport and militaries began to worry about the future availability of oil and the risk of depletion. Finding and controlling new resources became a vital necessity.

Rockefeller, with his personal assets in Standard Oil already exceeding $9 billion by 1911, was in control of the biggest oil monopoly in the world. In 1879, Robert and Ludwig Nobel (brothers of Alfred Nobel, the discoverer of dynamite and founder of the Nobel Prize) established an oil refinery in Baku and soon became known as the 'oil kings' of the East. Fifty years on, the Nobel Brothers Petroleum Company had become an empire within the Russian Empire. It possessed everything from oil wells, pipelines, refineries, tankers, barges, storage depots, its own railroad and even its own retail distribution network. Ludwig Nobel commissioned a new tanker ship to revolutionise the transport of oil across continents. Making good use of Alfred's dynamite, the Nobel brothers built a forty-two mile long pipeline from Baku to Batumi, a Black Sea port annexed by Russia after its 1877 war with Turkey. The Paris branch of the Rothschilds also got involved in Russia's oil industry, setting up their own Caspian and Black Sea Petroleum Company in 1877. In 1891, Marcus Samuel, a Jewish entrepreneur from East London, obtained a contract from the Rothschilds to sell Russian kerosene east of the Suez Canal. With the Asian markets safely in his pocket, Marcus Samuel set up Shell, then turned his sights to the Middle East and made massive investments there. In 1890, Aeilko Jans Zijlker, the enterprising manager of a Dutch tobacco company, discovered oil in Sumatra and established the Royal Dutch Company. In 1907 Shell and Royal Dutch merged under the dynamic leadership of Henri Deterding to become the oil giant Royal Dutch Shell.

Meanwhile, Shell founder Marcus Samuel had made it into politics. Using his friendship with Winston Churchill and Admiral John Arbuthnot Fisher, he became Lord Mayor of London in 1902. In the United States, the marriage between oil and politics was consummated when James Garfield, a Congressman who had invested heavily in oil, became President in 1881. Soon enough, the dramatic developments in Russia and their impact on the oil industry in the Caspian area would raise the importance of the Middle East tenfold, making it a hub of oil politics and imperial rivalries.

However, when in 1902 Admiral Alfred Thayer Mahan coined his term *debatable middle strip* for the 'Middle East', it was not oil that was uppermost on his mind. Widely esteemed as a naval strategist and military thinker, Mahan was assessing the region's geopolitical importance primarily under the angle of the security of the British Empire in South Asia. To him the entire zone was *debatable* in the sense that it could one day witness a fierce contest between Britain and Russia, or Britain and other aspiring maritime powers like the US and Germany. Similar considerations had already, for decades, been guiding the British moves in the Great Game, as borne out by this unequivocal statement in 1903 by Lansdowne, British Secretary of State for Foreign Affairs: 'We should regard the establishment of a naval base, or of a fortified port, in the Persian Gulf by any power as a very grave menace to British interests, and we should certainly resist it with all the means at our disposal'.

# The Anglo-Persian Oil Company

The year 1903 was also an important watershed in British–Russian relations for a number of other reasons, political and economic. Some of them had directly to do with British oil interests, which had become quite substantial after the merger of Shell and Royal Dutch. The period from 1892 to 1903 had been very conducive to foreign investments within Russia because of the economic policies pursued by Count Sergei Witte, Finance Minister under Czar Nicholas II. A mathematician by training, Witte believed in Russia's rapid industrialisation and wanted foreign capital to stimulate its nascent oil industry. However, the Russian regime under Czar Nicholas II was plagued by intrigue and conspiracy, with Interior Minister Vyacheslav Plehve, a warmonger and noted Jew-baiter, playing the leading part. Vyacheslav Plehve intensely disliked Witte. He intrigued with the Czar to have him removed from the government on grounds that Witte was part of a Jewish cabal. Witte was dismissed in 1903. In the same year, Baku witnessed its first major strike of oil workers. Soso Dzhugashvili, more famous under his later name of Joseph Stalin, was then operating in Baku under the pseudonym of 'Koba'. He was one of the organisers of the strike, which soon spread to other industrial centres. By then, Baku had already become a hub of communist conspiracies. The revolutionary magazine *Iskra* was being printed there, in a secret facility, for clandestine circulation in Russia.

The oil supplies from Baku were no longer assured. The frequent anti-Jewish pogroms and persecutions, orchestrated by the mischievous Plehve, were a further destabilising factor for the oil industry. Then came the Russo-Japanese war, which ended in ignominious defeat for Russia. Revolutionary agitation redoubled, with places like Baku taking the lead. Oil supplies from Russia steadily dwindled. The oil empires built by Marcus Samuel, Henry Deterding, the Nobels and the Rothschilds were on the brink of collapse. Their survival depended on finding alternative resources.

Even as Russia was fast slipping out of the hand of European oil interests, promising developments were taking place in Persia, that were to lay the foundations for the future oil dominance of the Middle East. The first oil concession in Persia was obtained in 1872, ironically enough, by the founder of the Reuters news agency, Baron Julius de Reuter. Reuter's concession was renewed in 1889. The nosiness of the first oil prospectors and their haphazard explorations brought remonstrations from Imperial Russia, which regarded Persia as its zone of influence. But the then Shah of Iran, Muzaffar al-Din, was short of money and keen to find oil investors. In November 1900, he sent his friend and economic advisor Antoine Kitabgi, a westernised gentleman of Armenian descent, to Paris to look for investors. In Paris, Kitabgi met with William Knox D'Arcy, a British lawyer, adventurer and trader who had made a huge fortune from gold mining in Australia. D'Arcy was taken in by Kitabgi's offer. The British government extended its indirect support. In March 1901, D'Arcy's representatives went to Tehran, over Baku, and negotiated oil concessions with the Shah's representatives, while Arthur Hardinge, the British envoy to Persia, carefully monitored the discussions. Hardinge was all admiration for Kitabgi's resourcefulness, his easy access to the Shah, his influence with the Shah's ministers and courtiers.

British official interest in these discussions was part of the diplomatic and political games which Britain and Russia were playing for control over Persia. In Curzon's own words, Persia was a 'chessboard upon which is being played out a game for the domination of the world'. Since the 1860s, Russia had followed a course of expansion that had brought much of Central Asia under its sway. It was now eyeing Persia for its warm-water ports with a view to get a strategic grip on the entire Middle East.

For Britain, this prospect of Russian expansion was abhorrent. The 1885 Russian attack on Afghanistan showed that the routes to India had to be defended. All these considerations explained why the British were so keen to help D'Arcy in getting the oil concession in Persia. Bribery and browbeating helped and, finally, on 28 May 1901 Shah Muzaffar al-Din signed a concession that allowed D'Arcy to explore and exploit oil in three-quarters of the country for the next 60 years. The Shah received £20,000 in cash and £20,000 worth of shares. Under the agreement, Persia was to receive 16 per cent of annual net profits.

George Reynolds, a graduate of the Royal Indian Engineering College who had previously drilled for oil in Sumatra, was in charge of D'Arcy's operation in Persia. Thomas Boverton Redwood, the author of *A Treatise on Petroleum* and a British oil policy advisor, closely supervised the exploration, even arranging a major loan from the British Admiralty. Being a strong advocate of the conversion of the Royal Navy from coal to oil, Redwood believed in the necessity of developing oil reserves for the British military. This is the background against which Lord Lansdowne's aforementioned statement of May 1903 must be seen: 'We would regard the establishment of a naval base or of a fortified port in the Persian Gulf by any other power as a very grave menace to British interests and we should certainly resist it with all the means at our disposal.' That declaration was, in the words of India's Viceroy Lord Curzon', Britain's 'Monroe Doctrine for the Middle East'. Lord Lansdowne and Hardinge supported D'Arcy's application for a loan to enable him to go ahead with his search for lucrative Persian oil. The Admiralty wrote to D'Arcy, cautioning him against approaching foreign oil interests, including Standard Oil and Rothschilds, and it persuaded Lord Strathcona to immediately arrange for a £50,000 loan. The British government also persuaded Burma Oil, founded by Scottish merchants in 1886, not only to underwrite the costs of exploration and production in Persia but also to establish a Concession Syndicate with D'Arcy as director. British military officers, strongly supported by contingents of South Asian soldiers, were to protect the drilling sites. Profit and politics became inextricably linked.

A gusher of oil at Masjid-i-Suleiman, which broke out on the night of 25 May 1908, brought D'Arcy's search for profitable, inexhaustible oil to a successful conclusion. The Concession Syndicate was quickly transformed into the Anglo-Persian Oil Company. By the end of 1910 it employed more than 2,500 workers. The Company built a modern refinery at Abadan, and a 138 mile long pipeline to transfer the crude oil from Masjid-i-Suleiman to the refinery. The vast majority of workers at the refinery and at the drilling sites were brought in from South Asia.

By now, the British government had huge stakes in the fortunes of Anglo-Persian Oil. As early as 1903, William Knox D'Arcy had wormed his way to Admiral John Arbuthnot Fisher, then Second Sea Lord, and had managed to convert him to the view that the Royal Navy needed to switch from coal to oil. Fisher was a staunch moderniser. He had already introduced the use of torpedoes, submarines and other state-of-the-art appurtenances of naval warfare. But the main battleships were still being fuelled by coal and were, therefore, at a tactical disadvantage against German battleships in terms of speed and scope of action. Admiral Fisher, Thomas Boverton Redwood (the British oil policy advisor) and Samuel Marcus were convinced that the Royal Navy could not match the German fleet in swiftness and manoeuvrability unless it switched to petroleum. Churchill also sympathised with their view. But, of course, the decision to switch depended on there being assured and plentiful petroleum supplies from loyal sources.

The discovery of vast oil resources at Masjid-i-Suleiman and the building of a sophisticated refinery at Abadan solved this problem. The need for haste was brought home by the so-called Agadir incident in July 1911, when a German gunboat steamed into the harbour of Agadir, on the Atlantic coast of Morocco, in an apparent challenge to the British and French monopoly on the maritime trade in Asia and Africa. The incident passed without a direct military altercation but made a deep impression on the British government, which decided to upgrade its naval capabilities. Winston Churchill became First Lord of Admiralty soon after the incident and decided, with full awareness of the implications, to change the navy's fuel from secure Welsh coal to the newly discovered oil in politically precarious Persia.

The decision was politically momentous and entailed an obligation on the part of the British government to secure long term supplies of oil. Admiral Fisher was appointed to lead a Royal Commission on Fuel and Engines 'to find the oil; to show how it can be stored cheaply; how it can be purchased regularly and cheaply in peace and with absolute certainty in war.' Fisher instructed Charles Greenway, Managing Director of Anglo-Persian Oil, to ensure that the company remained for all times strictly 'all-British' and that the concession embracing the entire oil fields of Persia [...] should not pass under the control of a foreign syndicate.' Foreign Secretary Edward Grey further explained: 'Evidently, what we must do is to secure under British control a sufficient oil field for the British Navy.' In June 1913, Churchill submitted a memorandum to the cabinet discussing the issues of oil fuel supplies for the navy and asking for a long-term contract to assure adequate supplies at secure prices. The memorandum ranted against big companies and monopolies, including Standard Oil, Shell and Royal Dutch, and went on to argue that the Admiralty should become 'the owners or, at any rate, the controllers' of oil in Persia.

To concretise Churchill's suggestions, the Cabinet decided to send a commission to Persia, under former Director of Naval Intelligence Admiral Edmond Slade, to investigate the facilities owned by Anglo-Persian Oil. The Company had been for some time under financial strains. The refinery faced serious technical snags and required large investments to keep afloat. Luckily for Anglo-Persian Oil, the British government simply could not do without the company and its oil concession. Without them the empire could not be defended. Admiral Slade told Churchill: 'It would put us into a perfectly safe position as regards the supply of oil for naval purposes if we had the control of the company and at a very reasonable cost.' He also said that 'it would be a national disaster if the concession were allowed to pass into foreign hands.'

In June 1914, Churchill moved a bill in the House of Commons proposing that the British government invest £2.2 million in Anglo-Persian Oil to acquire 51 per cent of the stock. The bill also proposed the nomination by the government of two directors on the company's board, with veto powers on admiralty fuel contracts and all political matters. After an acrimonious debate on the bill, with many members accusing Churchill of raising the spectre of monopoly and of engaging in 'Jew baiting', it was passed with an overwhelming vote: 254 to 18. Oil had become an instrument of British foreign policy and a key strategic commodity.

The British Empire, which had begun as an offshoot of the East India Company, was now the dominant partner of an oil company and ready to defend its interests by all means. We can see this logic at work in Britain's interest in the Suez Canal. In 1859, the British government had acquired 44 per cent of shares in the Suez Canal Company, originally a French concern. The Suez Canal was then Britain's water-highway to South Asia, the jewel in the imperial crown. A century later, in October 1956, Britain and France incited Israel to invade the Sinai Peninsula so that they could intervene militarily, under the pretext of separating the belligerents, and secure the canal which Nasser had just nationalised. By then, British India had split into independent countries for almost a decade. But what had been a highway of imperial control in 1859 was still a 'jugular vein of trade' in 1956 and had to be defended. Clearly, the transfer of power in the colonies had not spelt the end of imperialism and its diverse agendas of hegemony.

The metaphor is apt: the Suez Canal was indeed the *jugular vein* of British trade, and as long as the British Empire lasted, Anglo-Persian Oil was truly its blood bank. The requirements of their defence would take absolute precedence and bring much suffering to the people in the region. Winston Churchill, the First Lord of Admiralty during World War I, is reported to have said: 'We are prepared to shed a drop of blood for every drop of oil.'[3] Britain's acquisition of the League of Nations' mandate in Palestine, Transjordan, Mesopotamia and Syria also came out of that resolve, which has since continued to guide the West's geopolitical strategies in the region.

The demise of the British Empire after World War II altered the equations but did not shake the West's political will to defend its oil interests in the region, militarily if need be. The United States reaffirmed that resolve, loud and clear, with the proclamation of the 'Eisenhower Doctrine' in 1957, and so did President Carter when he declared, in 1980, that any 'attempt by any outside force to gain control of the Persian Gulf region will be regarded as an assault on the vital interests of the United States of America and [...] will be repelled by any means necessary, including military force'.

That such proclamations nowadays tend to emanate from Washington, with London concurring in poodle-like eagerness, merely underscores the transfer of imperial supremacy from Britain to the US. But there is no doubting the steely resolve behind the rhetoric. That became evident with the Iraq wars, which began in 1991 and have not ended yet, but have already unlocked the geopolitical space of the Middle East for further mutations. It also becomes evident when we examine how the recent discoveries of hydrocarbon resources in Central Asia have been reshaping Washington's and London's strategic thinking, even their spatial conceptions. New terms like *the Greater Middle East* and *Southwest Asia* have been in vogue for some time, which conveniently cover the Republics of Central Asia while excluding problematic countries like Turkey and Iran.

## The Political Geography of Conquest

Let us now briefly recount how the creation of Iraq under the British mandate laid the foundation for today's sectarian frictions and territorial contentions, which in turn are a standing invitation to outside intervention.

As we know, the liquidation of the Ottoman Empire, seat of the Caliphate, immediately after World War I, resulted in Gandhi's first major *satyagraha* against the British rule in India. The immediate aim, or pretext, was to remonstrate against what Gandhi had described as the 'British betrayal of the Muslim world'. The agitation witnessed an unprecedented degree of Hindu–Muslim solidarity.

Gandhi had pitched the ethics of his first *satyagraha*, known as *Khilaphat movement*, on the British pledge given by Lloyd George that at the end of the war the Ottoman Empire would not be dismembered. Of course, the pledge was conditional on Caliph Abul Hamid's honouring his promise of keeping Turkey neutral. In the early stages of the war, when it appeared that Germany might win, Ottoman Turkey, long known as 'Europe's sick man', got carried away and, without clearly weighing the consequences, allowed German ships to anchor off Istanbul. The Turks were impressed by the German technical know-how. Plans were afoot to build a railway line connecting Baghdad to Berlin and also to jointly prospect for oil in the Mesopotamian part of Ottoman Turkey. As a matter of fact, on 28 June 1914—the very day Archduke Franz Ferdinand of Austria was assassinated in Sarajevo—the Grand Vizier of Ottoman Turkey signed a memorandum promising the Mesopotamian oil concession to the Turkish Petroleum Company, a weird amalgamation of Anglo-German financial and political interests. The Turkish Petroleum Company had been put together by Calouste Gulbenkian, an Armenian millionaire trading in Caspian oil from London.

Gulbenkian had taken a degree in mining engineering from King's College, London and written his thesis on the technology of petroleum industry. In 1892, he had submitted a report to the Turkish authorities about Mesopotamia's oil potential, recommending German technical cooperation. Gulbenkian was also responsible for involving the Deutsche Bank as a partner in his Turkish Petroleum Company. The British, however, were determined to keep the Germans out of the Middle East.

With the hawkish Horatio Herbert Kitchener as Secretary of State for War, they were also determined to maintain their naval supremacy and control over all seaways to South Asia. The port of Aden, at the mouth of the Red Sea, was already in their possession. Alexandria, Egypt's most important port city on the Mediterranean coast, close to the Suez Canal, became a British naval base. Egypt, formally still an Ottoman province, had become politically volatile after Napoleon's 1798 invasion. It was declared a British protectorate in November 1914.

## Kuwait Becomes a British Protectorate

British eagerness to guard the 'debatable middle strip' also stood behind their clandestine agreement with the Bedouin chieftain of Kuwait. Kuwait was then a big patch of largely unpopulated desert at the upper corner of the Persian Gulf, and belonged to the Ottoman province around Basra. It derived its name from an 18th century fort (*Kut* in Arabic) which later housed a Turkish garrison. The first sizeable settlements go back to 1710 when, following a harsh drought, a Bedouin clan led by a chieftain with the common name of Al-Sabah drifted into this unprepossessing desert from its original home around Najf, in present-day Saudi Arabia. Over the years, the Al-Sabah became responsible for locally administering the area for the Ottoman Empire.

With Ottoman permission, the British had been using the port of Kuwait since 1775 as a station for overland mail service from India to the Mediterranean. In 1899, the Al-Sabah clan went through a bloody internal feud that resulted in the murder of the ruling chief by his cousin

Mubarak al-Sabah. Fearing chastisement from the Ottoman overlords and vendetta from influential members of the clan, Mubarak asked the British for protection. The request suited the British because Kuwait controlled Mesopotamia's access to the Persian Gulf. They were nervous about signs of a rapprochement between Ottoman Turkey and Germany under Emperor William II after the 1897 Greco-Turkish war. They were also worried about a joint German–Turkish project to construct a railway line from Berlin to Baghdad and eventually extend it to Basra over Kuwait.

So the British responded to Mubarak Al-Sabah's overtures. Colonel Malcolm John Meade concluded with him a secret pact promising British protection in exchange for British supremacy in foreign affairs. Al-Sabah also undertook not to 'cede, sell, lease, mortgage, or give for occupation or any other purpose any portion [of the territory] to the government or subjects of any other Power.' The pact clarified that 'Sheikh Mubarak bin-Sheikh Sabah of his own free will and desire does hereby pledge and bind himself, his heirs and successors.' Although the Pact remained secret for the next 14 years, the British fulfilled their part by keeping Mubarak safe both from Turkish reprisals and internal intrigues. In 1902, for example, when a Turkish force moved from Basra to occupy the territories under Al-Sabah's administration, a small Royal Navy contingent landed in Kuwait and chased the raiders away. Later that same year the British foiled a plot, by two of Mubarak's nephews, to overthrow him. A naval force under Commander Armstrong intercepted at sea a party of 150 armed Bedouins, burnt their boats, and punished the villages that had lent them. The British needed Mubarak; they were determined to help him stand his ground in Kuwait and resist external pressure. In 1907, they reinforced their secret agreement with him by signing a lease agreement, known as the *Bandar Shuwaikh Lease:* in exchange for a sum of £100 Britain obtained rights in perpetuity over the tract of land where Turkey and Germany wanted to construct their Baghdad–Basra railway. In that same year, the British appointed Captain W. H. Shakespeare as political officer for Kuwait. The appointment was part of a British plan to foment a serious Arab uprising against Ottoman Turkey in anticipation of the coming war.

The clouds of war had long been hovering over Turkey. Italy was claiming what remained of the Turkish territories in North Africa. In the Balkans, the Serbs, Bulgarians, Montenegrans and Greeks were all making swift progress towards independence. The Anglo-Russian Pact of 1907 further threatened Turkey's suzerainty over the Balkans. Emboldened by Turkey's beleaguered situation Britain announced its disapproval of the Berlin–Baghdad railway project and its resolve to maintain strategic control in the Persian Gulf to safeguard its trade interests. The British also formalised their involvement in Kuwait, by obtaining Turkey's official endorsement of the secret pact which they had concluded with the local chief fourteen years earlier. The Convention between Britain and Ottoman Turkey, signed in July 1913, provided that Kuwait, while remaining 'under the Ottoman flag', would become administratively autonomous; that the Imperial Ottoman Government would recognise the validity of the agreements between the Sheikh of Kuwait and Britain; and, that the Sheikh would retain his rights of private property in Basra in conformity with Ottoman law. The Convention also promised that Kuwait would not become a British protectorate 'as long as no changes are made by the Imperial Ottoman Government to the status of Kuwait, as defined in the Convention'.

About the same time, as already mentioned, a high-powered military deputation under Admiral Edmund Slade was touring the Persian Gulf region with several petroleum geologists to assess the oil prospects there. After the delegation submitted its encouraging report, Mubarak al-Sabah of Kuwait was made to sign yet another secret agreement, pledging exclusive oil rights to the British.

When World War I broke out in August 1914, Mubarak al-Sabah received a letter from the British Political Resident in the Persian Gulf instructing him to attack Umm Qasr, the only remaining shallow water port on the upper side of the Gulf. The letter quietly conveyed the British view that Kuwait had become 'an independent government under British protection'.

## The Role of Oil in the Mesopotamian Campaign

Anticipating Turkey's support for Germany, Britain dispatched a large force from South Asia to Mesopotamia, first to secure Basra, then to capture Baghdad. The idea was to safeguard the region's newly discovered oil resources, upon which war ships, armoured vehicles and military airplanes were now so critically dependent.

Persia's oil resources, controlled by the British dominated APOC (Anglo-Persian Oil Company), were already under exploitation. Since 1906, there were continual negotiations for petroleum rights in the Northern Mesopotamian province of Mosul and Basra. The parties involved were: William Knox D'Arcy, one of the founders of the APOC; Royal Dutch Shell, advised by the Armenian entrepreneur Calouste Gulbenkian; the Deutsche Bank; a group of American interests known as the Chester group; and, of course, the Ottoman authorities. The prospect of wrenching a contract for the exploration and exploitation of oil and gas in Mesopotamia had resulted in the formation in 1911 of the Turkish Petroleum Company (TPC). The capital participation was 50 per cent British, 25 per cent Dutch and 25 per cent German. The TPC received its Letter of Intent, signed by the Grand Vizier of the Ottoman Empire, on 28 June 1914, eleven days after the British parliament had passed the bill to acquire 51 per cent of the stock in Anglo-Persian, and on the very day that Franz Ferdinand was assassinated in Sarajevo.

Despite its name, the Turkish Petroleum Company had no Turkish partner. The Deutsche Bank was involved simply because the Ottoman authorities had greater trust in German technical skills. The German share in the TPC would later be transferred to France. Britain, then still the dominant imperial power, successfully manipulated the American Chester Group out of the deal. After the war, under American political pressure, the British agreed to take the Chester Group back into the TPC. But the American banks refused to finance the Group for fear that the dismemberment of Turkey would result in political instability and endanger the ambitious project. Eventually, a politically ascendant United States intervened and forced Britain, France and the Dutch to rename the TPC as the Iraq Petroleum Company so as to incorporate, at 16.6 per cent participation, the amalgamated American oil interests of the NEDC (Near East Development Corporation). The NEDC was jointly owned by Atlantic Refining Company, Gulf Oil Corporation, Pan American—AMOCO—Standard of Indiana, Standard Oil of New Jersey, and Standard Oil of New York. But these were later developments, which took place after the conclusion of the war.

In the critical initial stages, Britain maintained the most ruthless commitment to retain a pre-eminent hold over the oil resources of the region.

Marcus Samuel (founder of Shell) and William Knox D'Arcy (co-founder of Anglo-Persian) were directly advising Arthur Balfour (Foreign Secretary), Maurice Hankey (War Secretary) and Winston Churchill himself (then First Lord of the Admiralty and later Minister of Munitions) about the need to obtain unquestionable control over oil-rich areas as 'a first-class British war aim'. The tour of petroleum experts in the Gulf region, under Rear Admiral Edmund Slade, had resulted in a comprehensive policy memorandum that urged the British government 'to encourage and assist British Companies to obtain control of as many oil-producing areas [...] as possible'. The memorandum made a comprehensive appraisal of the global energy situation and identified Persia and Mesopotamia, including the Turkish province of Mosul, as having the largest potential oil fields in the world. Calouste Gulbenkian himself had pointed to Mesopotamia's huge potential in a report which he had submitted to the Ottoman authorities as early as 1892.

The Mesopotamian campaign ended to Britain's satisfaction but its earlier phase, under the command of Major General Charles Townshend, was a colossal disaster for nearly 50,000 South Asian soldiers who lost their lives. The British Expeditionary Force was drawn largely from the 'barracks in the Oriental seas'—Lord Salisbury's description of the Indian colony. It had been earmarked for action in Mesopotamia even before Turkey formally joined the war by attacking Russia on 29 October 1914. The force landed near Basra six days earlier, on 23 October, and within a month captured Basra by using the advantage of surprise. Then, under orders from India, the force moved up the Tigris–Euphrates valley towards Baghdad, occupying Amara on 3 June 1915 and continuing its northward advance. On 11 November it reached Tusbun (Ctesiphone of ancient Parthian lore) on the Tigris, 40 kms southeast of Baghdad. It was there that the Turkish troops mounted their devastating counterattack on an exhausted force that had been slogging along with insufficient logistics, poor communications, and much too rigid operational objectives. There ensued two weeks of fierce fighting which finally ended in the slaughter of Britain's Indian troops. On 1 December, Townshend ordered a retreat, but came under siege at a village called Al-Kut. On 29 April 1916, after 20 weeks of siege and futile attempts at rescue that resulted in more than 20,000 casualties, Townshend decided to surrender unconditionally.

By then more than 30,000 soldiers had perished. The 6th Poona Division had become a beleaguered garrison of the sick, wounded and hungry, dying daily in their scores. Townshend was taken prisoner and transferred to a luxurious palace in Constantinople, where he lived in 'comfortable captivity' for the rest of the war. All his soldiers were sent on a death march to prison camps or to work as labourers on a railroad. Out of the 6,000 Indian prisoners of war who had surrendered, nearly 3,000 died in captivity from disease or ill-treatment. Some British officers who encountered the straggling columns of survivors reported 'a dreadful spectacle [...] British troops in rags, many barefooted, starved and sick, wending their way under brutal Arab guards through an Eastern Bazaar [...] men slowly dying of dysentery and neglect.' The Chief Military Censor, whose task it was to monitor the morale of the troops, commented: 'Not since the days of Hannibal has any body of mercenaries suffered so much and complained so little.'

Ultimately, Britain sent a huge force, 166,000 strong, under General Stanley Maude, which again moved up the Tigris and after four months of fierce fighting captured Baghdad on 11 March 1917. After the war, Townshend returned to England to spend the rest of his life in peaceful retirement.

## The Plans for a Hashemite Caliphate and the Sykes–Picot Agreement

On their own, the 'barracks of the Oriental Seas' with their inexhaustible supply of cheap soldiers would not have been enough to ensure the British conquest of Mesopotamia and the establishment of a new empire of oil in the Middle East. To succeed in these objectives, Britain had to enlist the active support of sections of the native population. There had to be, too, a measure of cooperation among the old imperial powers with experience in the game of conquest, to beat back in concert new contenders like Germany. These requirements of imperial coalition, much as in our own days, were pursued largely by means of undercover politics, stealthy negotiations and covert military operations, whose full, authentic histories still remain unavailable. Only fragmentary episodes of this secret history have become known (mainly through disaffected inside sources), casting partial light on the confidential consultations between the British and ambitious Arab chiefs, or between the European allies, the United States and influential Zionist lobbies. Even so, enough facts have come to light, revealing a complicated story of double dealings, unprincipled alliances and incessant betrayals. Let us attempt a brief review.

Although the bulk of official documents about the Mesopotamian affairs for the critical 1909–15 period, in possession of H. I. Shakespeare, the political officer for Kuwait, have inexplicably been lost, it is acknowledged that clandestine contacts between British officials and local Arab leaders had been steadily developing since early 1900. These contacts were being coordinated and supervised by the British ambassadors to Constantinople, notably Nicholas O'Connor. But many others were involved, such as: John Gordon Lorimer, an officer of the Indian Civil Service who was also compiling the Gazetteer of the Persian Gulf, covering the period from 1870 to 1914; Percy Zachariah Cox, Chief Resident in the Gulf region from 1893 to 1914; Stuart George Knox and H. I. Shakespeare, political officers responsible for Kuwait from 1904 to 1915. Crucially involved was also one Harry St. John Bridger Philby, also known as Jack Philby. Originally an officer of the Indian Civil Service, he was moved to the Middle East during World War I on a sensitive mission. And of course, he also sired Harold Kim Philby, probably the most notorious double agent of the Cold War era.

After the outbreak of the war, several British actors, who later became the stuff of legend, entered the fray. While some of these characters were remarkable enough in their own right, their doings have been highly romanticised. The three most famous figures in this constellation were: T. E. Lawrence, better known as 'Lawrence of Arabia'; Gertrude Bell, famous in the Arab world as *Al-Khatun,* meaning 'the Great Lady'; and Gerard Leachman, who died at the side of his friend Ibn-Saud while fighting arch clan enemy Ibn-Rashid in 1915. Then there was Leonard Wooley, a colleague of T. E. Lawrence and archaeologist of distinction, who after the war led the excavations at Ur and made a significant contribution to our understanding of the Sumerian civilisation. There were also purely official figures, like British Viceroy Curzon, who paid a ceremonial visit to Kuwait in November 1903 and conferred a ceremonial sword on Mubarak al-Sabah; or Lord Kitchener, British Consul-General in Egypt who conferred with Amir Abdullah (son of Sharif Hussein of the Hashemite clan and guardian of Mecca and Medina) in Cairo in February 1914; or again Henry McMahon, Britain's first High Commissioner in Egypt, who personally supervised the clandestine negotiations with Arab leaders.

Apart from the Al-Sabah dynasty of Kuwait (Mubarak died in November 1915 but his sons upheld his policies), British imperial calculations in the Middle East revolved around the ambitions of two main Arab families. They were: [1] Sharif Hussein and his sons Abdullah and Faisal, who belonged to the Hashemite clan. The clan claimed descent from the Prophet Mohammed and traditionally controlled the central Arabian province of Hejaz with its holy cities of Mecca and Medina. Hussein was the *Sharif* or guardian of Hejaz. [2] Ibn-Saud, a desert warlord from the rocky region called Najd in the central part of present-day Saudi Arabia. He was the main political force behind the fanatical Wahhabi sect and fought intermittent battles not only with the Ottoman forces but also with fellow Arab clans that did not subscribe to the Wahhabi ideology.

The pact with Sharif Hussein and his sons Abdullah and Faisal, achieved largely through the influence and personal charisma of T. E. Lawrence, was based on the understanding that the British would transfer the Islamic Caliphate to the Hashemite dynasty. They would only retain Baghdad and Basra as special zones under British protection, to 'safeguard their mutual economic interests' through 'special administrative arrangement'. On its part, the Hashemite was to help the British in organising a broad Arab revolt against Ottoman rule.

The pact was apparently first mooted by Secretary of State for War H. H. Kitchener in late 1914 and finalised by Henry McMahon, Britain's first High Commissioner in Egypt, through an extensive correspondence with Hussein and his two sons. Scholars of the period make much of a handwritten letter by Kitchener to Sharif Hussein where he wrote:

> Till now we have defended and befriended Islam in the person of the Turks. Henceforth it shall be that of the noble Arab. It may be that an Arab of true race will assume the Khalifate at Mecca or Medina, and so good may come by the help of God out of all the evil which is now occurring. It would be well if your Highness could convey to your followers and devotees who are found throughout the world in every country the good tidings of the freedom of the Arabs and the rising of the sun over Arabia.

In June 1916, Sharif Hussein formally called on Arabs to rise in revolt against Ottoman rule, proclaiming himself 'King of all Arabs'. He trusted that the British would keep their word and recognise Arab independence under his Caliphate, excluding only a few areas where Britain could not act 'without detriment to the interests of her ally, France'. However, in a letter to Ali ibn-Hussein, dated 24 October 1915, Henry McMahon imposed the following conditions for the territories of Mesopotamia that would later become Iraq:

> With regard to the *vilayets* of Baghdad and Basra, the Arabs will recognise that the established position and interests of Great Britain necessitate special administrative arrangements in order to secure these territories from foreign aggression, to promote the welfare of the local populations and to safeguard our mutual economic interests.

If Henry McMahon and his superiors in London had imagined that Sharif Hussein, on the strength of his descent, was a natural leader of the Arabs, they were soon to be sorely disappointed. For the moment, however, the alliance served the British war objectives. Hussein and his sons, under active inspiration from Lawrence, were able to organise a large scale sabotage of Turkish supply lines. A group of Arab officers in the Ottoman army, led by Nouri al-Said and Jaar Askari, were enticed to defect and joined the Arab banner raised by Sharif Hussein. With the support of Arab bands, Lawrence was also able to capture the Red Sea port of Aqaba, near the point where Israel and Jordan now meet. It was a daring military expedition, across the desert called *Al-Houl*, the Terror. Lawrence was familiar with the desert route from a 1909 trip he had made in the region to study crusader castles for his graduation work. The capture of Aqaba helped Britain retain its control over the Suez Canal. It also precipitated the surrender of Jerusalem in December 1917, ending 400 years of Ottoman rule over Palestine.

Under the Sykes–Picot Agreement, Britain was to keep both Baghdad and Basra, with Mosul and parts of Greater Syria going to France. It was also to receive the Mediterranean ports of Haifa and Acre. Czarist Russia was to receive territories in northeastern Turkey, mainly the Armenian provinces, plus some Kurdish territory to the southeast and a vague assurance of control over Istanbul, in exchange for a pledge of non-interference in the rest of Mesopotamia. The territories marked out for

French acquisition in Greater Syria included Lebanon and Mosul. The Sykes–Picot Agreement, whose Articles I and II specifically referred to the Hussein–McMahon correspondence, radically contradicted the promises of an independent Arab State, or Confederation of States, under Hussein's Caliphate. The terms of this agreement might never have become known if the Bolshevik regime in Russia, after the October 1917 Revolution, had not decided to withdraw from the imperial bargain and to make it public.

## The Balfour Declaration

The October Revolution also precipitated the Balfour declaration of 2 November 1917 on Palestine, which expressed sympathy for the Zionist aspirations to establish 'a national home for the Jewish people'. The declaration had the eager support of Sykes, who maintained that it was important for the British to win over those Jewish groups in Germany, Russia and the United States which supported Theodor Herzl and his Zionist movement aiming at the creation of a Jewish homeland in Palestine. A larger number of Jews from Russia and other parts of Europe, mainly Germany, had begun migrating to Palestine following a spate of anti-Semitic pogroms in the 1880s.

Bible-reading British Statesmen associated Palestine with 'Judea'. They were conscious—not to say over-conscious—of the ancient connections between the land and the Jews. They also knew of the long history of anti-Jewish persecution in Europe. There was the haunting lore figure of the 'wandering Jew'. Byron's *Hebrew Melodies*, published in 1815, were popular in British conservative circles. Here is one of them:

> *Tribes of the wandering foot and weary breast,*
> *How shall ye flee away and be at rest!*
> *The wild dove hath her nest, the fox his cave,*
> *Mankind their country—Israel but the grave!*

The British politicians were also aware of rising anti-Semitism in Europe, especially in Russia, Germany and France. Thousands of persecution-fleeing Jews had been migrating to the United States and Britain. Many also came to Palestine as pioneers of the future state envisioned by Theodor Herzl, the founder of the Zionist movement. Herzl had argued, perceptively enough, that the creation of a national homeland on the ancestral land of the Jews would meet with favour in Christian Europe if it could relieve it of its unwanted Jews. Herzl himself made a positive impression on British leaders like Arthur Balfour, David Lloyd George and Winston Churchill when, in 1902 he put his case for ending the anomaly of Jewish statelessness before a Royal Commission that was examining proposals for a new immigration legislation. They became enthusiastic supporters of Jewish immigration to Palestine. The new situation arising out of World War I, especially the Bolshevik revolution in Russia, and the growing Jewish influence over the political circles of an ascendant United States, also contributed significantly to the Balfour Declaration, which was released on 2 November 1917. By then Chaim Weizmann, the Russian-born Zionist leader and scientist (he invented a synthetic acetone useful in the manufacture of explosives) was heading the British Admiralty laboratories. Weizmann, later to become Israel's first President, was already an influential voice in British political circles.

Meanwhile, the native inhabitants of Palestine were growing suspicious of the British–Zionist nexus. Their leaders were told that the small number of Jewish migrants only desired to live in peace with the Arab majority. But they were not convinced. They saw the incoming settlers as colonisers in league with the British government. Such were the tensions between native Arabs and Jewish settlers, even in the early stages, that President Woodrow Wilson's aide Colonel E. M. House concluded a sombre report with these words: 'It is all bad and I told [Lord Arthur] Balfour so. They are making [the Middle East] a breeding place for future war.' A special fact-finding commission, which Woodrow Wilson dispatched to the area, submitted a report full of pessimistic observations about future Arab–Jewish relations. David Ben-Gurion himself had no illusions. He told the governing body of Jewish settlers, known as Yishuv:

> 'Everybody sees a difficulty in the question of relations between Arabs and Jews [...] but nobody sees that there is no solution to this question. No solution! There is a gulf, and nothing can bridge it [....] We, as a nation, want this country to be ours; the Arabs, as a nation, want this country to be theirs.'

The Jewish settlers, though still a tiny minority, were single-minded, well organised, generally educated and adept in western ways of thinking and functioning. Their proto-government started developing its own system of education, taxation, fundraising, land and labour management. Most significantly, it took a disciplined approach to security, creating a secret militia internally known as Haganah. Their decision- and policy-making body, which styled itself 'Jewish Agency Executive' in English and *Yishuv* in Hebrew, was an offshoot of the original Zionist Commission. It was to receive British recognition in 1920. From the start, it worked like an actual government.

## The Wahhabi Warlord

As if the Balfour Declaration, which pledged Britain's 'best endeavours to facilitate [...] the establishment in Palestine of a national home for the Jewish people', was not enough to vitiate the future of the Middle East, the British were also in close contact with Ibn-Saud, the ferocious warlord of central Arabia and zealot of Wahhabism. Ousted from Riyadh by the House of Ibn-Rashid in the late 1800s, the Saudi clan had taken shelter in the inhospitable land of Kuwait. There Ibn-Saud befriended Mubarak al-Sabah. In 1900, with Mubarak's support, he set out to reclaim his ancestral lands of Najd from his clan rival, the strongly pro-Ottoman Ibn-Rashid. As noted in Lorimer's *Gazetteer of the Persian Gulf* and in secret documents belonging to the Gulf residency, the venture had the tacit support of the British.

Ibn-Saud was then only 21. On several occasions, British naval ships had to move into Kuwait to fend off raids which Ibn-Rashid and the Turkish governor of Basra organised jointly to wipe out the Saudi base in Kuwait and teach Mubarak a lesson for sheltering this seditious character. In 1902, through feats of extreme daring, Ibn-Saud managed to capture the castle of Riyadh and to get himself recognised as Imam and King of Arabia by the fanatical Wahhabi establishment, which had strong roots in the region. Over the years, Ibn-Saud's fortunes fluctuated under constant attacks from Ibn-Rashid's warriors and Turkish troops. Eventually, with covert British support, Ibn-Saud set up a religious-military organisation called *Ikhwan* ('brotherhood'), whose mission it was to bring the undecided under his sceptre and to fight and massacre his Muslim rivals as a matter of religious duty. After defeating a combined Turkish and Rashidi force in

1904, Ibn-Saud accepted Ottoman suzerainty, on British advice. That way, he hoped to improve his standing and gain political legitimacy, the better to crush his rivals. Although Ibn-Saud had been under British protection for a long time, he concluded a formal agreement with the British only in December 1915. He then received money and arms to fight and plunder the Arab territory still under Ottoman control.

The British alliance with Ibn-Saud was bizarre, not only for the reason that it squarely contradicted the political understanding reached with the Hashemite clan of Hejaz, but also because the Wahhabi fanatical school of Islam, which the Saudi clan championed, was plainly irreconcilable with the Western notions of democracy and political self-determination. Inaugurated in the 18th century by an obscure Muslim cleric, Mohammed ibn Abd al-Wahhab (1703–92), this grotesque aberration of religious revivalism is best understood as a convulsive response to the erosion of Islam's political power in the face of European expansion. From the start, the ire of the sect was directed against the 'vices' of mysticism, rationalism and intellectualism, accused of corrupting the purity of Islam and sapping its power. Although Abd al-Wahhab's own father and brothers condemned him as a fanatic and an ignorant, and denounced his weird puritanism as offensive to the true Islamic tradition, the Wahhabi movement gained a following in pockets of the Arab world and also in South Asia, by displaying a fierce spirit of resistance against Western encroachment.

The British should have known better than to cultivate the Saudis. For decades, their administration in India had faced the virulence of Wahhabi resistance. Wahhabi clerics declared Bengal 'land of infidels' (*Dar al-Harb*) soon after the British took over the state and introduced, in 1793, under Cornwallis and John Shore, the so-called Permanent Settlement, which spelled doom for the landed Mughal aristocracy. Although a first Wahhabi-inspired jihad in India, under the leadership of Syed Ahmed from the United Provinces, was stamped out with unprecedented ferocity, the followers of the sect significantly contributed to the Mutiny of 1857, under the symbolic banner of the Mughal Emperor. Over the next two decades, thousands of Muslim rebels, real Wahhabis or branded as such, were sentenced to capital punishment or transportation for life. During one such trial in 1871, a Wahhabi Muslim stabbed to death John Paxton Norman, Chief Justice of Bengal. Another Wahhabi convict in the Andamans, Sher Ali, murdered Viceroy Mayo while the latter was inspecting the detention facility.

This spirit of undaunted resistance against European domination, enduring in the face of extreme repression, earned the Wahhabi sect much admiration, even though, as a religious doctrine, it was too insane and totalitarian to gain widespread acceptance. In the Arab world, the sect might actually have died out after its sudden ebullience in the late 18th and early 19th centuries, had it not found a new ally in the person of Ibn-Saud who was dreaming of a popular revolt in Arabia against Ottoman rule. Mohammed ibn Abd al-Wahhab, in his own days, had already identified Ottoman rule over the holy land as a primary source of corruption—a vector of 'heretical' accretions like mysticism, interpretative jurisprudence and creative arts, which 'weakened' the pristine purity of the true faith. This was a convenient plank for the Saudi clan to stir Bedouin sentiments against the Ottoman power. When rebellion became a nuisance, the Ottoman authorities took notice and ordered reprisals. In 1818, a joint punitive expedition by the Egyptian and Turkish forces put down the stirrings of rebellion with a heavy hand. They even razed the city of Dhariyya, original home of the Saudi clan.

This would have been the end of the Saudi ambitions and their symbiotic association with the Wahhabi religious madness, but for the resuscitation they received, under British auspices, in Kuwait and later in Central Arabia. The British were looking for allies in the war against Ottoman Turkey. As we saw, they had already worked out a *quid pro quo* with the Hashemite clan, which carried the promise of a pan-Islamic appeal. But there was a risk here. Even at that stage, the British did not wish to encourage a wider Arab solidarity. So, they let Ibn-Saud organise his bands of Arab warriors (*Ikhwan*) on the basis of the murderous Wahhabi ideology. Their main targets, in the beginning, were the Shia community and its religious-political centres. The British extended financial and military support to Ibn-Saud, on the understanding that his bands would concentrate on fighting the Ottoman forces. Later on, after the establishment of Saudi Arabia following the collapse of the Ottoman Empire, the British forces assisted Ibn-Saud in wiping out those *Ikhwan* bands that rejected the European mandate under the League of Nations. The British also knew that Ibn-Saud's ultimate ambition was to capture Hejaz and to control Mecca and Medina. To do that, he had to oust the Hashemite sheriff of the holy cities—that very same Hussein, whom the British had encouraged to raise the flag of Arab revolt against Ottoman rule by promising him a new Caliphate. Clearly, Britain's war plans and choice of allies not only rested on cynical expediency, but also showed exquisite perfidy in planting the seeds of division for the post-war Middle East.

## Carving up the Middle-East

An estimated 13 million were dead at the end of World War I, a war that was fought on land, sea and in the air by machines powered by internal combustion engines and fuelled by 'earth oil'. Paris was saved from near certain occupation by the German army by the mobilisation of a 3,000 strong automobile squad under General Joseph Gallieni. By the end of the war, the British fleet of army vehicles included 56,000 trucks, 23,000 motorcars, and 34,000 motorcycles. British Colonel Ernest Swinton modified the recently developed agricultural tractor to build an armoured vehicle that was impervious to machine gun fire. This was the beginning of the tank. At the beginning of the war, the British air-force consisted of just about 250 planes. By the end of the war, Britain had built 55,000 planes; France, 68,000; Italy, 20,000; and Germany, 48,000. Assured supplies of oil, which Germany did not have, gave Britain a definite advantage.

The British government paid its tribute to the captains of the oil industry by hosting a dinner for the delegates of the Inter-Allied Petroleum Conference at Lancaster House in London, exactly ten days after the Armistice. Curzon raised a toast to the 'Allied cause' that 'had floated to victory upon a wave of oil'. The director of France's Comité Général du Pétrole was more to the point: 'The blood of the earth was not only the blood of victory; it is also the blood of peace, ever more in demand for reconstruction after the war.' Oil was also ever more in demand as fuel for the automobile—that vehicle of individual freedom. By 1929 the United States would claim 78 per cent of the world's cars, around 23.1 million, and consume 1.03 million barrels a day. By 1939, it would consume 2.58 million barrels.

There were also the thoughts of future wars. All eyes were riveted on the Middle East. Maurice Hankey, the British Secretary of the War Cabinet, was absolutely clear: 'The only big potential supply that we can get under British control is the Persian and Mesopotamian supply.' Winston Churchill, as we earlier observed, was willing 'to shed a drop of blood for every drop of oil'. So oil-hungry was Britain that it felt it had to revoke the terms of its agreement with France. At the Paris peace conference of February 1919, Sykes fell ill and died, and it was Winston Churchill who, under Prime Minister Lloyd George, became the arbiter of the occupied Arab territories. Georges Clemenceau, the then French Prime Minister, insisted that the pact should be honoured and that oil-rich northern Mesopotamia should go to France. Lloyd George pleaded with him to take Syria instead, also offering a share of oil production from Mosul. France needed Britain's support to pursue its vendetta against Germany. So it gave up its larger territorial claims. It had to be content with Syria, which it immediately divided into five pieces: Lebanon; the state of Damascus; the government of Aleppo; an autonomous area around Latakia and Cabal Druze; and the region of Alexandrite. Lebanon was declared independent. The region of Alexandrite was transferred to Turkey in exchange for a non-aggression pact with France.

On 24 April 1920, Lloyd George and France's new Premier, Alexandre Millerand, worked out a formal settlement at San Remo: France would get 5 per cent of the oil from Mesopotamia, which was to become a British mandate under the League of Nations. The vehicle for oil development remained the Turkish Petroleum Company, and the French acquired what had been the German share in it. In return, the French gave up their claim to Mosul. Britain made it absolutely clear that any private company developing the Mesopotamian oil fields would have to be under its control. The British and the French, together with Gulbenkian, also drew up a map of all the known oil fields in the Middle East (to the exclusion of Persia and Kuwait) to delimitate the area within which the oil agreement applied. All the signatories to the agreement had to respect the boundaries shown on that map and pursue further exploration and exploitation only after mutual consultation. The agreement became known as the Red Line Agreement because of the colour that was used to draw the map. Both countries also worked out a mandate under the League of Nations, by which Britain became responsible for Palestine and Mesopotamia, and France for Syria and Lebanon. Ostensibly, the 'mandate' was a trusteeship for grooming the local people towards the goal of self-determination. The agreement also mentioned, as an afterthought, the 'establishment of a Jewish national home'. The elasticity of the word 'mandate' allowed all sides to hide their true intentions. While suggesting a noble care-taker responsibility, it also carried sufficient assurances of imperial control.

Initially, Churchill was wary of disturbing too radically the administrative demarcations which existed under the Ottoman rule. Feeding his caution was the widespread unrest which erupted immediately after the war, and the clamour for political concessions raised by the most heterogeneous groups whose only unifying bond lay in their opposition to the British mandate. Tribal armies organised by Ibn-Saud began attacking the Shia holy centres at Karbala and in the Basra region. Bedouin tribes of the western desert started their own infighting. The Assyrian Christians, settled in the Hakkari Mountains, began to pour into Mesopotamia to escape persecution at the hands of Turks and Kurds. Iraq's nationalist groups became nervous when they realised that the British, instead of bestowing independence on the country as promised after the capture of Baghdad in March 1917, were now planning to install Sharif Hussein of Hejaz as their king. The Kurds were clamouring for independence. Sunnis and Shias were fighting each other, but were united in their opposition to the British rule. Organisations like the *Jamiyat an-Nahda al-Islamiya* (League of the Islamic Awakening) attracted both Sunni and Shia Muslims. In Baghdad itself a coalition of Sunni clerics, Shia merchants, secular nationalists and former Ottoman civil servants, known as *Haras al-Istiqlal* (Guardians of Independence) even issued a call to jihad, putting the British administration under serious strain. These outbreaks inside Iraq reflected a wider pattern of effervescence in the Arab world. Demonstrations, riots and strikes became endemic in Egypt. Ibn-Saud was poised to invade the Hejaz, to oust Sharif Hussein and his Hashemite clan, and take control of the holy cities of Mecca and Medina.

In Palestine, Jews and Arabs were clashing violently. The pogroms organised by the Arabs in the first week of April 1920 were particularly bad. The Jewish underground militant organisation called Haganah retaliated. The British High Commissioner for Palestine, himself a Jew, tried to be even-handed, regularly reiterating that the Balfour Declaration visualised a Jewish national home without compromising the aspirations of the Palestinian Arabs.

The British administration in the Middle East was under pressure to maintain order without draining the British exchequer. The British army, exhausted as it was from years of war, found itself unable to cope. Finally, Churchill once again had to call in Indian reinforcements, and to press heavy armoured vehicles and the air force to put down the Arab revolts.

After quashing the Arab uprisings, Churchill turned his attention to geopolitical matters. He appointed T. E. Lawrence (freshly lionised as *Lawrence of Arabia* by American journalist Lowell Thomas) as one of his main advisors on Arab affairs. Churchill gathered his panel of advisors and experts for a 10-day conference in Cairo, held in the Semiramis Hotel from 12 March 1921. About 40 persons attended. 'Everybody Middle East is here', wrote Lawrence. Sir Percy Cox, the High Commissioner for Iraq, referred to the Arab sheikhs insistently as 'those romantic old dears with dusters on their heads'. (These days, the coarser American GIs have taken to calling Arabs *rag heads*.)

Sharif Hussein's second son Faisal, who was a confidant of Lawrence, had returned from the 1919 Paris conference utterly disappointed with British perfidy. The British government, which had enough trouble on its hands, decided to appease Sharif Hussein, by suggesting that he get himself declared 'King of Syria' by a spurious National Congress in Damascus. But the League of Nations had placed Syria under the French mandate. The French, seeing no merit in his declaration, pushed him and his entourage out of Syria, compelling them to seek shelter in British Mesopotamia. The British now had to do something to placate the Hashemite family. Churchill, already consumed by his anxieties over the situation in Palestine, suddenly devised, as he thought, an ingenious solution.

Seventy-five per cent of the then province of Palestine lay east of the Jordan river, in what was then known as Transjordan. As we saw, the British did not have enough troops to control the conflicts between Jewish settlers and Arabs. While the Cairo conference was still in progress, news reached the participants that Abdullah, Faisal's brother, claiming to need a 'change of air for his health', had left Arabia with a retinue of Bedouin warriors and entered Transjordan. The British feared that Abdullah would attack French Syria, which in turn might give the French an excuse for invading Transjordan as a first step towards taking over all of Palestine. Churchill had to come up with a quick fix. So, as a temporary expedient, he announced that Transjordan would be administratively detached from the rest of Palestine, and that Abdullah would be appointed governor of

Transjordan. Churchill calculated that Abdullah would not seek trouble with the Jews who were burgeoning on the West Bank. He charged Abdullah to keep order in Transjordan until Britain's aircraft and armoured cars were in place. This 'provisional' solution became the basis of the kingdom of Jordan, now ruled by Abdullah's grandson Hussein. Today Jordan has a population of 5.3 million, of which more than 60 per cent are Palestinian refugees.

The appointment of Abdullah seemed to accomplish several objectives at once. It went part of the way towards repaying what Lawrence insisted was Britain's wartime debt to the Hussein family, although Sharif Hussein had pointedly refused to endorse the Balfour declaration and the manner in which the British were carving up the Middle East. He was also losing the battle for Arabia to his blood rival, Ibn-Saud. Britain hoped to mollify him by turning his two sons Abdullah and Faisal into kings of Jordan and Iraq.

The territory of Mesopotamia, which stretched from the Persian Gulf to Turkey and included the provinces of Basra and Mosul with their vast oil fields, was to witness some of the bloodiest uprisings against the British mandate. The man responsible for administering this troubled region, which joined three separate Ottoman provinces—Mosul, Baghdad and Basra—into a single unit, was Colonel Talbot Wilson, Cox's deputy. These territories, home to such incompatible groups as Shia and Sunni Muslims, ethnic Kurds, Assyrian Christians and Jews, was given the name of Iraq—either an Arabic form of *Uruk*[4] or a Persian word for 'lowlands'. In Arabic, Iraq also means 'the well rooted country'. In accordance with Churchill's plan, Sharif Hussein's elder son was proclaimed King of Iraq under the name of Faisal I. Like his brother Abdullah in Tansjordan, Faisal was charged with keeping Iraq quiet until the British were ready to police it with their aircrafts and armoured cars. High Commissioner Arnold Talbot Wilson did not like the arrangement. He warned that two million Shias and nearly half a million Kurds would never accept a Sunni Arab as their leader. In Wilson's judgment, 'far from making the Arabs on this side our friends, the recognition of Faisal as king of Mesopotamia can only be regarded in this country as a betrayal of its interests, and we shall alienate the best elements here.'

But in a way Faisal's lack of popular support also suited the British: the weaker his position, the more malleable a puppet he would prove in their hands. From the first, they made it clear to him that his becoming king was conditional on his signing two important treaties. The first treaty was signed on 3 January 1919. The co-signatory was Dr Chaim Weizmann, the Zionist leader (later to become the first Israeli President). The Agreement promised 'the closest possible collaboration in the development of the Arab State and Palestine'; the exchange of Arab and Jewish accredited agents between the Arab State and Palestine; a definite demarcation of boundaries; measures to 'encourage and stimulate immigration of Jews into Palestine on a large scale and as quickly as possible to settle Jewish immigrants upon the land through closest settlement and intensive cultivation of the soil'; a joint survey, under a Zionist Commission, of the economic possibilities of the Arab State and Palestine.

At the Cairo conference, before the proclamation of his kingship, Faisal also agreed to sign an Anglo-Iraqi Treaty, valid for 20 years, whereby he promised to be guided by British advice on all matters affecting British interests and his own fiscal policies; to have British officials in the country acting as advisers and inspectors; and to pay half the cost of supporting these British officials. The treaty also conferred on the Turkish Petroleum Company, later renamed as Iraq Petroleum Company (IPC), perpetual rights to produce oil in the whole of Iraq, with four schillings per ton of oil going to the Iraqi exchequer. In return for these generous terms, the king received £40,000 as a personal present. In 1925 Mosul was finally merged into Iraq, with the League of Nations' approval, following a decision to break up the Kurdish territory into four parts that would join the neighbouring states as 'southeastern Turkey', 'northern Syria', 'northern Iraq', and 'northwestern Iran'.

Until then the British had retained the option of declaring Mosul part of an independent Kurdish State or of leaving it with Turkey. The Kurdish independence leader Sheikh Mahmoud was deported to India. Arnold Wilson had just written a book where he vividly described the Kurds' aversion to being re-absorbed by Turkey or to be ruled by the new Arab territories, which the British were about to create. Talking about Southern Kurdistan, Wilson frankly admitted that there was a four-to-one majority there in favour of Sheikh Mahmoud's idea of an independent Kurdish State. An international commission of inquiry, formed under the auspices of the Council of the League of Nations, came to the same conclusion after spending nearly two months in Mosul province. Arnold wrote: 'If a conclusion were to be drawn from the ethnic argument, it would [be] that an independent Kurdish state should be formed, given that Kurds constitute seven-eighths of the population of the governorate.' Nonetheless, Britain managed to get the League of Nations' endorsement for detaching Mosul from the Kurdish part of Turkey and joining it with Iraq, after receiving from Faisal perpetual rights to explore and exploit all the oil in Iraq.

Britain also decided to formally separate Kuwait, a British protectorate since 1914, from the Basra province. Faisal and his Iraqi advisors were hardly privy to the understanding between the British and the Al-Sabah clan. Mubarak al-Sabah had died in November 1915, and his two sons Jabir and Salim also died in quick succession, after two short reigns: Jabir's from 1915 to 1917, and Salim's from 1917 to 1921. Salim took no part in the formal negotiations that followed World War I and allowed the British officials under Percy Cox to take all decisions on his behalf. The two brothers' successor, Ahmed al-Jabir al-Sabah, who ruled for nearly three decades, remained staunchly loyal to the British and turned down several offers by Faisal to merge Kuwait back into Iraq. Faisal understood that the decision to separate Kuwait from Basra was motivated by strategic considerations: depriving Iraq of a convenient outlet to the Persian Gulf. As one of the Middle East's larger countries, with its oil wealth, historical legacy and a relatively advanced political culture, Iraq had the potential of becoming a regional power. Other oil rich enclaves, like Oman, Qatar, the United Arab Emirates, Bahrain, or even Saudi Arabia, had no such potential. This was the reason why the British chose to block Iraq's access to the sea by retaining Kuwait as a protectorate. Iraq still had its small port of Umm Qassr on its southern coast. But to get there, ships had to pass through a narrow channel alongside the islands of Warbah and Bubiyan, which belonged to Kuwait and could be used in hostile circumstances to block all sea traffic to Iraq. Kuwait remained a British protectorate until June 1961 when it was declared fully independent.

Faisal, meanwhile, was unhappy. His entreaties to the British were falling on deaf ears. Even T. E. Lawrence, the man who boasted of designing the modern Middle East over dinner with Churchill and a few others, was turning a cold shoulder.

The British High Commissioner, as interim ruler of Iraq, drafted a constitution that conferred supreme powers on the King over his parliament: he could pass or withhold laws; call elections; prorogue parliament; and issue ordinances for the fulfilment of treaty obligations without parliamentary sanction. Then the British staged a carefully organised plebiscite which confirmed Faisal as king of the newly formed country. The Anglo-Iraqi treaty was ratified in 1922. The first parliament, elected that same year, under Prime Minister Abd al-Muhsin as-Saadun, decided to reduce the treaty period from 20 to 4 years. Saadun was dismissed. In June 1930, the treaty was renewed for a period of 25 years. It provided for a 'close alliance' and British guidance in 'all matters of foreign policy'. Basra and al-Habbaniyah were designated as British air force bases and British troops received freedom to move across the country.

All attempts by Faisal to bargain for less degrading terms failed against Churchill's arrogance and insulting attitudes. Churchill often wrote to Percy Cox asking him to convey to Faisal that while the British paid the piper, they expected 'to be consulted about the tune'. When Faisal asked for an independent review of the proposed terms of the Anglo-Iraqi Treaty, an exasperated Churchill complained to Cox: 'Six months ago we were paying his hotel bill in London, and now I am forced to read day after day 800-word messages on questions of his status and his relations with foreign powers. Has he not got some wives to keep him quiet?'

Of all the former Arab allies of Britain, there was only Ibn-Saud whose position remained to be settled. During the war, Ibn-Saud had consolidated his hold over much of central Arabia and was now planning military raids against Abdullah's Transjordan as well as Sharif Hussein's kingdom of Hejaz. He also claimed substantial portions of the territory that had been merged into Iraq—namely all the land west of the Euphrates river up to the Syrian border. In August 1922, Ibn-Saud's camel-cavalry force, on its way to invade Transjordan, was intercepted outside Amman by British airplanes and armoured cars. In the negotiations that followed, the British forced Ibn-Saud to accept a settlement aimed at protecting Iraq. The negotiations between Ibn-Saud and the British were led by Percy Cox who bullied Ibn-Saud in his desert tent until he broke down. According to several reports, an abject Ibn-Saud pleaded that Sir Percy was his father and mother, that he had raised him from nothingness to prominence, and that he would surrender half his kingdom, nay the whole of it, if Sir Percy so ordered. Percy Cox was satisfied and chose to be magnanimous, transferring large tracts of Kuwaiti territory—that would later yield oil—to Ibn-Saud's kingdom, which in 1932 became the kingdom of Saudi Arabia. Ahmed al-Jabir al-Sabah did not protest. The

British also gave him to understand that they would turn a blind eye if Ibn-Saud chose to annex Hejaz and take possession of Mecca and Medina. Ibn-Saud took the hint and organised a strong punitive expedition against Hussein in 1924, forcing him to abdicate and renounce his claim to the Caliphate. Hussein had offended the British by refusing to endorse the Balfour Declaration. Thus it was that Saudi Arabia, with its control over Mecca and Medina, became the West's bulwark against the first stirrings of secular Arab nationalism that were beginning to manifest themselves in Iraq, Syria and Egypt.

## The Partition of Palestine

The story of the partition of Palestine and the creation of Israel on 14 May 1948, which concluded the British mandate in the Middle East, has been narrated exhaustively in scores of scholarly or journalistic works. The whole sequence is well-known, from Hitler's rise in Germany and his murderous anti-Semitism up to the historic vote of Resolution 181 by the United Nations' General Assembly on 25 November 1947. The resolution called for a partition of Palestine into an Arab State of 4,500 square miles with about 800,000 Arabs and 20,000 Jews; a Jewish State of 5,500 square miles with 538,000 Jews and 397,000 Arabs; and a third international zone around Jerusalem. The recommendations of the Commission under William Robert Peel, released in July 1937, more than two years before the start of World War II, showed that the British had already made up their minds, long before the Holocaust had started, to conclude their mandate by creating a Jewish State through a partition of Palestine. After the conclusion of World War II, the coming into being of Israel had become doubly inevitable. The guilty conscience of the Western countries over their failure to avert the Holocaust; the influence of the Zionist groups over the administrations in the United States and (to a lesser extent) in the Soviet Union; the ambivalent attitude of Arabs during the war—all these factors tipped the scales decisively in favour of the new state-to-be.

The story is too well known for us to recount here. However, we shall attempt a quick review of developments in the decade and a half after

World War I to show that the British sympathy for the establishment of 'a national home for the Jewish people', even at the start of the mandate period, was primarily dictated by imperial interests: the policy was, in essence, an insurance against the challenges of a nationalist Arab resurgence in the Middle East.

In 1914, the Jewish presence in Palestine accounted for only 12 per cent of the population, but the Conservative government of Britain that took charge under Prime Minister Lloyd George considered these Jewish settlers as potential allies, out of several strategic calculations. The determination to retain control over the Suez Canal was one. But British distrust of Muslim political ambitions—despite the alliances with the Hashemite, Saudi and Al-Sabah clans—played an even greater part in cementing Lloyd George's friendship with A. J. Balfour and Chaim Weizmann. Weizmann, a well-known scientist and spokesman of Jewish interests in Britain, understood that the future of the Middle East would be decided not by the democratic aspirations of the natives, but by the strategic thinking and economic interests of the big powers. The British also calculated that the influence of America's Jewish community might help draw the United States into the war. The United States eventually did get involved in the war, and the Turkish forces in Palestine surrendered to General Edmund Allenby just five weeks after the Balfour Declaration. The next step came in 1919, when the British engineered the aforementioned pact between Faisal and Weizmann. The terms of the mandate, as worked out between Britain and France at San Remo in April 1920, also emphasised the 'historical connection of the Jewish people with Palestine' and called for the 'establishment of the Jewish National Home'. These terms were endorsed by the League of Nations on 24 July 1922. To succeed, the plan required Jewish immigration on a wide scale, as there were only 84,000 Jews in the whole of Palestine in 1922—less than 12 per cent of the total population. Given the demographic reality, if there was to be a state of Israel, it had to be achieved by other than democratic means. Even then the British mandate tellingly referred to the Jews in Palestine as a *community* and to the Arabs, who formed 88 per cent of the population, as *the other sections*.

As already mentioned, violent clashes between Jews and Arabs became routine from the very beginning of the British mandate. The Jewish self-defence organisation called Haganah was receiving weapons from the local

British administration under Herbert Samuels, the first high Commissioner of Palestine, who was himself a Jew. Samuels also encouraged Jewish immigration on a wide scale, and paid special attention to collective agricultural projects. The mandate administration under Samuels also tried to mollify the Arab elite through a complicated framework of patronage. Compliant representatives of the local Arab upper crust were rewarded with powers and perks. The Arab landed elite profited by selling their land to Jewish settlers at high prices. The poor peasants also, unable to withstand the economic depression that followed the war, gave away their land at low prices. In this way, the British managed to corrupt the Palestinian Arab elites and undermine the traditional system of Arab solidarity based on social bonds.

Winston Churchill, then Secretary of State for the Colonies, nurtured strong sympathies for the Jewish immigrants. He held that the Jews had every right to return to Palestine, with which they had historical and religious bonds going back 3,000 years. However, some radical Jewish elements, like Vladimir Jabotinsky, one of the main organisers of the Haganah, were unhappy with Churchill and the British administration for separating Tansjordan from Palestine, thereby reducing the land available for Jewish settlement.

Arab–Jewish clashes became more frequent and bloodier. The riot that broke out on the eve of Yom Kippur in September 1928 (comparable to the cow and pig fights between Muslims and Hindus in India) left hundreds of dead. The British either failed or didn't try to control these riots while they lasted, but took stern action against the Arab Muslims after the violence had run its course. But this policy of arresting Arab Palestinians and slapping on them death sentences after summary trials did not help to calm their tempers. The few official initiatives which the British took to curb the influx of migrants were thwarted under pressure from Zionist groups in London and the United States. For example, a Commission of Inquiry constituted in 1929 to determine the cause of the escalating violence came to the conclusion that about 30 per cent of the Arab agrarian population was already landless, and that further confiscation of Arab land would result in permanent impoverishment of the community. These findings led to the publication, in October 1930, of a White Paper that recommended a curb on Jewish immigration and legal restraints on the expropriation of Arab land. The White paper caused a Jewish uproar.

Chaim Weizmann, President of the Jewish Agency Executive in London, threatened to resign and initiate a complaint before the Permanent Court of Justice in The Hague. The threat compelled the British Prime Minister Ramsay MacDonald to address a well-publicised letter to Weizmann, dated 13 February 1931, which allows interesting insights into the British policy. The letter stated:

> The effect of the policy of immigration and settlement on the economic position of the non-Jewish community cannot be excluded from consideration. But the words are not to be read as implying that existing economic conditions in Palestine should be crystallised. On the contrary, the obligation to facilitate Jewish immigration and to encourage close settlement by Jews on the land remains a positive obligation of the mandate.

The letter further explained that the government was under an obligation to protect 'the landless Arabs'. But this was immediately qualified: 'The recognition of this obligation in no way detracts from the larger purposes of development which his Majesty's Government regards as the most effectual means of furthering the establishment of a national home for the Jews.' The Prime Minister's letter clarified that the government 'did not prescribe and does not contemplate any stoppage or prohibition of Jewish immigration in any of its categories'. Expressing sympathy for the Jewish policy to employ exclusively Jewish labour, the letter stated that 'the principle of preferential, and indeed exclusive, employment of Jewish labour by Jewish organisations is a principle which the Jewish Agency is entitled to affirm'. The letter concluded with the declaration that 'to the tasks imposed by the mandate, his Majesty's Government have set their hand, and they will not withdraw it'.[5]

Thus, the eventual partition of Palestine and creation of Israel after World War II were already contained, in germ, in the British interpretation of their League of Nations' mandate. The next decade and a half, which ended with the lowering of the Union Jack over Jerusalem in May 1948, was dominated by the manoeuvres around the big war. The Jewish immigrants in Palestine, about 84,000 in 1922, numbered 600,000 by 1948. Their militant organisations such as Irgun and Haganah joined the British army in large numbers and received special training to fight Nazi Germany. Well furnished with weapons and with 36,000 trained men in its ranks, the Haganah was no longer content with fighting the Palestinians.

It now turned against the British administration, knowing full well that it could count on the full support of the emerging world power, the United States. The assassination of Lord Moyne, the British Minister resident in Cairo, in November 1944, and the killing of 91 persons in the bombing of Jerusalem's King David Hotel that housed the British administration offices, on 22 July 1946, are only two high-points in a long campaign of terror by which the Zionists pursued, and achieved, Israel.

## Iraq's Turbulent Years and the Rise of Arab Nationalism

The history of Iraqi nationalism and its clashes with Anglo-American imperial interests, up to the advent of Saddam Hussein, though convoluted and contentious in its details, can be rapidly summed up. After King Faisal's death in September 1933, Iraq became formally independent, with membership of the League of Nations. The young country, however, was beset with endless conflicts arising from its structural incoherence.

The Sunni minority, about 35 per cent of the population, disproportionately dominated all walks of life. Sunnis had been used to this position of power since the days of the Umayyad Caliphate, and had continued to hold responsible positions in the Ottoman administration. The Shia, about 62 per cent of the population, felt discriminated against. The Kurds, too, in the northern province of Mosul, were unhappy with the division of their territory across Turkey, Iraq, Syria and Iran. Their discontent took the form of an anti-British revolt that was quickly and brutally put down. The leader of the Kurd uprising, Mustafa Mahmud Barzani, was first sentenced to death, but then banished to Kuwait because of his possible usefulness in the future. Basra, traditionally close to Iran in trade and commerce, resented its new economic isolation. Then there were the Assyrian Christians,[6] who had been living in the southern parts of Ottoman Turkey. During the war, they had sided with the British. After the war, many had migrated to Iraq, hoping for political support in the newly formed country. At first, they were allowed to join special units of the army that were paid and led by the British themselves. When these units were disbanded, following the declaration of Iraq's formal independence, the Assyrian Christians had nowhere to go. Their agitation for autonomy and for land where they might settle was handled harshly. King Faisal himself ordered the detention of their leader Mar Shamun until he renounced all his demands. The agitation petered out after Iraqi soldiers massacred a group of 800 Assyrians they had rounded up next to a police station in northern Iraq. The massacre, which happened while Faisal was terminally ill in a Swiss clinic, was applauded by Iraq's nationalist elements, who viewed the Assyrian agitation as a British intrigue. Faisal himself died a disillusioned man: he cynically called himself 'an instrument of British policy'.

Faisal's 21 year-old son Ghazi, who had lived with his grandfather before Ibn-Saud evicted the Hashemites from Hejaz in 1924, became the second king of Iraq. Shy, inexperienced in the affairs of state, and unfamiliar with the complexity of Iraqi society, Ghazi wore the crown without exercising any control. He apparently nurtured strong resentments against the British, their control and manipulations. Three years after his accession, a group of Kurdish and Shia army officers led by General Bakr Sidqi staged a coup to dislodge the government of Prime Minister Yassin al-Hashimi, who represented the Sunni interests. They replaced him with Hikmat Suleiman, a nationalist leader with ideas of socialist reform, who had earlier held the premiership for a brief spell but had been ousted for his anti-imperialist views. It is possible that the coup had King Ghazi's tacit support. Ghazi had set up a radio station inside the precincts of his palace, which used to relay critical comments on the Anglo-Zionist conspiracies and the British policy of keeping Kuwait as a protectorate, separate from Iraq. General Sidqi was killed by a group of military officers in August 1937 and King Ghazi himself died in a mysterious car accident on 3 April 1939. Mourners raised slogans accusing the British and their stooges, chiefly their new strongman Nouri, of having staged the accident to remove the king. The British ambassador to Iraq, Maurice Peterson, had himself noted in his diary: 'That King Ghazi must either be controlled or deposed.' These musings were probably stimulated by anticipations of the coming war.

Ghazi's son Faisal II, a 4 year-old infant, became the next nominal king while the real power was exercised by Foreign Minister Nouri as-Said through his influence on the regent Amir Abd al-Ilah, the infant king's uncle, known for his loyalty to the British. It was actually during his first brief tenure as Prime Minister, under Faisal I, that the British had managed to impose their 20-year treaty. Nouri's pro-British policies had caused widespread discontent, threatening an uprising against the king. So he was made to resign from his position as Prime Minister. But the British ensured that he stayed in the picture. In the sequel, he was to hold the premiership no less than 14 times, until his assassination in 1958. But the first Prime Minister under Faisal II was one Rashid Ali al-Gaylani, a nationalist who was inclined to align with Germany to shake off the British tutelage. In January 1941, Gaylani was forced to resign, and Nouri took his place. But Gaylani, with the support of a group of army officers, managed to seize power. He announced forthwith the dismissal of the regent who, together with Nouri and the infant king, left the country and fled to Cairo. Once again, the British dispatched Indian troops to Basra and managed to capture Baghdad towards the end of May. Nouri became Prime Minister once more. Gaylani escaped to Iran and got in touch with General Fernand Dentz, a nominee of the French Vichy government in Syria, to plan joint military operations against the British. The British, however, captured Syria in July 1941 and nominally turned it over to the Free French forces.

The British interest in Iraq and their other Middle Eastern creations was limited to their oil potential. Politics and governance, their perversions and failures, were of no concern to the imperial masters except to the extent that they impacted their control on oil. They had no illusions about the nature of governance under the corrupt regimes and rulers they had promoted and were sustaining. A report sent by the British ambassador in Iraq to the Foreign Office in London in the critical period of 1943 referred to a discussion with Nouri about 'the manner in which his team tolerated dishonesty, [...] corruption in the police, the unreliability of the army, the mishandling of the Kurds, the shameless land grabbing carried on by prominent personalities [...] and the wide gulf between the government and the people.' Another British Intelligence Service report described the Iraqi government as 'an oligarchy of racketeers'. But the report added that they were the only persons available to serve the British interests and so Britain had to put up with them.

Meanwhile, the oil resources, in Iraq and elsewhere in the region, were being systematically identified and secured. The oil potential of Iraq had never been in doubt. The drilling exercises in the northern region of Kirkuk, jointly initiated in 1927 by Anglo-Persian, Royal Dutch and several American companies, culminated in a violent gush of oil at a site called Baba Gurgur on 15 October 1927. The 1,500 feet deep well burst out, with a dreadful roar, into an eruption reaching up 50 feet above the derrick and carrying huge rocks from the bottom of the well. The entire countryside was under a flood of oil, with 95,000 barrels gushing out continuously for nine days. The oil companies and the town of Kirkuk itself risked being submerged by the inflammable liquid. Hundreds of Kurds and other locals were pressed into building dykes and walls to stop the deluge. After regaining control, Walter Teagle, the powerful representative of the American syndicate and president of Standard Oil of New Jersey, personally supervised the settlement that followed. The American interests were to be held by the Near East Development Company, a new creation. The other partners were to be Royal Dutch Shell, Anglo-Persian, and a French corporation. All would receive 23.75 per cent of the stock, and Gulbenkian would receive 5 per cent. For various reasons, Walter Teagle and his financial backers were not interested, right then, in launching a major developmental scheme in Iraq or generally in the Middle East. But their resolve to remain in control and safeguard the region from trespassers was absolute.

## Frank Holmes, Philby and the Role of American Capital

The development of the oil concession in Bahrain owed much to Frank Holmes, a mining engineer from New Zealand who came to the Gulf region during World War I as a British soldier. Holmes became acquainted with the region's oil resources while scurrying around the coastal towns to buy beef supplies for the army. After the war, Holmes befriended local Arab Sheikhs by promising to drill for water—a pretext, of course, for ascertaining the commercial potential of oil. Holmes knew that the Americans had the real money. So he disregarded British objections and roped in Standard Oil of California (Socal) into the concession in Bahrain. Under American pressure, the British did not insist on exclusive rights on oil and allowed Socal into Bahrain, but on the condition that Britain's political primacy would be maintained and that all communications between Socal and the Sheikh would be processed by Britain's local political agent. In

1932, a major discovery of oil in Bahrain, that tiny dot on the map of the Middle East, ensured America's enduring involvement in Saudi Arabia and Kuwait, whose geology was very similar.

Ibn-Saud, the ruler of Saudi Arabia, was desperate for money. He had gained his kingdom and all the wealth in the saddlebag of his camel, by aligning himself with Britain's strategic interests and by harnessing the frenzy of his Wahhabi warriors against the Hashemite sheriff of Mecca. In the early 1930s, however, an aging Ibn-Saud was beginning to worry about the future of his state: would it long remain the keeper of Mecca and Medina if it could not muster enough wealth to keep its Wahhabi following happy and build a strong enough apparatus of repression?

Ibn-Saud found an unexpected solution to his thorny problems with the help of a shadowy Englishman Harry St. John Bridger Philby or 'Jack Philby'. An officer of the Indian Civil Service recruited for service in the Middle East during World War I, Philby first came to Basra and Baghdad as a member of a British political mission. He then visited other Arab lands and, picking up Arabic with remarkable ease, became friends with Ibn-Saud, whom he first met in Riyadh in 1917. In 1925, while serving the British political mission in Transjordan, Philby quit the Indian Civil Service, returned to Saudi Arabia and joined Ibn-Saud's inner circle of advisors. In 1930, on Ibn-Saud's advice, Philby became a Muslim and took on the name of Abdullah. He also persuaded the king to invite Charles Crane, an American business magnate with a reputation as a philanthropist, to come over to Saudi Arabia and to employ a mining engineer, Karl Twitchell, also an American, ostensibly to explore the deserts of Saudi Arabia for water. Twitchell, instead, reported oil at Al-Hasa, soon after Socal hit petroleum in Bahrain. Twitchell then went off to the United States to muster capital and technology to develop the Saudi oil. He joined the staff of Socal and came back to Riyadh with Lloyd Hamilton, Socal's lawyer, to clinch the deal. But reports about the negotiations leaked out, and representatives of Anglo-Persian and Iraq Petroleum Company rushed to Riyadh to put in their bids, while a British Minister, Andrew Ryan, closely monitored the negotiations. But by that time Philby had already been enrolled by Socal as advisor. On top of his substantial salary, he had been promised fat rewards should Socal win the deal. So Philby, while keeping up parleys with the Iraq Petroleum Company and Anglo-Persian, did nothing to prevent Socal from clinching the deal with Saudi Arabia.

The agreement promised the Saudis an immediate down-payment of £35,000, plus £30,000 as a loan, plus £5,000 as advance payment for the first year's royalties. It also promised two future loans: a first loan of £20,000 after one year and a half, to be paid out of due royalties; and a second one of £100,000 when oil became a marketable commodity. The concession, valid for the next sixty years, covered an area of 360,000 square miles. Andrew Ryan, the British minister who had been monitoring the negotiations, was furious with Philby for letting Anglo-Persian down.

Even in Kuwait, on their own turf, the British could not resist the pressure to open the doors of oil industry to American interests. In December 1933, Anglo-Persian was forced to enter into a joint venture with American Gulf Oil on a fifty-fifty basis, under the name of Kuwait Oil Company. In December 1934, Sheikh Ahmed al-Sabah, Emir of Kuwait, finalised an agreement that conferred a 75-year concession to Kuwait Oil, against an outright payment of £35,000 and the promise of a minimum annual payment of £7,150 until the company found petroleum in commercially profitable quantities. There were also promises of higher annual minimum payments for after the beginning of commercial exploitation. The Kuwaiti desert did not disappoint: in February 1938 the company hit petroleum with an astonishingly large flow at the Burgan field in southeastern Kuwait.

The next month, in March 1938, Socal discovered enormous quantities of oil at a drilling site in Saudi Arabia, at 4,727 feet below ground. In April 1939, a Socal tanker picked up its first cargo of oil. The oil flowed through a pipeline, from the drilling site at Dhahran all the way to the marine terminal at Ras Tanura. King Saud in person turned on the flow, with great pomp and ceremony. To reward Philby for his labours, he presented him with a young woman, with whom he was to father a child at the age of sixty-five. But the days of real wealth for Kuwait and Saudi Arabia had to wait until after World War II.

The American capital which now controlled the oil interests in the Middle East was, at this point in time, not so keen to expand production from the region. Apart from issues of political stability, the oil companies were in the middle of a crisis resulting, paradoxically, from unexpected oil discoveries within the United States. The giant oil fields in East Texas, discovered in October 1930, had led to massive overproduction, bringing the price of the barrel from $1.85 in 1926 down to 15 cents in May 1931 and 4 cents in May 1933. Neither the price fixing agreements between the oil giants nor the introduction of official production quota were able to resolve the profit crisis in the industry. But although these early attempts at dividing markets to defend profits didn't have much of an impact then, they established the precedent of cartel formation, upon which the US would later fall back to undermine OPEC.

It was against this background of global oil glut that new drillings in the Middle East were revealing untold oil bounty in Iraq, Kuwait, Bahrain and Saudi Arabia. The decisions to acquire these concessions and to control the production facilities were politically and strategically (rather than commercially) motivated, and were dictated from Whitehall and the White House. But further production could only spell total ruin to an already shattered industry. To top it all, Iran's Shah Reza Pahlavi, as previously observed, had managed to improve the terms of his contract with Anglo-Persian by threatening to cancel it altogether. The coming war would provide remedies not only to the oil glut, but also to the rising spectre of economic nationalism in oil rich countries.

The United States was especially upset about a threat that seemed to be developing in its own hemisphere. The Mexican Constitution, drafted seven years after the ordeals of the 1910 revolution, declared that 'sub-soil resources' belonged to the Mexican State and not to the oil companies that owned the land above. The resulting tension reached its peak in 1927 when Mexican President Plutarco Elias Calles, fearing US military intervention, ordered General Lazaro Cardenas to burn the oil fields if the Americans came to invade the country. Although Mexico faced a stiff competition in oil production from Venezuela, its nationalist fervour did not abate. General Lazaro Cardenas, who succeeded Plutarco Elias Calles as President in 1934, established a Commission to examine various charges of tax evasion and economic irregularities against giant oil corporations. He not only forced the companies to raise wages for their workers, but also imposed on them retroactive penalties for understating their profits in the past. When the companies resisted, Cardenas nationalised the oil industry and, then, in March 1939 decreed the appropriation of properties of private companies. His action reflected a widespread and deeply felt resentment against the sort of imperialist capitalism which the oil industry stood for. In 1937, the Bolivian Government, too, expropriated the properties of Standard Oil's local subsidiary, guilty of tax fraud. These actions were seen as establishing a precedent that, according to a Shell director, 'would jeopardise the whole structure of international trade and the security of foreign investment'. In May 1938, Britain's Oil Board and the Committee of Imperial Defence not only expressed grave concern over these developments, but went on to identify the Dutch East Indies, Romania and Iraq as 'doubtful sources of supply' in 'certain eventualities'. These fears were fed by forebodings of the coming war and by worries over access to oil in wartime. The United States might well have taken military action against Mexico and Bolivia if the hovering threat of a world war had not tipped the scales towards restraint: the hemisphere had to be kept safe from German and Japanese interventions. The oil companies themselves decided to bide their time and to deal with the issues of expropriation only after the war.

## Oil as a Weapon and as a War Aim: The Case of Germany in World War II

World War II has been studied and over-studied, but insufficient attention has been paid to the advantage which the control of oil resources gave to the victorious side. Let us sketch here only some salient points. As earlier observed, Germany was unable to pursue its oil ambitions in Mesopotamia after losing World War I. Without access to secure petroleum resources, Germany was compelled to experiment with synthetic fuels, and that too with considerable success. Even before assuming absolute power in January 1933, Hitler paid close attention to the on-going research on chemical oil, and encouraged its development by I. G. Farben, the giant chemical corporation that specialised in coal hydrogenation. Coal had been Germany's main energy source. Even in the late 1930s, oil fulfilled less than 5 per cent of its power needs. Yet, so confident was Hitler in his vision of a new economy run on synthetic fuels that one of his very first decisions upon becoming Chancellor was to launch a grand scheme of highways for his Volkswagen, or 'people's car'.

The technology of hydrogenation (extraction of liquid from coal) had been pioneered by a German chemist, Friedrich Bergius, in 1913. The process involved adding large volumes of hydrogen to the coal under extraction, at a high temperature and high pressure, and in the presence of a suitable catalyst. The end product was a high grade liquid fuel, good enough to one day power the Luftwaffe. In the 1920s, Germany developed yet another, cheaper technology for breaking down coal molecules under steam into hydrogen and carbon monoxide, and then getting these to react to produce synthetic oil. This method was known as the Fischer–Tropsch process. I. G. Farben specialised in producing high grade fuel with the earlier Bergius process.

Ironically, I. G. Farben's initial partner in producing synthetic oil was Standard Oil of New Jersey. The president of Standard Oil, Walter Teagle, was so impressed by I. G. Farben's research and production facilities at Leuna that he gushed: 'I had not known what research meant until I saw it. We were babies compared to the work I saw.' Teagle hurried to the pilot plant in 1926 largely out of fear that synthetic oil would make Europe completely independent in energy needs, depriving Standard Oil of all its markets on the continent. So Standard Oil chose the join-them-if-you-can't-beat-them strategy. In 1929 it acquired the patent rights to all hydrogenation outside Germany, transferring 2 per cent of Standard's stock, valued at $ 35 million, to I. G. Farben. In 1931, Friedrich Bergius, the inventor of hydrogenation, received the Nobel Prize for chemistry together with Carl Bosch, another German chemical scientist from Cologne, for their trailblazing contribution to the chemistry and technology of high-pressure processes. Bosch became director of I. G. Farben in 1935, but he felt uncomfortable with the Nazi ideology, especially with the notion of his synthetic fuels serving to bolster the Nazi war machine. So he left the company.

In practical terms, the pilot project of I. G. Farben at Leuna was foundering because of the prohibitively high costs of the synthetic fuels compared to the market price of gasoline. But Hitler realised the importance of sustaining the production of synthetic fuels, and promised state subsidies, guaranteed markets and fixed prices as long as the production levels did not flag. Already at this stage, the air force (*Luftwaffe*) and army (*Wehrmacht*) were pressing for massive investments to improve the grade of gasoline, and to sustain the industry through state subsidies. They knew that without synthetic fuels, Germany would not be able to conduct the approaching war. By September 1939, just before the German invasion of Poland, 14 hydrogenation plants were producing 72,000 barrels of oil per day, nearly 50 per cent of the total oil supply.

The desire to capture the oil fields of the Caucasus was one of the main considerations behind Germany's decision to attack the Soviet Union in June 1941, just as seizing the petroleum resources of the Middle East was one of the objectives behind Rommel's thrust into North Africa. Both campaigns were supposed to converge triumphantly in Baku. The plan, had it succeeded, would have placed the Middle East's and Russia's oil resources under German control.

But the plan failed, and it failed partly because Germany did not possess sufficient hydrocarbon resources to sustain these campaigns. Under the euphoria of initial successes, the need for fuel supplies was ignored, despite repeated warnings by several generals. On the Eastern front, six to eight million Soviet soldiers had been killed or captured. But the Soviet manpower appeared inexhaustible, and so too seemed the will of the Soviet state to go on fighting. By December 1941, the German mammoth was bogged down in snow and mud 20 miles from the Kremlin in the outskirts of Moscow. The Wehrmacht, exhausted by the famous Russian winter, found itself unable to move forward for lack of oil when General Yuri Zhukov launched his first major offensive, severely denting German self-confidence. Hitler decreed a renewal of the campaign to capture the oil fields of the Caucasus, amidst fantasies of capturing Iran, Iraq, Central Asia, and finally India. The renewed offensive started in July 1942 and seemed to go well at first. In August, the German army captured Maikop, the Caucasus' westernmost oil centre. But the Russians had thoroughly destroyed the oil fields, supplies and equipment. By January 1943, the German army was not able to wring out more than seventy barrels a day. Even the capture of Russia's supply lines didn't ease the German needs for fuel, for the Russian tanks were fuelled by diesel whereas the German panzer units required gasoline. The German army's progress across the mountains became sluggish. Short of oil and with supply lines stretching thousands of miles, the Germans made one last desperate attempt to push through the mountains towards Groznyy and Baku, but they were repulsed.

By then, Hitler had probably lost all sense of reality. In February 1943, a large German army outside Stalingrad surrendered. Ground down without oil, its soldiers hungry and frozen, it was doomed. The battle marked the beginning of the German retreat in Europe. The final outcome of the North African campaign, as earlier noted, was likewise determined by a failure of mobility due to shortage of petrol. The campaign ended at El Alamein, less than 60 miles from Alexandria, where General Bernard Montgomery stopped the German advance. Rommel wrote to his wife: 'Shortage of petrol! It is enough to make one weep!' The British, besides, had been taking no chances with the German war plans. They had preventively deposed Reza Shah in Iran. For good measure, they had also toppled Iraq's nationalist government (installed after a coup by four colonels in 1941), bringing the country once again under direct British occupation.

Defeats in the East and in Africa ended the German fantasies of capturing the major oil fields of the Middle East and Caucasus. Under the impulse of Albert Speer, the Nazi regime reorganised its resources to increase the output of synthetic fuels. Between 1940 and 1943, the production nearly doubled, from 72,000 to 124,000 barrels per day, providing 92 per cent of the aviation's gasoline and 57 per cent of the total supply to the military. In May 1944, the Allied bombers began to target synthetic fuel factories, including the giant I. G. Farben plant at Leuna, which was reduced to a heap of twisted and broken metal. Speer told his Führer: 'The enemy has struck us at one of our weakest points.' Attacks on Germany's synthetic fuel plants continued. Even the German-held oil production facilities in Romania were being targeted. By September 1944, their production level had fallen to 5,000 barrels a day. Then the Russians captured the Ploesti oil fields in Romania. There was no fuel for the Luftwaffe to get its bombers and fighters into the air.

The end was near. Hitler committed suicide while Russian soldiers were almost stamping over his underground bunker. There was just about enough gasoline to burn his body, according to his last instructions. The dream of a thousand-year German Empire, which swallowed at least 35 million lives, evaporated—part of the reason being that there was not enough petroleum to keep it blazing. Albert Speer recounts how he understood that doom was at hand when he saw a convoy of 150 army trucks being pulled by four oxen each, because there was no other way for them to move.

## Japanese Oil Shortage and the Kamikaze Pilots

In the late 1930s, Japan produced only 7 per cent of the oil it consumed. The rest was imported: 80 per cent from USA and another 10 per cent from the Dutch East Indies. More than 60 per cent of the oil market within Japan was controlled by the Japanese subsidiary of Royal Dutch Shell and a joint venture by Standard of New York and New Jersey, known as Stanvac. The Japanese Government did its best to maintain some control over these foreign companies. It promulgated a *Petroleum Industry Law* which left it in control of all oil imports; gave it a free hand to fix market quotas and prices; and enabled it to make compulsory purchases and to force the foreign companies to keep six months of inventories of their oil stocks in commercial circulation. The fact remained, though, that Japan simply did not have enough oil to support its grandiose plans of conquest. To remedy this, the Japanese war strategy, in the beginning, concentrated on capturing the oil resources in the Dutch East Indies, Malaya, Indochina and the Pacific islands. It has even been suggested that the surprise attack on Pearl Harbour was itself designed to pre-empt flank assaults that might have foiled the planned invasion of the East Indies and Singapore. Also, by incapacitating the American fleet in the Pacific, the Japanese hoped, and for a time managed, to protect the oil route from Sumatra and Borneo to their home bases.

We already observed how, in the face of the Japanese advance, an American naval squadron had trained the Royal Dutch Shell staff at Balikapan in Borneo to destroy the oil facilities there.[7] However, by mid-March 1942, Japan had been able to take over the entire East Indies, home to all the oil resources of Southeast Asia. With no dearth of oil to replenish the Imperial fleet, Japan seemed invincible until the decisive battle of Midway, in which American bombers destroyed four Japanese aircraft carriers in mid-ocean. American submarines, equipped with deadly torpedoes, began to disrupt Japan's critical shipping links between the East Indies and its home islands. American submarines particularly targeted the Japanese merchant shipping and oil tankers, sinking approximately 86 per cent of the total fleet and seriously damaging another 9 per cent. A Japanese economist later described this phase of the war as 'a death blow to the war economy of Japan'.

Diminished fuel supplies radically affected the Japanese military capabilities. Japan tried to build new ships that could move on coal. This reversal to coal entailed a further loss of speed and tactical flexibility. The Japanese Imperial fleet then threw all its weight into saving the Philippines, but fuel shortages once again came in the way. Even the increased recourse to *kamikaze* missions at this stage of the war has been linked to the oil shortage: by crashing its planes into American battleships, the Japanese air force was saving fuel on the return flights! But the *kamikaze* tactics could not stop the Americans from capturing Manila. Soon, the Japanese had to evacuate Balikapan. After their defeat in Burma, which was sealed at the battle for Kohima, the Japanese had to leave most of the East Indies. In March 1945, the last Japanese oil tanker to leave Singapore was sunk on its way home.

Japan fought to the bitter end. It fiercely resisted the invasion of Okinawa in April 1945, sacrificing thousands of its soldiers in suicide attacks, to strike fear in the enemy. The fierceness of the Japanese resistance, it has been suggested, contributed to the American decision to crush the *Japanese Will* by using the atomic bomb. Even so, Emperor Hirohito proclaimed Japan's surrender only five days after the second atomic bomb incinerated Nagasaki on 9th August. The Pacific War claimed more than 20 million lives, including two-and-a-half million Japanese.

## Oily Succession to Imperial Supremacy

The transfer of imperial supremacy from Britain to the United States had begun soon after the end of the World War I. By 1934, the Standard Oil Company of California (Socal) and the Gulf Oil Company were firmly entrenched in Saudi Arabia, Bahrain and Kuwait. Britain fought the American challenge and tried hard to squeeze US stakes down to a minimum in the multinational Iraq Petroleum Company that had major interests in Iraq, Qatar and the 'Trucial States' (known today as the United Arab Emirates). However, British foreign officials soon began to concede that the influx of American capital might contribute to the stability of the region, and that the American partnership might help Britain fend off Russian or German advances in the region. Then the exigencies of World War II clearly established the United States as the main centre of economic and military power in the western world. The US involvement in the oil resources of the Middle East would no longer be limited to economic calculations. Rather, its financial investments, its management of technology or personnel; all this would be subordinated to America's new assumption of imperial supremacy.

In late 1943, even as the war was still raging, Everette Lee DeGolyer, a geologist who was to become the most important figure in the oil industry of his day, came to Saudi Arabia. A pioneer of the seismographic approach to oil exploration, DeGolyer had established a very successful consulting firm in petroleum engineering, DeGolyer and McNaughton, and was earning over $2 million a year. After traveling through the deserts of Iraq, Iran, Kuwait, Bahrain and Saudi Arabia, DeGolyer came back to Washington early in 1944. His report put the region's oil reserves at 300 billion barrels, with 100 billion barrels in Saudi Arabia alone. One of his associates told the State Department: 'The oil in this region is the greatest single prize in all history.' Until then, the United States produced 63 per cent of the global oil. DeGolyer predicted that 'the center of gravity of world oil production' would shift to the Middle East.

This was a prediction fraught with ominous consequences for the politics of the Middle East. The Secretary of Interior Harold Ickes had no doubts. Already in December 1943, he had declared: 'If there should be a World War III, it would have to be fought with someone else's petroleum.' No one in the high circles of the American administration had any doubt about whose petroleum it would be. Herbert Feis, the State Department's Economic Adviser, said pompously: 'The pencil came to an awed pause at one point and place—the Middle East.' The British policy makers had been clear about this since the beginning of World War I.

We may recall at this point that during the war, America's oil men in Saudi Arabia, some 100 of them, and their colleagues in Iraq, Iran and Kuwait, had been devoting themselves, not to oil production, but to oil destruction—they were planning to sabotage all known oil wells in case the German army managed to capture the region. These oil men worked closely with the Allied military and political authorities.

When Saudi Arabia needed money, the oil companies were reluctant to advance loans. At the same time, however, they were keen not to lose the concessions. So they engaged in some corridor politics in Washington, and eventually President Roosevelt suggested to the British that they take care of the Saudi king. The suggestion didn't go unheeded, and the British gave the king the equivalent of $2 million. The American oil men in Saudi Arabia then convinced the king that the bounty actually came from the United States. The British did not mind. They were slowly learning the wisdom of promoting American involvement in the region for security reasons, but also as a matter of long-term political and financial insurance.

But the American oil companies, especially Socal and Texaco, had already made large investments and were worried that the British might use their influence over King Ibn-Saud to marginalise them. They had also their concerns about the stability of a country barely two decades old, led by a king who was a British creation, with a burgeoning offspring but no clear provision for his own succession. For all these reasons, the American oil companies wanted the US government to take a direct hand in the affairs of Saudi Arabia. On 16 February 1943, the heads of Socal, Texaco and Casco, accompanied by H. L. Ickes, Secretary of the Interior, met President Roosevelt over lunch and managed to persuade him to extend financial assistance to Saudi Arabia, thereby flouting the regulations of the Lend Lease, a war time aid program which disallowed such assistance to non-democratic countries.

This decision to waive the restrictions built into the Lend-Lease programme was inspired by a government plan, initiated by H. L. Ickes, for the US to directly acquire the oil resources of Saudi Arabia. The plan had been hatched with the enthusiastic support of the US army and navy. In June 1943, Ickes quietly set up the Petroleum Reserve Corporation. Then, in concert with War Secretary Henry Stimson, Navy Secretary Frank Knox, and James Byrnes, Director of the Office of War Mobilization, Ickes worked out a proposal to buy up the concessions obtained by Texaco and Socal. Roosevelt endorsed the decision, which was conveyed to the Presidents of Texaco and Socal in August 1943, when these came into the President's office to discuss a possible American aid to Saudi Arabia in exchange for a guaranteed right to purchase oil. The oil barons were shocked by the proposal and quickly mobilised a wider opposition to the scheme. The US administration tried to appease Texaco and Socal by redesigning its proposal, now offering to buy only 51 per cent of shares instead of completely taking over Casoc (as the joint oil venture in Saudi Arabia was called). The negotiations dragged on till early 1944. By then, America's private oil industry had mobilised strong political support against the government's plan to go into the oil business. So H. L. Ickes came up with a new idea: the US Government would build a pipeline from Saudi Arabia and Kuwait to carry the oil across the desert to the Mediterranean for shipment to Europe and the United States. The US Government would spend $120 million on the project. In exchange, it would purchase oil at a 25 per cent discount, from a one-billion-barrel oil reserve to be set up by Casoc. The Joint Chiefs of Staff insisted that such a pipeline was 'a matter of immediate military necessity'. These plans were eventually shelved as the war in Europe drew to an end.

Thus, shortly before the end of World War II, the US administration gave up its parleys with the oil industry and dropped any idea of getting directly involved in the production and supply of Middle East oil. Instead, the US Government approached the British Government with proposals for jointly managing the world oil market. The two governments agreed that the oil reserves within the United States and Europe should not be exhausted. One should rather, for the time being, encourage production from the Middle East and ensure adequate supply arrangements to meet the post-war reconstruction needs. The two governments also agreed that everything should be done to avert a glut in the market that could easily result from the enormous production capacity of the Middle East. It was important to make the necessary arrangements before the war officially ended, so as to sidestep the constraints of the antitrust laws.

It was also important for the two countries to agree on a division of their oil interests in the Middle East. There followed a series of meetings and hard negotiations, involving Lord Beaverbrook (Lord Privy Seal), Lord Halifax (British ambassador in Washington), Summer Wells (US Undersecretary of State) and of course President Roosevelt and Prime Minister Churchill themselves. Roosevelt was frank. He invited Britain to keep all the oil in Persia, share the resources in Iraq and Kuwait, and leave the whole of Saudi Arabia to American interests. The proposal was further discussed by the two heads of state, often acrimoniously, each suspecting the other of devious afterthoughts. Eventually, both sides agreed on the proposed arrangements, whose objectives the State Department's Petroleum Adviser euphemistically described as being the 'orderly development and orderly distribution of abundance'. In plain words, the two governments were laying the basis for what Lord Beaverbrook privately called a 'monster cartel'. The American negotiators described the arrangement as 'an intergovernmental commodity agreement predicated upon certain broad principles of orderly development and sound engineering practices and directed towards assuring the availability of ample supplies to meet market demands'. The Anglo-American Petroleum Agreement was signed on 8 August 1944. The agreement led to the formation of an International Petroleum Commission, which was to draw up estimates of global oil demands; allocate production quotas to various countries; and make recommendations to the two governments on how to promote future developments in the industry. The governments were expected to implement the 'recommendations'. In essence, the Anglo-American Petroleum Agreement, presented before the American Senate as a 'treaty', legitimised price fixing and production rigging. But in the face of fierce resistance from the oil industry, which opposed international regulations and price standards, and to avoid court cases under the antitrust laws, the Roosevelt government eventually withdrew the treaty project in January 1945. The US administration also feared the adverse impact of a public controversy on the shadier side of the political relations between the former war partners. Besides, a crucial meeting between Roosevelt, Stalin and Churchill at Yalta, in Soviet Crimea, was in the offing. The issues to be discussed there were much larger ones, like defining the spheres of influence in the post-war world. Oil was only one of the points on the agenda.

In February 1945, immediately after the Yalta conference, Roosevelt and his team of advisers met Ibn-Saud aboard USS Quincy, anchored in the Great Bitter Lake in the Suez Canal zone in Egypt. Roosevelt and Ibn-Saud talked for five hours. They discussed oil, the Jewish homeland, and the future of the Middle East. Ibn-Saud was given assurance of America's interest in maintaining his country's integrity and protecting it from subversive influences. The official records made no reference to oil, but a report in the New York Times said: 'The immense oil deposits in Saudi Arabia alone make that country more important to American diplomacy than almost any other smaller nation.' Churchill did not want to be left out of the arrangements. He rushed to the Middle East and met with Ibn-Saud three days after Roosevelt's visit.

Roosevelt died soon after returning to the United States on 12 April 1945. Oil and Saudi Arabia remained matters of first importance under his successor Harry Truman. Navy Secretary James Forrestal led the briefings on Saudi Arabia at Potsdam. Forrestal was one of the champions of the Anglo-American Petroleum Agreement, which he still wanted to revive. There was no direct possibility of that happening, due to internal opposition from the oil industry, also because of the global political suspicion and criticism it was likely to stir up. But Forrestal missed no opportunity of urging Truman and his team not to reject the logic that had inspired the agreement, arguing:

> If we ever got into another World War it is quite possible that we would not have access to reserves held in the Middle East but in the meantime the use of those reserves would prevent the depletion of our own, a depletion which may be serious within the next fifteen years.

Forrestal's argument rested on the assessment of the Joint Chiefs of Staff that in the event of a hot war, the Middle East oil would hardly be safe from enemy interference. The solution they recommended was to import oil in peacetime to save American resources for wartime. This was also the key argument made in a major policy study by E. V. Rostow, a Yale Law School professor, under the title *A National Policy for the Oil Industry*. The subject was taken up for a more formal review and appraisal by the National Security Resources Board, a new Federal Agency. The Board endorsed Professor Rostow's policy recommendations and added its own categorical proposal to import enough Middle East oil to allow a million barrels of America's domestic production to be locked up as an underground military stockpile.

A very different set of recommendations, from more independent quarters, was drawing its inspiration from Germany's experiments with synthetic fuels. It pointed out that synthetic fuels could be produced not only from coal but also from other natural substances such as oil shale and natural gas. A *New York Times* article talked about a coming chemical revolution that could free industry from its dependence on foreign oil. Some influential voices within the Interior Department suggested a grand initiative, on a par with the Manhattan Project, aiming at achieving a production capacity of two million barrels of synthetic fuels per day. The Interior Department made an allocation of $85 million to initiate the necessary research.

The project was never pursued. The sheer abundance of oil from the Middle East made the project appear redundant. The United States was already collecting more in taxes from the oil companies than these paid in royalties to the countries whose oil they were exploiting. By 1949, Aramco alone was paying $43 million in taxes to the United States government. That same year, Aramco paid $39 million to Saudi Arabia.

## A Petro-Political Order for Europe's Reconstruction

The reconstruction of Europe was impossible without enormous quantities of oil. Coal was in short supply. Most power stations had been shut down. Industrial production was at a standstill. There was no money for the necessary imports. A devastated Britain was in no position to maintain its empire. It was determined to get rid of its South Asian colonies and to wind up its mandate in Palestine. It was certainly not equal to the task of policing the Mediterranean and the Middle East against possible Soviet designs. All the countries of western Europe were desperately waiting for the European Recovery Programme, known as Marshall Plan (it was first articulated by US Secretary of State George Marshall in June 1947) to become operative. But without petroleum the Marshall Plan could not be implemented. Estimates suggested that more than 20 per cent of the Marshall Plan aid had to be spent on oil imports. The rise in oil prices was an insupportable drain on aid dollars. Still, the only way to overcome the energy crisis was to switch power plants and other industries from coal to oil. Thus, whilst conversion to oil was a precondition for Europe's economic recovery, oil could not displace coal unless its price became competitive. These were some of the conundrums facing Europe and America in the immediate aftermath of World War II. They were to weigh heavily on the impending reorganisation of the petroleum industry in the Middle East.

In Kuwait, Gulf Oil and Anglo-Iranian had come together to create the Kuwait Oil Company. The State Department officials facilitated a purchase and sale agreement between Kuwait Oil and Royal Dutch Shell that enabled Kuwaiti oil to find established markets. The deal further consolidated American oil interests in the Middle East without repudiating the commitment Roosevelt had given to Churchill of seeking an accommodative arrangement in Kuwait.

Aramco (Arabian American Oil Company), a joint venture between Socal and Texaco, took charge of Saudi Arabia. By 1946, Standard of California had already invested $80 million in Saudi concessions. Another $100 million, at least, was now required for the pipeline across the desert to the Mediterranean that Aramco wanted to build in order to capture European markets. But steel was scarce and still controlled by the United States Government. Domestic oil interests within the United States were mobilising political support to block the allocation of steel to Aramco for fear that the cheap Middle East oil would destroy their control over markets. However, the US administration was aware that without the Middle East oil, the Marshall Plan for Europe's reconstruction would come unstuck.

The new pressures of the Cold War led Aramco to quickly increase its production levels: it was imperative to keep the Soviet Union off Europe's oil markets. The political fate of the continent was still in the balance. Italy and France had strong Communist parties, and the future of the newly divided Germany remained uncertain. Even the eastern Mediterranean did not appear politically safe. A Communist insurrection had just erupted in Greece, and Turkey too appeared unstable and vulnerable to Russian pressures. The unresolved issue of the Jewish homeland in Palestine was also adding to the tensions. Even the political future of Saudi Arabia was a matter of concern, with Ibn-Saud already frail in his mid-60s and his forty-five (or more) sons impatiently eyeing the succession.

The oil companies, no matter how powerful, could not act without direct and indirect support. Both Ibn-Saud and the US Government insisted that only American companies be allowed to develop the Saudi Arabian reserves. The State Department and the US Navy officials actively promoted American partnerships in Aramco. Standard Oil of New Jersey, a minor partner in IPC (Iraq Petroleum Company), was encouraged to become a partner in Aramco. Jersey in turn roped in Socony (Standard Oil Corporation of New York). The State Department intervened and advised Standard of New Jersey to sell its IPC shares to Socony and then enter Aramco alone. The step was necessary to keep the French and Gulbenkian, a 5 per cent partner in the IPC, from invoking the Red Line Agreement to challenge its independent operations. But the two companies resented the suggestion. During the war Gulbenkian had displayed pro-Vichy leanings and, as an 'enemy alien', had had his shares forfeited under the doctrine of 'supervening illegality'. But in the middle of the war, he had moved to Lisbon and, at the end of the war, his shares in the company reverted to him. Even so, Jersey and Socony argued that the doctrine of 'supervening illegality' had the effect of cancelling all agreements under the IPC. On 12 March 1947, the four American companies, Socal, Texaco, Standard Oil of New Jersey and Socony signed their agreement as partners of Aramco. France withdrew its objections to the deal in May 1947 but Gulbenkian challenged it by filing a suit in a British court. Before the litigation began, Aramco bought Gulbenkian's agreement by offering him a deal that he could not refuse.

The twelfth of March 1947 was marked by yet another important event. President Harry Truman made a major policy declaration. Addressing a joint session of Congress, he announced special aids to Greece and Turkey to help them resist Communist pressures. The speech outlined what came to be known as the Truman Doctrine. It marked, so to speak, the official start of the Cold War.

## The Anglo-Persian Oil Company and the Iranian Coup

The most daunting test for America's new assumption of imperial primacy in the region came from Iran. At the same time, it laid bare the symbiotic character of petroleum and political interests, and the military's instrumentality in securing them.

In 1941, as we already observed, while the German forces were still making rapid advances in the Caucasus and in North Africa, Reza Shah Pahlavi had been replaced on the Iranian throne by his 21 year-old son Mohammed Reza Pahlavi. Iran was still supposed to be an exclusively British sphere of influence. After the war, though, the Anglo-Iranian Oil Company did not have the financial resources to cope effectively with the sheer scale of oil operations in Saudi Arabia and Kuwait, and feared losing its markets to Aramco and Kuwait Oil Company. Moreover, Iran was considered vulnerable to Soviet pressures.

Soviet Foreign Minister Molotov, the architect of the Nazi–Soviet Pact, had once openly stated that the areas of the Persian Gulf south of Baku belonged to the Soviet sphere. That was understood to be the logic of the pact. As if to underscore the assumption, the Soviet troops, after occupying Azerbaijan in 1945, started making threatening incursions into parts of northern Iran while the Soviet Union demanded oil concessions in the country. It kept doing so right up to April 1946. The beginning of the Soviet withdrawal, under intense American pressure, was immediately followed by a meeting between the American ambassador in Moscow and Stalin. The latter explained that his attempts to extend Soviet influence in Iran were prompted by the need to protect the Caucasian oil fields, particularly Baku, from saboteurs. As a matter of fact, oil production in the Soviet Union had gone dangerously low in the 1940–45 period, requiring oil imports from the United States in the last and decisive phase of the war. The restoration of the Soviet oil facilities was going to require huge investments, and the reconstruction of the Soviet economy could not take place without sufficient oil. Stalin concluded the meeting by suggesting that a joint company be set up for oil exploration in Iran.

The suggestion was never entertained. Britain and the United States viewed all attempts by the Soviet Union to extend its influence in the Persian Gulf with extreme suspicion—as a continuation of the old Russian foreign policy that had characterised the Great Game. The Soviet Union maintained a close rapport with Iran's Tudeh party, which had been organising demonstrations and strikes—some of them at the Abadan refinery complex—to gain influence in Iran's central government. The American and British Governments were adamant about keeping the Russians completely out of the region. The British, however, did not have the wherewithal to counter the Soviet machinations. So they wanted the Americans to get involved, financially and politically, to shore up their own position in Iran. With these considerations in mind, the authorities in Washington and London encouraged the Anglo-Iranian Company to strike a contract with Standard Oil New Jersey and Socony, the two American companies also involved in Saudi Arabia. The contract was signed in September 1947.

Mohammed, the new Shah, shared his father's abhorrence of religious fundamentalism. He was also afraid of the well-organised Tudeh party and its links with Moscow. But he lacked anything like a genuine popular base. Having usurped his father's throne, he was completely dependent on his imperialist masters. The people of Iran associated Western capitalist interests with oil politics, that is to say with the Anglo-Iranian Oil Company. Politicians and public servants alike were well aware that the company had registered a profit of £250 million in the 1945–50 period, as against the paltry sum of £90 million earned in royalties by Iran in that same period. The British Government actually earned more money in oil taxes from Iran than Iran did in revenue from its own oil. The grinding poverty of the masses, their squalor and lack of basic facilities, side by side with the fantastic wealth amassed by the foreign companies and their puppet Shah, were to be the backdrop for the political discontent and upheavals of the next decades. Until the end of World War II, Iran—especially the southern part of the country—had been a British show, a pawn in the Great Game against Russia. After the war, America had taken over as lead player in the on-going game, now known as Cold War. But the Iranian people felt no need to distinguish the earlier set of white, English-speaking game masters from the new set of white, English-speaking bosses who replaced them.

The American Assistant Secretary of State in charge of Near-Eastern and African Affairs was one George McGhee, a geophysicist from Oxford and an oil man. In his Oxford days, he had befriended the daughters of John Cadman, the head of Anglo-Iranian and, upon leaving Oxford, had been offered a job in Iran as a geophysicist by the Company. But he chose to return to his own country and soon thereafter discovered a large oil field in Louisiana. George McGhee became a rich man and entered politics. He was only 37 when he became Assistant Secretary of State in charge of Near-Eastern and African Affairs. George McGhee was also a brash, abrasive character and the British, who had their own reasons for resenting him, dismissively called him behind his back 'that young prodigy'. People in Iran were even less impressed by the young American upstart who was managing their oil as well as their Shah.

In February 1949, even as the US was busy consolidating its positions in the region, a young Iranian man tried to assassinate Mohammed Pahlavi, firing several shots at close range, yet failing to kill him. Mohammed Pahlavi used the incident to impose martial law and to create an elaborate apparatus of tyranny and repression. In June 1950, post-war Iran witnessed its first major political convulsion when Mohammed Pahlavi put his Supplemental Agreement with Anglo-Iranian before the Majlis (the Iranian

Parliament) for ratification. An oil committee, recently constituted by the Majlis and led by Mohammed Mossadegh, denounced the agreement as a surrender to imperialist greed and called for the nationalisation of the company. Mohammed Pahlavi ignored the Majlis and appointed General Ali Razmara, Chief of Army, as Prime Minister. This coincided with a high-point in international tension, the Korean War having just begun. Iran's northern borders were the scene of frequent skirmishes between Iranian and Russian soldiers. George McGhee worked out a blue print for dealing with the eventuality of a Russian armed intervention in the country. The defence of Iran's oil fields and Abadan refinery, which then accounted for 40 per cent of the Middle East production, remained as much of a priority under the Cold War as it had been during the hot war, when it had prompted the British to depose Reza Pahlavi, back in August 1941.

The issue of the oil concession in Iran kept nationalist tempers boiling. In March 1951, Ali Razmara was assassinated near Tehran's central mosque, four days after addressing the Majlis and rejecting its demand for the nationalisation of Anglo-Iranian. Other pro-American politicians were assassinated in quick succession. In April 1951, the Majlis elected Mohammed Mossadegh, a nationalist lawyer from an aristocratic family, as the new Prime Minister. Mossadegh got the nationalisation bill passed. Mohammed Pahlavi had no choice but to sign the law. The British considered an armed intervention to secure the oil fields and the Abadan refineries, but the Americans talked them out of it, to avoid risking a Russian reaction. Averell Harriman, Truman's main foreign policy advisor and head of Mutual Security Administration, led an American delegation to Iran to find a negotiated settlement. Nothing came out of the mission. Prime Minister Mossadegh ordered all British employees at Abadan to leave the country, which they did on 25 September 1951. The British then imposed a rigorous embargo on Iranian oil. But the embargo had the effect of removing a large volume of oil from the global market at a time when oil was badly needed. By 1952, Iranian production had fallen to 20,000 barrels per day, compared to 666,000 in 1950.

In October 1951, Winston Churchill was returned to power as head of Britain's new Conservative government. Thirty seven years earlier, he had bought the British Government's stakes in Anglo-Persian, and he was now fully determined to defend the company. His Foreign Secretary happened to be Anthony Eden, the very man who in 1941, as Foreign

Secretary, had supervised the military intervention in Iran and the deposition of Reza Shah. Anthony Eden now wanted the Americans to use their influence to get Mossadegh dismissed. Mohammed Pahlavi told the American ambassador that he felt helpless before Mossadegh's popularity. The British government discussed the prospect of bringing about regime change, with American help. The final decision was taken after Eisenhower took over the American Presidency. The new Secretary of State John Foster Dulles and his brother Allen W. Dulles, the new chief of the CIA (he had led the Office of Strategic Services operations during the war) both gave their go-ahead.

'Operation Ajax' was on the roll. Kermit Roosevelt, Theodore Roosevelt's grandson, was put in charge of the operation from within Iran. C. M. Woodhouse of the MI6 worked as Roosevelt's assistant. General Fazlollah Zahedi, a Shah loyalist, was asked to arrest Mossadegh on the charge that he was planning a coup. But word about the plot leaked out and mobs flooded the streets of Tehran chanting anti-Shah slogans and smashing his statues. The Shah fled, first to Baghdad and then to Rome. On 18 August 1953, General Fazlollah Zahedi held a press conference to announce Mossadegh's dismissal on the Shah's order, and his own appointment as the successor Prime Minister. The military rallied in support and well-orchestrated mass demonstrations hailed the declaration. Mossadegh was put under arrest and a triumphant Shah returned to his throne.

Herbert Hoover, the former President's son and himself an important oil man, was asked to put together a consortium of companies that could take over Anglo-Iranian's interests. The major American oil companies insisted that they couldn't enter Iran to help out the US Government unless the Justice Department first withdrew the antitrust case it was planning to bring against them for acting as an international oil cartel. These legal threats had developed from the Federal Trade Commission's annual report in 1949, which exposed the corrupt practices of the oil companies. The State Department, the Department of Defence and the CIA together put their weight behind the oilmen. They all argued that the legal action would in effect assist the Soviet objectives. The National Security Council issued a directive to the Attorney General to drop the action in the national security interest. But the oil men were not satisfied. They wanted a guarantee of non-prosecution that would survive a change in the government. In January 1954, both the Attorney General and the

National Security Council gave the guarantee. With the road thus cleared, the grand consortium could at last be put together. It included Jersey, Socony, Texaco and Standard of California, Shell and Anglo-Iranian. Anglo-Iranian received $90 million straight, a 10 per cent-a-barrel royalty on the entire future production, plus a promise of $500 million. This was by way of compensation for giving up its independent concession. An agreement between the consortium and the Iranian Finance Minister was finalised on 17 September 1954. The Shah endorsed the agreement on 29 October 1954. The Iranian oil was back in business. As for Kermit Roosevelt, he later became chairman of the board of Buttes Gas and Oil, a company that operated barges, tankers and offshore rigging in various countries, aside from functioning as a CIA cover.

## An Example of Regional Policing

The Iranian example was to stand the Americans in good stead and help them enforce their petro-political order in the region, especially in the wake of the tensions attendant on the creation of Israel. In Saudi Arabia, Aramco feared that the pressure of Arab public opinion on Ibn-Saud to cancel the oil concessions might prove impossible to resist. But the United States was able to keep Ibn-Saud under control. Saudi Arabia's rapid enrichment depended entirely on it respecting the oil concessions. Then there were the Hashemite kings of Jordan and Iraq, whom Ibn-Saud had dispossessed of Mecca and who were openly equating his occupation of Saudi Arabia with the Jewish annexation of Palestine. The threat wasn't to be taken lightly: the Hashemites had once been Britain's favourites, and, if necessary, a new Arab coalition could be mobilised to recapture Saudi Arabia. Ibn-Saud was well aware of these factors. So, while continuing to do the Americans' bidding, he tried to counter Arab criticism of his dependence on the US oil companies by arguing that the oil royalties were needed to make the Arabs strong and capable of resisting Zionism.

The oil interests were thus safeguarded in the midst of all the Arab–Israeli violence and wars. The pipeline from Saudi Arabia to Sidon in Lebanon, covering a distance of 1,040 miles, was completed in 1950. From Sidon, the oil was carried to Europe in giant tankers. Europe's reconstruction was now well underway, even as the Middle East was becoming more and more entangled in the Jewish–Arab conflicts. Shielding the Middle East oil resources against all threats, whether coming from the USSR or from local Communists, became a primary objective of the Cold War era, for on that oil depended Europe's economic recovery, and later its prosperity. Saudi Arabia, at the epicentre of the oil interests, virtually became an American protectorate. In October 1950, President Harry Truman wrote to King Ibn-Saud:

> I wish to renew to Your Majesty the assurances which have been made to you several times in the past, that the United States is interested in the preservation of the independence and territorial integrity of Saudi Arabia. No threat to your Kingdom could occur which would not be a matter of immediate concern to the United States.

Thus it was that an artificial Islamic autocracy, founded in the wake of World War I by a Bedouin tribal leader with British help, became at the end of World War II, on the sole strength of its oil resources, the linchpin of Europe's reconstruction project and a valued Cold War ally of the US.

## The End of the Hashemite Kingdom

In Iraq, however, despite a faithful Nouri al-Said installed as Prime Minister by the British in 1941, things were not running so smoothly. After the war, the British tried to force Nouri to sign a Treaty that renewed the old arrangements which virtually made Iraq a British protectorate. But nationalist sentiments were strong and coalesced with widespread disaffection among students and the working class, keeping the government on tenterhooks. Nouri al-Said decided to crack down on all left-wing groups. Members of the Communist party were ruthlessly hunted down. The party's Secretary-General, Yusuf Salman Yusuf, popularly known as Fahd, was already in jail. He was accused of fomenting revolutionary unrest and sentenced to death along with some of his close colleagues. Their bodies were publicly hanged to scare people from raising republican slogans.

Then Nouri suddenly began to champion the cause of Arab unity, proposing a union of Syria, Lebanon, Palestine, Jordan and Iraq into a single confederal state. The proposal had been hatched under British inspiration to counter a resurgence of pan-Arab nationalism, which at that time was secular in nature and enjoyed widespread support, across much of the Arab world, especially among military officers who called themselves 'Free Officers'. Unknown to the authorities, Abdel Gamal Nasser, an Egyptian officer deployed during the war in Sudan, was one of the motivators of the pan-Arabic movement. He was already in touch with several like-minded officers in the region, including his compatriot Anwar al-Sadat. But the idea of an Arab federation, as floated by Nouri, made no progress—he was simply too tainted by his British association to be credible.

The virulent anti-imperialist mood generated by the coup in Iran made it difficult for Nouri to force a renewal of the 20-year long Anglo-Iraqi treaty that expired in 1950. The United States unwittingly contributed to the failure, by negotiating the so-called Baghdad Pact (or CENTO: Central Treaty Organisation), a multilateral defence agreement under the NATO umbrella, which had Pakistan, Turkey, Iran and Iraq as its main sponsors. In these negotiations, which culminated in 1955, Nouri played a prominent part, actively pressuring neighbouring countries into joining.

The Baghdad Pact provoked strong nationalist reactions across the region. Egypt was then in the grip of revolutionary ardour: in July 1952, Nasser's 'Free Officers' (under the nominal leadership of General Mohammed Naguib) had just overthrown the famously corrupt and ineffectual King Farouk al-Awwal. The kingdom of Egypt had been set up by the British in 1922 under Fuad I, the same year that the Hashemite kingdom had been created in Iraq. From the very beginning, both regimes had been battered by the waves of nationalist agitation. With Farouk gone after the 1952 Revolution, Nasser was now pushing ambitious agrarian reforms in Egypt. At the same time, he was championing a militantly secular form of nationalism that proved infectious and fanned the flames of anti-imperialist sentiments throughout the region. He also became a champion of the non-aligned movement. After the Bandung conference of Asian and African nations in 1955, Nasser even emerged as something of a world figure, on a par with Jawaharlal Nehru of India and Josip Broz Tito of Yugoslavia. In these circumstances, Nouri al-Said of Iraq was inevitably seen as a fraud, a regional lackey of Western interests, and his advocacy of the Baghdad pact only met with contempt.

Soon, Nouri overreached himself, bringing about the end of the Hashemite dynasty in Iraq, as well as his own. Provoked beyond endurance by Nouri's proposal to merge Iraq with Jordan (which was ruled over by another branch of the Hashemite family), on 14 July 1958 a group of army officers under Brigadier Abdul-Karim Qassem staged a coup which met very little resistance and culminated in the massacre at the al-Zuhoor palace in Baghdad. The 23 year old Faisal II, his regent Abd al-Ilah, and all the available members of the royal family were killed. Prime Minister Nouri escaped the palace disguised as a woman but was shot dead by an air force officer who recognised him. The bodies of the slain rulers were then cut up and burnt. The army officers who plotted the coup had been in touch with Nasser, who had promised support in case the signatories of the Baghdad Pact should interfere militarily. Interfere they didn't, but they might well have, if large public demonstrations all across Iraq had not affirmed widespread popular support for the coup. Iraq was proclaimed a republic and brought under a Sovereignty Council, *Majlis al-Siyadeh*, consisting of three members (a Sunni, a Shia, and a Kurdish leader) with Brigadier Qassem as Prime Minister.

Relations between Qassem and Nasser soon soured. Brigadeer Qassem, who was an Iraqi nationalist first and foremost and had little truck with ideological grandstanding, spurned Nasser's offer to join the freshly created United Arab Republic (a union of Egypt and Syria) which had come into being on 1 February 1958, ten weeks before Qassem staged his coup. Nasser had conceived of the idea as a substitute for Nouri's abortive scheme of Arab unity. Yemen, too, had announced its decision to join in March, and Nasser hoped that Iraq, as a new Republic, would enter the new federation and turn it into a viable Arab alliance capable of holding its own against the Big Power games in the region. Qassem not only spurned Nasser, but also sacked his own lieutenant, Colonel Abdus Salam Aref (he was Iraq's Deputy Premier, with the additional portfolio of Interior Ministry) and even got him arrested. Aref was an admirer of Nasser and ardently supported his vision of a United Arab Republic.

Iraq's refusal to join started a fissiparous chain-reaction: Yemen soon changed its mind about entering the Union, and even Syria separated from Egypt in 1961. That was a hard blow to Nasser, who had become an ardent protagonist of Arab unity after Israel's invasion of the Sinai Peninsula in October 1956. Nasser viewed Brigadier Qassem's rebuff as an act of betrayal. A first attempt to assassinate Qassem was staged in October 1959, with the participation of a 22-year-old Ba'ath party worker, Saddam Hussein. The attempt failed but Saddam managed to flee to Cairo.

To bolster his support at home, Qassem began to woo the left and to work closely with sections of the Communist Party. He also tried to boost his public standing by cleverly playing on other issues. Thus, he launched a major offensive against the ever restive Kurds, who had expected a measure of autonomy from the new regime, but he failed to quell the insurgency.

In 1960, Qassem hosted the founding conference of the Organisation of Petroleum Exporting Countries (OPEC) in Baghdad. OPEC vowed to coordinate oil production and pricing policies on a global scale. Qassem also caused an international stir by questioning Kuwait's sovereignty a few days after the Emirate was proclaimed independent, in June 1961. When the Iraqi tanks took positions near the border, the headlines of London's *Daily Mail* (26 June 1961) screamed: 'Qassem tries £100-million-a-year takeover.' That apparently was Kuwait's oil income at the time. The region then witnessed the biggest British military build-up since the Suez crisis. British troops, tanks and aircrafts were called in from Pakistan, Bahrain, Kenya, Aden, Britain, West Germany, Cyprus and the Far East. For whatever reasons, Nasser of Egypt did not impede the transit of British warships through the Suez Canal. In the end, the Arab League stepped in and Qassem ordered the withdrawal of his forces. As proposed by the League, a so-called 'Military Patrol Line' was drawn to protect the Iraq–Kuwait border: both countries had to refrain from constructing permanent installations close to the Line. In the face of combined opposition by the Arab world, Qassem did not have the strength to carry out his threat of invading Kuwait. But Iraq continued to deny Kuwait's claim of independence and with the support of the Soviet Union succeeded in stalling its membership of the United Nations for the next three years. With Soviet encouragement, Qassem's government also repudiated the older arrangements with the Iraq Petroleum Company and pressed for a substantial increase of Iraqi royalties. He promulgated a law, called 'Public Law 80', that prohibited further oil concessions to foreign interests. He also created a public sector company, the Iraq National Oil Company, to explore and develop new oil fields.

Nasser was not impressed. The Iraqi threat to invade Kuwait had created strong rifts within the Arab world and weakened his idea of a larger Arab federation. According to Nasser, Qassem's economic policies were also giving the Soviet Union too much scope for interfering in the region—an interference which, as a leader of non-alignment, he did not relish. On 8 February 1963, Qassem was killed in yet another coup, organised by the Ba'ath Party with the support of anti-Communist sections of the army. Leading the coup was Abdus Salam Aref, the noted Nasser admirer. He became Iraq's President, with Ahmed Hassan al-Bakr, Saddam Hussein's cousin, as his prime minister.

The first phase of the new government was marked by a systematic, unremitting persecution of Communist party members. It has been alleged that Saddam Hussein, armed with lists of Communist cadres and sympathisers, personally supervised their arrest, torture and execution. It has also been suggested that these anti-Communist operations were mounted at the insistence of the CIA. This, at any rate, was clearly implied by King Hussein of Jordan, in an interview with Hassanein Heikal, editor of Cairo's Al-Ahram newspaper:

> Permit me to tell you that I know for a certainty that what happened in Iraq on 8 February [1963] had the support of American intelligence. Some of those who now rule in Baghdad do not know of this thing but I am aware of the truth. Meetings were held between the Ba'ath party and American intelligence, mainly in Kuwait. Do you know that on 8 February a secret radio emitter beaming to Iraq was supplying the men behind the coup with names and addresses of Iraqi Communists so that they could be arrested and executed?

Thousands of Communists were killed. Some managed to escape. These anti-Communist purges ended only seven months later, in November 1963, when Aref broke with the Ba'ath Party.

Aref's new government re-affirmed the principles of Arab unity and socialism, paying merely lip-service to the former, but taking some vigorous steps towards implementing the latter. Under Aref, Iraq recognised Kuwait's independence, but maintained some of its claims about border areas along the Persian Gulf. Iraq's industrialisation and economic development received special attention, as did public education. Meanwhile, the Ba'ath party was urging the government to make up with the Kurdish insurgent leaders by offering effective decentralisation. The military faction that supported President Aref viewed these policies with alarm. It forced a split within the government that led to the dismissal of the prime minister in November 1963 and to a crackdown on the leaders of the Ba'ath Party.

Aref was known as a supporter of Nasser's idea of an Arab confederation. Once in power, however, he dragged his feet and begged Nasser for time to prepare the country for its merger with the United Arab Republic. He proclaimed socialist policies and appointed Abd ar-Rahman al-Bazzaz, a legal scholar and known champion of Arab nationalism, as his Prime Minister. Bazzaz negotiated a truce with the Kurd leaders: he offered to recognise the Kurds as a distinct nationality within the Iraqi homeland and to grant them administrative decentralisation. Aref was broadly sympathetic of these moves. He was also contemplating some radical democratic changes when he died mysteriously in a helicopter accident on 15 April 1966.

Abd as-Salam Aref was succeeded by his brother General Abdul Rahman Aref who, under pressure from the army, dismissed Abd ar-Rahman al-Bazzaz as prime minister. The 1967 war with Israel, which resulted in the Israeli occupation of Gaza, the West Bank, Egypt's Sinai Peninsula and Syria's Golan heights, further undermined the secular forces behind the pan-Arab nationalism in the region. The prospects for a peaceful arrangement with the Kurds, which Bazzaz had championed, faded away. Abdul Rahman Aref ruled precariously for about two years until the Ba'ath party, under Ahmed Hassan al-Bakr's leadership, ousted him from power on 17 July 1968.

The coup mounted by the Ba'ath party was bloodless and General Aref himself was allowed to leave for Istanbul. Ahmed Hassan al-Bakr became president, with his cousin Saddam Hussein as vice-president. On 1 June 1972, Al-Bakr nationalised the Iraq Oil Company after paying $300 million in compensation to foreign shareholders. For the next eleven years, Al-Bakr competently ruled the country, keeping the focus on economic development. Iraq's diplomatic relations with the US had been severed after the 1967 Arab–Israeli war. So Iraq now turned to France and the Soviet Union for technical assistance to develop its northern Rumaila oil field, also for credits to finance the project. The cooperation between the

Soviet Union and Iraq was mutually beneficial: the Soviet Union gained an important foothold in the region, and Iraq used the Russians' technical and organisational skills to revamp its economy. The eleven years under Al-Bakr's government were probably the most prosperous and peaceful period in Iraq's modern history. It all ended, abruptly and mysteriously, on 17 July 1979, when al-Bakr announced his decision to step down from the presidency, ostensibly on health grounds. His Vice-President (and cousin) Saddam Hussein took over the reins of government.

The true facts behind the transfer of power from Al-Bakr to Saddam Hussein remain unknown to this day. What is known, though, is that Saddam had once worked for the CIA and was a sworn enemy of Ayatollah Ruhollah Khomeini. For the next nine years, Iraq under Saddam Hussein would fight Iran, with America's backing, to sap the young Islamic Republic's revolutionary fervour, while the Mujahideen in Afghanistan, also backed by the United States, fought the Soviet forces until their final withdrawal, soon to be followed by the disintegration of the Soviet Union. In the event, four countries—Iraq, Iran, Afghanistan, and the USSR—bled themselves to exhaustion.

# Notes

1. The term was first used in an article by Mahan titled 'The Persian Gulf and International Relations', in *National Review of London*, September 1902. Mahan had then recently retired as Head of the National War College and become President of the American Historical Association. *A.N.*
2. The very term *Middle East*, according to historian Michael Oren, was also coined by Mahan. Indians, of course, refer to the area as *West Asia*, a term usually credited to Jawaharlal Nehru. *E.N.*
3. Let us sort out text and subtext here. At the front of their minds, Churchill and his listeners had of course images of *British* drops of blood, and could feel nobly uplifted, while at the back of their minds they were quite reassured as to the likely source of the blood to be shed. Political cynicism is rarely blunt; it prefers to play on ambiguity and double registers. *E.N.*
4. This ancient Mesopotamian city is associated with the mythological figure of Gilgamesh. It flourished from circa 5000 BC down to the end of the Parthian empire in 224 AD.

5.   From *The MacDonald Letter*, 13 February 1931.
6.   They derive their name from the ancient kingdom of Assyria in northern Mesopotamia, where their first communities developed. Western historians tend to lump them together with the Nestorians, but they themselves reject the label.
7.   See Chapter 1.

# 3

## *The ordeals of Arab nationalism: A discussion in Damascus*

In early September 2007, I went to Damascus, the capital of Syria, to attend a conference on human rights, or, rather, on the adverse impact that the massive increase in 'Counter Terrorism Measures' (CTM) was having, post-9/11, on human rights worldwide. After the conference, I decided to stay on for a while, so as to get the chance to meet some veterans of the Arab nationalist struggle and members of various resistance movements. Though based in Syria, not all my contacts were Syrian-born.

Under its halo of arid brown, Damascus is a beautiful city, scooped up in what appears like a huge tennis racket when viewed from the mountains to the west. Despite the tawdry character of the city's growth in the last decades, Damascus has managed to preserve something of its 5,000 years of living history. This shows everywhere: in the layered architecture, the heterogeneous population, the colourful street life. Some of the main sites, like the Umayyad mosque, said to house the head of John the Baptist, or the tomb of Saladin, are truly magnificent, and still ooze something of the glory that was Syria.

Today, even after losing its geopolitical weight, following the discovery of oil everywhere in the region save for on its own soil, Syria still matters politically. Damascus remains a focal point of Arab nationalism and an example of successful resistance to the West's hegemonic designs. Syria, which obviously is a Latin form of Assyria (from the Akkadian *Assur*), can look back on a long and rich history, as an important partner—in war, peace, and trade—to the ancient Phoenicians, Egyptians, Sumerians, Babylonians, Persians, Greeks, and then to the Romans, who conquered it under Pompey in 64 BC. Several Syrians actually became high Roman officials. There were even three Syrian Emperors: Elagabalus (218–22); Alexander Severus (222–35); and Marcus Julius Philippus (244–49).[1] As a geographical term, Syria denoted a rather vague and fluctuating territory, sometimes including and sometimes excluding the lands on the Mediterranean's eastern coast, much of Palestine, most of Mesopotamia, even parts of Egypt and Anatolia, such as the ancient city of Antioch (now inside Turkey) where Apostle Paul established the first Christian Church. In the 7th century, Damascus became the capital city of an Islamic Empire under the Umayyad dynasty, which added splendid palaces and mosques to the older castles and shrines. Their remains can still be seen.

Damascus lost its standing and security when the Abbasid dynasty took over from the Umayyads in AD 750 and established its capital in Baghdad. But Syria and Damascus re-emerged prominently on the historical scene during the Third Crusade, especially after Saladin, a warrior of Kurdish origin, made Damascus the centre of his campaigns in the year 1174. Over the next eighteen years, Saladin grew into a figure of legend, an ever-living icon of Islamic resistance against Western encroachments. He staged spectacular victories against the crusaders, while strictly adhering to humane norms of war and chivalry. Saladin took Jerusalem in 1187. He then invited the leaders of the local Jewish communities, notably that of Ashqalan (now Ashkelon, in Israel), to return and re-settle in the cities from which they had been expelled by the crusaders. In 1192, just one year before his death, Saladin concluded the Treaty of Ramla by which Jerusalem was to remain under Muslim rule but open to Christian pilgrims.

Unfortunately, the glory and material prosperity which Saladin brought to Syria and to Damascus did not long outlast him. This was an age of violent anarchy, with the crusaders, the *Hashshashin* warriors,[2] and then the Mongol hordes dealing death and destruction wherever they reached. In 1400, Damascus was taken by Tamerlane. Almost the entire elite population of the city was put to the sword. The artisans were deported to Samarkand.

Syria never quite recovered from the deadly blow inflicted by Tamerlane. It was absorbed by the Ottoman Empire and remained under

Ottoman rule until the end of World War I, when on 1 October 1918 Lawrence of Arabia staged his victory march on Damascus, in the name of his Hashemite friend Emir Faisal. But two years earlier, the French had made a deal with the British, of which Lawrence and his friend had no knowledge. The secret treaty, now known as Sykes–Picot agreement after the names of its two negotiators,[3] had been signed in May 1916: it promised Syria and Lebanon to the French, Iraq and all of Palestine to the British. After the war, the League of Nations formalised the division of spoils, with Britain taking the lion's share, largely from considerations of oil and geo-strategic control. The French occupied Syria in 1920 after defeating a ramshackle of an Arab army which swore by Faisal, of the Hashemite family. The British then moved Faisal to Baghdad, for him to function as nominal king—Faisal I—of the newly created Iraq.

In 1936, the French signed a treaty of independence with Syria. This allowed Hashim al-Atassi, an Arab nationalist, to become the country's first president. In formal terms, this marked the beginning of the modern Republic of Syria. But the French quickly reneged on the treaty and refused to leave. Soon after, World War II started and France fell to Hitler's troops in 1940. The Vichy government, installed by the Nazis, retained its control of Syria until July 1941, when elements of the French resistance, backed by British troops, took over. The French ruled Syria until April 1946, when it became an independent country.

The partition of Palestine and the birth of Israel brought chronic instability to the region. In 1949, Syria saw its first military coup—the first of a long series. Other misadventures followed, like Syria's short-lived union with Nasser's Egypt in February 1958 and its annulment in September 1961 after another coup. Then, after yet another coup engineered by the Ba'ath party (Arab Socialist Resurrection Party) in March 1963, the grand idea was mooted of a union of Syria, Egypt and Iraq. All agreed on a referendum and then disagreed and the union remained still-born.

In February 1966, a group of army officers imprisoned President Amin Hafiz and took over the government. Four months later, siding with Nasser, they went to war against Israel. That was the famous Six Day war, in which Syria lost its Golan Heights to Israel. Israel also took over the Sinai Peninsula and Gaza strip from Egypt, and the West Bank with Eastern Jerusalem from Jordan. At the time, Hafiz al-Assad was Syria's Defence Minister. In 1970, the Syrian Government dispatched troops against Jordan, after the king there had launched his *Black September* purges—a series of murderous attacks on the PLO to force it out of the country. But the Syrian troops retreated before taking any action, heaping discredit upon Amin Hafiz. Taking advantage of the fiasco and the rankling humiliation it had left in the army's ranks, Assad seized all the reins of power in November 1970. In October 1973, Syria and Egypt again lost, or half-lost, another round of war against Israel. This was the Yom Kippur War—still a defeat for the Arabs, but a far cry from the all-out trouncing of the Six Day War. After the *Black September* attacks, the PLO shifted its base from Jordan to Lebanon, upsetting the country's fragile political balance and eventually leading, in early 1976, to a regular civil war. At the behest of the Maronite Christians, Syria sent 40,000 troops to Lebanon, but soon got embroiled in the ever changing equations. Syria stayed in Lebanon for the next 30 years, and after successively supporting any number of factions and political constellations, it finally emerged as a firm ally of the Shia militias, now consolidated under Hizbullah.

In February 1982, Syria witnessed an armed uprising by Sunni fundamentalists close to Egypt's Muslim Brotherhood and based mainly in the city of Hama. The Assad government crushed the uprising with a heavy hand, leaving tens of thousands dead and the city half-razed. In 1991, Hafiz al-Assad, who had just lost the shield of the Soviet alliance and whose relations with Saddam Hussein had always been strained, joined the US-led coalition to expel Iraq from Kuwait. After the first Gulf War, Assad became involved in protracted negotiations with Israel, brokered by the United States. The first contacts took place at the Madrid summit in October 1991. After nine years of inconclusive parleys, Assad broke off the negotiations at his March 2000 meeting with US President Bill Clinton. He died three months later in June 2000.

His 34 year old son, Bashar al-Assad took over the presidency for a seven year term after a state-staged referendum in which he ran uncontested, taking nearly 98 per cent of the vote.

Bashar al-Assad was into his seventh year as President when I went to Damascus, in October 2007. Under his watch, Syria suffered two aerial attacks by the Israeli air force: the first in October 2003, ostensibly to wipe out a training facility for 'terrorists' near Damascus, and the second in September 2007, presumably to destroy a nuclear reactor under construction by North Korean technicians in the desert area of Deir ez-Zur. Syria also came under heavy criticism as well as political and economic sanctions from the United States and other Western governments, for supporting militant organisations like Hizbullah, Hamas and Islamic Jihad, and for meddling in the political affairs of Lebanon. Yet Syria remains undeterred and continues to offer sanctuary to persecuted Palestinians like Khaled Mashal, the intrepid Hamas leader. Mashal used to be based in Jordan until 1997, when he narrowly survived an assassination attempt. Two agents of Mossad (the Israeli Intelligence), acting on instructions from Israel's Prime Minister Binyamin Netanyahu, managed to spray a lethal poison on his neck. But the agents were caught and Israel was forced to part with the antidote in exchange for the release of its agents. After the attempt, Mashal briefly moved to Qatar, from where the US got him expelled, and then on to Damascus, where he is now permanently based. Together with Sheikh Ahmed Yassin, the Hamas founder who has since been assassinated, Mashal led the Palestinian opposition to the Oslo Accords, that peace deal which Yasser Arafat struck with Israel under Clinton's blandishments. Sheikh Yassin and Khaled Mashal have consistently upheld Hamas' intransigent line—which is the main reason for the movement's appeal.[4] The success of Hamas in the Palestinian parliamentary elections of January 2006 (most marked in Gaza) is largely attributed to Mashal.

Syria, a country of about 19 million people on 185,000 square kilometers of land, houses a large number of political refugees—some 600,000 Palestinians and 1.3 million others, including Sunnis fleeing Iraq. Despite being a military dictatorship, Syria is also known for its policy of religious and ethnic tolerance. It is actually led by a member of the Alawite minority.[5] Syria's motley population includes Syrian and Maronite Christians, Armenians, Kurds, Turks, Alawis, Druze, even offshoots of Ismaili sects like the *Hashshashin* of yore. All enjoy freedom of religion and equal civic rights.

My main contact in Syria was Dr Georges Jabbour,[6] Professor of Political Science at Aleppo University. Presently a member of Syria's Peoples Council (the country's supreme legislative body), Dr Jabbour has long been associated with the Arab nationalist movement and was close to the late Hafiz al-Assad. A member of the Greek Orthodox Church, he has represented his country at various international forums, including the United Nations. He was also associated with the Madrid peace process.

Dr Georges Jabbour invited me over to his private house. Some of his political friends, whom I shall leave unnamed, were also present. A man of polite erudition in his early 60s, Dr Jabbour spoke good English with a strong French accent, amidst good-humoured chuckles and strong Arabic interjections. He did not tire of my curiosity and endless queries. It was a free-flowing, unconstrained conversation, most of which I recorded and later transcribed.

I asked him about the plight of Arab nationalism, its disappointing record, apparent helplessness before Western hegemony and Israel's overbearing tactics. This was his response:

*Arab nationalism, in its modern form, was born in the second half of the 19th century. From the first, it was directed against the occupiers of our land, which at the time mainly meant the Ottoman Turks—our Muslim but non-Arab overlords. Our renascent nationalism was also wary of European designs. The French had already conquered Algeria in the 1830s. In Egypt also, after Napoleon's short-lived invasion, the British had established a more lasting presence. From 1882 onwards, they militarily occupied the country and ruled it in all but name, after defeating an Arab revolt (led by Ahmed Urabi, an Egyptian general and charismatic figure with a large following among the nationalist youth and the peasantry) which threatened to free Egypt of European interference. Arabs also knew about the first and second Afghan wars, which the British waged in 1838–42 and then again in 1878–80 to establish their stranglehold over the region. Thus, Arab nationalism arose from a dual opposition: to Ottoman occupation and to European designs. Yet, even at its inception, Arab nationalism was not a monolithic movement. From the start, it admitted a variety of political and ideological shades.*

*As a Syrian, I would like to illustrate the point with an example that captured the attention of that early Arab nationalist philosopher, Sati al-Husri. Up to 1891, the patriarch of the Greek Orthodox Church for Syria—the church to which I belong—used to be Greek. The Orthodox Greek Christian community of Damascus objected. They submitted a petition asking for a patriarch who could speak their language. The Church discussed the petition and conceded the demand. Since then, the patriarch of our Greek Orthodox Church has always been an Arab. For comparison: the patriarch of the Greek Orthodox Church in Jerusalem continues to be a Greek and the members of the Church in Palestine go on objecting, to no avail. Thus, towards the end of the 19th century Arab* nationalism had scored a success in Damascus which remains unattainable in Jerusalem at the start of the 21st century.

The episode is significant because it reminds us that we Syrian Arabs are an assimilated people, with a long exposure to religious and cultural diversity, through centuries of trade, migrations and conquest. Arab nationalism, as we conceive it, is an assertion of self-determination, firm in its refusal of external interference, but tolerant of our internal diversity and wedded to the egalitarian principle of respect for all minorities. Sati al-Husri talked about linguistic unity as the foundation of Arab nationalism, capable of bridging the religious and ethnic divides. But even this primacy accorded to the Arabic language should remain compatible with our internal linguistic diversity. Syria has villages where Aramaic—the language in which Jesus of Nazareth and his disciples conversed—is still in use (mainly for liturgy). Syria is also home to quite a few other languages and dialects, such as Kurdish. Even the Turkish language has not been outlawed, and is still being freely spoken, written, and printed in some border areas, although Arab nationalism, in its modern form, was chiefly directed against the Ottoman yoke.

But again: within the broad spectrum of Arab nationalism, there were all sorts of shades, some of them reflecting the dominant discourses in European politics. This was inevitable.

The progenitors of Arab nationalism in the 20th century are Michel Aflaq, a Syrian Christian, and his Sunni colleague, Salah ud-Din al-Bitar. They were the ones who founded the Ba'ath Party in the early 1940s and who developed its ideology. They used the Arab language as the common plank for anti-imperialist solidarity, but without a whiff of hostility towards the religious and linguistic minorities in the region. They were also strong proponents of secularism, industrialisation and social welfare. For Michel Aflaq, the founder of Islam was a great prophet who paved the way for Arab cultural unity and political ascendancy.

The same holds for Antun Saada, the founder of the Syrian Social Nationalist Party, known as SSNP (or PPS, standing for Parti Populaire Social in the French mistranslation). A Greek Orthodox, he became one of the early pioneers of a brand of Arab nationalism that emphasised the common heritage, linguistic and cultural, of all Arabs as the basis of their anti-imperialist solidarity, without denying their internal diversity. Antun Saada was also fiercely secular, insisting on a strict separation of religion and politics. Western political scholarship, monopolised as it is by

Anglophiles and Francophiles, has unfairly portrayed the founder of the SSNP as a fascist, sympathetic to Hitler, without recognising that all patriotic Arabs were looking for tactical alliances with the enemies of Britain and France, the two countries which had divided the Arab world between themselves. Nasser and his aide Anwar al-Sadat of Egypt had also established contacts with agents of the Axis powers, mainly Italians, to plan a coup with their assistance and oust the British from the country. This is well-known yet no one doubts their patriotic credentials. Antun Saada was also a votary of Syrian unity. He did not advocate a grand Arab nation, but an anti-imperialist front of independent Arab states like Syria, Egypt and Iraq. It is because of such views that the SSNP suffered persecution under the French, who had it banned, and that it was later reviled, after independence, amidst the euphoria of pan-Arab unity spread by Nasser. The Sunni Islamists also opposed the party's secular orientation. To Israel, of course, the SSNP was anathema, because the Zionist project was anathema to the SSNP. The monarchies and sheikhdoms set up by the British also looked askance at the party because of its republican fervour. Betrayed by the rulers of Iraq in July 1949, Saada was executed in Beirut.

Then there were also Socialists and Communists of all kinds who tried hard to reconcile the Arab nationalist credo with the Marxist vision of life—with questionable intellectual rigour and without much visible success. In Egypt there was Salama Musa, a Coptic Christian by birth, a socialist by conviction and ardent believer in modernisation, who founded Egypt's Socialist Party in 1920.

In Lebanon, Yusuf Ibrahim Yazbek and Fuad Shamali founded the region's first Communist party. After its ban by the French, they went on to establish, in secret, the Syrian Lebanese Communist Party.

In Syria we had Khalid Bakdash, a Syrian Communist Party cadre who led the underground resistance against the French occupation. He made history by becoming, in 1954, the first member of a Communist party to be elected to an Arab Parliament. He had to flee Syria in 1958, when Nasser and his idea of a grand Arab union were at their zenith. He returned to the country after Hafiz al-Assad seized power.

Then there was Akram al-Hawrani, a controversial figure, who formed the Arab Socialist Party and campaigned for agrarian reforms, later cooperating with all kinds of political figures and eventually teaming up with the Ba'ath Party. There were all kinds of secular, socialist strands which are now almost completely extinct. The traditions of the political left are kept alive only in the theoretical sphere, by men like Ilyas Murqus (who died in 1991), Samir Amin, Hassan Hanafi, Hussein Morowa and Mahdi Amil (both were assassinated in Beirut in 1987), Hisham Ghassib and so on. But let us not get entangled in the details of Arab political thought.

The main point I am trying to make is that the Arab people's reaction to the occupation of their lands by the Ottomans or the Europeans was, at first, decidedly rational, political and secular in character. It was also, inevitably, inchoate. To develop and mature, it needed time, which it had, but also an environment of intellectual and political autonomy, which it was denied. I should not have to repeat that Islamic philosophy and logic can look back on a rich tradition. Time and again, it has shown itself capable of synthesising and surpassing earlier intellectual contributions. Let me mention but two names: Ibn Sina (Avicenna) who absorbed Aristotelian thinking and transformed it into an original philosophy; and Ibn Khaldun, the noted historian and forerunner of several social science disciplines, widely acknowledged as 'the father of social science' even in the West.[7] Surely, with such traditions to build on, the Arabs could have overcome the intellectual challenge of their encounter with Western civilisation—if only the West had not spoiled their chances by occupying their lands, thwarting their development, disrupting their institutions.

Europe's modern involvement in the region was, at heart, political and economic. Nonetheless, the Europeans continued to view the Middle East, the Ottoman state, Egypt, and above all the land of Palestine, through the distorting lenses of their own, highly idiosyncratic religious geography, at the centre of which was the Holy Land, the birth-place of Judaism and Christianity, the heartland of the unfinished Crusades, which had to be carried on by a new alliance between Zionism and the European Enlightenment. This reconstruction of a religious geography of the Middle East, as the land of biblical events, was a helpful prelude to the politics of re-conquest, clearly heralded by the Balfour Declaration of November 1917, in which Zionists and Europeans could cooperate.[8] The Sykes–Picot agreement, signed in 1916, displayed all the crassness and stealth of Western diplomacy—with everything revolving round the division of spoils—which has remained unchanged to this day. But the re-conquest inevitably entailed a recourse to military methods. Military success, in turn, required a degree of local complicity and cooperation, which could only come from the most retrograde elements in the Arab landscape—reactionary *clerics and feudal chiefs. That was the thinking behind the European alliance with the Hashemites from Hijaz, the Emirs of the Gulf and the Wahhabis of Saudi Arabia. So far, these tactics have worked. They have kept Palestine under occupation. They have maintained the Arab people politically divided and intellectually confused. Early on, the British recognised Arab nationalism as an emerging force which could seriously endanger their designs. Instead of fighting it head-on, they seemingly embraced the idea, harnessed its power to finish off the Ottoman empire, and then corrupted it from within, through deceit, division, bribery. But Arab nationalism continued to flutter under various banners.*

*The cause of Palestine, whose people became stateless after the creation of Israel, was one such banner. During World War II, Hadji Amin al-Husseini attained brief prominence by courting the Axis powers, hoping for support. In Iraq, Rashid Ali al-Gaylani, a distinguished nationalist politician who became the country's Prime Minister in 1940, led the revolt against the Anglo-Iraqi Treaty of 1930. The British and the French portrayed him as a Nazi and had him ousted. But like Antun Saada, Rashid was simply an Arab nationalist. He was the one who first floated the idea of a League of Arab States. The British crushed Rashid Ali al- Gaylani, but embraced his idea of an Arab League, after twisting it to suit their requirements. If you consult the history of the period closely, you will see that immediately after crushing Rashid Ali al-Gaylani the British issued a declaration about 'facilitating Arab cooperation'. Isn't that shrewd politics!*

Even before he could round off his argument, Dr Jabbour was chuckling!

I objected: weren't the years 1940–41 absolutely critical for the British war effort in the Middle East? Weren't the Nazis at the outskirts of Alexandria, when the British had the good luck of beating them back in the tank battle at El Alamein? Who could expect the British to put up with regimes and uprisings that looked to their arch enemies for support? Wasn't that the reason why the British deposed Reza Shah in Iran in September 1941?

Dr Jabbour went on unperturbed:

*Certainly the British had good reasons to be worried about their adversaries. But I am not talking about the war. I am talking about the Arab nationalism and the light in which it has been depicted in the biased narratives of Western* scholars who did not know or care to know the Arab viewpoint. In their love for the European and Zionist missions, they have demonised the Arab resistance movements and distorted the historical perspective. Arab nationalist leaders, as I said before, looked to the enemies of Britain and France for support in their quest for national liberation. To portray them as fascists is, in my view, not only unjust but also boorish.

I know Syria and Lebanon well and can tell you that despite the deep abhorrence of the French occupation there were strong voices opposing the Nazi propaganda and its local proponents. Have you heard of the 'League Against Nazism and Fascism' in Syria and Lebanon and the journal Al-Tariq, which the League published from 1941 onwards? It was a leftist initiative, also joined by several nationalists who did not subscribe to Marxist or socialist thinking. On 9th April 1933, some time after Hitler became Reich Chancellor, there was a public demonstration in front of the German consulate in Beirut: they burnt the German flag and chanted anti-Nazi slogans. In 1935, with Mussolini poised to invade Abyssinia, left-wing intellectuals in Syria and Lebanon formed the 'Committee for the Popular Struggle in Defence of Ethiopia', as a platform for spreading anti-fascist consciousness. Yusuf Khattar al-Hilu, a prominent Syrian Communist,[9] did much to counter the fascist propaganda in Arab lands. During the Spanish Civil War, Arab leftists joined the International Brigades in non-negligible numbers. In 1936, Khalid Bakdash, a Syrian Communist leader, sided with the left-front government of Léon Blum in France, and applauded the new treaty between the Syrian nationalists and the French Government, out of a conviction that European fascism had first to be defeated in Europe for the liberation struggles in the colonised world to develop along genuinely egalitarian lines.

The political left in Syria and Lebanon, while strongly anti-Zionist where Palestine was concerned, was uncompromising in its opposition to Nazism. Beirut housed a Syrian–Lebanese conference against fascism in the first week of May 1939. It was attended by more than two hundred delegates, representing several political and non-political organisations. Raif Khuri, an independent Lebanese intellectual, was largely responsible for the event's success. Unfortunately, in August 1939, there burst the bombshell of the Molotov–Ribbentrop Pact, which Stalin signed to save the Russian Revolution, and his own skin. It bewildered Arab nationalistic thinking. It put the Arab resistance in the impossible position of having to oppose, simultaneously, the two sides contending for world domination. There followed a spate of repressive measures, that especially *targeted the leftist elements—precisely those that had been active against the fascist forces. Then, in the summer of 1940, Hitler overran France. In terms of global politics, it was a truly confusing situation. But even then an underground newspaper, Nidal al-Sha'ab, distributed in both Syria and Lebanon, carried an article stating the Arab position with unexceptionable clarity: 'No British, no Germans, no Italians; but bread, freedom and independence.' For Arab nationalism, these were truly testing times—but then things haven't become much easier since.*

*The Free-French troops, backed by the British, regained possession of Syria in July 1941. Those left intellectuals and Communist sympathisers who had been jailed under the Vichy regime were gradually released. Many of them, led by Umar Fakhuri, Yusuf Yazbik and Raif Khuri, resumed their fight against the Fascist ideology, and that too despite the serious socio-economic difficulties of the period, which were of greater import to the public. The editor of the Beirut daily Al-Nahar, Jibran Tuwayni (he was not a Communist) wrote a pamphlet, titled 'The Arabs and the Allies: Why are we with them and what do we expect from their victory?' The pamphlet was widely circulated and sparked off a heated debate about Fascism. Then there was this monthly magazine, Al-Adib, published from Beirut by Albert Adib. The first issue of the magazine appeared in January 1942. It became the main forum for the defenders of democracy and liberal values, and among those were forceful Arab nationalists like Qustantin Zurayq, Idmun Rabbat, also left-leaning intellectuals like Iliyas Abu Shabka or Qadri Qalaaji.*

I interrupted Dr Jabbour: weren't the Arab defenders of the Allied cause in an awkward position, given that the French had just amputated Syria of a sizeable part of its territory two years before the start of World War II? Hadn't the French used—or abused—their UN mandate to give away to Turkey an important chunk of northern Syria, with the ancient city of Alexandretta, thereby divesting the Syrian city of Aleppo of its natural outlet to the sea?

*Indeed, we Syrians can never forgive the French for this act of meaningless treachery. The calculation was that the backhander would so delight the Turks that they would side with the Allied forces in the upcoming war. As a result, we lost a historically important city along with large chunks of our province of Liwaa Aliskenderuna, which the Turks call Hatav. It also made it easier for Turkey to filch our precious waters from the rivers Euphrates and Tigris. We seldom rake up these issues now, because we have enough troubles with Israel* and do not want to infuriate our powerful northern neighbour. But speaking of territorial amputations, France did even worse: it separated Lebanon from Syria, this time out of sectarian considerations. This misguided decision would cause endless conflicts.

But it is of course the question of Palestine that rankles most on the mind of all Arabs, including us Syrians. Directly or indirectly, it has been the one cause behind most of the conflicts in the region, and that won't change until a just and principled solution is found.

At this point Dr Jabbour's other guests joined in the discussion, and I too contributed a number of questions which I now realise must have struck them as supremely naïve.

I began: Obviously, modern Israel arose at the heart of the Middle East in response to events that were totally external to that same Middle East, and are only too well-known. There was the long history of European anti-Semitism, which in Herzl's time reached a pitch of intensity sufficient to push Jews in their droves to Palestine—a place which was etched into their collective consciousness as the 'promised land', but which, otherwise, would have held little appeal to European Jewry. Then, two generations later, anti-Semitism reached an all-time peak with Hitler. The Holocaust stunned the world and created an unstoppable momentum for Israel. Thus far, the sequence is clear. But what about the sequel? By 1948, Palestine's Jewish population hardly exceeded 650,000, as against more than 1.5 million Palestinian Arabs who enjoyed the sympathies and support of some 100 million Arabs throughout the Middle East. Why this bitter enmity ever since? Was conflict pre-ordained? Why was it not possible for the Jews of Israel and the Arabs, of Palestine and beyond, to evolve a reasonable *modus vivendi* and coexist without too much friction or even to mutual advantage? After all, didn't both Jews and Arabs share at least one strong bond: that of being Europe's victims?

Dr Jabbour answered me in a slow and sobre tone, but with a twinge of exasperation that contrasted with the ease and confidence with which he had spoken so far:

I do not want to talk about the Biblical narrative—God's 'promise' of land to the patriarchs and their progeny—because that would get us entangled in issues of history and theology, for which we have no time, no competence, and no taste. You are right about the anti-Semitic bigotry and intolerance of Christian

*Europe, but that intolerance applied equally to Jews and Arabs, both being 'Semites'. The term of course is of recent coinage,[10] but Europe, instinctively, had long equated these two branches of the Semitic family in the same aversion. It is another matter that the two cousin races, Jews and Arabs, also seem to have entertained an adversarial relationship, no one knows for how long. Here again, for those who like Biblical parables, we have the story of Abraham and his two sons—Isaac, the legitimate child, borne by his spouse Sarah, and progenitor of the Hebrews; and Ishmael, the accursed one, borne by the maid Hagar, and forefather of all Arabs.*

*In fabulous history, the Jews have been migrating and returning, migrating and returning yet again. They supposedly left the land of Canaan, the Bible's name for Palestine, for Egypt in ca. 1700 BC. There they became slaves to the Pharaohs until Moses came and brought them freedom. He led them back to the 'promised land' in ca. 1250 BC, where they settled after engaging in thorough ethnic cleansing. None of this, incidentally, is borne out by archaeology or independent chronicles. With the King of Assyria, Sargon II as spelt in the Bible, we are on slightly firmer ground. This Sargon is said to have invaded Palestine in 721 BC and to have driven ten of the twelve Jewish tribes towards Mesopotamia. According to the Hebrew tradition, the event marks the start of Jewish dispersion—'Galut' in Hebrew, 'Diaspora' in Greek. Then again the Bible tells us that in 586 BC the King of Babylon, Nebuchadnezzar, entered Jerusalem, the centre of the remaining two tribes, destroyed Solomon's temple, and drove the entire population into exile. Let us accept all of this for the sake of argument.[11]*

*The subsequent history of the region shows that there were people who lived there, fought wars, defended and preserved the land with their blood and toil, from Persian antiquity down to World War II. Some Jews, a minority of fluctuating size, have also been living there, through the vicissitudes of history, sharing the place with others, Muslims, Christians, Druzes, and so on. We do not know for sure whether, at the dawn of recorded history, the Jews really dispersed or, assuming they dispersed, when, how or why they returned. We only know that thereafter they lived with roughly the same rights as others, and shared the resources of the land in much the same way as others.*

*To us, this history is far more reliable, and feels far more real, than the private Jewish epic of divine bequest under Moses and loss under Nebuchadnezzar. The people who fashioned that history, even those not chosen by Jehovah, also possess, do they not, certain rights and claims deserving of respect. The children of Ishmael, even if cursed by Jehovah, found inspiration from the Prophet Mohammed and went on to develop an impressive history of their own, to which the Jewish diaspora contributed only tangentially. As for the mix, of whichever descent, who lived in Palestine, endured through all its historical tribulations, survived the ebb and flow of conquests, tended their fields and tilled the soil, even if in their own clumsy or inefficient ways—aren't these entitled to some respect, too? Don't they deserve some protection against those aliens who suddenly take it into their heads to make their 'aliya'—their 'return' (literally, 'ascent')—and think nothing of snatching the land by force or deceit, and then either banish the indigenous people or, unable to expel them all, treat the rest as third-class citizens?*

Dr Jabbour was still speaking slowly but his scorn and exasperation were now audible. I did not quite understand all his nuances. So I asked him to explain which Jewish immigrants, of what period, he was referring to. At first, from the middle of the 19th century, there had been this persecution-driven trickle of Jewish migration from Eastern Europe and Russia, which became a surge only after Theodor Herzl organised the Zionist movement. Surely, I suggested, the early migration did not constitute a menace to the Palestinian people living in the waning days of Ottoman rule. By all available accounts, the early immigrants, the pioneers of the *Yishuv*, the founders of the *kibbutzim*, even did a lot of good to Palestine's agriculture, I ventured. I knew it was a sensitive subject to discuss with Arab nationalists. But I wanted to hear what they had to say. The following is the gist of their response. Dr Jabbour spoke first, the others chiming in now and then.

*I wonder what are your sources of information about the early Jewish migrants to Palestine and their first settlements there. The bulk of the literature on the subject emanates from a generation of doggedly blinkered authors, all Zionist sympathisers to a man. Most of it amounts to little more than a scholarly elaboration of the Zionist claims, which have never been seriously and critically appraised.*

*In 1970 Shimon Peres published a book titled* David's Sling: The Arming *of Israel. In this book, Peres claims that Palestine was an empty wilderness, with only a few pockets of Arab settlements, and that Israel's cultivable land was salvaged from swamp and shrub by the Herculean labour of Jewish settlers. That other old-timer of Israeli politics, Levi Eshkol,[12] claimed that the Zionists made the desert of Palestine bloom—seeing which the envious Arabs plotted to take it back. Much of the Western scholarship on the subject is a rehashing of this make-the-desert-bloom cliché. From the beginning, especially in the decisive years after World War I when things were still in a state of flux, the Zionists managed to convince the European powers that Palestine was a desolate wasteland—a desert without people which the Jewish immigrants could take over without hurting anyone, and turn into arable land. These are crass lies, which large sections of Western opinion, in their prejudice against Arabs, have gobbled up as gospel truths. These lies in reality hide a mentality of conquest— a self-righteous attitude which lies at the core of the conflict between Jews and Arabs.*

*Have you heard of a book, actually a novel, called* Altneuland *('Old-New Land'), penned by Theodor Herzl, which appeared in 1902? If you read the book, as I have, you will realise that all European scholarship on the geography, demography and birth of Israel is merely an elaboration of the prejudices and fantasies which the father of Zionism spelled forth in this book. The novel revolves around the adventures of Friedrich Loewenberg, a young Jewish lawyer from Vienna, and his rich American patron Kingscourt, who visit Palestine twice within a span of twenty-two years. The first time, everything about Palestine strikes them as repugnant, decadent, dirty, stinky and vile. The country is plain desolation, sand and swamp. The people are hideous: dirty Arabs, destitute Turks, all looking like brigands, and some timid Jews. The towns and cities are dirty; packed with ragged, beggarly crowds, sick and hungry, jostling for survival with hapless brutality. Even Jerusalem, which by moonlight looks spiritual, by daylight appears as grimy and disgusting as Jaffa. Loewenberg and Kingscourt go away thinking that centuries of misuse and oriental corruption have made the land of Palestine unfit for civilised habitation. Then they come back twenty-two years later, when Jewish settlements have become established. It is a new land altogether, thoroughly European, cosmopolitan, clean, prosperous, modern and culturally rich. There are even a few Arabs left, alongside newcomers from China and Africa, but they no longer look so dirty and hideous. Jerusalem, lo and behold, has awakened from death into lustrous life, once cleansed of its Arabs. The novel has a scene of Passover celebration, meant to highlight the ecumenical humanism of Jewish Israel. Attending are a Russian Orthodox priest, a Franciscan monk and an English clergyman. But there is no Arab to join the celebration, not even a Christian Arab. This was Herzl's vision of Israel. Founded on prejudices and fantasies, the vision could come to life only through a caesarean birth. It required, by necessity rather than by accident,* the colonial outlook and ruthless mentality with which Zionism, from the start, was imbued.

Before we talk about that mentality, let me reiterate some basic facts that are well-established and acknowledged even in Western scholarly circles. In 1882, the total number of Jews living in Palestine was less than 25,000. At the outbreak of World War I, their number had gone up to 70,000. The first census carried out by the British in 1922, during the mandate period, returned the figure of 80,000 Jews in a total population of 752,000. By 1946, the Anglo-American Commission counted 600,000 Jews while the total population was estimated at 1.85 million. How and why did it come to this swell in Jewish migrants?

You talked about the atmosphere of prejudice and persecution as being the backdrop of the Zionist project. No one with a sane mind can deny that. But were the Jews the only victims of prejudice, intolerance and denial of rights? Surely, the trade in African slaves, carried out by Europeans throughout the 18th and early 19th centuries, which reduced millions of people to the status of beasts, was an even clearer outgrowth of racist ideology, and even more inhuman.[13] Race riots and public lynching remained common practice in the United States right up to the early 20th century. Then, did not the Balkan Turks suffer collective punishment, ethnic cleansing, and, at times, even mass murder at the hand of the Serbs throughout the 18th and early 19th centuries? Surely, you know what happened to the indigenous peoples of America, Australia and New Zealand when the Europeans colonised them. To pick but one example: have you heard of the Choctaw Trail of Tears, a forced march which in 1831 drove the Choctaw American Indians out of their ancestral land? It was personally led by the then US President Andrew Jackson and resulted in thousands of deaths. You may not have heard about the genocide of Muslims in China that took place in the mid-19th century under the Qing Dynasty. Several millions were killed. You have obviously never heard about it because Chinese Muslims are not a subject worth the attention of historians. You may also not have heard of the extermination of nearly half a million Cossacks in Russia in the early years of the Bolshevik Revolution. You should know about the near total extermination by the Germans, between 1904 and 1908, of the Herero and Namaqua peoples in South-West Africa, in today's Namibia. Nearly 75 per cent of their population perished. Those who remained were forced into concentration camps, the first ones to be built by Germans in the 20th century.[14] The genocide of Armenians during World War I, which consumed nearly 1.5 million lives, is well-known (outside Turkey, that is) and so is the extermination of Romas (Gypsies), along with Jews, under the Nazis. *Where were the safe havens for these many groups, all victims of racial prejudice and intolerance? Where could all these people go to save themselves, escape persecution and ensure their collective survival? They could and can only struggle to better their lot, social and political, in those locations in which they are historically trapped—as the Palestinians have been doing from the days of the Balfour Declaration, so far in vain, and without much sympathy from the outside world.*

*The Jews' attitude to the Holocaust and their way of linking it to the birth of Israel as its pre-ordained, inevitable prelude, is bizarre in its twisted logic, and hardly makes sense in terms of human rights. Jewish historians like Y. Talmon, Evyatar Friesel, and political figures like David Ben-Gurion himself, have been projecting the Holocaust as some sort of an apocalyptic acquittal of the Jews from the curse of Exile, a visitation of redemptive suffering that won them the realisation of the promise of Israel. Evyatar Friesel unabashedly wrote that 'shock and guilt in the face of the extent of the tragedy' practically impelled 'the nations' to assist in the establishment of the Jewish state and to grant it immediate recognition.*

*But that logic, however flawed and inhuman, came to be accepted and because it was accepted, it worked. The report of a British Commission of Experts headed by Sir John Woodhead, published on 10 November 1938, ruled out a partition of Palestine in categorical terms. The utmost it offered was a Jewish enclave of only 1,250 sq. km., a coastal strip of land to include some kibbutz settlements between the towns of Rehovot and Zichron Ya'akov. In the end, however, good sense and sound logic were swept aside. Palestine was partitioned, and Israel came into being.*

*Israelis today, of course, keep harping on the Holocaust, but it is even more disquieting to observe how the founders of the state barely managed to conceal their gratefulness for what they saw as a windfall. I know it for a fact that less than a month after the Kristallnacht, in December 1938, the Jewish National Council of Palestine held a meeting in which Ben-Gurion analysed the recent events in Germany. In his conclusion, he came down vehemently against plans, then being discussed at various governmental levels, to have large numbers of Austrian and German Jews transferred to safe countries. Ben-Gurion actually said that even if it were possible to save all Jewish children in Germany by transferring them to England, he would still reject the proposal. He would rather save only half of them by transferring them to Palestine. This is on record, in the protocol of the meeting. Ben-Gurion was one of those masterminding the* secret drive for illegal mass migration into Palestine. Read his biographer, Shabtai Teveth, and his Kinat David, or David's Zeal in the English edition. Ben-Gurion made no bones about his belief that 'disaster was his strength'. You may not believe it, but it is on the record, in Shabtai Teveth's book, that two weeks before Hitler came to power, Ben-Gurion, addressing a meeting of his party, did ask: 'Has the time not come to turn the mass Jewish distress, the destruction of Jewry in several countries, into a lever?'

Now, how does that question, posed even before Hitler formally came into power—I mean, as Chancellor—by one of the founders of Israel, sound to the ears of a human rights activist? Can a person, whose main concern it is to save human life, to the largest extent possible, talk of using 'human distress' on a mass scale as a lever for political objectives? Teveth also writes that Ben-Gurion viewed World War II as 'a rare opportunity to achieve the Zionist solution'. Do you think he would have done anything, even if he possessed the power, to either avert the war or save the European Jewry? Well, you should be aware that the British Government seriously reviewed a number of proposals for settling persecuted Jews in Cyprus, Uganda, also in the El-Arish region of the Sinai Peninsula, on the Mediterranean coast. All of them were rejected by the Zionists because they were single-minded about Palestine, not about saving Jews from persecution.[15] Then you said something about the earlier phases of Jewish immigration being beneficial to the country and its agriculture. You must be talking about that claim by Levi Eshkol about making 'the desert bloom'. Well, that is a flat lie— a lie which hides the mentality of settler colonialism and betrays contempt for the humanity and the rights of indigenous people.

Article 6 of the League of Nations' Mandate over Palestine clearly required Britain to 'encourage [...] close settlement by Jews on the land' while 'ensuring that the rights and position of other sections of the population are not prejudiced'. But what happened? You mentioned the kibbutz movement. Now, what was that? The movement was founded on a queer cocktail of Zionist-socialist ideology. One of its main exponents, Ber Borochov, an Ukrainian Jew and self-confessed Marxist, in the name of the dignity of labour shrewdly prohibited the Jewish settlers from employing Arabs for agricultural work. The phrase was 'conquest of labour' (or even 'Redemption through manual labour').[16] The idea was to ensure from the start that the Jewish settlements be free from Palestinian presence. The Jewish National Fund and Palestine Jewish Colonisation Association, run by billionaire Jews from Europe and America, were absolutely unyielding on this principle. It had been laid down by Herzl himself. He had written that *the native inhabitants of whatever land would be allotted to the Jews would be 'gently persuaded to move to other countries'. The slogan of early Zionism was 'building the land of Israel on collective foundations'. The land for settlement; the capital for its acquisition and the start-up investments; the cattle and machinery; the legal support machine—all infrastructure as well as the labour, everything had to be Jewish or in Jewish hands. It was in strict adherence to these guidelines that the Zionists of the post-Balfour immigration wave began to establish their first major 'settlements', some with as many as 2,000 members.*

*In 1882, the Jews of Palestine owned only 25,000 dunums of land, that is, 25 sq. km.*[17] *They owned 420,600 dunums in 1914; 594,000 in 1922; 1,058,500 in 1939; and 1,604,800 in 1941.*

*A Commission of Inquiry,*[18] *set up by the British in 1929, submitted its unequivocal conclusions one year later. Its report said: 'The plain facts of the case are that there is no further land available which can be occupied by new immigrants without displacing the present population.' Yet another Commission, headed by Robert Peel, was set up in 1936 in the wake of bitter Arab–Jewish clashes. It too concluded that from 1932 onwards there was simply no land left for the British authorities to settle displaced Arab tenants. I do not have the precise figures right now, but I know that the Jewish National Fund alone had acquired more than 3.5 million dunums of land by the start of the 1960s. By then, the total area transferred to the ownership of the Jewish State Development Authority was approximately 15.5 million dunums. Under law, all that land was exclusively meant for Jewish settlements and barred to Arabs.*

*'Exclusive Jewish labour' meant the boycott of landless Palestinians. 'Exclusive Jewish produce' implied an embargo on Palestinian produce. Absentee Arab landlords sold large tracts to Zionist syndicates which in turn insisted that the tenant farmers be evicted before funds changed hands. These tenant farmers had subsisted on the land for generations but now they had to move without any compensation or alternative livelihood. The pauperisation of tenant farmers, following their eviction and denial of labour opportunities, inevitably aroused hostility. Rural indebtedness assumed grievous proportions. Even small landowners had to sell off their land to survive. The census of 1931 put the total number of landless agricultural families at 30,000, out of a total of 120,000 families dependent on agriculture. So, from the start the Zionist concept was to displace and replace the Palestinian population, rather than exploit it in the classical colonial pattern. With their financial muscle and capacity to invest in superior technology and build monopolies, the Zionists also debarred Arabs*

*from entering into industry and business. In this way the Zionists gradually established monopolies in construction, mining, transport, commerce, and even in the liberal professions, using their many advantages and the patronage willingly extended to them by the Mandate administration.*

*The large Arab landholders who sold some of their estates to Jews acquired large sums of money, which they diverted into cash-crops, mainly citrus plantations, and into improving irrigation facilities. The poor sank into indebtedness. Even as the Palestinian society was suffering fragmentation, dislocation and social disorientation, the Jewish community was steadily consolidating, subsisting on an autarchic economy, using mainly Hebrew, developing institutions that amounted to self-government, and soon acquiring its own military.*

I interrupted Dr Jabbour and his friends to ask whether, in their view, the Zionist project had always moved on like a monolithic juggernaut, uniformly insensitive to the humanity and rights of Palestinians. Weren't there variant voices among these Jewish migrants who were coming from such diverse backgrounds? Weren't there people who dissented with this mentality of conquest?

*Of course, there were! There always were Jews, inside Palestine and outside, who opposed the Zionist mentality and balked at Zionist methods. In fact, there is nothing that I have said which Jewish critics of Zionism haven't already said. And this has been so from the start of the 'return'. But the fact is that these dissenters did not and do not have the power of persuasion to stem the racist agenda of conquest which mainstream Zionism represented and which it carried out, and still carries on, implacably, from the days of the founders to our own.*

*There were some less aggressive Zionists, who believed in cultivating friendly Arabs, either for tactical reasons or because they genuinely valued inter-communal harmony. But they were ignored, and ended up feeling isolated and defeated. One such early moderate was Chaim Margalit-Kalvarisky, a Polish-born Jew who migrated to Palestine as early as 1895. After studying agricultural management in France, he became a land purchase agent for the Jewish Colonisation Association. As a land purchaser, he had to deal with prominent, well-to-do Arabs. Given his crucial calling, he also carried much weight within the Zionist circles, and had access to the likes of Ben-Gurion and Chaim Weizmann. A pragmatic man, Kalvarisky pleaded for a softer approach. Without questioning the basic Zionist objectives, he cautioned against inflaming Arab opinion, if only to forestall a violent backlash. He wanted to cultivate influential but moderate Arab friends, and persuade them of the advantages that accrued from the Jewish presence. He was also in favour of funding moderate Arab leaders, to entice them into active politics and thus create an environment favourable to the Zionist project.*

*But Kalvarisky was pursuing a hopeless cause. All his efforts availed nothing: no Arab could accept the framework of conquest in which the Zionist enterprise was rooted. Within the Zionist circles themselves Kalvarisky met only with rejection—the hawks would not brook his moderation and felt only contempt for all this woolly talk about winning Arab consent. The Zionists did not mind bribing influential Arabs. But they opposed talks. They knew that there was no scope for accommodation within their scheme of politics.*

*There were others, staunch Zionists who believed in establishing a Jewish collective in the 'promised land', yet wanted to hold on to their humanistic values. They fully appreciated the disruption and affliction which the Zionist enterprise was inflicting on the local population. They did their best to find a middle road, a principled way of fulfilling their dream without wronging the Arabs. They failed. One of them was Dr Arthur Ruppin, a native Jew of Palestine who played a significant role in establishing the early Zionist settlements without ever losing sight of the Arab side of the moral equation. Before World War I, Ruppin toyed with the idea of resettling the displaced Palestinian Arabs to other parts of Syria (Palestine was then part of Syria). He actually submitted a written proposal to the Zionist Executive to make the corresponding financial provisions. But he withdrew the suggestion at the end of the war when the Ottoman province of Greater Syria got divided between the French and the British mandate areas. He had also come to realise the basic immorality of a population transfer to make room for the Jewish settlers. So he wrote to the Zionist leaders, asking them to set aside a part of the land they were acquiring to accommodate the evicted tenant-farmers. The proposal was turned down outright. Later, Ruppin toyed with the idea of creating a 'bi-national' state, in which Jews and Arabs could live separately but with equal rights. That proved impossible, because the basic ideology of Zionism is so self-centred. It can thrive only on the de-legitimisation of the other, the denial of his rights. As Vladimir Jabotinsky said, there was no possibility of compromise. Ruppin, a humanist, could not understand this and was swallowed by the Leviathan he had helped to create.*

*There was another class of Jewish immigrants who realised the impossibility of compromise, but drew the opposite conclusion: they rejected the idea of a Jewish state. Dr Judah Leon Magnes, the founder President of the Hebrew University in Jerusalem, was one of them. His rejection of the Jewish state was rooted in an orthodox perception of Judaic law, or Torah, which holds that the purity of a religious pursuit is incompatible with the corruptions and brutalities of a nationalistic mission.*

*Magnes was an interesting man. Born in California in 1877, he studied theology and later helped found the American Jewish Committee in 1906. He was a scholar and an active community organiser. Together with Albert Einstein and Sigmund Freud, Magnes conceived the project of a Hebrew University of Jerusalem. He moved to Palestine in 1922 and became the University's first chancellor and, later, its President. He viewed aliya as a matter of individual choice rather than a negation of the Diaspora, which he felt was of equal significance to Jewishdom. He was also strongly committed to the idea of equal rights for all inhabitants of Palestine and disapproved of a theocratic conception of state that would privilege Jews. Even after realising the political impossibility of an immediate reconciliation between Jews and Arabs, he urged the British and the Americans, in 1942, to prevent the division of Palestine. In 1948, he resigned from the American Jewish Joint Distribution Committee, which he had himself established, when the organisation turned down his request for help to the Palestinian refugees. He died in 1948, disillusioned but unbending in his refusal to align himself with any Jewish project 'that cannot be justified before the conscience of the world'.[19]*

*Magnes was close to a constellation of likeminded Jewish intellectuals who believed in a peaceful coexistence of Arabs and Jews and in the feasibility of a bi-national regime. In 1925, some of these—Martin Buber, Hugo Bergmann, Gershom Scholem, Henrietta Szold and Albert Einstein—inspired the formation of a political group known as Brit Shalom—'covenant of peace'. People may think that these men strove in vain and died defeated. That would be a short-sighted conclusion. It is by drawing on the legacy of these truly great men that we may one day—God knows when—move beyond our present predicament of war, brutality, authoritarianism and apartheid.*

*So, you see, I am not saying anything that has not been voiced by conscientious Jews from the past, and by several who live among us. Rabbi Samson Raphael Hirsch, a 19th century leader of Germany's orthodox Jews (he lived in Frankfurt) said that 'to actively promote Jewish immigration to Palestine is a sin'. His epigones, still active under the name of Neturei Karta ('Guardians of the Walls') are among the fiercest critics of Zionist Israel. Their leader Rabbi Moshe Leib-Hirsch is on record as saying: 'We will not accept a Zionist state even if the Arabs do.'[20]*

I wanted to take the discussion back to the issues of Arab solidarity with the Palestinian cause and the repeated setbacks that cause has suffered, beginning with the initial catastrophe when, after World War II the Palestinian leadership rejected the UN partition proposal and, despite receiving military support from their Arab neighbours, the Palestinians were roundly defeated in the 1948 war. I asked Dr Jabbour to comment on these episodes.

He was no longer his relaxed, unruffled self. Unlike the man I had seen at the beginning of the discussion, he was now sitting stiff and erect, deep furrows on his forehead, eyes humourless, his hands clutching the armrest of his chair. His voice was a little louder, but it remained steady and courteous. He began with a question of his own:

*Did you know that the Muslim Brotherhood, then quite influential in Egypt, had written a letter to the British authorities to state its position—namely, that the issue of Palestine could be resolved only by ending further Jewish immigration and granting full independence to the country? Before that, the letter added, the leaders of all sections should come together to agree on a framework for the new state, without compromising on the principles of equal rights and adequate protections for all racial and religious minorities. Is that not pretty much what those wise and prudent Jewish voices had been demanding?*

I interrupted Dr Jabbour to ask what explained the outcome of the 1948 war. How could a fledgling Israel prevail, and prevail so completely, over the combined Arab forces? The war earned Israel twice as much territory as it had been originally awarded by the UN in its Partition Resolution. The resolution had made no provision for the deployment of an international force to oversee the orderly transfer of sovereignty. Sensing trouble, Syria had taken the initiative of forming a volunteer force,[21] before the outbreak of the war, to help the Palestinians hold on to their territories. After the outbreak of hostilities, these Syrian volunteers joined the regular armies of Jordan, Egypt, Lebanon and Iraq, which moved jointly to invade Israel. The dismal outcome of this war is now commemorated by the Palestinians, indeed all Arabs, as *al-Nakba*—'the Disaster'.[22] What explains the rout of the combined Arab armies?

'The question is silly and misconceived,' exclaimed Dr Jabbour, raising his voice to a high pitch. For the first time, he was visibly angry. He sat in silence for a few seconds to compose himself. When he spoke again, his voice was level and calm.

*There is enough literature on the subject. Despite its pro-Israeli bias, it should give you some sense of facts, and allow you to raise more pertinent questions. The facts of the matter are as follows. Soon after the British decision to evacuate Palestine, which was taken on 20 September 1947, Alan Cunningham, the last important High Commissioner of Palestine, began planning the British withdrawal in such a way as to ensure the establishment of a strong, territorially dominant Israel. The British coordinated their moves with the Haganah, Irgun and the Stern Gang—the three Zionist militias that had risen to prominence during World War II. The British Foreign Secretary Ernest Bevin also conferred with Tawfiq Abu al-Huda, the Prime Minister of the Hashemite kingdom of Transjordan: his Bedouin army was to get involved in the looming war, ostensibly to help the Palestinians, but with the real objective of seizing the territories east of the river Jordan which the UN had assigned to Palestine. Then the British administration went on to deliberately promote anarchy and civil war conditions, knowing full well that in any violent confrontation the Zionists would have the upper hand, given the superiority of their armed organisations.*

*Bloody riots kept erupting in Jerusalem, Haifa, Tiberias, Safed, Tel-Aviv and Jaffa from the beginning of December 1947. In January 1948, the Haganah launched systematic raids against Arab villages. To paralyse the remnants of the administration, it blew up the Semiramis hotel in West Jerusalem, killing, among others, the Spanish consul there. The British also spread exaggerated rumours to the effect that Arab armed forces, acting as a Liberation Army, were infiltrating the Palestinian territories. King Abdullah of Transjordan, a British puppet, ordered his borders closed. Then, the better to spread anarchy and to invite the Zionist militias to take matters into their hands, the British administration under evacuation declared itself unable to supervise the borders. At the same time, the remnants of the British army were taking strong positions along the Syrian borders, especially in eastern upper Galilee. By April 1948, the Zionist militias had effectively cleared large parts of Iberias, Haifa and Galilee of their Arab population, by terrorising them into flight.*

*The British authorities, particularly Alan Cunningham, knew about the Jewish plans for ethnic cleansing—code named Operation Nahshon and Plan Dalet—that had been prepared long beforehand, and finalised in January 1948 under the direct supervision of Ben-Gurion. After clearing Haifa of all its Arabs, the Haganah, Irgun and the Stern Gang imposed an effective embargo on essential supplies, including food, in other Arab towns such as Nablus and Jenin. In the first week of April 1948, Irgun and the Stern Gang carried out a joint operation in the Arab village of Deir Yassin, on the western edge of Jerusalem, murdering hundreds, torching the houses, and compelling the survivors to flee. The village was within walking distance of the British headquarters in Jerusalem. But the authorities chose to take no action. In the middle of April, the British military authorities persuaded the Arab population of Safed (assigned to Palestine under the partition plan) to leave the city, escorted by their own units under evacuation. They did the same to the Arabs of Haifa, which was virtually under Haganah control. Major General Hugh Stockwell personally supervised these operations. In the last week of April 1948, the Irgun and the Palmach, a highly trained wing of the Haganah, captured the Arab quarter of Manshiya in Jaffa and the Sheikh Jarrah quarter of Jerusalem. Yitzhak Rabin personally led the attack on Sheikh Jarrah. If you compare the British passivity in 1948 with their ruthless suppression of the Palestinian uprisings between 1936 and 1939, it becomes clear that the evacuation was nothing but a cover for the British handover of the entire Palestinian territories to the Zionist forces—a surreptitious way of delivering the country, key in hand, to the Yishuv. It was an extraordinarily disgraceful conclusion to the Mandate, which the British had acquired, remember, 'to lead the local people towards self-determination'!*

*Even as Cunningham and his confidants left Jerusalem in secret and flew out from the Kalandia airport, to the north of the city, Yigal Allon, the Palmach commander, was sending his storm troopers to raid and take over all Arab neighbourhoods of West Jerusalem, Jaffa, Acre, Western Galilee, Safed, Eastern Galilee and Beit Shen. A total of 863 villages and settlements, in and around Acre, Beersheba, Baysan, Gaza, Hebron, Jenin, Jablus, Nazareth, Al-Ramla, Ramallah, Safad Tiberais, Tulkaram and of course Jerusalem, were systematically depopulated.*

Several Zionist writers have themselves written about the organised violence which triggered the Palestinian exodus. Notable among them are Jon Kimche's Seven Fallen Pillars: The Middle East, 1915–50[23]; Harry Sacher's Israel: The Establishment of a State[24]; Harry Levin's Jerusalem Embattled: A Diary of the City Under Siege[25]. There are other accounts, including one penned by Menachem Begin in Hebrew under the title Ha-Merid (The Revolt)[26]. In it, Begin gives away some of the well thought-out plans for ethnic cleansing which had been in place long before the declaration of Israel's independence. Little had been left to chance.

The Zionists now claim that the Palestinians fled their homes on the advice of the village elders, or in panic over the spate of defeats which the Arab armies *began to suffer soon after the outbreak of the war. This was a later invention, an outrageous lie, forged by a Goebbels-like character from the Zionist 'revisionist camp', one Dr Joseph Schechtman, to counter the adverse impact which the massive refugee problem was having on the conscience of the world. You referred to the Arab armies—volunteers and regulars—that invaded Israel. In fact, it was the other way round: the decision to intervene was in response to the massive exodus caused by the Zionist raids, and the execution of the operations was clumsy in the extreme—uncoordinated and quarrel-ridden. Until 12 May 1948, most of the Arab governments were talking and thinking in terms of a diplomatic solution to the proposed partition. At the time, the Zionist radio stations themselves were acknowledging that Arab diplomatic initiatives were afoot to install a federal government in Palestine that would be supervised by Syria, Lebanon, Egypt, Transjordan and Iraq.*

At this point I cut in to ask if the Arab armies had really intervened only after Israel's declaration of independence, in the face of the Palestinian exodus, and why they failed to regain the land which had been demarcated as Palestinian under the UN partition proposal. Dr Jabbour did not mind the interruption, and continued to explain in a distinctly calm mode.

*To begin with, you must remember that if Israel failed to seize the entire West Bank and Gaza it was because of the intervention of the Arab armies. But let us first grasp the basics. Syria, of course, was consistently and uncompromisingly anti-Zionist. It played an active part in setting up a liberation army, under the leadership of Fauzi al-Qawuqji, a Lebanese officer who had served in the Ottoman army. He was widely respected for his anti-imperialist zeal. But his 4,000 army was untrained, unequipped, and possessed only antediluvian weapons. In the last week of April 1948, Qawuqji left the Palestinian front for Damascus and complained there about the scandalous lack of arms, ammunition, rations, clothing and communication. I honestly don't think that the Syrian state was then in a position to meet his requirements. Be that as it may, after Israel's declaration of independence, Syria took the lead in calling for a joint Arab military intervention, which duly followed. Despite organisational deficiencies and poor weaponry, the Syrian forces made some advances north of the Sea of Galilee, and even captured some areas awarded to Israel under the UN partition proposal.*

*But you cannot discuss this war and understand its outcome without appreciating the political weakness of the Arab states, their duplicity, and the petty calculations which crippled their military moves. The main point to bear in mind is the close relation which King Abdullah of Transjordan had maintained not just with the British but also with the Jewish Agency and the Zionist underground militias. Abdullah in person had secretly met with Golda Meir on 17 November 1947. The meeting and the tenor of the discussions are part of the record, as preserved in the Central Zionist Archives. Ezra Danin and Eliyahu, who attended the meeting as Golda Meir's assistants, identify Abdullah somewhat confusingly by the code name 'Meir'. According to the record, the King promised that he would not allow the Arab forces to collide with the Jewish forces. He would concentrate on preventing bloodshed, keeping public order, and would cooperate with the Jewish authorities. The records further mention that Meir (i.e., Abdullah) would be willing to assist the Jewish authorities if these helped him to enlarge his lands in Transjordan. Colonel Abdullah el-Tall, a Jordanian officer who brokered this and other such meetings, later confirmed in a written account that the King had been acting against Arab and Palestinian interests. On the Israeli side, one Lieutenant-Colonel Israel Baer (who was later accused of collusion with the Soviet Union and imprisoned) accused Ben-Gurion of striking clandestine, dishonest alliances with the Arab states, especially the Hashemite kingdoms of Iraq and Jordan.*

*You may not have heard of it but three Jewish historians—Dan Schueftan, Yad Tabenkin and Uri Bar-Joseph—have independently reached similar conclusions. Dan Schueftan actually revealed that the Zionists and the British were considering a 'Jordanian option'—allowing Jordan, as a trusted ally, to annex some of the Palestinian areas and to police the Palestinians there. Jordan was only waiting for the arrangement to materialise.*

*The chief of the Jordanian army at that time was an eccentric and very corrupt Englishman, John Glubb, better known as Glubb Pasha. Do you think he would have fought the Jewish troops? There is evidence that he and his close advisers had actually been meeting senior Haganah leaders long before the 1948 war. One of Glubb Pasha's close confidants, Colonel Desmond Goldie, had a long, private talk with General Shlomo Shamir of the Haganah only two weeks before the end of the British mandate. When the fighting began, the Jordanian forces made some token forays to mislead the Arab world. The same holds true for the Iraqi volunteer forces. They simply stayed in their camps. As for the Lebanese army, it was dominated by the self-centered Maronite Christians, hankering as usual after political supremacy. The Lebanese force was not only very small, but also sharply divided in its reading of the unfolding events, and* in two minds about the attitude to adopt. *So you see how disjoint this 'joint' Arab military intervention of 1948 really was, how confused, how inefficient!*

*Pitted against all this muddle, military disorder, and mutual mistrust in the Arab ranks were the very well-trained, well equipped, and single-mindedly ruthless Jewish militias—the Haganah and all the other outfits—whose traditions of military training went back to the earliest beginnings of the Zionist expansion in Palestine. It is a fact, even if not widely known, that the Zionists had established their first undercover military organisations already in the Ottoman period. A group called Bar-Giora was active already in 1903. Yitzhak Ben Zvi, later to become Israel's second President, was one of its leaders.*

*The Haganah was formally set up in 1920 and soon gained political importance through the advocacy work carried out by its labour wing, the Histadrut. In 1936, the Haganah played a prominent part in suppressing the Palestinian uprising. By then, it was a well-equipped military, with a permanent command structure and a total of 17,000 members, both men and women. It had 5,000 rifles, 10,000 small arms and 300 light machine guns. Two men, Shaul Avigur and Eliahu Golomb, were mainly responsible for building up the militia at that stage.*

*A more extreme right-wing group, the Irgun Zvai Leumi, split from the Haganah. In the period of the Palestinian revolts, several other secret groups (some local constabularies or police units attached to individual settlements) came into being. British experts like Orde Wingate trained them with redoubled zeal after the murder of a British officer in Galilee, in September 1937, supposedly at the hands of Palestinians. The Haganah quickly built up mobile units, night squads and guerrilla detachments, partnering with the British army, but taking its orders only from its National Command, a secret body of six leaders, with the ultimate authority resting with Eliahu Golomb. Under the supervision of a special unit of British officers led by Orde Wingate, the Haganah men perfected the tactics of mounting surprise attacks on rebellious villages and learnt how to carry out punitive actions that would result in depopulation. These tactics would come in handy in 1948, to establish a racially pure Israel through the ethnic cleansing of Palestinian Muslims. Yakov Dostrowsky, who during World War I had served in the Jewish Legion of the British army, was appointed Chief of Staff of the Haganah.*

*The Mossad was also born in those years. Originally a unit of the Haganah, it supervised the smuggling of illegal immigrants. Taking its directions from Moshe Sharett and Ben-Gurion, it brought in more than 100,000 Jews, at first without the knowledge of the British authorities. Then World War II, especially the fear of a German invasion over Turkey or Egypt, brought closer cooperation between the British and the Zionist military agencies, resulting in the birth of Palmach, a mobile unit devoted to special operations.*

*Then came the head-on confrontation. The history of Zionist terrorism against the British is well known. In November 1944, Lord Moyne, who had apparently refused a Nazi offer to release a large number of Jews in exchange for some lorries, was assassinated by members of the Stern Gang. By then, however, the Jewish militias were too strong to be suppressed. In 1944, the Haganah alone had nearly 38,000 men under arms, more than 10,000 rifles, nearly 500 machine guns, hundreds of submachine guns, thousands of revolvers and pistols and the capacity to manufacture explosives and mortars. Menachem Begin was the commander of Irgun.*

*This, in short, was the build-up of events that brought al-Nakba ('disaster') to the Palestinians, and 'triumph' to the Zionists. The prevalent discourse about 1948, alas, is usually vitiated by a deep ignorance of the true historical sequence, and by the wilful distortions peddled by those responsible for these crimes. There is also the very contemptible yet very human tendency to despise a cause that didn't prevail, to equate defeat with moral opprobrium. But at the same time we know, deep down, that these struggles for justice and dignity, even when abortive, are never completely in vain. In ways hard to fathom, they do matter for our human future, no less perhaps than outward victories. Of this I am convinced.*

I wanted to return to the present: to the perspectives of Arab resistance, and to where Syria fitted in the picture. The country has remained consistently anti-imperialist and anti-Zionist. Despite suffering serious territorial setbacks—losing the Golan Heights in 1967 and failing to recover them during the 1973 war—Syria remains apparently undaunted. It patronises the two most visible resistance movements in the region: Hizbullah in Lebanon and Hamas in Palestine. Its relations with Iraq and Jordan have remained strained, and those with Saudi Arabia and the other oil-states in the Gulf are equally tense. In 1971, after Jordan liquidated the PLO bases in the brutal *Black September* crackdown, Syria allowed large numbers of Palestinians to settle on its soil (while an even larger contingent sought refuge in Lebanon). Despite trade sanctions and a precarious international standing (it remains on the US list of 'terror-sponsoring nations') Syria continues to support Hamas and Hizbullah, and to offer sanctuary to its most threatened leaders. It also shows no sign of ending its strategic partnership with Iran—the leading Shia power, heartily disliked by the Sunni diehards and treated as a pariah state by the United States and Israel. To counter Israeli designs in Lebanon, especially after the military invasion of 1982, Syria involved itself deeper and deeper in the affairs of its former province. It assisted in the creation and arming of Hizbullah: it protected Ali Akbar Mohtashemi, Iran's ambassador in Damascus and, flouting international disapproval, gave him plenty of latitude to build up Hizbullah's organisational and military capacities. Later on, after the first Gulf War, and under heavy US pressure, Syria joined the Middle East Peace Conference in Madrid in October 1991, co-sponsored by the USA and the USSR. But otherwise Hafiz al-Assad remained resolute. He never budged from his position. He uttered a final *no* to President Clinton's offer, at Geneva on 26 March 2000, that Israel return the entire Golan Heights minus a small north-eastern strip bordering on Lake Tiberias.

Hafiz al-Assad said *no* and died. His young son Bashar al-Assad, who succeeded him as Syria's President, has so far not said anything very different. Where does Syria get the pluck to resist the global powers? It is medium-sized and not noted for its economic strength. It is not a democracy, nor is it a particularly devout Islamic society. Arab nationalism, as an ideology, has lost much of its post-Independence force and cannot, on its own, account for this unyielding streak. So, what is the source of Syria's spirit of resistance? Does it imply a definite vision of life? What does it portend for the future? My questions were rather general, and I had already taken up more than two hours of Dr Jabbour's time. Yet he displayed no signs of impatience and went on with his explaining, in his sobre, sparkling tone:

*I'll answer you as a Syrian and as a student of Syrian history. Inevitably, my own perspective on politics and my patriotism colour my representation of my country, and I may overestimate its role in the Arab resistance. But I can tell you only what I know and think. We already talked about the origins of our aspirations for independence in the waning days of the Ottoman Empire. Freedom then meant freedom from Turkish dominance, and the Europeans might conceivably be viewed as allies. But we Syrians soon became disenchanted with European trickery and fraudulence, when we found out that while McMahon had been promising the whole of Ottoman Syria to the Sharif of Mecca, in a formal and official correspondence extending over a period of eight months[27], the British Government was simultaneously dividing the country between itself and France, and then promising a homeland to the Zionists. We Syrians also observed the greed for oil and its consequences. We saw how it dictated the interventions in Iran, and what manner of a state was created in Saudi Arabia. We saw the French at work, too. The moment they entered Syria, they began to mutilate it. They first separated Lebanon, giving it an independent political status that was calculated to ensure Maronite Christian supremacy. Then they gave away Alexandretta to Turkey. Then after World War II, a Zionist Israel was born, turning the sons of Palestine into homeless and stateless refugees. We have talked about it. No sooner did Iraq shake off the monarchy foisted on it by the British than it plunged into fratricidal wars driven by territorial greed and sectarian lunacy—I mean this Sunni–Shia enmity—thereby inviting upon itself imperialist aggression and occupation. The largest Arab state, Egypt, seemed to hold great promise after World War II, but the absence of democratic traditions and the ingrained evil of personality cult led to the swift disintegration of the united Arab state that Nasser so badly wanted.*

*Syria, for its part, has adopted a view of Arab solidarity that is respectful of national distinctiveness. Although we are not a Westminster type of democracy, our state is firmly grounded in the principle of equal citizenship, untainted by considerations of religion, ethnicity and language. As a matter of fact, Syria is the only country in the region to be ruled continuously, for over 35 years, by members of a minority community, the Alawi—until recently one of the poorest and most downtrodden groups. Assad's family belongs to a small tribe, the Kalbiyya, one of the four Alawi tribes, which together account for only 20 per cent of the population. What we have here is a process of empowerment of previously marginalised sections, which has gone almost completely unnoticed by the outside world. The Alawi, who consider themselves a sub-sect of the Ismaili but whom most Muslims regard as distinctly deviant, have known religious persecution throughout history. Since Hafiz al-Assad took charge of the country in 1970, rather than seeking revenge, the Alawi have assiduously followed a policy of toleration of all faiths.*

*Under Hafiz al-Assad Syria has known its longest stretch of stability since the days of the Umayyad dynasty. Here was a pragmatic politician, equally good at anticipating global trends and at reacting to surprise events. But he was also a sterling character, who held on to a number of principles. Several Arab regimes, Saddam's Iraq chief amongst them, tried to isolate Syria by denouncing its closeness to Iran. Yet Syria did not vacillate. Syria opposes fratricidal conflicts within the Arab world. It condemned Iraq's annexation of Kuwait in*

August 1990 and did not stand against Desert Storm, the military intervention that reversed Kuwait's invasion. But Syria opposed the 2003 invasion of
Iraq. Despite its own serious economic problems and at the risk of upsetting its
precarious demographic balance, Syria has absorbed nearly one million and a
half Iraqi refugees, most of them Sunni—a huge burden for a country our size.
Syria recently withdrew its troops from Lebanon. (Remember, our troops had
moved into Lebanon in June 1976, at the height of the civil war, at the express
behest of the Maronite President, Suleiman Frangieh.) All these developments
took place under the younger Assad, Bashar,[28] who is a trained ophthalmologist
with no previous connection to the military. Yet the world does not recognise
any virtue in any of this. Or maybe it doesn't care to notice.

You asked about the 'vision' behind all this. Well, the first thing is to survive
with dignity in the face of Israeli and American bullying, threats and attempts
at destabilisation. Syria is doing that. You may recall that immediately after
the fall of Baghdad, Colin Powell came to Damascus to put before Bashar
al-Assad a list of dos and don'ts with which Syria had to comply if it was to
escape military action. Bashar did not buy the threat. He remained steadfast,
without doing anything provocative or foolhardy. The United States and its
allies accused Syria of standing behind Rafiq Hariri's assassination. A German
judge, Detlev Mehlis, appointed by the UN to lead the investigation, pointed the
finger of blame at Bashar's brother Maher al-Assad (head of the Presidential
Guard) and at his brother-in-law, Asaf Shawkat (in charge of military security).
Israel, the US and all their hired pens also keep blaming Syria for supporting and financing Hamas, Hizbullah, Islamic Jihad, even the Iraq resistance.
But Bashar has stood his ground. He has established himself as a reliable,
self-confident ruler.

As mentioned earlier, the memory of Syria's past greatness—in territorial
size and historical achievements—remains indelibly printed in our minds.
Understandably, Syrian nationalism has often craved for a return to this past
glory, epitomised in the term of Bilad al-Sham, 'Greater Syria'.[29] However,
no sooner were we freed from the Ottoman yoke at the end of World War I
than European brinkmanship broke up our society and redrew our borders. We
cannot dream of reversing this baleful legacy of the colonial period, we cannot
even hope to carry out more pressing reforms, if we remain mired in nostalgia,
wistfully hankering after our past. We need a measure of realism if we are to
deal with the immediate challenges; such as resisting Israel's expansionism or
ending the Palestinians' six decades of homelessness and persecution.

*The long flirtation with the idea of a pan-Arab state after World War II and Syria's short-lived merger with Egypt (which collapsed in 1961) brought us only disappointment and diverted our attention from more pressing needs, such as reforming our societies, closing the doors to Western interventions, checking the foreign appropriation of our resources, and reining in the berserk bully next door—I, of course, mean Israel. To move towards these objectives, we will have to discard sectarian antipathies. We will have to establish a political and societal framework which is plural and essentially democratic, maybe not with all the trappings of textbook democracy, but democratic at least in the respect that matters most—conferring equal citizenship to all, irrespective of sectarian, ethnic or linguistic affiliations. Well, if you take an honest look around the region, you will see that Syria, despite all its ordeals, has come closest to exemplifying this conception of state and society. Listen to Arab discourse, ask people high and low, and you will realise that Syria remains a beacon to Arabs, and the backbone of anti-imperialist struggles.*

*As you know, the main political formation here is the Ba'ath Party. It was founded in 1947 by Michel Aflaq and Salah al-Din al-Bitar, and in 1952 it amalgamated with the Arab Socialist Party (ASP) after adopting the motto of 'unity, freedom and socialism' and re-christened itself as 'socialist party for Arab rebirth'—Hizb al-Ba'ath al-arabi al-istiraqi. It is this inclusiveness of the Ba'ath, this embrace of all sections, that first made it so attractive to minorities like the Alawites, Druze and Ismailites, as well as to the downtrodden sections of the majority population of Sunnis. In Syria, this vision which informed the early Ba'ath is still alive and breathing.*

*The turmoil and trauma wrought by Israel and its Western backers have hugely hampered our progress. The Ba'ath has had its black sheep, too. Saddam Hussein of Iraq rose as a strongman of the Ba'ath but was bought over by the CIA before he joined the government of Abdus Salem Aref in 1963. With his cousin Ahmed Hassan al-Bakr as Prime Minister, he further ingratiated himself with the CIA by arresting, torturing and executing members of various left groups. Yet, many of the Ba'ath Party's historic leaders, including Michel Aflaq, either did not know or closed their eyes. In 1967, after the Six-Day war debacle, Aflaq sided with Saddam, only to get disillusioned soon. Hafiz al-Assad, who at the time headed the Syrian Air Force, was a pragmatist who valued political stability and survival above doctrinal quarrels and political adventurism of the Saddam sort. In retrospect, we can see that whereas Iraq stumbled from catastrophe to catastrophe, Syria survived as a stronghold of Arab resistance. It didn't capitulate to the United States and Israel. It retained its internal cohesiveness and pluralism. This, in my view, is to the everlasting credit of Hafiz al-Assad, who stepped in at a critical juncture of our history. Unlike Egypt and Jordan, Syria didn't become a doormat to Israel and the United States. Uncowed, it continued to act as a sanctuary to the Palestinians and to support their struggle for their inalienable rights. At the same time, Syrian society didn't stand still: industrialisation proceeded apace; we built our infrastructure; improved our public health system and education; progressed towards equal opportunity for women; and achieved a measure of public freedom. Syria also remained secular and plural—no mean achievement, considering what is going on elsewhere.*

*Hafiz al-Assad didn't shy from using strong methods against those, driven by extreme ideologies, who threatened to plunge the country into anarchy. But unlike Saddam Hussein, he never indulged in political vengeance for vengeance's sake. He would subdue his opponents, implacably so, when these engaged in violence, and then would let them be. I repeat: Syria might not have survived as a secular space, while jealously guarding its independence, had it not been for the pragmatic leadership of someone like Hafiz al-Assad, who steered the course for more than three decades, through the rough and tumble of Middle-East politics. For six years now, it has fallen to Bashar al-Assad, his son, to lead the country. In all essentials—primacy of internal stability and support for the forces of Arab resistance—he has upheld the vision of his father. In September 2000, although young and new in office, Bashar stood firm in his support for the Palestinian Intifada triggered by Ariel Sharon's provocative visit to the Al-Aqsa mosque. After the attacks of 11 September 2001 Syria, unlike Pakistan, withstood all American pressures to join in the 'war on terrorism', while maintaining its secular line. In early 2003, when the US was poised to invade Iraq, Bashar didn't allow himself to be swayed by memories of the bitter enmity between his father and Saddam, and refused to endorse the American intervention.*

*The Bush administration, while embracing a rabid Wahhabi-Islamist state like Saudi Arabia as an ally, assigned Syria to the 'axis of evil' and to the 'terrorist camp', on grounds that Syria refused to brand the Palestinian and Lebanese resistance as terrorist.*

*Bashar's decision, in April 2005, to withdraw Syrian troops from Lebanon was yet another example of pragmatic statesmanship. But one year on, in August 2006, President Bashar publicly congratulated Hizbullah for withstanding Israel's brutal air attacks with flying colours and for compelling Israel to sign a ceasefire agreement on rather humiliating terms. In a public speech, he made* it clear that there was no alternative to resistance as long as Israel and its allies were not ready for a 'just peace'. Bashar has also shown admirable tolerance, even respect, for the democratic opposition to his regime. On 16 October 2005, a call for a 'democratic national change' was issued in Damascus, with the endorsement of an array of opposition groups.[30] Several national figures, staunch advocates of democratic reforms, supported the declaration that called for:

> Mobilising the energies of all Syrians to bring change and lift the country out of the mould of a security state into that of a political state, so that it may consolidate its independence and unity, and allow its people to hold the reins of their country and participate freely in running its affairs.

The declaration also called for the election of a Constituent Assembly to draw up a new constitution, guaranteeing the separation of powers; safeguarding the independence of the judiciary; and fostering national integration on the principle of equal citizenship. Altogether, it was a bold declaration, and all the signs are that Bashar al-Assad basically agreed. You should look up the text of a speech he made in Damascus in March 2006, to representatives of Arab political parties from all over the Middle East. He talked about the connections between Islam and Arab civilisation, also about Christianity and Arabism. I remember his words. He said, 'First comes Islam, which is tightly bound to Arabism: Islam cannot be expunged from the substance of Arabism. Second comes Christianity, which emerged from our midst and was first spread around the world in Aramaic, an Arabic language.' These are bold, courageously syncretistic words.

Another significant aspect of the Damascus declaration was its endorsement by the Muslim Brotherhood—given the bitter memories of the Hama massacre.[31] The current leader of the Brotherhood in Syria, Ali Sadreddin al-Bayanouni, now consents to 'Islamic pluralism'. Here is what the declaration says on the subject:

> Islam, which is the religion and ideology of the majority, with its lofty spirit, higher values, and tolerant canon law, is the mainstay of our cultural life, its most prominent but not exclusive component. Our Arab civilisation has taken shape within the framework of Islam's ideas, values, and ethics, but also in interaction with Syria's other historic cultures, through moderation, tolerance, mutual give-and-take, free of fanaticism, violence and exclusion...."

To see such diverse political groups rally behind this vision of unity and reconciliation is encouraging indeed. There are great promises here, for healing *our political fractures, freeing our resources, and strengthening our resolve to stand up to external challenges. No doubt, the path ahead is thorny and strewn with all manner of obstacles, external and internal. Bashar himself has to make compromises to survive—an accomplishment in itself, considering the power and resources of his foreign adversaries. Many Syrians, under the disguise of reformist postures, tend to align themselves with the American call for regime change. Others, mainly those who have lived in Western countries, equate reforms with 'free market' and dismiss the politics of Arab resistance as a dis-traction. A glaring example is the so-called* Syrian Reform Party *(Hizb al-Islah al-Suri) led by a businessman settled in America, Farid Nahid al-Ghadiri. In January 2004, with the support of the American administration and the CIA, this group tried to gather together in Brussels various opponents to the Syrian regime, who thrive in Western countries. They launched their* Alliance for Democracy *(al-Tahaluf min ajl al-Dimuqratiyya). Then you have this Abd al-Aziz Sahhab Muflat, another businessman based in America, who formed his own* Democratic Awakening Party *(Hizb al-Nahda al- Watani al-Dimuqrati). In March 2005, the US State Department invited these assorted worthies for a meeting to discuss 'regime change'. But all these gimmicks cut no ice with the Syrian people: they instinctively reject such interference. The West has been lambasting Syria for its authoritarianism, without wincing in embarrassment over the fact that its allies, Israel, Saudi Arabia, Jordan and Egypt, among others, tend to be far more undemocratic and totalitarian than Syria. Egypt alone holds thousands of political dissenters in its prisons. Israel is democratic enough, but only to its Jewish citizens. Clearly, democracy, secularism, human rights and all the Western blather are just so many shields behind which the forces of hegemony hide their daggers, waiting for tactical opportunities to strike. I have no doubt that Israel and its political hostage, the United States, would embrace Syria as an ally and partner, and settle overnight all bilateral quarrels to our satisfaction, including the return of the Golan Heights, if only we promised to break with Hizbullah and Hamas, and to end our friendship with Iran. Nor in my view would Israel and the US mind befriending the most extreme Wahhabi and Salafi regime, as they do in Saudi Arabia, if that regime gave up the policies of resistance and accepted the occupation of Palestine. Well, Syria has withstood all pressures so far and I believe it will go on doing so, until it sees its causes prevail—which means an end to hegemony, and justice to the Palestinians.*

# Appendix A

## The Biblical narrative and (sparse) archaeological evidence[32]

- *Post-exilic history.* The Bible account of Israelite history after the reign of King Solomon (i.e., over the nine centuries BC) is generally believed to be based on historical fact because it is partly corroborated by contemporaneous Egyptian and Assyrian chronicles.
- *Earliest texts.* The oldest scrolls carrying Biblical fragments (from the Book of Numbers) were carbon-dated to ca. 600 BC, i.e., to the decades before the Babylonian exile. But most historians still hold that the Bible, in its present canonical form, was written down during or shortly after the exile.
- *Pre-Solomon obscurity.* No undisputed Hebrew records survive from the times of King Solomon or earlier. The ancient Israelites wrote mostly on perishable papyrus rather than on clay tablets (as the Babylonians always did) or stone slabs (as the Egyptians sometimes did). More puzzling is the complete silence of ancient Greek historians and Egyptian sources on early Hebrew history.
- *Jeremiah:* In 1986, scholars identified an ancient seal that had belonged to Baruch, son of Neriah, a scribe who recorded the doomsday prophecies of Jeremiah in 587 BC. Another seal belonged to Yerahme'el, grandson of King Jehoiakim (ca. 600 BC), mentioned in the Book of Jeremiah.
- *King Solomon:* In February 2010 archaeologist Eilat Mazar announced the excavation in Jerusalem of what she believes is a 10th-century city wall and royal structure with Hebrew inscriptions that would point to the existence of a royal palace and fortified city under a Hebrew king in the 10th-century BC (that would be around the time of Solomon, according to the Bible).
- *King David:* In 1993 archaeologists uncovered in the Golan (at an ancient mound called Tel Dan and identified with the Biblical 'tribe of Dan') a 9th century BC inscription on a chunk of basalt which, according to Avraham Biran, reads 'House of David' and the 'King of

Israel' (although some experts, as you would expect, disagree). The rest of the inscription, dated a century after David's reign, appears to describe a victory by a neighbouring King over the Israelites. In 2000, André Lemaire reported a related 'House of David' discovery on the Mesha Stele (also known as the Moabite Stone), the most extensive inscription ever recovered from ancient Palestine, which was found in 1868 at the ruins of biblical Dibon (capital of the kingdom of Moab) and later wound up in the Louvre. Here again the inscription appears to record a victorious raid by an enemy of Israel, King Mesha of Moab, who finds mention in the Bible.

- *Joshua and the conquest of Canaan:* Historians generally agree that Joshua's conquest (*Exodus, Numbers, Joshua*), if at all, would have taken place around 13th century BC. But most archaeologists see little evidence for this. Kathleen Kenyon[33] and Magen Broshi[34] found no evidence for the devastation of Jericho in the 13th century BC. 'Jericho, Hazor, and Ai'[35] were deserted from the beginning of the 15th century BC until the 11th century BC and so was most of the land surrounding these two cities [...] The central hill regions of Judea and Samaria were practically uninhabited.' No invader would have had to kill and burn to settle. Hence the prevailing view among historians that the settlement of Canaan was a gradual, drawn-out process, involved both locals and a mix of outsiders. In the view of Israel Finkelstein,[36] 'some came from the Hittite country, some from the desert to the east and some from the south,' and some may have come 'from Egypt, and brought with them the idea of monotheism'. That the Israelis fought their neighbours for territory is all too likely, but only after they were firmly established in Canaan'.

- *Egypt, Moses, Exodus:* In 1990 Frank Yurco[37], working on a stele from Luxor, dated to 1207 BC and celebrating a military victory by the Pharaoh Merneptah, deciphered its hieroglyphic inscription as meaning: 'Canaan is captive with all woe; Ashkelon is conquered; Gezer seized; Yanoam made nonexistent; Israel[38] is laid waste, its seed[39] is no more,' and felt justified in identifying the figures on a nearby wall relief as ancient Israelites. Yurco's rendering of the inscription, which is now widely accepted, suggests that the Israelites were a distinct population more than 3,000 years ago.

However, so far not the slightest Egyptian mention of a Hebrew presence in their midst has been found. There is, therefore, no proof whatsoever that the Exodus took place, or that a figure resembling Moses actually existed and laid the foundation of the Israelite faith. Nor is the supposed 40-year sojourn of the Israelites in the Sinai desert backed by a single piece of archaeological evidence.

- *The Patriarchs:* In the case of the Patriarchs (Abraham, Isaac, Jacob) the lack of direct evidence is, of course, complete. Their extraordinary longevity, as well as the fact that several kings and known figures, whom Abraham supposedly encountered, existed at widely separated times, shows that we are not dealing here with chronicles, however embellished. This doesn't mean, either, that the stories were entirely made up. Scholars like Kenneth Kitchen[40] have pointed out that many elements in the Biblical narrative, from the quoted price of slaves to the style of warfare to the laws of inheritance in Abraham's day, are amazingly consistent with what is known from other sources.

- This, in short, is how things stand at the moment, despite the best efforts by Israel's archaeologists to create, as the joke goes, *facts under the ground,* and despite their having combed for twelve years[41] the Sinai desert for traces of the wanderings of Moses and his flock. The discovery of pre-Solomonic royal archives could of course change all that at one stroke. So far, however, none have been unearthed in Israel, which is all the more surprising since surrounding countries have yielded many from the same era. As a frustrated Israeli archaeologist[42] put it: 'It's like striking oil. Everywhere but here.'

# Appendix B

## Syria's exceptionalism?[43]

The most testing challenge to Hafiz al-Assad's thirty-year rule—its defining moment, in a way—was the ferocious Islamist uprising in Hama.

- The revolt followed years of antagonism between the conservative Muslim Brotherhood and the nationalist regime of President Assad.
- The Muslim Brotherhood had tried to unseat the regime through targeted political killings and urban warfare. The first major assault came in June 1976, when a rebellious army captain, Ibrahim al-Yussuf, led the massacre of Alawi students at the Aleppo artillery school.
- After a subsequent attempt on the President's life, his brother Rifaat entered the city of Talmor with his Defence Brigades and had up to a thousand Muslim brothers machine-gunned to death.
- During a search of Hama to try to root out dissident forces, Syrian troops came across the hideout of a local commander and were ambushed. As troop reinforcements were rushed to the city, the mosques called for a holy war against Assad's regime on 3 February 1982. The Muslim Brotherhood led the rebellion with guns, knives and grenades. Female suicide bombers hurled themselves against government troops. Hama's Islamists slaughtered entire families of Ba'ath party officials.
- The leadership's response was harsh. 'Death a thousand times to the hired Muslim Brothers', Assad shouted in fury. 'Death a thousand times to the Muslim Brothers, the criminal Brothers, the corrupt Brothers.'
- The Syrian army, once again led by Rifaat, destroyed half of the city (the old, rebel-held part of Hama) with tank shellfire and killed up to 20,000 people.
- Rifaat was seen as the natural successor to his brother, who ruled for three decades, but was accused of preparing to take over the country with his special forces. He was driven out of Damascus.

Many Syrians at the time felt that the brutality of the insurgency and the chilling prospect of a Salafist takeover more than justified the harshness of the regime's clampdown. With an apparently unquenchable civil war raging in neighbouring Lebanon, and given Syria's own potential for sectarian strife, the draconian emergency laws (still in force) which Hafiz al-Assad introduced in the wake of the Hama uprising could even pass for a reasonable price to pay for the years of stability that followed.

A reasonable price it may have been, but certainly a stiff one: a glance at the yearly reports of *Amnesty International* and *Human Rights Watch* suggests that in point of arbitrary arrests, detentions without trial, torture during interrogation, 'disappeared' people at home[44] and exiled dissidents assassinated abroad[45]; restrictions on freedom of movement[46], expression and association; rigged elections; an opaque web of secret services constantly espying the citizenry and each other; skewed governance under a rubber stamp parliament; and all the usual evils of dynastic rule—in all these respects Syria under Hafiz ranked among the most repressive Arab regimes, topped only by Saddam Hussein's Iraq, Saudi Arabia and Libya, and closely followed by Egypt.

Bashar Al-Assad's accession to the Presidency in 2000, and his early promises of gradual liberalisation, were met with immense relief and raised great expectations, which, however, were quickly disappointed. The ban on independent publications was lifted, but the only two private newspapers allowed to cover political events were owned by businessmen closely tied to the government. The emergency laws were not abrogated. The announced reforms were constantly postponed, under threadbare pretexts: priority to the country's economic development; external threats and destabilisation attempts from various quarters; and the old bogey—once credible, but now wearing thin—of the lapse into anarchy that would inevitably follow if the lead were to be taken off the sectarian cauldron. All in all, dissatisfaction with the regime seems to be growing, and may soon prevail over whatever anxieties still linger in the national psyche about the threat of intersectarian strife, or the danger of a Salafist takeover—especially since Syria's feared *mukhabarats* (intelligence agents) can be seen to target journalists, human rights critics,[47] and proponents of free speech far more frequently than Islamist extremists. In the eyes of its own citizens, and even more so in those of other Arabs, the Syrian autocracy may still compare favourably with the Egyptian one—better a dictatorship that stands for Arab pride than one exemplifying national humiliation—but this is increasingly felt to be a poor consolation for the indefinite deprivation of freedom.

# Notes

1. Syrian traders were active throughout the Roman Empire, as far as Gaul, and in St. Augustine's time Rome's most famed Latin rhetor was one Hierius, a Syrian who had previously dazzled Athens with his Greek oratory. Later on, the Syriac language, an evolved form of Aramaic, became the carrier of a rich Christian patristic literature, and is said to have exerted a decisive influence on the Arabic language (in script and vocabulary) in its formative stages. A highly controversial thesis—so controversial that its author, a German scholar, prefers to hide behind the pseudonym of Luxenberg—even claims that many obscure Quranic statements make much better sense when interpreted in the light of a Syriac substrate, and that key Quranic expressions are liable to receive a completely different reading. Thus, the *huri* of Paradise, according to Luxenberg, are not *white-eyed virgins* but *white grapes.* Luxenberg's thesis has come under savage criticism, not just from Muslims, but also from independent scholars like François de Blois. *E.N.*
2. A fanatical sect with a weakness for hashish smoking, which gave the English language the word *assassin.*
3. Francois Georges-Picot of France and Mark Sykes of England.
4. Hamas' declared policy is one of non-recognition of Israel. *In petto,* most Palestinians take this to mean fighting Israel until it withdraws to its pre-1967 borders and makes significant concessions on the exiled Palestinians' right of return. *E.N.*
5. The Alawis are a distinctly heterodox Muslim sect. They describe themselves as a branch of Shia Islam, but mainstream Shias reject the claim.
6. Dr Jabbour was sent a provisional draft of his interview for approval, but gave no reply. We cannot vouch, therefore, that the following rendering reflects his views exactly and in every particular, and apologise in advance for possible inaccuracies. Some contributions by the other guests present at the meeting may, for conciseness, have been conflated with Jabbour's own, and it would seem that neutral pieces of information (figures, dates, quotes, book details etcetera) were supplemented after the event by the author. *E.N.*
7. On Ibn-Khaldun, see the end-of-chapter notes after Chapter V.
8. Regarding the skewed relationship—truly asymmetrical, but not in the sense that Dr Jabbour implies—between Dr Weizmann and Lord Balfour, and more generally between the Zionist pioneers and their gentile 'backers', see the end-of-chapter notes.
9. He represented his party at the Seventh Congress of the Comintern (Communist International) held in July–August 1935 in Moscow.

10. The term *Semitic* (after the biblical *Shem,* one of Noah's sons) was coined by
linguists in the late 18th century as a rigorous denomination for a language
family that comprises Babylonian, Arabic, Hebrew, Aramaic, Syriac, among
other languages. It was later taken up by historians, who applied it, more
questionably, to the *carriers* of those languages. It then entered the mainstream,
to be used and abused by race theorists. *E.N.*

11. About the present state of archaeological research into Biblical history, see
Appendix A.

12. An Ukrainian Jew from Kiev who migrated to Palestine during World War I,
Levi Eshkol succeeded Ben-Gurion as Israel's Prime Minister in 1963 after a
stint as Minister of Agriculture and then of Finance.

13. With respect, the good Dr Jabbour could pick his examples, and direct
his indignation, much nearer home. He forgets, no doubt inadvertently, to
mention the Arab slave trade which lasted, without interruption, for more
than eleven centuries. In the early phase, the main slave contingents were
Berbers, Turks, even Europeans (mostly of Slavic stock—hence the conflation
of *Slavic* and *slave);* but soon enough sub-Saharan Africa became the main
hunting ground for Arab slave traders (so that *abd* often became synonymous
with *black African).* Overall, it is estimated that a total of between 11 and 18
million black Africans were captured by Arabs and dispatched (through the
Red Sea, Indian Ocean and Sahara desert) to serve Arab slave masters or be
sold on the slave markets of Central Asia. For a comprehensive investigation,
see *Le Génocide Voilé: Enquête Historique,* by the Senegalese historian Tidiane
N'Diaye (Paris: Gallimard, 2008). For comparison, the figure for the European
slave trade across the Atlantic is usually put at between 11 and 13 million.
As a legal Muslim institution, slavery persisted in some places (Saudi Arabia,
Sudan, and Mauritania) well into the second half of the 20th century. This of
course is to say nothing of such modern forms of slavery as the exploitation
of Bangladeshi and South-Asian workers in the Gulf States. *E.N.*

14. The first 'modern' concentrations camps were set up by the British during
the Boer uprising (1899–1902) to intern Afrikaner prisoners and civilians en
masse, and claimed more than 27,000 lives. *E.N.*

15. Here is the place to interject, like the schoolmen of old, thrice and at the top
of our voice: *distinguo, distinguo, distinguo!* We must indeed draw the sharpest
distinction between what the Zionists of the Ben-Gurion generation did to the
Palestinians—about that, there can be no two views—and what they did to
their own people. Ben-Gurion's position couldn't have been clearer or franker:
The Jews' subjection must end, and ours is a scheme to end it. This is a once-
in-a-millennium chance. We cannot blow it. We have staked all our on its
success. If the price to pay for ending centuries of exile and humiliation is a

terrible but momentary bloodshed, so be it! One may of course question all of Ben-Gurion's premises (as the present book convincingly does), but if one accepts them, as he himself wholeheartedly did, his conclusion becomes hard to dispute. For the record, I must state here that Kumar himself held quite germane views. Although he inevitably varied on many issues in the course of his militant career, he never repudiated this core belief, which he voiced at the threshold of his public life, in 1975, while defying Indira Gandhi's Emergency regulations: 'Better a terrifying climax than an endless terror without climax.' E.N.

16. We have here, in a nutshell, Marxist earthiness, echoes of Judaic themes, and sentimental Tolstoyan ethics. That was then, of course, and now is now. The *kibbutz* movement with its ideology is presently a spent force, and it is mainly foreign labourers (Romanians, Thais, Filipinos, among others) who now 'redeem themselves' by tending ex-Palestinian farmland. E.N.

17. The *dunum* was a unit of land measurement used in the Ottoman period, equivalent to one thousand square meters, or about one quarter of an acre.

18. It was headed by Walter Shaw, a prominent jurist, and included three members of the British Parliament.

19. Quoted from an address delivered by Judah L. Magnes in September 1929 during the opening session of the Hebrew University of Jerusalem. See Arthur A. Goren, *Dissenter in Zion*, a bibliography of Judah L. Magnes (Harvard University Press, 1982), p. 62.

20. In actual fact, these colourful—albeit clad in black—figures have nothing in common with the aforementioned humanists. They live in a time warp; represent the most exclusivist and inward-looking strand of Judaism; and their rejection of Israel has precious little to do with any supposed 'toleration' of Arabs or non-Jews. E.N.

21. Under the leadership of Fawzi al-Qawuqji.

22. It is often alleged that the expression *al-Nakba* was consciously patterned on *ha-Shoah,* in negative emulation as it were, but Gilbert Achcar, author of *The Arabs and the Holocaust* (New York: Metropolitan Books), denies such origin and intention, arguing instead that the designation arose spontaneously. E.N.

23. Published by Seeker and Warburg of London in 1950.

24. Published by William Clowes and Sons of London in 1952.

25. Published by Victor Gollancz of London in 1950.

26. Published by Achiasaf, Jerusalem, in 1950.

27. Between July 1915 and March 1916.

28. After Hafiz developed a heart condition around 1983, his younger brother Rifaat, who as the head of Syria's 'internal security forces' had overseen the

repression in Hama, was seen as the natural successor. But he overplayed his hand; paraded his tanks rather too conspicuously in Damascus; was accused of plotting a coup; fell out with Hafiz; was (characteristically) spared but driven out of the country; and now lives in London. *E.N.*

29. *Bilad al-Sham* is often equated with *al-Mashrek* (the 'East' minus Iraq, i.e., present-day Syria, Lebanon, Jordan and Palestine all put together), implying something symmetrical to, and as weighty as, *al-Maghreb* (the 'West', i.e., the whole of the southern Mediterranean).

30. These included the Democratic National Grouping in Syria, the Committee for the Revival of Civil Society, the Future Party (led by Sheykh Nawwaf al-Bashir), the Kurdish Democratic Alliance, and the Kurdish Democratic Front in Syria.

31. See Appendix B. The Syrian branch of the Brotherhood had played a leading role in the 1982 Hama uprising, and had borne the full brunt of the ensuing massacre. For the next two decades, at least, membership of the Muslim Brotherhood was, under the Syrian law, an offense punishable by death (in theory at least; towards the ends, the ban was being lamely implemented).

32. This brief summary is based on various entries in Wikipedia and draws heavily on a survey by Michael D. Lemonick that appeared in *TIME* magazine on June 24, 2001.

33. A British archeologist who excavated at the Jericho site for six years.

34. A Dead Sea Scrolls curator.

35. Canaanean cities allegedly destroyed by Joshua.

36. An archeologist at Tel Aviv University.

37. An Egyptologist at the Field Museum in Chicago.

38. *i-si-ri-ar*, which is this context can reasonably be read as *Israel.*

39. Egyptologists tell us that *seed* here should not be taken as *progeny* but quite literally as *grain stores.* Mentioning the destruction of *grain* was the Egyptians' way of describing how crushing the defeat of their enemies was: faced with food shortage or famine, they would be incapable of waging war for the next season.

40. An egyptologist at Liverpool University.

41. During the Sinai's occupation by Israel, from 1967 till 1979.

42. Amnon Ben-Tor, of the Hebrew University.

43. This short note draws on *Amnesty* and *Human Right Watch* reports, and quotes extensively from articles by Nadim Houry (16 July 2010) and Robert Fisk (24 June and 17 July 2010) that appeared in *The Independent.*

44. Robert Fisk quotes a 117 page report compiled by Radwan Ziadweh, *Years of Fear,* which states that as many as 17,000 Syrians may have been 'disappeared'

during the rule of Assad senior, and adduces many instances of extra-judicial execution. Fisk cautions that the report, being published in Washington with the support of Freedom House, an institution largely funded by the US State Department, should be treated with great caution, but adds that it is simply too detailed to be dismissed in its entirety.

45. At least during the five years that followed the Hama uprising.

46. Human rights activists are routinely denied visas.

47. Thus, in the summer 2010, criminal courts sentenced two of Syria's human rights lawyers, Muhannad al-Hassani, 42, and Haytham al-Maleh, 78, to three years in jail for criticising Syria's human rights record.

# 4

## *Refugees in resistance: Memories and dreams from exile*

*We must use terror, assassination, intimidation, land confiscation, and the cutting of all social services to rid the Galilee of its Arab population.*

—David Ben-Gurion[1]

I didn't want to leave Damascus without meeting representatives of the Palestinian diaspora there. Fortunately, a friend, who is currently based in Oxford but grew up in the region, put me in touch with two such Palestinians—civil society leaders both, and both with their livelihood in Damascus. Along with their families, they had been forced to flee their native villages near the Sea of Galilee in 1948. Abu Husam, the younger of the two, now over 65, was only 6 years old at the time. His was a large family, with no less than nine siblings. Along with three brothers, Abu Husam went to what is now Jordan, where two of his uncles had been living. His younger brothers and the rest of the family left for Lebanon. Faced with harassment and discrimination, they moved from there to the Golan Heights, then part of Syria. After the 1967 war and Israel's capture of the Golan, they had to move again, this time to Hums in Syria. Together, the nine brothers and sisters and their progeny now form a family of some 60 members, male and female. Abu Husam grinned, 'We procreate a lot.'

The older man, Adnan Abdul Rahim, now nearly 70, was born in Safad, close to the Lebanese border. He was 9 years old when Safad was subjected to ethnic cleansing and the family had to move. They first went to Lebanon, after a 40 kilometre walk across the border, then to Tripoli, and then again to Hums in Syria. They eventually settled down in a village near Damascus in the early 1960s. Adnan Abdul Rahim's elder brother was fortunate in finding a job in the Syrian capital when the family shifted there. Like Abu Husam, Adnan Abdul Rahim was a PLO veteran, who had been involved with the Palestinian resistance in various capacities.

I invited the two of them to my hotel room for discussions. They came over one evening after *iftar* (the breaking of the Ramadan fast), and stayed into the wee hours of the morning, talking with me non-stop until dawn drew near. Then they retired to have their morning meal before the day-time abstention.

As mentioned, both men hailed from Eastern Galilee, a place which, in 1948, was systematically cleansed of its Muslim Arabs by the provident founders of Israel. Benny Morris, a celebrated historian at Ben-Gurion University and former diplomatic correspondent for the *Jerusalem Post,* has devoted two major works to the subject—*The Birth of the Palestinian Refugee Problem, 1947–1949,*[2] and again *The Birth of the Palestinian Refugee Problem Revisited*[3]—by drawing from Israel's State Archives to expose the careful planning behind the ethnic cleansing. In the first book Morris quotes Ben-Gurion addressing the Haganah leaders, in April 1948:

> We will not be able to win the war if we do not, during the war, populate Upper and Lower, Eastern and Western Galilee, the Negev and the Jerusalem areas, even if only in an artificial way, in a military way [....] I believe the war will also bring in its wake a great change in the distribution of the Arab population.[4]

According to Morris, 700,000 Palestinians fled their land to escape Israeli military attacks. *The Birth of the Palestinian Refugee Problem* very ex-plicitly demonstrates how the Zionist raids on forty-one Palestinian villages resulted in the forced expulsion of all their inhabitants and caused wild panic in the 187 neighbouring villages, leading to a mass exodus there too.

Predictably, the book came under virulent attack from Zionist his-torians. So Morris published a second book, to present more archival evidence of atrocities by the Zionist troops, including mass murder and rape. Although Morris was himself born in 1948 in a *kibbutz,* in a family of prominent Jewish immigrants from the UK, traditional Israeli scholars, like Efraim Karsh, never forgave him for disproving the official Israeli fiction that Arab Muslims had 'quit their villages voluntarily'. Morris also came under fire from the other end of the ideological spectrum. Thus, Norman Gary Finkelstein, a noted American political scientist and a Jew himself,[5] took Morris to task for not going all the way in evaluating the historical evidence, and for being half-hearted in his criticism of the early Zionists and their Nazi-like conduct.[6]

Finkelstein was born in America to Holocaust survivors. Both his parents were Orthodox Jews from Poland. His mother lost her parents, siblings and first husband in the Holocaust. His father survived the siege of the Warsaw Ghetto only to be taken to Auschwitz, which he also survived. Of his own admission, Finkelstein's radical criticism of Israel stems from the seething indignation which as a child he used to feel over the US atrocities in Vietnam—a rage all the fiercer for resonating with the experiences of his parents. Finkelstein, as also other Arab historians of repute, have criticised Morris for understating the intensity and pervasiveness of Zionist violence, which did not erupt, uncontrolled, in the heat of action, but was part of a pre-planned, thought-through strategy for achieving a population transfer.

Another radical Jewish historian, Ilan Pappé,[7] has criticised Morris on the same grounds. Ilan Pappé is an outspoken advocate of one secular state for both Jews and Palestinians, and a supporter of the right of return for *all* refugees.

I began by asking my guests, both natives of Eastern Galilee, what they had seen and remembered of the mass exodus in this outlying part of Palestine.

Abu Husam was only 6 years old when his family left Palestine and does not remember much. He only recalls hearing of a massacre of Palestinians in a nearby village, which prompted his parents to leave 'temporarily'. As it was, his father would die in Syria, his wish of returning to his native village, unfulfilled. On his death-bed, he instructed Abu Husam to take his bones back to *al-Falasteen,* for reburial there after the country's liberation.

Adnan Abdul Rahim had been born in Safad and was already 9 years old when his family underwent ethnic cleansing. Nearing 70, he has a vivid memory, and a clearer recollection of events. He spoke in a low, husky bass, with emotive fluctuations from resurfacing memories of distant pain.

Safad (at 800m above sea level, the highest point in Galilee) had been an important city, both as a place of early Zionist settlement, and a scene of early disturbances. It was also significant because of its deep resonance in the Jewish imagination. As legend has it, it was founded by a son of Noah after the Great Flood of Biblical lore. It is mentioned in the work of Josephus, the celebrated first century historian, as an important fortified city, under the name of *Sepph*. It retained all its importance, both as city and as fortress, in the period of the crusades, first under the Knights Hospitallers, who called it *Saphet,* and later under a Mamluk Sultan of Egypt and Syria,[8] who captured the city and renamed it as *Safad* or *Safat.* In the 16th century, Safad also became famous as a centre of Jewish mysticism. It saw the establishment of the first printing press in the whole Ottoman Empire.

Thus, up to modern times, Safad flourished as a centre of learning and trade. But in August 1929 it was the scene of the first major clash between Zionists and Muslims. Some Zionists in Jerusalem, for their Yom Kippur celebrations, had created a furore by building screens at their Wailing Wall, which abuts the Al-Aqsa Mosque. Muslims call it the 'Western Wall' and also claim it as theirs. The affair escalated into a bloody riot. Throughout Palestine, about the same number of Jews and Arab Muslims were killed, approximately 250 on each side. Many more were injured. In Jerusalem only 17 Jews died. In Hebron and Safad, which were overwhelmingly Muslim cities, there were many more Jewish casualties: in Hebron nearly 65 and in Safad about 20. The entire Jewish population there might have been killed if Arab Muslims, in their thousands, had not hidden them in their own houses.

Adnan recalls what happened in 1948. At the time, Safad's Jews only numbered about 1,700 against 12,000 Arab Muslims. Zionist historians depict the battle for Safad as a tale of heroism, in which a small minority of Jews stood up to a large Arab force bent on finishing them off. Adnan has other recollections. He recalls the spirit of gloom and anger that gripped the city, the cultural and administrative capital of upper Galilee, and 85 per cent Muslim, when on 29 November 1947 the UN decided to allocate it to the future Jewish State. There were strikes and demonstrations, all carried out by Arab Muslims. The Jews remained extraordinarily quiet because, as Adnan later found out, they had been preparing for the decisive showdown already for several years, under the instructions of the Haganah.

Some Arabs had also been talking war, especially members of organisations like *al-Najjada* (the helpers). But they only talked and did not dare to defy the British authorities, for the brutal repression of the Arab uprisings in the years 1936–39 was still fresh in their memories. By late 1948 the Palestinian leaders, under the banners of the Higher Arab Committee and local National Councils, prided themselves in having raised a defence force for Safad, with 444 local volunteers. But these organisations were riddled with leadership controversies and petty divisions, and could not be effective in any manner. All their talk of war had no impact on the running of daily life, given that Arabs and Jews shared all common resources—water, electricity, health, trade, transport, and postal services.

In December 1947, a Haganah officer on patrol in the Arab areas was attacked and killed. In retaliation, the Haganah executed three Arab Muslims. Minor scuffles and skirmishes ensued. It seems that some Syrian soldiers came in as volunteers to shore up Safad's defence forces. Adnan vaguely remembers one Ihsan Kam-Ulmaz, a militarily incompetent bully, given to bragging and hectoring. He said he was loyal to the Mufti of Jerusalem.

Meanwhile, the Haganah and its Palmach battalions were going about their military preparations, quietly and effectively. Several garrisons were established in strategically sensitive locations, from where they mounted hit-and-run raids on remote villages, mainly to seed panic. Adnan recalled an attack carried out on 18 December 1947 by one commander Moshe Kelman, of the Third Battalion of Palmach, on a village called Khisas. A Jew had apparently been killed at a location some kilometres away from Khisas, without there being any obvious connection between the attackers and the village population. In the course of the retaliatory raid by Palmach, more than ten villagers were killed and dozens of Arab houses set on fire.

Adnan also recalls another major attack on 14 February 1948, again the work of Palmach's Third Battalion, against a village by the name of Sa'sa. The village lay in an overwhelmingly Arab zone, 12 kilometres northwest of Safad and 15 kilometres east of Haifa, and served as an important junction on the road between Lebanon and Palestine. The raid was launched after dark. Eleven villagers were killed; more than 75 were badly injured; and nearly 50 huts were torched. The idea was to take the initiative away from the Arabs and to impress on them that Jewish militias could roam the Arab territory unimpeded and put its population to flight. Such attacks intensified over the next weeks. There was no visible Arab defence, nor was there much organised rescue or relief. When the more brutal attacks started for good, the Muslim population was already shaken and demoralised.

On 12 March 1948, the ubiquitous Moshe Kelman launched a nocturnal attack on village Husseiniya, in the middle of the fertile Hula valley, cupped up between the Golan Heights to the east and Upper Galilee to the west. The avowed aim was to 'annihilate it'. Dozens of people were killed, and all houses but one were blasted off with explosives. This was the first Arab village to suffer this fate—complete annihilation—a full two months before Israel's declaration of independence.

Several such attacks followed. The Arabs of Palestine became completely listless, gripped by fear for their collective and individual survival. The British forces were still there, and technically responsible for maintaining public order. In reality, they did not have the nerve to take on the Zionist militants, whose lethal capacities they knew at first hand.

Adnan remembered the name of one Colonel Gordon Watson, the British district commander. All he cared for was to avoid direct clashes with the Zionists. To appease them, he turned down all Arab requests for defensive preparations. Adnan learnt of all these details later on, from his parents and uncles. He also learnt that the British forces were internally divided on how to respond to the developing civil war. For example, he heard that while some officers like Colonel Gordon Watson would maintain a facade of neutrality, appeasing the Zionists and preventing Arab self-defence preparations, others, like Captain Lambert[9] went much further and actively assisted the attacks on Arabs.

The British forces stationed in Safad evacuated the city on 16 April. The Haganah launched vicious attacks on the Arab quarters. Local members of the Arab Rescue Force, led by Fawzi al-Qawuqji fought back and even compelled the Haganah to vacate some forward positions overlooking the Arab quarters. But the Arab Rescue Force needed reinforcements which never came. The Haganah ranks, meanwhile, were being reinforced by special Palmach battalions. On 18 April, the Haganah issued a general recruitment call to all men from age 15 to 50 and all women from 15 to 35, demanding absolute, unquestioning obedience to military orders.

Adnan heard from his parents and his uncles that the Arab Rescue Force, a motley array of some 800 soldiers and volunteers, theoretically under the high command of Adib Shishakli (a Syrian officer), was hopelessly divided. Their officers kept quarrelling over trifling matters. There was endless bickering over the issue of command. There were also desertions and minor mutinies, and little energy left for action. The few initiatives, defensive or offensive, which the Rescue Force took did the Palestinian population more harm than good. Rivalries between commanders of the Rescue Force became so bitter that each competing faction began spreading rumours of an impending massacre of Palestinians, accusing the other side of being hands in glove with the Zionists.

Adnan heard that the rivalry between Sari Fnaish, appointed by Adib Shishakli as commander of the Arab Rescue Force, and his predecessor Ihsan Kam-Ulmaz, loyal to the Mufti of Jerusalem, was especially unsettling to the morale of the local population. As for the *real war,* the war which the Arab Rescue Force was supposed to wage against the Haganah, its outcome was sealed in advance by the internal dissentions; poor armoury; deficient intelligence; and, above all, the complacency of the commanders and their blissful ignorance of Zionist military tactics. Desertions increased. Sari was said to be beholden to King Hussein of Jordan; that very same Hussein who was (rightly) suspected of having an understanding with the Zionists. Jordan would have a free hand to annex what is now known as the West Bank, in return for Hussein's benevolent neutrality and indirect assistance in the creation of Israel.

At this point, the Palmach Commander Yigal Allon toured Safad and its surroundings, took the measure of Arab disarray, and recommended swift military action to 'speed up the evacuation' of all Arabs according to *Plan Dalet*—a master-plan that had been hatched under Ben-Gurion's direct supervision. Sari Fnaish then began to beseech Shishakli for reinforcements, better arms, ammunition and rations, none of which arrived.

Moshe Kelman launched a frontal attack on 1 May 1948, largely with a view to impress on the Palestinian residents what fate lay in store for them if they did not leave. It was an operation of signal brutality, which completely obliterated the village of Ein Zeitun, close to Safad. All the houses were destroyed. Those who could not flee were killed, even those who surrendered, including the children, nearly 40 of them. Some soldiers of the Arab Rescue Force watched all this from their locations a few hundred meters away. They were paralyzed with fear, as if spell-bound in the face of this will to conquer, unseen before, that swept all before it and made no allowance for human sentiments.

The total strength of the Arab Rescue Force was less than 800, of which 450 were non-Palestinian Arab volunteers, the rest being local recruits. They had only 200 primitive shotguns—one gun to be shared among four! Many of the volunteers had already deserted. The Jordanians were lukewarm, or worse, because of the Hashemite undercover deal with the Zionists. Egypt was then under King Farouk, a man of vain temper, a lecher given to lavishness and hedonism, with no time to spare on distractions like Israel or Palestine. He had been educated in England, and was a brother-in-law to the Shah Pahlavi of Iran. He was also a sworn enemy of the Muslim Brotherhood, which had taken a strong stand against Israel. Ismail Sidqi, a politician close to Farouk and twice Prime Minister,[10] went out of his way to pronounce that 'Israel, being separated from Egypt by a large desert, should not be of any concern to Egyptians.' However, his confidant Mahmud Fahmi al-Nuqrashi, who had succeded him as Prime Minister, decided to symbolically join the Arab opposition to Israel, so as to keep intact Egypt's bid to the leadership of the Arab world. Since Iraq, like Jordan, was under a Hashemite king, its troops showed no more zeal than Jordan's. The Lebanese Maronites, too, had a secret understanding with the founders of Israel. As for the Druze militias, pitiless in battle, they had come down openly on the Zionist side. So there was really no war, just a bedlam and the hot air of war-mongering. The Haganah and the Palmach forces, on the other hand, were disciplined, properly trained, war-hardened, well supplied. Above all, they were under a competent, ideologically committed command. After the destruction of Ein Zeitun, they concentrated on terrorising the Arab residents of Safad. They kept firing mortar shells into the civilian areas, to spread shock and panic. At the same time, they had taken good care to leave open some routes of escape into Lebanon and Syria, which the people of Safad were now taking, in headlong flight.

Thus, Safad was lost to the Palestinians even before Israel was formally established on 14 May 1948. On 5 May, Sari had written to Fawzi al-Qawuqji to warn him that he would have to withdraw from the city unless he received immediate reinforcements, armoury, ammunition and supplies. His soldiers were already taking to flight, like the civilian population they were supposed to protect. Sari himself fled Safad on 6 May 1948 in the morning, when the Palmach battalions launched their decisive attack on the city. Leaderless, without anything like an operational command, the Arab volunteers were unable to make a stand. They either ran off or took to hiding.

Within four days, the Zionists were in full control of Safad. Adnan later heard that Sari Fnaish had all along been taking his orders from the King of Jordan and the British chief of the Jordanian army, John Glubb, nicknamed *Glubb Pasha*. Thus, the rumours about a secret understanding between Jordan and the Zionist leaders had been accurate. It was Sari's job to wreck the Arab resistance from within and to foil the return of the Mufti of Jerusalem to a position of leadership.

According to Adnan Abdul Rahim, what happened to Safad was fairly typical of what happened in the rest of Palestine. Nor did it happen by accident. It was part of a well-organised plan, code-named *Plan Dalet*. The plan was designed at the highest level, under David Ben-Gurion's direct supervision. Taking part in its execution were all the great heroes of Israel: Yigal Yadin, Israel Galili, Yosef Weitz, Moshe Dayan, Yigal Allon, Yitzhak Sadesh, Yitzhak Rabin, Shimon Avidan, Yitzhak Pundak, Moshe Kalman and all the rest. The plan rested on a methodical study of Arab settlements, rural and urban, and aimed at effecting the mass expulsion of the Palestinian population through massacre, terror and systematic destruction of their homes. The plan also identified those Palestinians with leadership qualities or associated with the Arab national cause, and earmarked them for assassination. The Plan was ruthlessly implemented. It resulted in the expulsion of nearly 700,000 Arab Muslims from all over Palestine and made possible the establishment of a Jewish majority State.

Adnan looked at me with wide, moist eyes, and repeated:

*This is how I left, along with all my family. This is how all other Muslim Arabs of Safad left their land, to remain homeless and stateless ever since. Only 150 old women and a few young men stayed back. The Israelis killed all the men and pushed the old women across into Syria. Safad was emptied of all Muslim Arabs.*

I asked what happened to the Christian Palestinians. Adnan said:

*Most of them lived in Galilee and in Jerusalem. Many stayed back. So did the Christian Arabs of Nazareth and Haifa, and so did the Druze. The Israelis treated the Druze well, saying they were not Arabs. I am giving you the general picture. There were, of course, exceptions and many Christians, too, suffered terrible loss in the 'catastrophe' of 1948. One of them, as you must know, was my leader. His name was George Habash, and in 1951 he became one of the founders of the Arab Nationalist Movement. And then there was Wadie Haddad, also a Greek Orthodox, and, like me, a native of Safad.*

I asked Adnan to tell me how a non-Muslim like George Habash could become such a prominent leader of the Arab nationalist cause. Abu Husam spoke before Adnan could answer:

*Well, as I said, he was my leader. I admired him from the time I joined school in Damascus. I was only 12 years old at that time. Later, I got to know him personally and worked with him. George Habash was born in the historic town of Lydda, now renamed as Lod, 15 km southeast of Tel Aviv. In 1947, the UN Partition Plan demarcated Lydda, which had a population of around 20,000 with one-fifth of Christian Arabs, for amalgamation in the future Arab State. At the outbreak of the war, the Arab voluntary force, led by Fawzi al-Qawuqji, succeeded in taking Lydda. But in early July 1948, the Zionist militias (now merged into the Israeli Defence Force) managed to retake the town, and also the neighbouring Ramla, in a ruthless operation code-named Dani. Yitzhak Rabin was in charge of this action which left hundreds of dead, both Muslim and Christian. George Habash, then a 22-year-old student of medicine at the American University of Beirut, happened to be in Lydda on a family visit when the Israelis retook the town. Yitzhak Rabin then signed an order calling for the expulsion of all Arabs from Lydda and the nearby Ramla, another historically important centre with a population of 12,000 Muslims and a few thousand Christians. Thousands of Arab Muslims from Jaffa (a major port city on the shores of the Mediterranean south of Tel Aviv, awarded to the slated Arab State under the Partition Plan) had fled to Lydda and Ramla to escape the terror which Irgun and Haganah had unleashed.*

*Members of the Muslim Brotherhood had been trying to defend the city with its population of 100,000: more than 50 per cent of these were Muslim but with nearly 17,000 Christian, mainly Greek Orthodox. By the time the Zionist militias captured Jaffa in the middle of May, the population had dwindled to 4,000! The Arab Muslims, under constant bombing and mortar rain, had been fleeing in intermittent waves, to Lydda, or Ramla, or farther. This whole region had been a stronghold of the 1936–39 Arab revolt, which the British troops, with the help of the Zionist militias, had ruthlessly put down. Jaffa suffered aerial bombings; the methodical destruction of its old Arab quarters; and the cutting off of its water supply to beat the population into submission. Israel was now taking revenge.*

*After the capture of Lydda, Yitzhak Rabin ordered all Arab inhabitants to be marched under escort out of Israel. It became a death march, with hundreds dying from thirst and hunger, trekking for days under a scorching sun. Some 60,000 Arabs, both Muslim and Christian, were expelled in this way. George Habash survived the march and lived on to work for the Arab cause. King Abdullah of Transjordan took more than 9,000 square kilometres of the Palestinian West Bank and renamed it as the* Hashemite Kingdom of Jordan. *The Gaza Strip, with its 218 odd square kilometres came under Egyptian rule. Refugee Palestinians went off to Lebanon, Syria, Jordan, Gaza, the West Bank, and other far-flung places in the Middle East.*

I inquired if Adnan Abdul Rahim knew Wadie Haddad personally. Adnan nodded tentatively as he began to speak:

*Well, I saw him once but never spoke with him. Our politics were different. He was the leader of the military wing of a radical socialist forum called* Popular Front for the Liberation of Palestine, *which grew out of the* Arab Nationalist Movement. *I was with the PLO, especially attached to the Fatah. George Habash and Wadie Haddad were friends and political partners. I mentioned Haddad because he was born in Safad, my own ancestral city. Like Habash, he was 21 when he had to flee across to Lebanon in 1948, just as I and my family had. Haddad was a medical doctor who, like Habash, worked for years tending to Palestinian refugees in Jordan.*

*He was arrested by the Jordanian authorities in 1956. After fleeing Jordan and settling down in Syria, Haddad was the main radical influence in the* Arab Nationalist Movement, *which became the* Popular Front for the Liberation of Palestine *after the disastrous war of 1967. He was probably the one who pioneered the hijacking of airplanes; the first hijacking being that of an Israeli plane in 1968. Haddad's violent tactics may have precipitated the bloody purges of Palestinians which Jordan started in September 1970. He was suspected of having close ties with 'Carlos', the Venezuelan-born revolutionary Ilich Ramirez Sanchez, who is currently languishing in a French prison.*

I asked Abu Husam and Adnan Abdul Rahim what they did after leaving Palestine.

Abu Husam told me that he had joined a school in Damascus and become involved in the Arab nationalist movement, very early in his life, adopting George Habash and Abdel Nasser as his heroes. He also studied Marx and thought of himself as a 'scientific socialist'. By 1962, he finished his college education and became a school teacher in Damascus.

*Nasser then was at the pinnacle of his popularity. He had concluded arms treaties with a number of Soviet bloc countries. He had also recognised the People's Republic of China. The United States was miffed and withdrew all the financial aid it had promised Egypt for the construction of the Aswan Dam. Nasser retaliated by nationalising the Suez Canal. This seriously threatened British interests. Britain then made a pact with France and Israel, instigating the latter to launch a ground attack on Egypt, which it did in October 1956. Britain and France then launched their joint air attack and eventually secured control of the canal.*

*Britain and France came under international criticism, which only enhanced Nasser's popularity. Everyone was talking about Arab unity and a union of Arab States under Nasser. Even the PLO (established in June 1964 with Ahmed Shukeiri as its first chairman) supported 'pan-Arabism'—that exhilarating vision, half dream half programme, of all Arab nations once again being re-united under the roof of one state. The disaster of the 1967 war, which saw the occupation of the West Bank and Gaza Strip and resulted in a second wave of expulsion of Palestinians, displacing more than 300,000 of them, broke the reverie. It also bred disillusionment with a political culture dealing in barren rhetoric, to which both Ahmed Shukeiri and Nasser seemed to belong. It was in this environment of anger and disillusionment that a new set of leaders like George Habash, Yasser Arafat, Wadie Haddad and others, all advocates of militant resistance, rose to prominence.*

I wanted to ask about the early PLO, as formed in 1964. How homogeneous was it? Was it not more of an umbrella organisation, a federation of political factions?

It was Adnan Abdul Rahim who answered:

*Before 1967, the PLO was a complex organisation accommodating the diverse and sometimes contradictory political perceptions and interests of various Arab States, their leaders and other prominent individuals. Nasser was the towering figure then. The United Arab Republic, established in February 1958, seemed a grand experiment—that is, until it collapsed in September 1961.*

*Regarding Palestine, Nasser realised that Israel, in concert with its Western backers, was pitching for a mock-solution to the Palestinian refugee problem so that it could gradually legitimise its presence on Palestinian soil. Jordan, hoping to obtain more territory from the West Bank, was hands in glove.*

*In April 1948, Syria underwent a military coup by Army Chief Husni al-Za'im against the government of Shukri al-Quwatli. The coup was clearly backed by the CIA. Za'im was a member of Syria's Kurdish minority and as such did not harbour strong Arab sentiments. His first important political initiative was to make an overture to Israel for a substantial and comprehensive peace deal. He promised to resettle nearly 300,000 Palestinian refugees in the country on a permanent basis if the United States provided enough financial assistance. Fortunately, Za'im was overthrown before he could implement his peace plan. He was deposed four and a half months after staging his coup.*

*Nasser understood the significance of the proposal Za'im had made. He could see that with support from Jordan and Saudi Arabia, Israel could attempt to permanently resettle all the refugees and then flood Palestine with Jewish migrants from the Eastern Bloc countries. There was also this proposal by the Swede Dag Hammarskjöld, Secretary-General of the UN from 1953 to 1961. In a report submitted to the UN General Assembly in June 1959, Dag Hammarskjöld appealed for international financial support for the absorption of the Palestinian refugees within the existing Arab states. In May 1961, President John F. Kennedy personally wrote to the heads of all the Arab states to endorse the proposal and promise his personal commitment to their implementation.*

*Realising that with the refugees resettled, the issues of the right of return and illegal occupation of the land would become largely irrelevant, Nasser played a major role in guiding the Arab League discussions towards the establishment of the PLO, with participation of Palestinian elements from all Arab states and from the occupied territories. Nasser made it clear that the Gaza Strip, then under Egyptian administration, belonged integrally to the future Palestinian state-to-be. Nasser also criticised Jordan's annexation of the West Bank and raised the question of the right to self-determination of the Palestinians living in Jordan. He made no bones about his view that Jordan was an artificial State without historical precedence, created by a British imperialist fiat. Jordan was peeved but could not do much, since Arab public opinion was overwhelmingly behind Nasser.*

*Eventually, a meeting of approximately 400 prominent Palestinian figures was convened in Jerusalem in May 1964 and saw the establishment of the PLO with the avowed objective of liberating Palestine through armed struggle. The PLO was created as a loose umbrella organisation, with a legislative body and an executive committee that were supposed to coordinate the activities of a number of pre-existing organisations such as Fatah, the Democratic Front for the Liberation of Palestine (DFLP), and the Popular Front for the Liberation of Palestine (PFLP). There were also several smaller groups with a secular and* socialist orientation, like the Palestinian People's Party (PPP), the Palestine Liberation Front (PLF), the Palestine Democratic Union (FIDA), the Palestinian Popular Struggle Front (PPSF), the Arab Liberation Front (ALF), and other groupings more or less aligned with this or that Arab state. Even King Hussein of Jordan attended the Jerusalem conclave. Ahmed Shukeiri, a high profile diplomat originally from Lebanon and loyal to Nasser, became the first PLO chairman. A man of high-flown rhetoric, he enjoyed wide contacts within the Arab world, having been assistant secretary-general of the Arab League from 1950 to 1956 and then Saudi Arabia's ambassador to the UN from 1957 to 1962. He resigned his position as PLO chairman after the 1967 war, to make way for Yahya Hammuda, who acted as Chairman from December 1967 to January 1969, when Yasser Arafat took over.

Initially, the PLO was anything but a cohesive body. It faced open hostility not only from the predictable quarters such as Saudi Arabia and the Gulf states, but also from militant figures who had previously been in the forefront of the Arab resistance against Zionism. Mohammed Amin al-Husseini, the Grand Mufti of Jerusalem from 1921 onwards, who had fled Palestine in 1936 to escape arrest by the British, was one of them. After escaping Palestine the Mufti went on to Germany where he met Hitler and sought his support for the Arab cause. He was caught by the French and convicted as a war criminal to three years of imprisonment. But he managed to escape and received political asylum in Egypt. The Mufti's influence gradually declined and the 'catastrophe' of 1948 did little to restore his prestige. His hand was suspected behind the assassination of King Abdullah of Jordan on 20 July 1951. The Mufti was not allowed into the country and his followers and sympathisers were ruthlessly put down. But Abdullah's grand-son King Hussein, who came to power in 1952, made a show of pardoning the Mufti, receiving him as a guest at his Jerusalem residence in 1967.

Early in 1964, the Mufti, backed by Saudi Arabia, hankered after the leadership of the future PLO and, unable to obtain it, opposed its formation on all kinds of grounds. Ironically enough, Yasser Arafat himself, an admirer of Al-Husseini, was then highly sceptical of the PLO. He regarded it as a mere platform for echoing the views of its sponsors, i.e., the Arab states led by Nasser. Born in 1929 in Cairo to Palestinian parents from Gaza, Arafat was then 35-year old. After fighting alongside the Muslim Brotherhood against the Israeli troops, mainly in the Gaza area, he had made his mark as a leader of the General Union of Palestinian Students in Cairo, and later as one of the founding members of Fatah in Kuwait, where he moved in 1957. His closest associates from that period, who were to stand by Arafat to the end, were Salah Khalaf, also known as Abu Iyad, and Khalil al-Wazir, renowned as Abu Jihad. Both were members of the Muslim Brotherhood and admirers of its founder, Hassan al-Banna. Although the formation of Fatah, in 1958 or 1959, happened in the heyday of Arab Nationalism, when Nasser was leading the show, its declared objective was to obtain the liberation of Palestine by an armed struggle that was to be carried out by the Palestinians themselves. In its formative period, Fatah also turned down offers of financial support from the Arab states, to avoid coming under political pressure. It relied on Palestinian oil workers and businessmen based in Kuwait and other Gulf countries for financial contributions. Mahmoud Abbas, then based in Qatar, was responsible for building these networks.

In 1964, when Fatah reluctantly joined the PLO, it was desperately trying to put together a group of soldiers who could infiltrate the occupied territories and carry out armed attacks. Arafat, unlike other leaders, often personally led such forays, earning the admiration and loyalty of the armed groups. This became perhaps his main strength within the organisation. Alas, Arafat's intolerance of opposition also became evident very early on in his revolutionary career. In 1966 Yusuf Orabi, a Palestinian leader from Damascus, close to Hafiz al-Assad, died after being flung out of a multi-storied building in the Syrian capital where he was meeting with Arafat and Abu Jihad to discuss a possible merger of the two organisations. At the time, Assad was Syria's Air Marshal and had Arafat and some of his colleagues detained for investigation. But Arafat had influence and enjoyed the sympathies of the then Syrian President Salah Jadid. So, he escaped detention and prosecution. Salah Jadid's deposition by Assad in September 1970 had something to do with the former's sympathies for Fatah and Arafat. Assad ousted Salah Jadid from power through a military putsch. Assad himself called his coup a 'corrective move'. By then Arafat was the chairman of the PLO and had the ears and sympathies of an ailing Nasser. But Assad would never forget the assassination of Yusuf Orabi; he never forgave Arafat for it.

I interrupted Adnan Abdul Rahim to ask how Fatah and Arafat could become so prominent so soon, when they were facing such odds: an uprooted Palestinian people; Arab states either sympathetic but weak, or openly hostile as in the case of Jordan and Saudi Arabia; and an unassailable, vengeful Israel.

After finishing school in Damascus in 1956, Adnan joined the university there to study English literature. That is where he became involved with the Palestinian struggle. Adnan joined the Fatah. He became acquainted with its leaders, including Arafat and Abu Jihad when they moved to Damascus to recruit followers among the local refugee population. So he knew the inside story.

*Arafat was a man of action, and so were his early associates, Abu Iyad, Abu Jihad and the rest. They believed in organising grass-root resistance and carrying out daring armed actions before making political statements and seeking publicity. Arafat had a long record of armed actions, beginning in 1948, in Gaza. That is where he first met with Khalil al-Wazir (Abu Jihad) and Salah Mesbah Khalaf (Abu Iyad). Both had been born in Jaffa and had gone to Cairo in 1950 to join the Muslim Brotherhood. They continued to take part in fidayeen guerrilla actions, mainly from Gaza. They went about their grass-root work with all the daring and discipline which the Muslim Brotherhood had instilled in them. That gave them a definite edge over other groups. Basically, they did a thorough job of building a political and military organisation. They were also eclectic in cultivating friends and patrons far and wide, to avoid excessive dependence on the actors in the immediate neighbourhood. For example, Arafat and Abu Jihad went to Algeria in 1962 where they made friends with Ahmed Ben Bella. It was in Algeria that the Fatah established its first military training camp. They also went to China, in 1964, where they engaged various Chinese leaders, including Zhou Enlai, in discussions about the Palestinian cause. All of this came together to ensure that the Fatah and later the PLO, when it came under Arafat's stewardship, were able to stand their ground and survive vicissitudes, adversity and opposition. Nasser himself, the Arab narcissist, became a staunch supporter and admirer of Arafat, especially after the 1967 war. He did everything in his power to assist the PLO and rescue it from trouble, like after the fatal confrontation with Jordan in 1971.*

I asked Adnan to explain briefly what happened in Jordan.

*After the disastrous war in 1967, Jordan at first allowed the PLO to operate from its territory: the King hoped to pressure Israel into negotiating a deal. Fatah had already been active in Gaza and the West Bank. It had set up secret recruitment centres there and was leading intermittent attacks inside the occupied territories. Other Palestinian groups were also active. There was the Popular Front for the Liberation of Palestine, organised by George Habash and Wadie Haddad. There was also the Marxist Democratic Front for the Liberation of Palestine, organised by Nayef Hawatmeh, a Palestinian Marxist born in Jordan to Greek Orthodox parents. As for the PLO, it had its base camps in the small*

*Jordanian town of Al-Karameh, just across the Allenby Bridge that spans the Jordan River, and in a nearby hamlet called Safi.*

Soon, Jordan became unhappy with the rather too conspicuous PLO presence and all these uncontrolled guerrillas who were throwing their weight about. It sent its forces to ask the Fatah units to vacate the territory. Under instructions from Arafat, the Fatah refused to comply and ordered the Jordanian troops to either leave or fight. The Jordanian troops withdrew. Clearly, Jordan had acted under pressure from Israel.

On 21 March 1968, the Israeli army crossed the Allenby bridge into Jordanian territory and attacked the PLO camps in Al-Karameh and Safi with the clear intention of destroying them and killing the PLO leaders, including Arafat. But the PLO had advance intelligence of the Israeli attack. Some Jordanian officers in touch with the CIA had tipped them off. So the PLO fighters were prepared for the unequal encounter. It was a regular battle. The Israeli forces comprised one armoured brigade, one infantry brigade, one paratrooper battalion, one engineering battalion and five artillery battalions. Israel also used helicopters to lift its paratroopers into the sites of acute action. Jordan became worried that the Israeli forces might march up to Amman. So it sent its army to help resist the invasion. Arafat and his close associates personally led the battle plan. The Israeli troops were forced to withdraw. Casualties were heavy on both sides. But it was the first military defeat for the Israeli army, which lost thirty-three soldiers; four tanks; three military trucks and two armoured cars. One of their helicopters was shot down. More than 150 Israeli soldiers were wounded.

The PLO too suffered serious losses. Some 200 out of its total strength of 1,000 died. About 150 guerrillas were taken prisoners. Nonetheless, it was the first Palestinian or even Arab victory in a direct confrontation with Israel. The Israeli commander of the operation, Uzi Narkiss, had to resign. Arafat became a hero worldwide. TIME magazine carried his picture on its cover page. Thousands of Palestinians and other Arabs joined the PLO. Even Nasser's new-found affection for Arafat had a lot to do with the glory and publicity which the Palestinian guerrilla leader had earned at Al-Karameh. The fact is that, in February 1969, Nasser intervened personally to secure the PLO chairmanship for Arafat.

Jordan now began to fear the PLO. The majority of the Jordanian population was Palestinian and felt more loyal to the PLO than to the monarchy. King Hussein first tried to win over Arafat by inviting him to become his Prime Minister. Arafat publicly refused the offer, explaining that his mission was to establish a Palestinian State, according to the PLO charter. Hussein felt humiliated.

Then something very dramatic happened. Members of the Popular Front for the Liberation of Palestine (PFLP), a constituent of the PLO under the leadership of George Habash, successfully hijacked one TWA aircraft from Frankfurt to New York and two Swissair aircrafts leaving Zurich to some destination in the United States. They demanded the release of the Palestinian prisoners held in Israel, Germany and Switzerland. The PFLP tried but failed to hijack a fourth plane belonging to El-Al, Israel's national airline. One of the hijackers, a Nicaraguan, was killed and the second, a woman by the name of Leila Khaled, was overpowered. This was a flight from Amsterdam to New York. The flight was diverted to London's Heathrow airport, landing Leila Khaled into the hands of the British authorities.

On 8 September, PFLP men hijacked yet another British plane on its way from Bombay to Rome, diverting the plane with its 300 passengers to Beirut to demand the release of Leila Khaled. The hijackers had already demonstrated their resolve by blowing up one of the hijacked planes at Cairo, after releasing all the crew and all passengers. Two other airplanes were flown to a small military airstrip in Jordan.

Israel and the United States refused to negotiate the release of the hostages who were, mostly, British citizens. The British Government, under Edward Heath, carried out secret negotiations. The PFLP men showed flexibility by unconditionally releasing all women and children. But they blew up the two planes they were holding at a Jordanian military airstrip (Dawson's Field) on 12 September, to make it clear that the British must release Leila Khaled and get the Swiss and German Governments to free their own Palestinian detainees, if the remaining hostages were to survive. The British Government caved in and ordered the release of Leila Khaled on 13 September.

Israel was furious. King Hussein, already humiliated by Arafat, now feared a Syrian military intervention, which could result in the toppling of his regime and its replacement by a Palestinian State. He requested the UK and the US to pass on to Israel his plea to bomb the Syrian military if it tried to intervene. Assad, who anticipated yet another Arab disaster, decided to seize power in Damascus. In his view, the Arab cause could not survive yet another catastrophe—a war triggered by one Arab country and enabling Israel to destroy another Arab country.

This in short was the background to the confrontation between Jordan and the PLO. It started in September 1970. Golda Meir was then Prime Minister of Israel. She pressured Jordan to take on the PLO militarily. King Hussein, *who had long been nervous about the PLO presence and the threat it posed to his regime, gave in. After accepting secret military assistance from Israel, he declared Marshal Law on 16 September 1970. The Jordanian army attacked the PLO bases and offices. It carried out targeted massacres of Palestinians, with the objective of scaring the rest out of the country. Scores of thousands fled to Syria or Lebanon. It was a bloody affair, in which thousands of Palestinians perished.*[11]

*Nasser tried hard to end this Arab–Arab war. He convened an emergency meeting of the Arab League in Cairo on September 21, bringing Arafat and King Hussein head to head for a deal. Most Arab States condemned Jordan's brutal clamp-down. Muammar al-Ghaddafi of Libya was specially scathing in his criticism. But King Hussein was not prepared to stop the military campaign until the PLO and its sympathisers had left his country. Nasser could not bear to see the decimation of the PLO, and that too at the hands of a diminutive king ruling over an artificial country carved from Palestinian land with British help—a kinglet who was now taking his orders from Israel! The Cairo meeting lasted one full week. It ended on September 27, with the King and the PLO agreeing on a ceasefire. But Hussein insisted that the PLO and its sympathisers had to vacate all Jordanian cities and towns and henceforth confine their operations to the border areas.*

*Nasser died of a heart attack on 28 September 1970.*

*Despite the Cairo Agreement, battles between the Palestinians and the Jordanian forces raged on till July 1971. No one knows the exact numbers of casualties. Thousands of Palestinians died. Scores of thousands had to flee, mainly to Lebanon. The PLO also had to shift its bases to Lebanon.*

*A guerrilla group calling itself 'Black September' was born to avenge the massacre. It was credited with several high profile assassinations, including that of the Jordanian Prime Minister Wasfi al-Tal in Cairo on 28 November 1971. It was responsible for the killing of eleven Israeli athletes at the 1972 Summer Olympics in Munich.*[12]

*It was also in the wake of the Black September massacres that Sabri Khalil al-Banna, better known as Abu Nidal, broke away from the Fatah, to pursue his own path, vowed to even more radical violence. He was condemned to death in absentia by the PLO itself.*

*This, in a nutshell, was the fate of the Palestinians of Jordan in 1970: an exodus within an exodus, a tale of expulsion from a land that was rightfully theirs, perpetrated by a post-colonial regime, a papier-mâché monarchy, at the*

express request of the Zionist murderers and land-grabbers. These ⟨
a watershed in Palestinian destinies. They were, you might say, a le...
an after-tremor of the great quake. They did receive some cursory jo...
coverage at the time, for sure, but their real import, I am afraid, has com...
escaped the attention of historians outside the region.

Abu Husam, who as a youth had joined, not the Fatah, but the DF...
(Democratic Front for the Liberation of Palestine) founded by Naye...
Hawatmeh, made it clear that he was no admirer of Arafat and his leadership. He felt that from 1971 onwards Arafat became too compromising.
He was prepared to deal not only with corrupt, deceitful Arab leaders like
King Hussein himself—despite all he had done—but even with Israel, on
the premise of a so-called two-state solution. But what could a two-state
solution mean in practice, other than a powerless, moth-eaten Palestinian
state existing side by side with an Israel of unmatched military might
that would continue to treat its Palestinian citizens after the apartheid
rule book? According to Abu Husam, the real turning point was the
Egypt–Israel war, which Anwar al-Sadat launched in October 1973 and
half-won. The indecisive outcome of this 'Kippur war' opened the door
to negotiations—a process that culminated in the Camp David Accords
of March 1979 by which Egypt recognised Israel and established normal
diplomatic relations in return for the Sinai Peninsula, which Israel had
captured in 1967.

I wanted to know what explained this one example of successful diplomacy. What was it that made peace possible—a peace of sorts—between
Israel and Egypt, or should we say, between Israel and Egypt's rulers?

A number of factors, Abu Husam said, combined to make this happen.

*Firstly, even the early Zionists had nurtured some grudging affection for
Egypt, which came from the irrational sphere of the Zionist memory: all this
stuff about the Pharaoh letting Moses and his people go out of slavery and settle
in Canaan, today's Palestine, some 3,350 years ago.*[13]

*There were also strategic factors of more immediate relevance. Anwar [al-Sadat]
had been in touch with the Americans even before the Kippur War. [By telling]
shown unequivocally where he stood within the Cold War equation by [expelling]
all the Russian military advisors from Egypt. Kissinger quickly g[rasped that]
Sadat's strategic calculation behind his launching of a limited war [was to bring]
Israel to the negotiating table and force a return of the Sinai. In [the first phase]
of the war, Israel was caught off-guard and suffered a severe b[eating, leaving]*

ɔ00 of its soldiers on the battle-field. Some 300 Israeli soldiers
ed by the Egyptians and held as prisoners of war. Then the fact is
:l was not terribly interested in the Egyptian desert, except perhaps
ess to the Suez Canal or for gaining strategic depth.
ne 1967 war, in a way, had already fulfilled the Zionist dream of Eretz
ael—it had brought the occupation of the entire Judaea and Samaria, with
all the places of Biblical resonance like Hebron, Jericho, Anatot and Shiloh. It
had brought the Golan Heights, giving Israel exclusive control over the source
of the Jordan River, a boon it was not prepared to part with. Peace with Egypt
became possible, in short, partly because there were no real obstacles in the
way—but also because it weakened the Arab front and therefore enhanced the
Zionist prospects to perpetuate occupation.

We then went back to discussing the PLO and Arafat.

According to Abu Husam, immediately after the Kippur war, Arafat
began making subtle policy shifts with respect to Israel, which carried the
seeds of Oslo. To a clear-sighted observer, all the compromises to come
were already foreshadowed at the Seventh Arab Summit Conference in
Rabat, Morocco, which convened in October 1974. The conference established the PLO as the sole legitimate body of all Palestinians. It pressured
and cajoled Jordan into withdrawing its claims over the West Bank territories, which it had physically lost to Israel, and into recognising their
'Palestinian-ness'. In return, Jordan received a huge grant of more than
$300 million for four years. On the surface, it was a diplomatic triumph
for the PLO. In reality, the resolution adopted at the conference implied
a tacit acceptance of Israel as a State and the readiness to establish a
Palestinian national authority only over those territories 'that would get
liberated'. In practical terms, it could mean nothing more than the Gaza
strip and a severely indented West Bank. Arafat must have recognised the
implication and reconciled himself to the loss. Of course, at that time,
almost nobody would describe the outcome of the Rabat conference in
these terms. But some Marxist leaders like George Habash and Nayef
Hatmeh could see the trends.

sonally, Abu Husam had a grudging admiration for Arafat's achieve-
me⟩s a diplomat:

 naged to get himself invited to address the UN General Assembly
on 13 mber 1974. He delivered a powerful speech, where he said: 'I have
come t an olive branch and a freedom-fighter's gun. Do not let the olive

express request of the Zionist murderers and land-grabbers. These events marked a watershed in Palestinian destinies. They were, you might say, a lesser Nakba, an after-tremor of the great quake. They did receive some cursory journalistic coverage at the time, for sure, but their real import, I am afraid, has completely escaped the attention of historians outside the region.

Abu Husam, who as a youth had joined, not the Fatah, but the DFLP (Democratic Front for the Liberation of Palestine) founded by Nayef Hawatmeh, made it clear that he was no admirer of Arafat and his leadership. He felt that from 1971 onwards Arafat became too compromising. He was prepared to deal not only with corrupt, deceitful Arab leaders like King Hussein himself—despite all he had done—but even with Israel, on the premise of a so-called two-state solution. But what could a two-state solution mean in practice, other than a powerless, moth-eaten Palestinian state existing side by side with an Israel of unmatched military might that would continue to treat its Palestinian citizens after the apartheid rule book? According to Abu Husam, the real turning point was the Egypt–Israel war, which Anwar al-Sadat launched in October 1973 and half-won. The indecisive outcome of this 'Kippur war' opened the door to negotiations—a process that culminated in the Camp David Accords of March 1979 by which Egypt recognised Israel and established normal diplomatic relations in return for the Sinai Peninsula, which Israel had captured in 1967.

I wanted to know what explained this one example of successful diplomacy. What was it that made peace possible—a peace of sorts—between Israel and Egypt, or should we say, between Israel and Egypt's rulers?

A number of factors, Abu Husam said, combined to make this happen.

*Firstly, even the early Zionists had nurtured some grudging affection for Egypt, which came from the irrational sphere of the Zionist memory: all this stuff about the Pharaoh letting Moses and his people go out of slavery and settle in Canaan, today's Palestine, some 3,350 years ago.*[13]

*There were also strategic factors of more immediate relevance. Anwar Sadat had been in touch with the Americans even before the Kippur War. He had shown unequivocally where he stood within the Cold War equation by expelling all the Russian military advisors from Egypt. Kissinger quickly grasped that Sadat's strategic calculation behind his launching of a limited war was to bring Israel to the negotiating table and force a return of the Sinai. In the first phase of the war, Israel was caught off-guard and suffered a severe battering, leaving more than 2,500 of its soldiers on the battle-field. Some 300 Israeli soldiers were captured by the Egyptians and held as prisoners of war. Then the fact is that Israel was not terribly interested in the Egyptian desert, except perhaps for access to the Suez Canal or for gaining strategic depth.*

*The 1967 war, in a way, had already fulfilled the Zionist dream of Eretz Israel—it had brought the occupation of the entire Judaea and Samaria, with all the places of Biblical resonance like Hebron, Jericho, Anatot and Shiloh. It had brought the Golan Heights, giving Israel exclusive control over the source of the Jordan River, a boon it was not prepared to part with. Peace with Egypt became possible, in short, partly because there were no real obstacles in the way—but also because it weakened the Arab front and therefore enhanced the Zionist prospects to perpetuate occupation.*

We then went back to discussing the PLO and Arafat.

According to Abu Husam, immediately after the Kippur war, Arafat began making subtle policy shifts with respect to Israel, which carried the seeds of Oslo. To a clear-sighted observer, all the compromises to come were already foreshadowed at the Seventh Arab Summit Conference in Rabat, Morocco, which convened in October 1974. The conference established the PLO as the sole legitimate body of all Palestinians. It pressured and cajoled Jordan into withdrawing its claims over the West Bank territories, which it had physically lost to Israel, and into recognising their 'Palestinian-ness'. In return, Jordan received a huge grant of more than $300 million for four years. On the surface, it was a diplomatic triumph for the PLO. In reality, the resolution adopted at the conference implied a tacit acceptance of Israel as a State and the readiness to establish a Palestinian national authority only over those territories 'that would get liberated'. In practical terms, it could mean nothing more than the Gaza strip and a severely indented West Bank. Arafat must have recognised the implication and reconciled himself to the loss. Of course, at that time, almost nobody would describe the outcome of the Rabat conference in these terms. But some Marxist leaders like George Habash and Nayef Hawatmeh could see the trends.

Personally, Abu Husam had a grudging admiration for Arafat's achievements as a diplomat:

*He managed to get himself invited to address the UN General Assembly on 13 November 1974. He delivered a powerful speech, where he said: 'I have come bearing an olive branch and a freedom-fighter's gun. Do not let the olive* branch fall from my hand. I repeat: do not let the olive branch fall from my hand.'

As speeches go, this was a beautiful one: well-turned, politically uplifting and all. Arafat talked in passionate terms about the establishment of a single secular state for all people—Palestinian Muslims, Christians and Jews, but without hinting at the compromise that was implicit in the Rabat Resolution. Who knows, this omission may have been the reason why Israel thereafter continued to lambast him and his PLO. Anyway, some parts of the speech were really inspiring and are still worth remembering. Passages like these:

> If the immigration of Jews to Palestine had had as its objective the goal of enabling them to live side by side with us, enjoying the same rights and assuming the same duties, we would have opened our doors to them, as far as our homeland's capacity for absorption permitted. Such was the case with the thousands of Armenians and Circassians who still live among us in equality as brethren and citizens. But that the goal of this immigration should be to usurp our homeland, disperse our people, and turn us into second-class citizens—this is what no one can conceivably demand that we acquiesce in or submit to. Therefore, since its inception, our revolution has not been motivated by racial or religious factors. Its target has never been the Jew, as a person, but racist Zionism and undisguised aggression. In this sense, ours is also a revolution that may benefit the Jew as well, as a human being. We are struggling so that Jews, Christians and Muslims may live in equality, enjoying the same rights and assuming the same duties, free from racial or religious discrimination.

Arafat had something to say about terrorism, too:

> The difference between the revolutionary and the terrorist lies in the reason for which each fights. Whoever stands for a just cause and fights for the freedom and liberation of his land—be it liberation from invaders, settlers or colonialists—cannot possibly be called a terrorist. Otherwise the American people in their struggle for liberation from their British colonial masters would have been terrorists; the European resistance against the Nazis would have been terrorism; the struggle of the Asian, African and Latin American people would also be terrorism; and many of you who are in this Assembly hall were considered terrorists. Ours is actually a just and proper struggle, consecrated by the United Nations' Charter and by the Universal Declaration of Human Rights. As for those who fight against just causes, who wage war to occupy, colonise and oppress other people, they are the real terrorists....

Arafat also spelt out his dream of a Palestinian State, and what it would mean to the people of the land. He said:

*I proclaim before you that when we speak of our common hopes for the Palestine
of tomorrow we include in our perspective all those Jews, now living in Palestine,
who choose to live with us there in peace and without discrimination....We offer
them the most generous solution, that we might live together in a framework of
just peace in our democratic Palestine.*

Abu Husam marked a short pause, as if reminiscing with a hint of
melancholy, and continued.

*All well and good. But unfortunately the PLO and the coterie around Arafat
began to move away from this ideal. The disastrous developments in Lebanon
(made worse by Arafat's inability to get on with Damascus) merely accelerated
the drift.*

*At the beginning of the civil war in Lebanon, I personally moved to Algeria,
to earn my living there as a school teacher, while remaining active in the
Democratic Front for the Liberation of Palestine. Of course, after the Black
September purges in Jordan, most Fatah cadres and followers moved to Lebanon,
and so did the other resistance organisations farther to the left.*

*As I said, Arafat had his problems with Syria. Lebanon therefore was his
natural choice. Nasser also, with his grasp of geopolitics, encouraged Arafat to
move his base to Mount Hermon: from there, he could gradually take control
of the Shabaa valley bordering Syria, and establish strong positions in southern
Lebanon down to Hasbaya. The PLO camps later spread to the coastal areas,
up to Tripoli, where a large number of first-wave Palestinian refugees, I mean
1948 refugees, had already settled. Nasser, despite his frail health and dented
prestige after the1967 debacle, made all these arrangements on behalf of the
PLO. He pressured the Lebanese Government into conceding to all PLO members
the right to move into, and about, Lebanon; to carry their own weapons; and
even to launch attacks against Israel. No other Arab leader could have wrung
from the Maronite leadership that kind of space for the PLO.*

*Nasser may have been a peacock and a narcissist, but the outcome of the
1967 war made him realise that he had exhausted his life without achieving
all that much; that his days were numbered; and that, all things considered,
he would better serve the Arab cause by providing for a strong, independent Palestinian resistance than by hobnobbing with the Arab states, such
as they were. One last consideration probably tipped the scale in favour of
Lebanon as the main theatre of future Palestinian resistance: Nasser and
Arafat knew that Israel had long nurtured its own ambitions of controlling
Lebanon.*

In 1982, I gave up my teaching position in Algeria, leaving my family behind, and moved to Lebanon to fight the Israeli invasion. The PLO men picked me up at the airport and drove me to the Bekka valley—not to fight, but to engage in administrative work. Although I was disappointed to be denied active combat missions, mine was a unique vantage point: I saw a lot of what happened at first hand, and learnt even more at second hand, because I stayed on in the valley for a full eight years, till the middle of 1990. Thus, I witnessed the eviction of the PLO in 1983 and its relocation in Tunisia. I was also a witness to the rise in Lebanon of Amal and later of Hizbullah.

I came back to Damascus in the middle of 1990 and, since then, I have been leading the Palestinian campaign for the right of return. As a Marxist, I don't feel comfortable with some of the ideological positions of Hamas. As a Palestinian, however, I admire Hamas for breathing fresh life into our resistance; you might almost say, for resuscitating it. I do believe that the spirit of resistance, which Hamas currently upholds, will eventually prevail, even if not in my lifetime. I do believe that a secular, democratic state will eventually come about for all Palestinians alike—those who now live in Israel as second-class citizens, as vermin almost; those who vegetate in that archipelago of concentration camps known as the 'occupied territories'; and all the others who were uprooted in 1948 or 1967 or twice over, and who now pine far from home.

Adnan Abdul Rahim, also a Marxist, but with an existentialist streak, joined the Fatah mainly because he disapproved of the politicking and shilly-shallying of the Arab Communist parties, their unprincipled strategies and shifting alliances within the Arab states.

*After working for a while with the Front for the Liberation of Palestine, I soon left the Front, in 1968, to join the Fatah. But, in 1979, disillusion again caught up with me. I was getting weary of the Fatah and its ways. I couldn't stomach the corruption, this obsession with the pecking order, all these petty power hierarchies and petty turf wars which riddled the organisation, in Lebanon and outside. Arafat wanted me to go to New York as a PLO representative at its UN office. As a preparation, I picked up a scholarship to go to Budapest and do a PhD there. I stayed in Budapest for three years and then came back, only to get trapped in the horribly byzantine Fatah infighting, which eventually brought about the PLO's eviction from Lebanon.*

*There were other, external factors, to be sure: Israel, France and the United States were all pushing hard for Lebanon to eject the PLO. But that doesn't absolve us of all responsibility: the fact remains that the PLO was doing a first-class job of tearing itself apart. In this internal PLO revolt, I sided with the rebels, those who questioned Arafat's leadership. Why so? Well, for two reasons, I suppose. First, I couldn't close my eyes to the fact that our puffed-up Fatah leaders had taken to behaving more like ministers or heads of state than revolutionaries. They would stay in big cities, enjoy themselves, and get the new recruits to do all the fighting, bear all the brunt of Israeli retaliations. Then I joined the rebels also for the reason that Arafat, at the height of the Lebanese Civil War, had struck with Israel and America an agreement which enabled him and all his cadres to move unmolested, first to Algiers and then Tunisia—to 'tourist spots', far away from the raging conflict.*

*Personally, I had been close to one of the leaders of the rebel faction, one Abu Khalid. I believed in his personal integrity, his courage of conviction. I later discovered, to my mortification, that he was mixed up with the Syrian regime and that the rebellion itself was being partially funded and remote-controlled by Syria, to undermine the independence of the Palestinian resistance. As I said, I was thoroughly disappointed with the PLO leadership. I was sick and tired of watching the top echelons operating in comfort from Beirut, that tourist heaven, while Israel's iron fist was crushing the PLO operatives in the embattled south of the country. The commanders were either not there when it mattered or they escaped in time to avoid the death struggles. Later, in 1982, when Israel marched into Beirut to carry out its large-scale massacres of Palestinians—the high-points being Sabra and Shatila—our valiant leaders were nowhere to be found. They had escaped, all to a man. So you can understand why I sympathised with the rebellion. When I discovered that the rebels were themselves on Syria's payroll, that was the last drop.*

*So I ended my formal, political involvement with the PLO. I am still contributing my mite to its humanitarian activities—helping with educational facilities for the refugees; supporting the campaigns for the right of return; even, now and then, attending international conferences. Many of my personal friends have settled in Tunis, and so I went there to visit them a number of times. But I always came back to Syria, closest to my homeland. In Syria, I have had some contacts with the present torchbearers of the Palestinian cause, men like Khaled Mashal, and I am trying to keep abreast of the evolution of Palestinian resistance. But my own involvement, to be honest, has become peripheral.*

I felt privileged being able to have such a long exchange with these two elderly men, so laden with experience, so devoted to their cause and yet, after a lifetime of militancy, so nuanced in their judgments.

But I still felt intrigued by the Palestinian experience in Lebanon. Adnan himself had hinted that his family, after moving to Lebanon in 1948, felt so unwelcome there that it had to move to Syria. Then Abu Husam had just brought up the issue of Israel's long-held ambition of controlling Lebanon. I knew that the Lebanese Civil War had been precipitated by the massacre of a busload of Palestinian refugees, in April 1975, by a right-wing Maronite Christian group. Then came the two Israeli invasions, in 1978 and 1982, and the rout of the PLO. That much I knew, but the detailed sequence was still hazy to my mind. So I asked Abu Husam for a brief. He started by elaborating on Israel's old designs on Lebanon.

*On the eve of the 1948 war, Ben-Gurion had clinched a secret agreement with Lebanon. While pretending to join the Arab front against Israel, the Lebanese would discreetly assist the Zionist militias in their ethnic cleansing of Palestinian Muslims, especially in Galilee. The pact had been signed between Lebanon's dominant Maronite Christians and the Jewish Agency. Two decades on, when the PLO moved to Lebanon after the Black September purges in Jordan, Israel revived those contacts. Five years later, after invading south Lebanon up to the Litani River in March 1978, Israel began to impart military training to a fanatical Maronite militia, the so-called SLA (South Lebanese Army) led by one Saad Haddad. This was almost Ben-Gurion's vision come true: the old plan to physically control south Lebanon up to the Litani River and to install a pro-Israeli Maronite government in Beirut to hold the rest of the country. Israel came close to achieving these goals in 1983. And though eventually it failed, it proved once again how adept it was at using the endless complexities of Lebanese politics to snuff out the Palestinian resistance.*

*Lebanon's full-blown civil war started in April 1975, but it had been simmering for a long time. It had its roots in the popular discontent with the sectarian-based order introduced by the French, which allocated all wealth and power to a small minority of landlords and merchants belonging to the Maronite, Sunni and Shia elites. The so-called 'National Pact' of 1943, designed by the French, ensured that all key government positions went to the leading families of the three sects, with the Maronites getting the lion's share. Under the pact, the president of Lebanon had to be a Maronite Christian, the prime minister a Sunni, and the leader of parliament a Shia. The poorer segments of these sects were simply ignored. In the meantime, however, the country had seen the rise of an aspiring middle class which resented this cosy power-sharing arrangement. There was also a strong labour movement seeking socio-economic justice. The*

Shia population in the south became particularly restive. Then there came the Palestinian influx, especially after 1971, which injected a revolutionary ferment into the mix.

Israel was controlling the extreme right-wing Maronites.[14] It helped them set up well-equipped and well-trained armed outfits. In April 1975 one of these Christian militia massacred Palestinians. The idea was to excite popular resentment against the large influx of PLO cadres who were bringing with them the threat of Israeli retaliations against the country. Israel, in short, was after a repeat of Jordan; it wanted a Lebanese Black September.

It did not work out that way, probably because the Lebanese bedlam was too complex to be amenable to a clear polarisation of that kind. The Lebanese army itself broke up into factions. Syria staged a military intervention. Since, at first, it was intervening at the behest of the Maronite Christians, Israel did not mind. Later, after entering the Lebanese arena and getting its military presence endorsed at Arab League summits, Syria would change sides.

In March 1978, the Israelis launched their first military invasion of south Lebanon, right up to the Litani River, because they were fretting about the civil war which was not quite going their way. Thousands of Palestinians were killed in the course of the military operations. Then, under pressure from UNSC resolutions, Israel physically withdrew from the region, but only after handing over the place to the SLA militia (South Lebanese Army). The sheer brutality of the invasion and the subsequent atrocities committed by the SLA forces were to be the ferment out of which grew the first palpable mobilisation of the Shia community. It first assumed the form of Amal or Movement of the Deprived (literally, 'amal' is Arabic for 'hope') and later that of the rival Hizbullah ('God's Party').

Meanwhile, Israel wasn't relenting in its harassment of Palestinians. It used the SLA to attack them. It even took on the UN peacekeeping contingent stationed in the south when the latter interposed itself to protect the Palestinian camps. It pressed on with its lethal aerial attacks, killing thousands in the south, also in Beirut. It wanted to fray Lebanese nerves and bring the Lebanese, at long last, to expel the Palestinians. Israel also carried out terrorist attacks, such as massive car-bomb explosions, in the vicinity of Palestinian camps, right up to the middle of 1982. When none of these tactics helped, Israel decided to go the whole length. On 8 June 1982, it launched its military invasion of the entire Lebanon, south and north. The invasion brought the rout of the PLO and its expulsion from the country.

*The then US President Ronald Reagan sent Philip Habib to negotiate the PLO evacuation and Israeli withdrawal. Israel had prepared itself well. Bashir Gemayel, a pro-Israeli Maronite, had already been elected to the Presidency. The American diplomacy promised the deployment of a multinational force to supervise the evacuation of the PLO.*

*Fatefully for Israel, Bashir Gemayel was assassinated. Israel took revenge by organising large-scale massacres of Palestinians at Sabra and Shatila. The PLO, its cadres and Arafat himself duly left Lebanon's shores. But, in a deeper sense, the invasion misfired, because it brought about the birth of Hizbullah. As one of its first and most spectacular actions, Hizbullah carried out massive bombings against the American and French troops stationed in Lebanon. Demoralised, the multinational force withdrew from the country in February 1984.*

I wanted to hear Adnan's account of the Sabra and Shatila massacres, as well as his views about the wider issue of responsibility: how to bring to book not just the perpetrators of such atrocities but also the thread-pullers.

*Well, let me tell you about an American Jewish nurse, Ellen Siegel, who had volunteered to work with the Palestinian Red Crescent Society at the Palestinian refugee camps in Beirut. She came to Beirut in August 1982, immediately after the conclusion of the US-brokered deal about the PLO evacuation of Lebanon in exchange for Israel's undertaking to stop battering Palestinian inhabited areas. Ellen ended up working at a medical facility next to the Sabra refugee camp. She actually lived inside the facility. During the massacres, she was herself nearly killed by the Maronite militiamen, who had rounded up all the foreign medical personnel. They hated anyone who helped the Palestinians to the point of wanting to kill them. Ellen Siegel and her associates were saved in the nick of time by the intervention of senior Israeli officers who knew of, supervised and controlled every move and action of the Christian militia. Ellen Siegel later testified before a Commission of Inquiry which Israel, under the pressure of international and domestic clamour, had set up under Justice Yitzhak Kahan, President of the Israeli Supreme Court. Ellen gave a chilling eye-witness account of the coordination between the Israelis and the Christian militia during the massacres, which took place between 15 to 18 September. She fixed the responsibility squarely on Ariel Sharon, then Minister of Defence; on the Army Chief Rafael Eitan; on the Commander of the Northern Sector Amir Drori; and on the Division Commander General Amos Yaron. The Commission, which included General Yonah Efrat of the IDF (Israeli Defence Force), published its report in February 1983. The report raised doubts about the veracity of Ellen*

*Siegel's testimony by dwelling on her pro-Palestinian sympathies. Even so, the report concluded that Defence Minister Sharon was indirectly responsible for the massacres, in that he failed to anticipate the bloodshed likely to follow when he allowed the Christian militias into the Palestinian camps to 'mop up the PLO guerrillas'. I don't want to go into the gory details of the massacres, which lasted for 48 hours on end and took nearly 3,000 lives. If you are interested, you can read eyewitness accounts.*

I requested Adnan, who despite all his years in the Fatah was so critical of the PLO's poor showing in the face of the Israeli invasion, and scathing of the PLO's decision to move to Tunisia, to elaborate on the revolt which Arafat faced, and survived. How did it unfold; what were its consequences? Adnan brooded in silence for a while and then spoke in his slow, husky way:

*There was tension within the PLO from the days of the Rabat Resolution of October 1974, which called for the establishment of a Palestinian author-ity alongside Israel. The PLO had been founded on the rejection of the Zionist State. Now the resolution implied Israel's recognition! The Rabat conference had also, shockingly, invited King Hussein of Jordan to participate—the very man who, under pressure from Israel, had carried out the bloody purges of Black September. Arafat, every bit the diplomat, had acquiesced in his participation. That was hard to swallow. Black September, the PLO's subsequent move to Lebanon, and then the bloody civil war, these were among the most traumatic experiences of the long-suffering Palestinians. Then many felt that the bad blood between Arafat and Assad of Syria (Arafat's fault, basically) had contributed to the latter's decision to send his forces on behalf of the right-wing Maronite militias. Israel invaded Lebanon twice, in 1978 and 1982, and twice, under Arafat's gaze, the PLO forces collapsed. To cap it all, Arafat had accepted to vacate Lebanon even as, protected by the Israeli troops, mad Maronites were carrying out the Sabra and Shatila massacres. While the evacuation of the PLO forces was still in progress, Arafat went to Cairo and met with Sadat, the man who in 1977 had made his much-publicised trip to Jerusalem and who later opened up diplomatic relations with Israel. Little wonder, then, if rebellion against Arafat was brewing.*

*But the leaders of the rebellion weren't themselves above reproach. They were mostly military men who bore a measure of responsibility for the collapse of the PLO's resistance. Arafat took advantage of this and eventually succeeded in quelling the rebellion. But let us not rush ahead. The main leader of the rebels* was one Said Abu Musa, a former Colonel in the Jordanian army, who had received his military education at Sandhurst Military Academy in Britain. He had been the second in command of the PLO forces in Lebanon. Sympathising with him were a number of senior military officers, of diverse ideologies. There was Abu Khaled al-Umla, a Marxist I knew personally, who was close to Said Abu Musa. There was Ahmed Jibril, one of the founders of the PFLP (Popular Front for the Liberation of Palestine) and a former Syrian military intelligence officer. Then there was that key figure, Abu Nidal, also known as Sabri Banna, who was based in Damascus. And there were a handful of others. All of them accused Arafat and his coterie of corruption and capitulation. All of them received support and encouragement from Syria and, perhaps, for a while, also from Ghaddafi.

But Arafat had his charisma and no one could match him in persuasive rhetoric. He eventually prevailed and had the military lobby isolated, after months of internecine war, which resulted in hundreds of deaths. The antagonism between Assad and Arafat, who could not afford so many enemies, was probably a factor behind the latter's rapprochement with Jordan. Arafat also accepted, albeit clandestinely, the Reagan Plan which eventually led, in 1993, to the Oslo Accord between Israel and the PLO. This disappointing Oslo Accord, and its even more disappointing aftermath, rekindled the feelings of disenchantment with Arafat's politics of appeasement. But by then the PLO's rebellious spirit was spent and it was now Hamas, an offshoot of the Muslim Brotherhood, which took up the torch of resistance in the occupied territories of Gaza and the West Bank.

I requested Adnan to briefly recount the history of the Oslo process.

Arafat needed time to deal with the internal revolt. He wasn't firmly in control of the PLO until the middle of 1988. He then clinched a truce with Lebanon's Amal militia, which promised not to attack the PLO-run Palestinian camps. Arafat also had to deal with Jordan's claims over the West Bank. After a long and tortuous process of diplomacy, with many ups and downs (such as the expulsion of the PLO representatives from Jordan's capital Amman in February 1986) Jordan finally agreed, in the middle of 1988, to waive all its claims over the West Bank.

This was yet another 'triumph' for Arafat, but one he could not have achieved without help from the United States, and probably at a price.

Arafat was also very lucky in having Khalil Wazir, one of his ablest deputies, work as the PLO's liaison man in Jordan throughout these tricky negotiations. Khalil Wazir also headed the Fatah's Bureau for the Occupied Homeland. In this *capacity, he was responsible for work at the grass-root level inside the occupied territories, such as setting up local resistance units, social and professional associations, among other things. He launched a dynamic Youth Movement, the Harkat al-Shabibah, that took an active part in stirring up the first Intifada, which started in December 1987.*

*The Intifada began as a non-violent uprising and Israel all of a sudden found itself under tremendous international pressure to exercise restraint and open negotiations. But Arafat spoke and behaved as if he had personally fomented the Intifada. The uprising, in fact, had been largely spontaneous. Many grass-root organisations, including Hamas, had been involved. But Fatah had enough organisational strength to sustain its claim of being the prime mover. The fact is that Khalil Wazir, Fatah's man responsible for the Occupied Territories, was assassinated in Tunis, in April 1988, most probably by Mossad agents. Arafat was now ready for the next move.*

*On 15 November 1988, the Palestine National Council met in Algiers to announce the establishment of an independent Palestinian state. The announcement implied the PLO's acceptance of Israel and of its right to live in peace and security. Yasser Arafat also formally endorsed the American conditions that the PLO would enter negotiations with Israel to reach a political settlement on the basis of the UNSC resolution 242. That resolution called on Israel to withdraw its troops from the occupied territories and on the Palestinians to renounce terrorism. Ronald Reagan immediately authorised diplomatic contacts with the PLO.*

*In fact, these contacts had been going on in secret for a long time. The first significant US–PLO confabulations had been arranged by Saudi Arabia, in 1977, while Cyrus Vance was US Secretary of State. But the time was not ripe yet for Arafat to openly recognise Israel: it would have contradicted the PLO's foundational charter and could have led to his leadership being challenged.*

*Israel clearly knew of Arafat's ambiguities and probably took them into its strategic considerations, choosing to leave him alive even when it could have removed him from the scene as, for example, during the Lebanese invasion.[15] The patience—Arafat's and Israel's—paid off. Immediately after Reagan's authorisation, 150 UN member states greeted the announcement of the State of Palestine. In January 1989, the PLO received an invitation to address the Security Council, an invitation which normally comes only to member states.*

This, to my mind, was the real background to the Oslo process, which the PLO was able to join only after the Gulf War. At the same time, Arafat, in his unthinking blustering moods, was making small missteps, which worked to his disadvantage, like during the Kuwait crisis. The United States were then on a triumphant, seemingly unstoppable course: first in Afghanistan, where the Russians had to withdraw after eight years of inconclusive war, then in Iraq, where the US resolved to chastise Saddam Hussein for taking over Kuwait, its oil enclave. The First Gulf war destroyed Iraq's civil infrastructure and over the next decade brought untold hardships to its people, and an unquantifiable number of deaths through starvation and disease—but that, as Madeleine Albright would say, was by the by. Having displayed its lethal power, America now felt free to launch its peace initiative in the Middle East.

But at the time of Kuwait's invasion, Arafat came down in support of Saddam Hussein, and so the PLO was conspicuously excluded from the international peace conference, held in Madrid in October 1991. To snub Arafat and tell him what a dispensable quantity he was, the United States invited several Palestinians from the West Bank and the Gaza strip to attend the conference, but as members of the Jordanian delegation. This was to drive home the point that, if need be, the fate of the West Bank and Gaza could always be decided through confederal arrangements between Israel, Jordan and Egypt.

Yitzhak Shamir, the Likud hardliner and then Israeli Prime Minister, also attended the conference and lashed out as usual at 'Palestinian terrorism'. All in all, the 1991 Middle East Madrid summit redounded to a thorough humiliation for Arafat.

In June 1992, the Labour Party, led by Yitzhak Rabin, came to power in Israel. The foreign minister Shimon Peres and his deputy Yossi Beilin were strategic thinkers. They were taking a long-term view and wanted the PLO to come to a lasting deal with Israel. The Oslo process dragged on behind a shroud of secrecy, between the Israeli negotiators and PLO representatives handpicked by Arafat. They met surreptitiously for some fifteen rounds of talks, from January to September 1993. Abu Mazen and Abu Ala were then heading the PLO delegation.

Israel floated the idea of 'Gaza first'. Arafat should have rejected the proposal outright since the framework of the negotiations was supposed to be based on the UNSC Resolution 242 which called for Israel's withdrawal from all the territories seized in 1967. Arafat did not do that. He wanted the see the birth *of a Palestinian State, and himself at its head, before his death. So he astutely suggested 'Gaza and Jericho first'.*

*Israel's Labour Goverment sensed Arafat's desperation. The deal that finally emerged left much of the West Bank, including the Allenby Bridge that connects the West Bank to Jordan, under Israeli control. Yitzhak Rabin had been closely following the rise of Hamas in the occupied territories and was troubled by the spirit of intransigence and desperate dedication which the new movement disseminated. This growing fear of Hamas may have softened, ever so slightly, Israel's customary intransigence. Anyway, the deal that came to be known as the Oslo Accord was signed on 13 September 1993, on the Lawns of the White House, concluding with the famous handshake between Rabin and Arafat.*

*It was not much of an accord, not even a settlement. It was more a statement of principles, a basis for further negotiations. It provided for some interim governance arrangements. Arafat was taking responsibility for policing Gaza and Jericho and preventing anti-Israeli violence. Israel retained sovereign authority over defence and foreign affairs. The interim Palestinian Authority was to be responsible for health, education and social welfare at the municipal level. The declaration also proposed municipal elections in the Gaza strip and West Bank, to set up a democratically elected (rather than appointed) Palestinian Council. The accord did not specify the final political status of the territories—that was left to 'further negotiations'. It said nothing about the right of return of the three waves of Palestinians refugees, or the eventual borders of the future Palestinian State, or the fate of the Zionist colonies in the West Bank and Gaza strip. It did not even clarify whether the Gaza strip together with the West Bank would constitute an independent Palestinian State, or would fit into some form of confederal arrangement linking Israel, Jordan and Egypt.*

*The Oslo Accord, as signed on 13 September 1993 by Mahmoud Abbas, alias Abu Mazen, was very clear on one point, though: the PLO, under Arafat, offered Israel political recognition and undertook to protect it against Palestinian violence. In return, the Israelis were promising to keep up the dialogue, but without any specified framework. The accord also stipulated a five-year transitional period for the PLO to prove its capacity to govern and enforce law and order. Thus, while Israel was recognising the PLO as the 'sole legitimate representative' of the Palestinian people (according to the Arab League's charter of 1974), the declaration was couched in such vague and conditional terms that it amounted to a delegitimisation of the Palestinians' resistance project.*

*Inevitably, the compromise provoked strong opposition, from expected but also less expected quarters. Radical Palestinian groups were loudest in their rejection: the PFLP of George Habash; the DFLP of Nayef Hawatmeh; and, of course, Hamas and Islamic Jihad. But even liberal elements within the PLO and independent Palestinian intellectuals like Farouk Kaddoumi (the PLO's foreign minister), Edward Said (the famous US-based academic) and Mahmoud Darwish were critical. Kaddoumi pointed out that the accord was a double let-down: it betrayed the collective Palestinian aspiration to statehood and the right of return of the exiles—all those who had been uprooted in wave after wave of expulsions. But it was Edward Said who hit the nail on the head when he said that all secret deals between a very powerful and a very feeble adversary always led, step by step, to a capitulation of the weak partner, to a shameful surrender of his basic principles, which no amount of vain rhetoric could paper over. Arafat was indeed full of bloated rhetoric and vain projections about the looming 'final settlement' and 'general Israeli withdrawal' from all occupied territories, including Jerusalem.*

*The Israeli Defence establishment had no intention of implementing even the limited transfer of authority to the PLO, in Gaza and Jericho, which the Oslo declaration had promised. Ehud Barak, then chief of the Israel Defence Force (IDF), openly said that too much had been conceded to the PLO and that the security implications of those concessions, once understood, would prevent their implementation. The prophecy became self-fulfilling. The IDF found reasons galore for not withdrawing its forces. But it insisted that the Palestinians police, check, and punish all acts of violence. The Israeli forces remained deployed on strategic roads, in all border areas, in all 'restive' Palestinian settlements, and around all Zionist settlements. The derisory character of the Palestinian self-rule was illustrated by the fact that only in May 1994 was the first group of 30 Palestinian policemen allowed to enter the Gaza strip, but from Egypt, and only to assist the Israelis in maintaining order. Israeli military laws and regulations were to prevail, except when modified by mutual agreement. Failing such agreement, it was Israeli, not international, law that applied.*

Adnan stopped talking and held my gaze for several seconds, his small, sharp eyes set in deep pouches. I asked him what he was thinking of. He stayed silent for some more seconds, and then asked me if I had heard of the Hebron incident of February 1994. I had, but wanted to hear his relation of it. He began:

*There was a massacre of Palestinians in Hebron, a Biblical town inside the West Bank. It took place on 24 February, an important day in the religious calendars of both Muslims and Jews. For the Muslims, it was a Ramadan day of prayer and fasting. For the Jews, it was Purim, a major religious festival. The massacre was carried out by one Baruch Goldstein, an American-born Jew and medical doctor by training. The scene was the historic mosque dedicated to Ibrahim the Patriarch, revered by both Jews and Muslims. Recall that all Arab Muslims look up to Ismael, Ibrahim's elder son, as their first ancestor. According to tradition, or legend, Ibrahim was of course the Jewish proto-patriarch, the progenitor of the race. Jews and Muslims assume that he lived at the site where the Ibrahimi mosque now stands, and that his remains were buried there, and later those of his son Isaac and grandson Jacob (Yakub). So Baruch Goldstein entered the mosque—the Tomb of the Patriarchs for the Jews—dressed in an Israeli military uniform and armed with an assault rifle and two magazines of 30 shots each, which he proceeded to empty into a praying congregation of more than 800 worshippers. He didn't stop until he was lynched to death by the survivors. Twenty nine died and more than 150 were injured.*

*Baruch Goldstein hadn't chosen this day of 24 February arbitrarily. The origins of the Jewish festival of Purim can be traced back to ancient Persia. The book of Esther, of the Hebrew Bible, narrates how the young Jewish beauty Esther, Queen of the Persian King Ahasuerus (who didn't suspect her Jewish descent) and her cousin Mordechai saved their people from an impending massacre. The King's evil counsellor Haman orchestrates cunningly to massacre all the Jews of Persia. But at the end of the episode it is Haman himself, with his ten sons and 500 of his Jew-hating followers who are hung. Here is how the Book of Esther 9–5 relates the edifying story: 'The Jews smote all their enemies with the sword, slaughtering and destroying them, and did as they pleased to those who hated them.' Before carrying out the massacre Baruch Goldstein greeted the congregation with 'Happy Purim'. His funeral was attended by a large number of Orthodox Jewish settlers who hailed him as a righteous martyr.*[16]

*The Hebron massacre led to angry exchanges between Arafat and Rabin, and resulted in the establishment of the* Temporary International Presence (TIPH) in the City of Hebron, with military personnel from Italy, Denmark and Norway, *to provide security to the local Palestinians. Several auxiliary agreements followed, like the one signed by Yitzhak Rabin and Yasser Arafat in May 1994, which spelt out a framework for the extension of Palestinian self-government to the rest of the West Bank. Finally, there came the* Interim Agreement on the West Bank and Gaza Strip, *signed in Washington on 28 September 1995 by Rabin and Arafat in the presence of Bill Clinton, Hosni Mubarak of Egypt and King Hussein of Jordan. The agreement promised the transfer of legislative authority to a Palestinian Council, following general elections, and the withdrawal of Israeli troops from the Palestinian zones designated as Area A; the simple transfer of civilian authority in Area B, with continued Israeli military presence to supervise security; and the retention of the Israeli control, both civil and military, in Area C, which included the vicinity of Jewish settlements and borders areas.[17] The agreement also promised a united Jerusalem and implicitly required the demilitarisation of Palestine. Binyamin Netanyahu, the hardline Likud leader denounced Yitzhak Rabin as a contemptible appeaser in the Neville Chamberlain mould.[18] Rabin's effigy, in SS uniform, was publicly burnt. The Interim Agreement, also known as Oslo II, was denounced as a surrender to evil and a national humiliation. Eventually, Rabin was assassinated by a Zionist fanatic, on 4 November 1995, at a public function attended by more than 100,000 people, five weeks after signing the agreement.*

I interrupted Adnan to ask if he knew who murdered Rabin and how the people of Israel reacted.

*The name of Rabin's murderer is Yigal Amir. He had worked for the Israeli security establishment. He is an educated man, who has thousands of fervent admirers throughout Israel, who worship him as something between hero and saint. There are reports that senior officers responsible for Rabin's security had helped Yigal Amir. This is also what his wife, Larissa Trembovler, believes. Speaking of Larissa Trembovler: she is a biologist from Moscow, who made her aliyah to Israel in 1989 and went on to do a PhD in Jewish and Arab philosophy. Then she met with Yigal Amir in jail and managed to marry him after divorcing her husband with whom she had four children. Larissa's infatuation with Yigal Amir speaks volumes about the depths of approval for his act, even in enlightened Zionist circles.*

I asked what happened after the assassination. Did the Labour Party benefit from a wave of popular sympathy for an old Zionist leader who had died attempting to bring peace to the land?

*If there was any sympathy for Rabin, it did not show in the election outcome.[19] The opposition Likud, led by Binyamin Netanyahu, trounced Labour at the polls and formed the next government in May 1996. By then the Oslo agreements were as good as dead. They could not be revived even after Ehud Barak and his Labour Party won the next elections, in May 1999. The Jewish* settlements kept expanding in the West Bank. Arrests and curfews continued unabated. So did the confiscation of Arab lands to make room for Zionist settlements. And so did the pauperisation of the Gaza strip. Barak's long-standing opposition to the Oslo agreements was well-known. He was more interested in reaching a deal with Syria, which he took seriously as a military power. But Hafiz al-Assad was unbending. Under pressure from Bill Clinton, Barak signed an agreement with Arafat in September 1999, for the implementation of an earlier, unimplemented accord that had been signed under Netanyahu, again under American pressure. The agreement proposed the usual stuff: a new timetable for interim measures, a framework agreement by February 2000 and a final peace treaty by September 2000. By the time President Bill Clinton hosted his trilateral summit at Camp David, in July 2000, with Arafat and Barak, the latter had lost his parliamentary majority, three of his coalition partners having quit the government in protest against his readiness to meet with Arafat.

At Camp David, Barak wanted Arafat to agree to the annexation by Israel of all Jewish settlements in the West Bank, approximately 25 per cent of the land. He also wanted military control over the Jordan valley. On Jerusalem, he offered a partition of the city with Israeli control over Haram al-Sharif which the Jews call the Temple Mount. On the right of return, he would not offer anything more than family reunification, after official scrutiny, not exceeding 500 people a year, and only in the Gaza strip and West Bank areas under Palestinian control. Barak also insisted that the settlement would be final: once accepted, there would be no scope for further claims against Israel.

There was no way Arafat could have accepted Barak's proposals. So Camp David failed, with both Barak and Clinton blaming the failure on Arafat's intransigence.[20] The rest is history.

On 28 September 2000, Ariel Sharon, the Likud leader and Sabra-and-Shatila hero, made a much publicised pilgrimage to the Al-Aqsa mosque, ambling and preening himself around al-Haram al-Sharif, which the Muslims revere as their third holiest shrine, with a retinue of thousands of followers and hundreds of security personnel. This was a deliberate provocation, calculated to spark off Palestinian protests, which Israel could then use to re-occupy the land that had been conceded to the Palestinian Authority. This is exactly what happened. Riots erupted. The Israeli military retaliated ruthlessly, and the second Intifada took off, dovetailing into a wave of violence and suicide attacks of unprecedented intensity.

I requested Adnan and Abu Husam to tell me a little about Hamas, its origins, and the reasons for its current success.

*Hamas, like its rival twin, the even more radical* Palestinian Islamic Jihad *(or PIJ, founded by Fathi Shaqaqi and Abd al-Aziz Awda) gained popularity in the 1980s. It takes its inspiration from the* Muslim Brotherhood, *which had already contributed so decisively to Fatah's initial success by building grass-root networks in Gaza and the West Bank. Hamas was officially founded in December 1987, soon after the eruption of the first Intifada. It looks up to the founding fathers of the Muslim Brotherhood, pious and scholarly men who had also their steely side: they believed that there could be no restoration of Arab dignity without a spirited opposition to foreign rule, colonial or neocolonial, and the cultivation of democracy at home. The oldest such figure is the Egyptian Hassan al-Banna, who founded the Brotherhood in 1928 and was assassinated on orders from King Farouk in February 1949. Then there was Sayyid Qutb, the Egyptian philosopher of Islamic resistance, who was executed in Egypt in August 1966, under Nasser. A third Hamas hero is Sheikh Izzedin al-Qassam, a Syrian preacher who died in Palestine, in the 1930s, while resisting the colonial administration and the Zionist expansion. The name Hamas, incidentally, is an acronym that can be rendered as 'Islamic Resistance Movement'.*

*Hamas might never have emerged as a serious threat to Israel had not the latter, rather foolishly, made a practice of exiling local Palestinian protesters in Gaza and the West Bank, from the early 1980s onwards, to southern Lebanon. Fathi al-Shaqaqi, a co-founder of Islamic Jihad, was one of these early deportees who used their time in exile to understand the rise of Hizbullah and drew lessons from it. As late as December 1992, the Israeli Government, then under Yitzhak Rabin, deported 415 Palestinians to Southern Lebanon, following an attack on the Israel security forces that had claimed five lives. Unbeknownst to Israel, all deportees were Hamas members. By the time the Al-Aqsa Intifada started in September 2000, all of them had managed to re-enter the occupied territories (the Oslo Accord enabled them to do so). But they had learnt a lot from the Hizbullah model. Indeed, back in the early 1980s, Hizbullah had perfected its tactics of devastating bombings, which it used to great effect, to demoralise and ultimately evict the multinational contingents and later the Israeli occupying forces.*

*In collaboration with Islamic Jihad, Hamas began to use suicide bombings on a regular basis, in retaliation to Israeli outrages. For example, Hamas used the tactic to avenge the Hebron massacre in February 1994 and later the assassination of one of its leaders, Yahya Ayyash, in January 1996. The second Intifada saw a dramatic escalation in suicide bombings, from twenty-eight in the 1993–2000 period to 125 between October 2000 and September 2004. This was Hamas' way of trying to achieve a balance of terror within the conditions of asymmetric warfare imposed by Israel. All along, Hamas maintained its position that if Israel stopped killing Palestinian civilians, it would reciprocate by ceasing its attacks on Israeli civilian targets. This is the militant face of Hamas.*

*Hamas also has a democratic face, which the world noticed for the first time when it won the 2006 elections, clearly defeating the PLO candidates. Hamas' success had much to do with its consistent positions on Palestinian rights, including the right of return, but it had even more to do with its long record of grass-root work and its dedication to the principles of social justice. For years, Hamas had been helping the impoverished and the needy, discouraging the tendency towards hoarding and capital accumulation in favour of egalitarian growth. All this may have a Marxist or socialist ring to it, but in Hamas' case the inspiration lies elsewhere: namely, in a unique understanding of a certain strand of Islam and Islamic political tradition. While the PLO leaders were playing high table politics, Hamas was concentrating on building its networks in mosques, schools and colleges, village councils and municipalities, setting up charities and social work institutions. Sensing competition, the Fatah cadres tried to take on the Hamas workers—not by vying with them in grass-root work, but by relying on their superior weaponry and the support of the Israeli armed forces and intelligence.*

I asked, the poll victory aside, what were we to make of Hamas' decision to contest the 2006 elections, which took place within the framework of the Gaza–Jericho accord, which in turn accepts Israel as a State and breathes not a word of the right of return. Does that not contradict Hamas' vocal rejection of the Oslo process?

*Yes, there is a contradiction, which was thoroughly debated by the Hamas leadership, with strong views for and against contesting. I guess there was a slim majority opposed to the participation. But then the top leadership, especially Sheikh Ahmed Yassin, one of Hamas' founding fathers, stepped in and tipped the scales in favour of participation, arguing that the advocates of radical resistance couldn't afford to be absent from the nascent Palestinian institutions, leaving the field wholly to the other party.*

*Sheikh Ahmed Yassin, a pious Islamic scholar in his late 60s, was an invalid on a wheel chair (he was a quadraplegic) when Israel mounted a helicopter attack, over the exit of a Gaza mosque where he had been leading a prayer meeting on 22 March 2004, killing him along with nine other members of the congregation. Yassin had just been mooting the idea of a prolonged truce if Israel was prepared to stop its attacks on Palestinian civilians. He had also been pleading for an end to the fratricidal war between Fatah and Hamas.*

*Abdul Aziz al-Rantisi succeeded Sheikh Yassin as Hamas leader, and as the next Israeli target. Originally a refugee from a village close to Jaffa, he had studied medicine in Cairo and returned to Gaza to set up a paediatric clinic. He was one of the batch of 415 Palestinians whom Israel deported to South Lebanon in 1992. After returning to Gaza in 1993, he was re-arrested by Israel and jailed for the next four years. After his release, he was soon re-arrested, this time by the Palestinian Authority. While in his PLO jail, he came under an Israeli airforce attack that aimed to kill him. He survived the attempt and came out of jail, only to escape another Israeli assassination attempt in June 2003, which claimed the life of his bodyguard and some common Palestinians. Al-Rantisi was finally killed within one month of his assuming the Hamas leadership, in April 2004. He was succeeded by Mahmud al-Zahar, yet another physician. Al-Zahar had already suffered a number of assassination attempts, losing his 30-year-old son in September 2003, when an Israeli F16 bomber targeted his modest residence in Gaza, killing several residents of the neighbourhood. He and his daughter were injured, but survived the attempt. The current Hamas leader is Ismail Haniya, who doubles up as Prime Minister in the Hamas-led Government of Gaza.*

*All these Hamas leaders, and others who have not been assassinated yet, are ordinary Palestinians expelled from their land. Either born or brought up in refugee camps, they know, at first hand, the ordeals of life under occupation. And they are determined to resist the occupier come what may.*

I asked Adnan and Abu Husam one last question: how do they, with their Marxist background and worldview, relate to Hamas, whose outlook is grounded in a variant of Islam, that of the Muslim Brotherhood? Both remained silent for a while before Abu Husam responded:

*We cannot but sympathise with any group that keeps up the flame of resistance against Israel and its occupation of Palestine, especially after the bankruptcy of the socialist old guard and the treason of the pseudo-nationalists, who have traded their principles for a plate of lentils: limited, meaningless power, spiced with material corruption and moral turpitude. I, for one, confess that I still find myself unable to talk with the Hamas leadership because our political languages are so different. However, as a Palestinian determined to recover my right of return, I feel more in sympathy with the Hamas leadership than with many of my earlier Marxist comrades in the PFLP (Popular Front for the Liberation of Palestine) or DFLP (Democratic Front for the Liberation of Palestine), or with my personal friends in the Fatah and PLO. Still, friends are friends, and we still meet, now and then, in the coffee houses of Damascus and Beirut, to talk about the good old days. As to the future, well I am at least grateful for Hamas to have re-opened the doors of hope, after the PLO had shut them close, leaving all Palestinians at the dead-end of capitulation.*

The discussion which I have tried to summarise here took place over three long night sessions, from 7 pm to the early morning hours, in the month of Ramadan according to the Muslim calendar, in the month of September according to ours. On the last day of my stay in Damascus, I went out with Adnan for an early morning meal, which we fraternally enjoyed.

I then returned to Beirut to meet with a number of social activists, media men and academics whose names had been recommended to me and from whom I expected a better understanding of the Hizbullah phenomenon.

# Notes

1. Michael Ben-Zohar, *David Ben-Gurion: A Biography* (New York: Delacort, 1978).
2. Published by Cambridge University Press, New York in 1988.
3. Published by OUP, Oxford in 1990.
4. Benny Morris, *The Birth of the Palestinian Refugee Problem, 1947–49* (Cambridge University Press, 1988), p.181.
5. In May 2008, Finkelstein was refused entry into Israel on the ground that he was in touch with "'elements hostile to Israel'".
6. Once the 'scandal' over his first books had served its purpose and earned him name recognition, Morris slowly reverted to form. The metamorphosis is now complete: he has repudiated his earlier liberal stance and espoused extreme rightist views. E.N.
7. Pappé was born in Haifa to Jewish parents from Germany who had managed to immigrate to Palestine in the early 1930s.

8. Al-Malik al-Zahir Rukn al-Din Baybars al-Bunduqdari, popularly known as Baibars.

9. He led the First Battalion of the Irish Guards and was responsible for liaising with the Haganah.

10. He had served as Egypt's Prime Minister twice under king Farouk, from June 1930 to September 1933 and again from February 1946 to December 1946.

11. According to contemporary witnesses (like American journalist Kay Bird, who watched the events at close quarters) not all Israeli schemers and plotters were rooting for King Hussein and yearning for his army to crush the Palestinians. Some, possibly more far-sighted, wished for the opposite outcome, which in their view would have resulted in the creation of a Palestinian state, with a solid Palestinian majority and a manageable Bedouin minority, on Jordan's territory (to which bits of the West Bank might have been aggregated), thus 'solving' or at least defusing the refugee problem. On the anecdotal side, Kay Bird quotes (or makes up?) a diplomatic cable supposedly sent from Amman to Washington after the Black September massacres: "The PLO is dead, wiped out, and finished as an effective fighting force. But I have to remind Washington that this part of the world has been the scene of at least one resurrection." *E.N.*

12. The Black September commando actually wanted to use the Israeli hostages to force the liberation of scores of Palestinians held in Israeli jails. According to veteran Israeli peace activist Uri Avnery, the 11 athletes were killed during the bungled rescue operation by the German police, in the cross-fire, and probably by stray German bullets. Avnery bases his claim on a confidential German report, which was never released to avoid embarrassment, but whose contents, or so he claims, are no secret to the conoscenti. *E.N.*

13. This is a most bizarre take! There is no affection at all in the Bible for Egypt (unlike there is, for example, for Persia) or that particular Pharaoh: they are clear figures of evil, in the Bible and in the whole Talmudic tradition (in the biblical narrative, the Pharaoh didn't "'let the Hebrew go'"; he was forced to, after a severe battering—the seven plagues). But the Sinai episode is remarkable for other reasons. The Israelis might have been interested in the oil there, as an insurance against future blockades. Or they might have kept the peninsula long enough to pump all the oil before withdrawing. So here at least we have an occasion where oil didn't trump all other considerations. The fact of the matter is that the Israelis always had very precise and limited territorial ambitions. They were very clear about what they coveted, and the Sinai just wasn't part of that. Unfortunately, the West Bank was and is, with a special fixation on places like Jericho, Hebron, and of course Jerusalem. *E.N.*

14. Actually, percipient authors on Lebanese affairs are convinced that in this Gemayel–Begin alliance, the rather naive Begin was largely nose-led by

Gemayel. Lebanon's politics are extremely murky, and so are Israel's for that matter, but manipulation is seldom a purely one-way affair. *E.N.*

15. The claim is very dubious. In fact, Israel repeatedly tried to liquidate Arafat. Thus, in 1982, acting on inaccurate intelligence that Arafat found himself in a certain high-rise building in Beirut, the Israeli air force bombed it to rubbles. In all, Arafat survived a dozen attempts on his life, mostly from Mossad. While in Tunis, he lived almost permanently in a (grounded) plane to ward off assassination plots—from other Palestinian factions, but mostly from the Israelis. Regarding his death in November 1982, from an unclear medical condition, Uri Avnery has repeatedly voiced his conviction (which he admits is unsupported by direct evidence) that Arafat was poisoned by Mossad, possibly with American assistance. *E.N.*

16. They erected a mausoleum around Goldstein's tomb, which became a site of pilgrimage for the ultra-orthodox, until the Israeli authorities got it bulldozed, in 1999, for decency's sake. Rabbi Yaacov Perin, who eulogised Baruch Goldstein at his well-attended funeral, said inter alia: 'One million Arabs are not worth a Jewish fingernail.' Unhinged types can be found in all communities, but the significant point here is that the Rabbi could say this before an audience of thousands, and was allowed to proceed unhampered. *E.N.*

17. Here is how Uri Avnery, the doyen Israeli peace activist, describes the three areas A, B, C:

> Area A, which was turned over to the Palestinian Authority, is a zone which the Israeli army invades only from time to time. Area B is governed formally by the Palestinian Authority, but ruled in practice by Israel. Area C, the largest one, remains firmly in the hands of Israel, which acts there as it wishes: expropriates land, sets up settlements, builds walls and fences, as well as roads for Jews only. *E.N.*

18. Neville Chamberlain was the British Prime Minister who signed the Munich agreement with Adolf Hitler in 1938. His name has become a by-word for the cowardly appeasement of adversaries who, by their very nature, cannot be appeased. *E.N.*

19. Throughout the short campaign, Labour's Shimon Peres, as caretaker Prime Minister, vied with Netanyahu in war-mongering (bombing south-Lebanon, appearing on TV in military fatigues, etcetera) to boost his prospects at the polls. In disgust, Arab Israeli voters (who might have tipped the scales) and moderate Israelis massively abstained. *E.N.*

20. Tellingly, this version of events went almost unchallenged in the mainstream Western media. *E.N.*

# 5

## *The Hizbullah model:*
## *Militant tactics and political savvy*

A small country of West Asia on the eastern coast of the Mediterranean, Lebanon holds a territory of 10,452 square kilometres and is home to an estimated 4 million people. The area was the cradle of one of the earth's most ancient cultures, the trading civilisation of the Phoenicians (from circa 2300 BC to 539 BC). Modern Lebanon, surrounded as it is by Israel to the south and Syria to the north, has remained trapped in the wars of the Middle East ever since its creation. This patchwork of a country seems to be able to live with war and in war, with others and with itself. Its population is so divided into religious communities, sects and sub-sects—not counting an estimated 350,000 migrants and refugees, mainly from Palestine, with all their factions—that its internal power struggles and the hegemonic designs of its neighbours combine to form an almost inextricable nexus of intrigue, violence and treachery, which somehow doesn't seem to detract from the vitality, even vibrancy, of Lebanese life.

The Lebanese Civil War alone, which began in 1975, lasted fifteen years and nearly tore the country apart, is estimated to have killed about 150,000 people and wounded another 200,000. It formally ended in October 1989, with a constitutional accord finalised at Taif (a mountain resort in Saudi Arabia's Mecca Province) that promised the establishment of a genuinely democratic system of governance, but introduced none of the changes that could have made it possible. So the strife continued and the civil war merely switched to low-intensity mode.

There was nothing low-intensity, though, about the Israeli bombardments of July 2006. The Israeli air-force carried out nearly 1,000 air strikes over Lebanon, raining down nearly 5 million cluster bombs and destroying what it could of Lebanon's civilian infrastructure, including Beirut's airport. Israel was 'retaliating' against the kidnapping of two Israeli soldiers, across Lebanon's southern border, which Hizbullah militants had carried out to seek the return of Lebanese prisoners held by Israel. The war ended—if that's the word—in August 2006 with UN Security Council resolution 1701.

In reality, the wars, all the parallel wars, continue, not only between Hizbullah and Israel, but also between various Lebanese factions. Targeted assassinations are still high in favour with all actors, local and foreign. One of their most conspicuous victims was Prime Minister Rafiq Hariri, a billionaire politician close to Saudi Arabia and a darling of Western capitalist interests. He was killed on 14 February 2005 in Beirut when a huge quantity of explosives were detonated by remote control as his motorcade drove by.

The Christian population has long constituted a slim majority but it is an open secret that it no longer does. In the image of Lebanon itself, it is both fractured and fractious, being divided into Armenian Catholic, Armenian Orthodox, Assyrian Coptic, Chaldean, Greek Orthodox, Maronite Catholic, Melkite Catholic, Protestant, Roman Catholic, Syrian Catholic, and Syrian Orthodox groups. Each community—none more so than the Maronites—is itself fraction-ridden. The Muslim population presents the usual Sunni–Shia divide, the Sunni being in a minority, but socially dominant. Then, there are the Druze.[1]

There are no official figures for the numerical strength of the different sects, because Lebanon has not had an official census since 1932. The reason for the reluctance of the Maronite-dominated Government to hold a census is of course its fear that a census would disprove the official fiction about the Maronites (or even the Christians) being a majority, and result in a loss of privilege within a system of confessional power distribution foisted on the country by the French and based on balances and quotas—some explicit, others implicit. One such rule—no less binding for being unwritten—is that the President of the country must be a

Maronite Christian (with a majority of senior governmental positions also going to Maronites); the Prime Minister a Sunni; and the Speaker of Parliament a Shia. The system claims to ensure a fair representation of Lebanon's eighteen recognised socio-religious communities, but it rests on no serious demographic data.

Lebanon long grappled with a constitutional crisis after October 2007 when the presidential term of Emile Lahoud expired. Lahoud, of course, is a Maronite but—such are the niceties of Lebanese politics—a pro-Syrian one. So the pro-Syrian faction insisted on a constitutional amendment to extend his term, which the pro-Hariri coalition, backed by the United States and France, vehemently opposed. As a result, Lebanon remained without a legitimate president for about six months. In May 2008, member countries of the Arab League, led by Qatar. brokered a deal to get a consensual figure, Michel Suleiman, elected as president. The general elections, slated for June 2009, will pit the pro-western alliance led by Rafiq Hariri's son Saad Hariri against the radical alliance.[2] Hizbullah stands for a comprehensive resistance to 'imperialist hegemony' and the 'US–Israeli project' in the region. The alliance led by Saad Hariri stands for free market economy, a non-aggression pact with Israel, and the disarming of Hizbullah.

Soon after reaching Beirut, I contacted Dr Fawwaz Traboulsi, Associate Professor of History and Politics at the Lebanese American University. A well-known Marxist scholar and author, Traboulsi also writes weekly columns for the influential newspaper *As-Safir*. He agreed to see me at a coffee shop on Hamra, a fashionable street in downtown Western Beirut, not far from the hotel where I was staying. Before meeting with Hizbullah sympathisers and Hizbullah militants, I was keen to gain a sect-neutral perspective on Lebanese politics. Here is the gist of Traboulsi's elaborations, as recreated from the notes I took down during our two discussions.

I wanted to hear his views on the sectarian divisions that bedevil Lebanese politics and interfere with the usual polarisation between haves and have-nots. Traboulsi held forth at length about the historical origins of sectarian divisions, but suddenly paused to look at me, even as I was frantically taking notes. He asked me to write down a short anecdote called 'enemy brothers', which appears in a chronicle on Lebanon written in 1860, under the Ottoman rule, by Iskander ibn Yaqub Abkariyus. Traboulsi used the anecdote as a parable for the exacerbation of sectarian strife under foreign influence. The anecdote, as I later found out, also features in Traboulsi's *History of Modern Lebanon*,[3] and concerns a major flare-up between the Druze and the Maronites in 1860. This hostility was triggered by European interest in silk production and trade. According to Traboulsi, at the symbolic level, the episode remains a valid key to the perennial civil strife in present-day Lebanon. For accuracy, I refer to *History of Modern Lebanon:*

> During the fighting, a Druze got hold of a Christian. They battled and resisted each other and went on fighting until they reached the waterfront from which they fell into the water still exchanging punches and blows. A huge wave unfurled and dragged them into the open sea where they were swallowed up by the tide. The next morning, their corpses were recovered on the beach scrunched up in a tight embrace and gripping each other's hands.[4]

To Traboulsi, the symbolism was transparent: the surging sea waves stood for the tidal assaults of global markets and imperialist militaries, and the brotherly embrace (which here took place in death, but needn't await death...) stood for cross-sectarian unity, built on the solid basis of a common agenda for equal socio-economic rights...[5]

Traboulsi's book records how outside interventions and global capitalist meddling in Lebanon did in fact produce, time and again, social mobilisations which held, or seemed to hold, the promise of bringing about a unity of purpose among the underdog elements of all sects, but which so far failed to achieve that elusive unity. The failure, according to Traboulsi, goes back to the country's very creation, and the purpose behind that creation: the French used the pretence of safeguarding the rights of the main religious minorities (Christian, Druze, Alawi and Shia) in mandate Syria to carve out a Christian-dominated Lebanon. In Lebanon itself, the sectarian power sharing was institutionalised in 1943 under the informal agreement known as *National Pact*. The system, according to Traboulsi, was designed to absorb any stirring of social unrest, any mobilisation of the downtrodden, within a hierarchic framework of patronage, power distribution and allotment of public office. An opaque arrangement of this sort belies the principles of transparent democracy and equal citizenship. It can only perpetuate division and corruption. Under the system, we recall, the country's President is always a Christian Maronite; the Prime

Minister a Sunni and the Speaker of Parliament a Shia. Although the system is heavily tilted in favour of the Maronites, it is also able to co-opt the emergent leaders of all communities with the lure of public office—a cover for public plunder—and assorted fleshpots.

When I raised the subject, Traboulsi was emphatic:

*This system does not find mention in the written constitution of Lebanon. It endures because it suits the imperialist powers and enables them to do their undercover deals with a handful of oligarchs who monopolise public representation under their respective sectarian banners. Some thirty families belonging to various sects have been controlling the politics and economy of the country over the last six and a half decades. They have used their extraordinary private wealth and control over the levers of power to keep the society divided and mired in chaos. The unwholesome surfeit of the oil economy; the neglect of industry by oligarchs interested only in easy profits in the tertiary sector; the imperialist manipulations and conspiracies during the Cold War era; the Israeli designs of strategic and political control—all these have contributed to the mess and muddle that Lebanon has become.*

I asked Traboulsi to comment on the widespread distrust, even antagonism, that exists in Lebanon towards the Palestinian refugees and, in no small measure, contributed to the civil war.

*The creation of Israel was a disaster for the Palestinian people. As far as Lebanon is concerned, the swarming of Palestinian refugees also led, indirectly, to calamitous consequences, but that wasn't fated to be. On the contrary, the Palestinian presence could have precipitated revolutionary changes and helped turn Lebanon into a progressive, democratic society. The influx of Palestinians, some 120,000 from Galilee alone, with their non-negligible financial resources had the potential of undermining the socio-economic control that the sectarian oligarchs had exercised. Therefore, anti-Palestinian sentiments were stirred up.*

*The population figures for Lebanon in 1951 were approximately 1.2 million. With practically no industry to speak of and an underdeveloped public service sector, there was little scope for job creation in the skilled or unskilled labour sectors. Under these circumstances, it was somewhat natural for the Lebanese to feel nervous about foreigners coming in and settling down in such large numbers. The oligarchs, who had their own reasons for not wanting a labour intensive economy, did their best to turn this fear of the 'job-snatching foreigners' into a national hysteria. They were paranoid of Palestinian talent, and ill at ease with their fundamentally secular outlook.*

For example, the Lebanese oligarchs did their best to wreck Intra Bank, one of the most successful banking experiments, which a Palestinian Christian, Yusuf Baydas, had been running in Palestine. The bank, which had been the biggest and strongest of all such financial institutions for nearly two decades and maintained a very high number of small accounts, was declared insolvent in October 1966. This bankruptcy was the fruit of a close cooperation between western economic interests, the oil rich countries, the Israeli defence establishment and the Lebanese oligarchs who baulked at the success of a Palestinian entrepreneur. The crash of Intra Bank triggered a furious flight of capital from Lebanon. Those who engineered the crash were not bothered.

After the Arab defeat of 1967, the PLO's expulsion from Jordan in 1971 and the swelling of the Palestinian refugee population in Lebanon, Israel established close links with the Maronite right-wing elements and got them to whip up anti-Palestinian sentiments, by harping on the threat of Lebanon turning into 'Fatah-land'. Thus, the people of Lebanon, who in the 1960s had been overwhelmingly sympathetic to the Palestinian cause, were manoeuvred into turning against the Palestinian presence. The massive attacks on Lebanon's civilian and military infrastructure, which Israel carried out at regular intervals (and which it managed to justify as retaliation against PLO actions launched from Lebanon or, if not, 'planned' there), also contributed a lot to this collective change of heart. For example, in December 1968 Israel destroyed thirteen Middle East Airlines planes parked at Beirut airport in retaliation against the hijacking by a Palestinian group of a plane en route to Athens. The right-wing Christian army of Lebanon, I have to say, played this Israeli-scripted game very effectively. On 23 April 1969, it opened fire on public demonstrations held in Sidon and Beirut, in support of the Palestinian cause, precipitating a crisis of which the Maronite right-wing took full advantage.

In 1970, Gamal Abdel Nasser was still around and could persuade the Lebanese leadership, especially army chief Emile Bustani, to accommodate the interests of the Palestinian resistance. But by 1975, Lebanese society had become fiercely polarised between the Christian right-wing with its Phalange party and the Palestinians with their sympathisers—which, alas, did not include the Lebannese working classes.

I wanted to hear Traboulsi's take on the 'Shia awakening': the gradual rise of the poor segments of the Shia population that started mainly in South Lebanon and suburban Beirut, in the 1960s, after the arrival on the scene of Musa al-Sadr and the launching of *Amal* (or *Movement of the*

*Deprived;* the name actually means 'hope' ). The rise of Hizbullah and its amazing success (as an armed resistance group fighting Israel, but also as a growing political force within Lebanon) is also part of this 'awakening' which took place over the last four decades and is still gathering pace.

*The phenomenon is carried by a potent urge for social revolution and the desire to end the oligarchic rule—a desire that is shared by the suppressed sections of all religious denominations. These aspirations are unable to find secular political channels because of the realities of state repression, the power of capitalist corruption and the nexus between the state interests and the various religious establishments. The Shia population of Lebanon, particularly in the South, has long been a suppressed community, possibly the country's largest underclass, and it is but natural that it should rise and take the lead in challenging the status quo. But this rejection of the established order, this revulsion from the privileges, power and pomp of the ruling classes, is by no means limited to the Shia community. It is equally at work in the Christian segments of the Lebanese population. For example, in the same period in which Musa al-Sadr was making his mark on the Shia population, a number of Christian denominations in the country were questioning the system of governance, at once feudal and capitalistic, which the old Church leaders had been aligned with. Thus the* Christian Student Youth *and the* Rally of Committed Christians, *inspired by the sort of 'liberation theology' that was making waves in Latin America, were taking a bold stand for social equality, democracy and an end to oligarchic rule. The bishop of the Greek Orthodox Church in Beirut was also openly critical of our abusive, unequal socio-political order in its cosy symbiosis with Lebanon's sectarian fragmentation.*

*The same phenomenon was in evidence within the Druze community under the watch of its ethnarch, the late Kamal Jumblat, a progressive socialist who was assassinated in March 1977. Even the Sunni political alliances were not irresponsive to the demands for social reform. Saeb Salam, a Sunni, was Prime Minister from 1972 to 1973 when Lebanon was descending into civil war. He had been elected on a platform of fiscal reforms, development of national industry, price control, limitations on profit rates and speculative hoarding. President Suleiman Frangieh and his team of ministers, however, had strong links with the merchant association, the national oligarchs, owners of pharmaceutical companies; bankers; dealers in oil, and top army generals who acted as compradors for the Israeli and western arms industry. In the end, Saeb Salam had to resign when the President refused to take action against the army, which, in*

*April 1973, had allowed an Israeli commando under the then Lieutenant Ehud Barak to shoot dead three PLO leaders in broad daylight, in a public place, close to a police station.*

*The civil war in Lebanon was not inevitable. The people of Lebanon were neither anti-Palestinian nor in favour of Israel and its western mentors. Nor, in the last analysis, is the 'Shia awakening', which sustains Hizbullah, a strictly sectarian phenomenon. It rather reflects the rise of an underclass, its aspiration to greater democratic solidarity, and its rejection of capitalist greed. It also expresses a whole nation's fatigue with outside interference. The movement may yet succeed in righting many of Lebanon's wrongs, if only it doesn't deviate from its goals and doesn't allow itself to be cowed by the firepower of its implacable enemy.*

I left the coffee shop and walked back to my hotel wondering if Hizbullah's current political alliances really mirrored the kind of 'consciousness' that Professor Traboulsi was talking about, with his rather too neat Marxist categories. The most intriguing of all such alliances was the one with Michel Aoun's FPM (*Free Patriotic Movement*). From Hizbullah's point of view, Aoun was a most improbable partner: a Maronite Christian, at first squarely aligned with the anti-Syrian faction, he had headed the Lebanese army before becoming prime minister from September 1988 to October 1990.[6] He then invited Syria's wrath by proclaiming himself president. Syria responded by bombarding the Presidential palace, forcing Aoun into a 15-year long exile in France.

By the time Michel Aoun returned to Lebanon, in 2005, the political equations had changed. Syria, when it had driven him into exile, had been enjoying, for a brief spell, the backing of the United States (under Bush senior) for supporting the first Gulf War against Saddam Hussein. But by 2005, Syria had again fallen foul of the US and regained its status as pariah state in the eyes of the West. Syria was being blamed for Hariri's murder and had just withdrawn its army from Lebanon. In these changed circumstances, a changed Michel Aoun began talking about the importance of building a secular, political culture in the country. Hizbullah, too, had been pushing in the same direction, pressing for the abolition of Lebanon's sectarian-based system of elections and governance. Under that system, the National Assembly with its 128 members is equally divided between Christians and Muslims. All the eighteen recognised sects in the country get a fixed share of seats, with the Maronite Christians taking the maximum, namely thirty-four. The whole system is clearly absurd, given that Lebanon has not had a single census since 1932 to determine the numerical strength of the different sects. All knowledgeable sources suggest that the Shia population has, for a long time now, been the majority. This being so, I wondered why Hizbullah, which despite its disclaimers is, at least in part, a sectarian organisation, was not demanding a census to establish the numerical superiority of the Shia and then press for a re-adjustment of their representation in the national assembly and government. That would open the way for Hizbullah to form a Shia-dominated government. Why, then, wasn't the movement asking for a census?

There were a few other questions about Hizbullah which I wanted to probe: its ideology of resistance; its position on Israel and Jews in general; its long-term vision for the wider Arab world; and its attitude to the mixed blessing of oil.

Dr Abdo Saad, head of the Beirut Center for Research and Information, was the first person close to, and knowledgeable about, Hizbullah, with whom I was able to meet and talk freely. He also introduced me to his daughter Amal Saad-Ghorayeb, Associate Professor at the Lebanese American University in Beirut and author of a well-received book on Hizbullah.[7] But before meeting with Amal I had two long sessions with her father, who readily answered all my questions, without a trace of political reserve or sectarian caginess.

Abdo Saad, a lean, spiky, white-haired man in his late 60s, is a vivacious conversationalist and an ebullient thinker, who speaks his thoughts out loud as they occur to him, going back and forth, sometimes contradicting himself, then graciously admitting the inconsistencies and modifying his arguments, as much in dialogue with himself as with his interlocutors.

I began the interview by asking what he thought of the prevalence of authoritarian regimes in the post-colonial Arab world. The question was not pre-planned or even well thought-out; it just presented itself, but had the effect of throwing Abdo Saad into an intense rumination.

*I have often asked myself these questions. Why do we in the Arab world tolerate tyranny? Why do we remain politically and socially backward even when advancing economically? I failed to find any literature that really answered the question. So I started my own research, especially into British and European history, starting from that big turning point, the signing of the* Magna Carta *(the Great Charter of Freedom) in 1215. How did the Charter come about? It came about because rebellious barons and Church leaders, anxious to assert their rights and citizenship privileges, compelled King John to issue an explicit Charter of rights, with such items as the writ of habeas corpus, and to put his seal on it. Not before the Charter was signed did the rebellious English barons renew their oath of allegiance to the King. The Magna Carta also contained in it the germ of the theory of 'social contract' because its clause 61 provided for the establishment of a committee of 25 barons—the incipient parliament—which could overrule the decisions of the King. Absolute no longer, the King was henceforth required to abide by the collective Will of the Committee. As we all know, the implementation was anything but smooth. The terms of the Magna Carta had to be continuously renegotiated and renewed, down to the enactment of the Bill of Rights in 1689, in the wake of the Glorious Revolution. By then, civil society was strong and courageous enough to tame the powers of the throne, or let us say State, and impose a framework applicable to all alike: the rule of law.*

*The French Revolution took place exactly one hundred years after the enactment of the English Bill of Rights. It too had a bumpy ride, with phases of popular rebellion, anarchy, wars, regicide, terror. Then came the 'Thermidorian Reaction' against the wave of revolutionary terror, with Robespierre's execution as its high point. The Directory took over, and the first bicameral parliament was called into being. But soon enough, political instability and too blatant a display of corruption bred disenchantment. Finally, the decision was with the army and Napoleon Bonaparte got himself crowned as Emperor in 1804. Thus, fifteen years after the onset of the Revolution, things seemed to have come full circle. France had turned its back on the republican ideals, and the erstwhile watchwords of the Revolution rang more than a little hollow.*

*In 1943, 154 years after the French Revolution, Lebanon held democratic elections under the authority of the Free French Government, whereupon the elected majority declared Lebanon an independent country. General Charles de Gaulle, a 'liberator' at home but not abroad, had all the elected members of the new Lebanese Government thrown into prison. But the United States pressured France to honour Lebanon's declaration of independence. That is how our first independent government came into being. The Western war alliance, which had prevailed against the Axis powers, was now making a show of respecting 'democracy' in its colonies, to deflect the charge of hypocrisy and justify its war aims after the event, as it were. But I am telling you: sixty-four years after its declaration of independence, Lebanon is still not a sovereign, democratic country, not in any real sense. The Government of Lebanon is still doing the bidding of outsiders.*

Abdo Saad's impassioned ramblings were getting me rather confused. What meddlesome 'outsiders' was he referring to? Did he mean Syria? Or Israel? Or the bad old imperialist powers again? I begged Abdo Saad to be precise and to the point.

*Let me start with the writ of* habeas corpus. *It grants any subject, 'free or fettered', the right to appeal, and it bans unlawful imprisonment. Well, the habeas corpus has been around for nearly 800 years, but look at what the world's 'leading democracies' are forcing Lebanon to do with respect to 'unlawful imprisonment'!*

*Rafiq Hariri was killed on 14 February 2005 by a truck bomb triggered by a remote controlled device. There has been a riot of speculation as to the identity of the culprits and their possible motives. In April 2005 the UN Security Council adopted a resolution (no. 1595) to institute an international investigation headed by Detlev Mehlis, a German judge. Mehlis began his inquiries and witness interrogations in February 2005, but had to step down in December 2005 amidst controversies regarding the quality and impartiality of his investigation.[8] The chief witness on whom Mehlis had relied to reach his conclusions (incriminating Syria), one Hassan Taher, later retracted his testimony en bloc, declaring that he had been bribed and threatened by Lebanese politicians to testify against Syria. Another key witness, Zuhair ibn-Mohammed Said Saddik, also changed his statements, radically contradicting himself, and was jailed in France on charges of perjury and suspected involvement in the assassination. After Detlev Mehlis' resignation, the UN appointed Serge Brammertz, a Belgian jurist, to lead the commission. Brammertz too resigned in January 2008 without completing the assignment. Serious doubts about the investigation's integrity and reliability were expressed even by UN officials. Nonetheless, four senior Lebanese generals were arrested in 2005 on mere suspicions, without concrete charges: the former head of the Presidential Guard Mustafa Hamdan, Security Services Director Jamil Sayyid, Domestic Security Chief Ali Hajj, and Military Intelligence Chief Raymond Azar. Since their arrest, all four have remained in jail without trial.[9] So, what becomes of this much vaunted writ of habeas corpus—of this right of appeal against unlawful imprisonment—if the UN itself sanctions imprisonment on political grounds, without charges, without trial, even without serious evidence of wrongdoing?*

Abdo Saad was visibly angry and agitated. He got up from his chair and started pacing up and down the room for a few moments. Then, having composed himself, he resumed his seat, and his argument.

*We all know about the goings-on at Abu Ghraib and Guantanamo Bay, 792 years after the enactment of the Magna Carta. So, it would seem that in the UN's view none of these exalted principles apply to the Arab world. Neither do Montesquieu's theses about the separation of powers, the preservation of civil liberties and the rule of law. The Arab world apparently belongs to a grey zone of exception, a zone where civil liberties have no relevance, where the rule of law and the equality of all before the law are somehow suspended! Why? What is the logic behind this relegation of the Arab world beyond the pale of the law and its protective shield?*

*Well, you begin to get clues when you read someone like Alexis de Tocqueville, the 19th century political philosopher from France, famous for his studies on American democracy. When it came to America, he was broadly supportive, with minor reservations, of the equality principle which drives democratic progress. But North Africa was another matter! The same Tocqueville not only supported the colonisation of Algeria, in full knowledge of the barbaric methods used by the French to subjugate the country ('far more barbaric than those of the Arabs themselves') but he went out of his way to justify the recourse to the harshest, most brutal means of conquest. He even advocated the suspension of all political freedom there, the institution of racial segregation and the limitation of citizenship rights to the sole European settlers. During his visit to Algeria in 1837, Tocqueville wrote: 'I have no doubt that we can raise on the coast of Africa a great monument to the glory of our country.'*

Abdo Saad had calmed down. He fell silent for a while, then said:

*We are all making a grievous mistake in trying to pattern our democracies and our laws on western models. I referred to Tocqueville because Lebanese Francophiles never tire of quoting him as the great exponent of the equality principle, always drawing from his work on America, but conveniently forgetting about his stance on the Algerian question and on European colonisation in general. Even a cursory examination of Tocqueville's views on Africa, slavery and the French colonisation of Algeria show that, to him, democratic advances and progress towards constitutionalism were to be limited to the Western sphere. They had no relevance to the outside world, fated for conquest and colonisation by 'superior civilisations'. These 'superior civilisations' had the 'natural right' to hold the subject races under despotic rule and* to harness their resources, human and natural, in furtherance of their own interests.

Most 19th century political philosophers, even those of liberal persuasion, more or less agree on this point. John Stuart Mill, one of the first champions of women's right to vote, had this to say in his famous treatise On Liberty (1859): 'Despotism is a legitimate mode of government in dealing with barbarians, provided the end be their improvement.'

This proviso about 'improving the barbarians' speaks volumes about the civilisational hubris behind the colonial enterprise. The presumption was that despotic rule, unrestrained violence, and exploitation by the European races would actually redound to the good of their victims! Tocqueville first went to Algeria in 1841. He could see for himself with what barbaric means the French were attempting to subdue the natives. Yet he chose to defend the conquest in unadorned terms. He wrote:

> I have often heard men whom I respect, but with whom I do not agree, find it wrong that we burn harvests, that we empty silos, and finally that we seize unarmed men, women, and children.... These, in my view, are unfortunate necessities, but ones to which any people that wants to wage war on the Arabs is obliged to submit.

Of course, his 'Essay on Algeria' (1841) and other writings on the subject remained unpublished until 1962.[10] Anyhow, the noteworthy point about his vindication of savagery is the argument that 'war on the Arabs is not possible without it'.

Tocqueville, like many other well-known European political thinkers of the period, was a firm, rapturous believer in the European imperial project, as his private correspondence shows. My point is, until we fully grasp the arrogance and dishonesty behind this European conceit of bringing civilisation to the savages and light to the benighted, we cannot hope to win redemption from imperial hegemony (which today, of course, assumes different forms) or achieve genuine, functional democracy and respect for the rule of law.

Take, for example, a letter that Tocqueville wrote in April 1840 to his English friend Henry Reeve, a liberal intellectual, writer and journalist, who was also Tocqueville's translator. The political context was the war that the British East India Company was waging against the Qing Dynasty of China, to force it to accept the opium trade and cede Hong Kong to the company. The British had been bringing in large quantities of opium into China, a country familiar with the medicinal properties of the drug but with strong laws against its abuse. As *opium abuse began to assume epidemic proportions, China objected and, since its objections went unheeded, in 1839 it banned the sale of opium, a measure that also applied to all foreign traders. The British defied the ban, sent in their gunboats and started a regular war. In August 1839 they seized Hong Kong. China lost the war and the British had their way. In August 1842, China was forced to sign the Treaty of Nanjing, whereby it agreed to lower its trade tariffs, reverse the opium ban, cede Hong Kong to the British, and undertake to pay them 'reparations'.*

*In April 1840, when Tocqueville addressed his letter to Henry Reeve, the trend of the war was already clear. Tocqueville wrote:*

> I can only rejoice in the thought of an invasion of the Celestial Empire by a European army. So at last the mobility of Europe has come to grips with Chinese immobility! It is a great event, especially if one thinks that it is only the continuation, the last in a multitude of events of the same nature all of which are pushing the European race out of its home and successively submitting all the other races to its empire or its influence. Something more vast, more extraordinary than the establishment of the Roman Empire is growing out of our times, without anyone noticing it; it is the enslavement of four parts of the world by the fifth. Therefore, let us not slander our century and ourselves too much; the men are small, but the events are great.

*In case you doubt the passage's authenticity: the letter, with many others of the same ilk, is included in* Tocqueville's Selected Letters on Politics and Society.[11] *I am harping on about Tocqueville because of our French connection, but the point also holds true for other European thinkers of the period, not just, mind you, the conservatives amongst them but also, perhaps even more so, the proponents of political revolution or evolution.*

*Marx praised the British conquest of India for taking (no matter how indirectly and unintentionally) the subcontinent forward in the direction of progress and hauling it out of sloth, superstition and ignorance. You know what Tocqueville said about the prerequisites for bringing civilisation to India? He said that just as Plato had contemplated banishing everyone older than ten, the better to raise the pre-teens into ideal citizens of an enlightened city-state, so also the British should wholly expunge all traditions and institutions of India before it could attain civilisation and progress. Here again, you can find the passage, black on white, in* Tocqueville's Collected Works.[12] *Max Weber, too, advocated imperialism, strongly urging Germany to acquire 'power above all' and not to let 'English uniformity' or 'Russian bureaucracy' dominate the world.[13]*

*So you see how foolish it is for those of us who seek to build genuine democ-racy, strengthen human rights and entrench the rule of law in the colonised world, to look to the masters of European political theory for inspiration, or even to borrow their conceptual tools! Imperialist interventions, including those which happen in our own times (often under UN cover, as now in Lebanon) are almost invariably justified in the name of 'defending western security'. The irony of it all was captured by Henri-Benjamin Constant[14] in a pithy formula: 'Some governments, when sending their armies from one pole to the other, still talk about the defence of their hearths; one would think they call all the places to which they set fire their hearths.'[15]*

Abdo Saad was clearly a well-read man. He was also clearly wrought-up. I could see him seething at the thought of so much hypocrisy among western thinkers, such brazen Eurocentrism, such blanket refusal by the self-anointed carriers of civilisation to apply their own standards to the conquered races, all this smug arrogance and quiet assumption of supe-riority. But I was still puzzled as to where Abdo Saad was heading with his fiery invective, valid as it was. Was he simply denouncing Europe's double standards? Or was he recommending a more radical rejection of western political paradigms? So I asked him to elaborate, which he did, slowly and clearly.

*These contradictions and duplicity should be recognised for what they are. They stem from a psychology that breeds exceptionalism. Europeans do not feel they have to respect the human rights of Arabs, Africans, Amerindians and Australian aboriginals. Seen from here, this is obvious. What few of us see, however, is where this exceptionalism springs from; how inseparable it is from a certain consciousness mould, from notions of superiority (of race, religion, political ideology, civic development, etcetera) which immediately translate into hierarchies of rights and entitlements. In adopting this consciousness, we also imbibe the exceptionalism that goes with it, even if unwittingly and in altered forms.*

*Take Lebanon, for example, after it gained its independence from France in 1943. Lebanon is now supposed to be a democracy. But look at its history. The victims and perpetrators have changed over time, but the one thing that hasn't changed is the abuse of power, denial of rights, intolerance of dissent, and habit of bloody repression. These have been the constant hallmarks of our politics. Given the opportunity, yesterday's victims become today's perpetrators, as if such skin-changing were the most natural thing in the world. Why?*

*In my opinion, this tendency to abuse power—what little of it you have—goes back to the thought patterns we inherited from 19th century Europe, from our 'teachers' on democracy, governance, and on what constitutes 'progress'. The sources may vary and those drinking at the sources may call themselves Marxists or nationalists or this or that, but the results are much the same. The authoritarianism or tyranny that you see across the Middle East do spring, in my opinion, from the grip which 19th century European political thinking has acquired over the minds of our leaders and statesmen. Has not the same been happening in India also? Haven't India's leaders, after wrestling their freedom from the British in the name of self-determination and democracy, been fighting sections of their own people, especially in peripheral areas, for claiming the very same rights? That is why we must, at all costs, evolve an alternative political consciousness. We must try new approaches to the challenges in front of us—from the restructuring of our state–society relations, to matters of social solidarity and minority rights, to the fighting back of imperialist designs.*

Well, where do you see such 'alternative consciousness building' at work?, I asked. Abdo Saad was emphatic.

*I see it at work in Hizbullah! The movement's origin, its spirit and methods, its history of resistance to tyranny, external and internal, all these are strictly self-evolved and owe nothing to European models or theories. Hizbullah's internal culture also requires that we subordinate all narrow interests and self-privileging—the sources of exceptionalism—to a set of 'universal maxims' which constitute our ideological bedrock. I am confident that Hizbullah's valiant experiment in political resistance will soon inspire emulation outside Lebanon and succeed in imparting a new impulse to our societies. Hizbullah has already set a striking example by successfully resisting a regional superpower like Israel. It is now providing inspiration to scores of other organisations which fight for self-determination, in Palestine and beyond.*

Since I was soon going to meet Abdo Saad's daughter Amal, who had made an in-depth study of Hizbullah and written a book about it, I decided to keep my questions about the movement's history for her. Right now, I was thinking about Abdo Saad's plea for the rejection of 19th century European ideologies in favour of indigenous approaches, and his (rather tall) claim that the substitution might render the resistance movements immune to the temptations of 'exclusivism' or 'exceptionalism' to which they so often succumb, especially when victorious, at the expense of 'excluded' groups.

Clearly, we were touching here on the distinction between *violence* and *power*. Following Hannah Arendt and others, we may define *power* as the human ability to act in concert. Power then is *legitimate* when it is rooted in consent; more precisely, when it rests on laws which the citizenry understands and complies with. Legitimate power, which is also the only form of truly effective power, thus rests on consent, which translates into the tacit recognition that those in authority do deserve obedience. Command through terror, on the other hand, or through threat and violence, may enforce obedience, but it can never achieve that quality of power which requires consensus and earns the respect of a people happy to obey.

So, Abdo Saad's claim about new forms of resistance commanding 'popular support' and therefore immune to 'ugly deviations' (such as turning on those weaker still), was assuming a lot: it assumed a pre-existent ideology; an authority representing that ideology; a mass of followers consensually upholding its goals and tenets; and an even broader support base in the ambient population. I asked Abdo Saad whether Hizbullah really fulfilled these preconditions; whether it fully qualified as 'legitimate resistance' in the above sense. Abdo Saad reflected for a while and then started speaking in the first person plural, indicating his identification with Hizbullah:

*I already told you, we do not depend on 19th century European political philosophy for our understanding of history and its 'destination'. And that too for a good reason: our historical and existential experiences simply do not compare to Europe's. Ours is a completely distinct background from that which inspired political philosophers like Hegel, Jean Bodin, John Stuart Mill, Marx, Max Weber, Montesquieu, Thomas Hobbes, Tocqueville, and the rest of them. For that reason alone, their narratives, analyses and prescriptions do not resonate with our experience and cannot serve as a vehicle for our aspirations.*

*Hizbullah rose to prominence in an era of disenchantment not just with the West, but also with Marxism—that critique of the West by the West. From the start, Hizbullah adopted a different framework, rooted in Islam: that of resistance as society or resistance society. Now, this is a framework that may be slightly off-putting or hard to grasp for those unfamiliar with our Shia tradition. So let me tell you briefly about that tradition, and Lebanon's pre-eminent part in shaping it. The fact is that back in the 16th century Lebanon, southern Lebanon to be specific, made a historical contribution in consolidating Safavid*

Iran as a Shia state and in permeating its institutions with the spirit of Shiism. The driving force behind this mighty change was the Islamic Sufi order known as Safaviyeh. It was in this period that scholars and clerics from south Lebanon, mainly Jabal Amil, flocked to Iran to assist the Safavid officials in their drive to institutionalise Shia practices, in religion and politics, and to promote their observance at the popular level.

Seen from that perspective, Iran's modern interest in Lebanon has nothing incongruous about it: it is, so to speak, the repaying of a spiritual debt. In fact, the return to Lebanon, especially after the 1979 Iranian Revolution, of some of those descendants of 16th century migrants, falls into a well-established pattern of interactions between the two countries. In any case, this return to the ancestral home, in its hour of need, to help it resist Israeli aggression, doesn't at all feel like 'interference' to us, nor should it to anyone conversant with our intertwined histories.

Now, to understand the meaning of 'resistance society', you must appreciate that Hizbullah has been working with the Shia population not on a purely sectarian basis, but rather on the premise that the Shia represent the most disadvantaged and marginalised section in Lebanon. The Shia tradition, as you must know, is riveted to the martyrdom of Imam Hussein. In keeping with the symbolic charge of this foundational event, Shiism tends to identify with the oppressed and the underprivileged. It regards their upliftment and empowerment as its sacred duty. The way to do this is through what, in modern parlance, we might call 'social mobilisation'—except that mobilisation in Shiism is never a purely top–bottom affair. It is part and parcel of a comprehensive framework of thought and practices that do not exclude moral values or the meaning(s) of life. Even more crucially, from a practical viewpoint, it relies on institutionalised forms of deliberation, communication and action, a system we call wilayat al-faqih (a loose and somewhat restrictive rendering would be: 'consulate of the jurists'), in close interaction with the umma, or community.

Concern about the legitimacy of governance has always been a central theme of Shia jurisprudence, because Shiism sees 'just governance' as a prerequisite for peace and prosperity. I'll spare you the doctrinal and political history of these concepts; it would be too arcane for a layman to follow, also of dubious relevance. But let's get hold of the central point, which is this: the institutionalisation of 'deliberation, communication and action' that binds the wilayat al-faqih and the umma aims to keep a meaningful and workable balance between high principles and practical possibilities. And the way it attempts to do so is by *keeping up a dialogue between* wilayat al-faqih *and* umma. *Another trait of Hizbullah is what we might call 'principled flexibility': when the* de facto *realities (say, a state order of shaky legitimacy) appear to be amenable to gradual reforms, Hizbullah readily takes the reformist course. When not, it takes the revolutionary road, or that of direct action.*

*But let me repeat: a key tenet, which Ayatollah Salihi and many others have emphasised, is that the* umma *must approve the authority of the* wilayat al-faqih *before the latter can claim obedience.*

*In this sense, the institutionalisation of deliberation,* shura, *as a prelude to purposeful action, is a uniquely democratic exercise. It subordinates the* ex cathedra *rulings of clerical hierarchies to a substantiation by the community 'in faith', that is, in free, trusting assent. Of course, under doctrinaire scrutiny, the system may appear thorny and convoluted. But it has glorious antecedents. Without wanting to sound pedantic, this view had already been clearly articulated by 11th century Islamic scholars like Abu al-Hussein ibn Abd Allah ibn Sina Balkhi, better known under his Latinised name of Avicenna. In one of his most famous works,* Al-Shifa al-Ilahiyyat (Book of Healing), *Ibn-Sina declared:*

> *The one who sets the precedent (or tradition-maker—the Prophet) must introduce his successor and must oblige people to obey him. No one can succeed the Prophet without his appointment, or a consensus of experts who publicly confirm that he is brave, honest, evidently independent in decision making, an original thinker and problem solver, and the most learned in religious law. However, the people must publicly agree with this consensus.*

*You cannot think of a more democratic conception of authority than this view of* wilayat, *already strong in 11th century Islamic discourse, which insists that the interpretation of the tradition cannot be valid without public endorsement.*[16] *This is the framework of 'resistance society' which Hizbullah steadfastly follows, despite being branded by Israel, the US, Canada and the UK as a terrorist organisation. It is on this basis that Hizbullah relates to other organisations engaged in similar struggles, like Hamas, which is not a Shia movement. It is on this basis that Hizbullah counsels the Shia of Iraq to reconcile with the Sunni, rather than allowing themselves to be instrumentalised by outside forces.*

*Al-Sayyid Hassan Nasrallah, the current Secretary-General of Hizbullah, often points to the example of Afghanistan as a warning to those who might be tempted by military alliances with the West, no matter how tactical or temporary. The Afghans fought the Russian occupation with American support and drove the occupiers away—at least, one set of occupiers. Yet the neat outcome, for the Afghan people, has been unmitigated disaster.*

*Years before the Twin Towers attacks of 9/11, Hizbullah had been voicing its condemnation and outrage over the atrocities committed by the Taliban and their Arab allies in Afghanistan. In November 1997, Hizbullah took Ayman al-Zawahiri (head of the Egyptian Islamic Jihad and allegedly the number two of Al-Qaida) to task for condoning the killing of foreign tourists and civilian by-standers in Egypt, and also for fomenting political assassinations in Egypt, aimed at overthrowing the regime: such methods being, in Hizbullah's view, fundamentally un-Islamic and undemocratic.*

*Coherent with its doctrine of 'resistance society', Hizbullah unambiguously condemns the Wahhabi violence and the indiscriminate terrorism practised by groups like Al-Qaida. Hizbullah also takes responsibility for the welfare of the people who constitute its 'resistance society'. It spares neither time nor strategic planning nor financial resources to provide social services to those living in Al-Dahiya (the slum quarters of southern Beirut) or in south Lebanon or in the Bekaa valley along the Litani and Orontes rivers. It takes care of their educational, health and housing needs. It also looks after the relatives of those who have laid down their lives in fighting Israel's invasions and occupation.*

*Hizbullah has developed a network of semi-independent organisations involved in research, publication, public dialogue and popular communication. It has set up radio and television stations and a publishing network. Our adversaries may dismiss all this as propaganda, but we see it as part of our Shia threesome of 'deliberation, communication and action'.*

*Take an honest look at Hizbullah and see all it has to offer. The movement has set an example of effective resistance to Israel. It has set exacting moral standards and abides by them. It has shown active sympathy for the victims of war. In its political discourse, it reaches out to all sections and emphasises Muslim unity. Don't we have here a harbinger of hope such as the Arab world has not seen since 1948? I for one truly believe that Hizbullah can become a model of resistance and democratic engagement for the rest of the region.*

Abdo Saad had briefly mentioned Hizbullah's fine balance between flexibility and intransigence: the movement may sometimes compromise with unsavoury realities in the hope of inspiring reforms from within, or, when nothing avails, it may plump for revolutionary action. It is all a matter of *discernment*. I wondered how these principles applied to the Arab–Israeli conflict. On the one hand, both Hizbullah and Hamas have talked about Zionist Israel as a clear evil that should be removed if peace, justice, stability and democracy are to take roots in the region. On the other hand, both Hizbullah and Hamas have been conducting political negotiations with Israel. Periods of violent military engagement have alternated with prolonged truces, negotiations, and prisoner exchanges.

So I asked Abdo Saad point-blank: was he able to visualise peace and coexistence in the event Israel agreed to vacate the occupied territories and accept the Palestinians' right of return? That would solve a seemingly endless conflict on the basis of two self-governing but interdependent states. Hizbullah and Hamas, and scores of independent Palestinian and Arab voices, have argued that Israel in its present shape is an artificial creation sustained by military might—its own, but above all that of the United States. Israel, so the conclusion goes, is bereft of all legitimacy—moral, historical, political. But I represented to Abdo Saad that the argument could just as well apply to Arab states like Jordan, Iraq, Kuwait or Saudi Arabia. Are these any less artificial? Weren't they arbitrarily carved out by the British, to reward their allies or to function as safe enclaves for oil extraction? So I asked Abdo Saad: shouldn't the flexibility principle apply here? Shouldn't Arabs make their peace with that massive and, to all appearances, irremovable, piece of *de facto* reality that is Israel, in the hope of inspiring reforms from within, alleviating as far as feasible the legacy of six decades of horror, and giving peace a chance in the region?

From Abdo Saad's facial expressions, as he sat there brooding over my question, I could guess his mental strain and emotional turmoil. Here is what he answered, at last:

*Hizbullah will never recognise Zionist Israel even if the whole world pressures it into so doing. This is my belief, and I will explain why I think so in a while. That said, it is also my belief that Hizbullah won't attack Israel unless attacked by it—but Israel should return the Sheba farms to Lebanon and the Golan Heights to Syria, and free all the Lebanese prisoners it holds.*

*As for the Palestinian cause, it is a cause for the Palestinian organisations, such as Hamas, to pursue and fight for. Hizbullah stands in solidarity with them and will do everything within its ability to help them. For example, in January 2004, Hizbullah compelled Israel to return 400 Palestinian and 29 Lebanese prisoners in exchange for a kidnapped Israeli spy and the remains of three soldiers captured several years earlier. Besides, the very existence of*

*Hizbullah strengthens Hamas' hand against Israel. But Hizbullah will not, on its own, fight the Palestinians' war in their place. It will continue to support the Palestinians living in Lebanon in every conceivable manner, by providing them with medical care, education and other social services. At the symbolic level, which also matters, Hizbullah maintains the sites of the 1982 massacres at Sabra and Shatila as places of commemoration. Hizbullah's television channel, Al-Manar, has always been open to Palestinian voices, to the Palestinian memory, to the Palestinian perspective, which are systematically expunged from the hegemonic discourse on the Middle East as dictated by Israel and taken up by its army of propagandists and hired pens. Documentary series like Huna Filasteen (This is Palestine), which Al-Manar broadcast in 2002, brought the memories of refugees, their ordeals and aspirations, to the forefront of historical debate. Hizbullah, of course, has never made a secret of its view that 'intifada and resistance' are the only ways open to the Palestinians for achieving their rights. Hizbullah unambiguously rejects the Oslo Accords as unprincipled and deceptive. In February 2006, immediately after Hamas won the elections in Palestine, Nasrallah spoke of forming a coalition of resistance movements which would unite Gaza, Beirut, Damascus and Tehran (he even mentioned Venezuela and 'brother Chavez'). All this assistance, all this moral and material support for the resistance, is part of the 'duty of solidarity'. Solidarity as understood by Hizbullah is not a matter of sentiment, but of level-headed, solid groundwork. It is like the 'granite foundations of a skyscraper'. This solidarity is based on the convergence of long-term interests, on a shared vision, on honesty of intent, as well as plain human brotherhood. But Hizbullah will not wage the war for Palestinian freedom from the Lebanese territory. That defensive position is the stand that Hizbullah has taken, and it will maintain it.*

But it is also my belief that Israel will never make even these minimal concessions which I mentioned a moment ago as Hizbullah's conditions for a lasting truce. Secure in its assumption of military superiority, Israel will sink further and further into hubris, and continue to take aggressive military actions, as it did in July 2006 when it tried to eradicate Hizbullah. There is something implacable and odious about Israel, a doubly irrational exclusivism—not born of reason and not amenable to reason—which seems to prevent that state from seeking humane solutions to the Palestinian problem and which impels it to pursue, instead, insane experiments in subjugation and eradication.

For example, it is my conviction that Israel played a decisive part, twice over, in pushing the Americans towards military intervention and regime change in

*Iraq. The intention, mainly, was to deflect the world's attention from a gigantic experiment in recasting the demography of Palestine, which Israel undertook in the wake of the Soviet Union's collapse. Even as the US started bombing the Iraqi troops in Kuwait, the Jewish Agency was making frantic efforts across the former USSR to facilitate mass migration from Russia, Eastern Europe and the Caucasus into Palestine, to finally tilt the demographic balance in favour of Jews, not just within Israel's borders but in the whole of Palestine. Israel joined the Oslo and then the Madrid peace process disingenuously, on false pretences. It joined only because that was the condition attached by the US for granting its $10 billion aid package to help settle the new migrants from the East. Even as the dreadful events in Iraq dominated the news and the (non-existent) 'prospects of the peace process' filled the political debate, a huge contingent of Russian-speakers—about twenty per cent of the population in occupied Palestine—suddenly and silently swelled the Jewish ranks.*[17]

*Such foresight and planning in demographic management is uncanny, almost satanic. For parallels, you would have to go to Nazi Germany. While Arafat and his admirers were prattling about the 'Oslo breakthrough', the population of the West Bank, unnoticed to the world, was undergoing a sea change.*

*The demographic change also had military implications. When the Israeli Defence Force, in the wake of the Intifada, stepped up its exactions against Palestinians, many Israelis became restive and began to question the morality of these actions. In August 2004, a former Deputy Chief of Mossad, Shmuel Toledano, publicly accused the military of losing its morality. Earlier, in September 2001, six members of the Israeli Defence Force, led by Matan Kaminer, had refused to join the on-going military operations in the occupied territories, particularly in Gaza. As the level of criticism and the multiplication of conscientious objectors were becoming an embarrassment for the military establishment, Israel mobilised former Soviet veterans, with combat experience in Afghanistan and Chechnya. A special unit of 1,200 commandos, Battalion Aliyah, was formed under the command of Roman Rathner, a former resident of Belarus, who had long been fantasising about 'Soviet Jews revitalising the flagging Zionist mission'. Well, vitality aside, the fact is that in numbers and military capacity, Battalion Aliyah more than offset the eyesore of conscientious objection.*

*Yet, the Zionist enterprise remains insecure and uncertain of its future. And it feels insecure not just because it depends on occupation, ethnic cleansing and apartheid—it has long ago reconciled itself to all this—but also, and above all, because it is irreducibly alien to, and at variance with, everything local—the people, their history, language and culture. That is, ultimately, the reason why Israel had to build its mini Great Wall of China: to protect its own alien self from the local people.*

*There are also the Oriental Jews, known as Mizrahim, who were coaxed, cajoled and browbeaten into leaving their birth places in Egypt, Jordan, Iran, Iraq, Lebanon, Morocco, Syria and Yemen to migrate to Israel soon after its creation. Once trapped in Israel, they found themselves treated as a lesser breed; though of course privileged over Palestinian Muslims.*

*Despite the influx of more than one million Jews from the former Soviet Union, the Zionists are aware of the natural pressures of demography which will eventually reverse whatever advantages they may now possess. They know that the Palestinians living inside Israel in apartheid-like conditions will eventually make common cause with those living in the West Bank, Gaza, Egypt, Jordan, Lebanon, and Syria. The Zionists are also aware that this cross-border Palestinian front could receive a forceful boost from two sections of Jews: the Sephardim, many of whom, following their expulsion from 15th century Spain, had settled in the Ottoman dominions, and the Mizrahim, who, as I just said, were tricked into leaving their livelihood in the lands of the Maghreb and Mashrek to shore up the newly created Israel. Since then, these two categories, especially the Mizrahim, have been living there as lesser citizens. All feel patronised and discriminated against by the Zionist aristocracy—the children and grand-children of those Ashkenazi Jews from central and eastern Europe who founded Israel.*

*Then there are the Fallashmura, the so-called 'forgotten Jews' from Ethiopia, nearly 100,000 of them, who occupy the lowest rung in the Israeli hierarchy. Then again, higher on the ladder than the Fallashmura and Mizrahim but lower than the Sephardim, you have other groups, like the Jews from Latin America, mainly Argentina, which between 1948 and 1995 contributed some 50,000 migrants.*

*All these categories of Jews may also be regarded as victims of Zionism, even if their victimhood is less blatant than that of the Arabs. You see, the Ashkenazim, after suffering centuries of persecution and 'labeling' in Europe, have apparently internalised the persecutor–persecutee relationship. No sooner did they get a state of their own than they replicated the vicious pattern, not just against the Palestinian Muslims but against anyone and anything 'Arab-like', be it culture, language or politics. No wonder then if their contempt extends to those whom they dismissively label as 'Oriental Jews' and who actually constitute the majority of Israel's Jews.*

*If all these groups were to unite on the basis of their common victimhood, or at least to develop a modicum of solidarity, their sheer demographic weight could spell doom for the Zionist project. Israel would then face a drastic choice: either embrace a course of political reform leading to equal citizenship for all— hardly thinkable at the moment—or go down the Fascist road with all that it implies: subjugation, apartheid and racial cleansing as life norms, assisted when necessary by terror and murder.*

*Well, the Zionists have clearly chosen the latter option. Hizbullah and Hamas have taken note, and refuse to compromise with them because, in plain terms, they are evil.*

Abdo Saad was beginning to sound tired. He paused for a while and then told me about an episode that took place in early 1996, in the course of a military operation code-named *Grapes of Wrath* which Israel had launched against Hizbullah. The Israeli air-force bombed a UN base in the south Lebanese village of Qana, where 100 civilians had taken shelter. The raid killed one and all: nearly one hundred lives were snuffed out at one go. Cana—apparently the same as today's Qana—is mentioned in the Gospels as the village where Jesus of Nazareth performed his miracle of turning water into wine. At the site of the destroyed UN base in Qana, there is now a cemetery, Abdo Saad told me, with a commemorative inscription that reads: 'Qana is the Kerbala of the 20th century; it is a place made holy by the Lord Jesus and defiled by the Zionist Satan.'

I could see that Abdo Saad was exhausted, probably as much from the strain of conversation as from the daylong fasting. Still, I was puzzled by the point he had just made about the fierce Zionist antipathy for everything indigenous. It reminded me, *a contrario*, of his earlier depiction of the Hizbullah spirit; the movement's rejection of Eurocentric ideologies, and its spurning of the western yardsticks for progress. Then, after bringing up the Zionist aversion for oriental Jews, Abdo Saad had hinted at the possibility of a far-going re-alignment, some sort of Arab–Sephardim–Mizrahim solidarity that could eventually pave the way for a one-state solution, based on secular and egalitarian principles. That sounded like a leap of faith to me, and I wanted to press him a little more on this. So I asked him to substantiate his claim about the Zionist loathing for 'oriental Jews'.

Abdo Saad looked at his watch and told me, with a wry smile, that he would have to leave in ten minutes. I nodded even as he began to elucidate.

*It may sound strange, but the fact is that even under European persecution, the Zionist forerunners of Israel were absolutely clear about their role as frontline representatives of western culture and power in the East. Ben-Gurion was quite candid when he declared to George Antonius, the well-known author of* The Arab Awakening *(1938): 'We want to return to the East only in the geographic sense, to create there the foundations of European culture.' Herzl and his successor Max Nordau were just as frank when stating that their mission was to expand 'the moral boundaries of Europe to the Euphrates'. We can only wonder what these Ashkenazim surmised under the 'moral boundaries of Europe'—a moral that had just produced the Holocaust as its latest fruit. We will not attempt to unravel that mystery.*

*The derision and contempt which the European pioneers of Israel felt for the native Palestinians are well-known. So let us talk about what is not so well-known—the Zionist loathing for oriental Jews. Immediately after Israel's creation, the Zionists felt an urgent need for demographic reinforcement and could not afford to be too choosy. So after trying, with moderate success, to attract Jews from all four corners of the 'civilised world', they turned their attention to the Mizrahi Jews scattered across the Middle East and North Africa, and applied all means, fair and foul, to get them to settle in Israel.*

*The term Mizrahim was coined by the Ashkenazi Jewry to refer to 'oriental Jews'—this 'uncouth, unkind, uneducated' lesser breed. The outpourings of Ashkenazi scorn for them didn't abate when the first waves of oriental Jewish migrants began to take over the dwellings and lands of expelled Palestinians. In 1949, Arye Gelblum, a well-known Jewish publicist, wrote these lines in Ha'aretz (22 April), the most influential newspaper of the Israeli left:*

> We are dealing here with a people whose primitivism is at its peak; whose level of knowledge is one of virtually absolute ignorance; and worse, who have little talent for understanding anything intellectual. Generally, they are only slightly better than the general level of the Arabs, Negroes and Berbers in the same regions.

*Ben-Gurion was just as scathing. He surely meant every word of what he said, when he pronounced, without a hint of sarcasm or provocation: 'The Mizrahi immigrants are without a trace of Jewish or human education [....] We do not want Israelis to become Arabs. We are duty-bound to fight against the values of* the Levant, which corrupts individuals and societies, and preserve the authentic Jewish values as they crystallised in the Diaspora.'

Ben-Gurion's words were meant for the Yemenite Jews who, at his behest, were airlifted into Israel in 1949 in an operation codenamed Magic Carpet. It is now known that just as the European settlers in Australia stole aboriginal children from their parents to give them a 'civilised upbringing', so also the Ashkenazim kidnapped hundreds of Yemeni children to have them educated in special institutions, as proper Israeli citizens.

The state of Israel also organised the theft of manuscripts—truckloads of them—dealing with Jewish history, law and philosophy of the last 1,000 years, which the old Jewish families of Yemen had been assiduously preserving for centuries. Yitzhak Ben-Zvi, Israel's second President, justified the measure by arguing that the Jewish nation had to recover its knowledge treasures. Shlomo Korah, the grandson of a respected Jewish scholar of Halachic law and Kabala who had his large library of manuscripts stolen when he migrated to Israel in 1949, declared that never in their long history had the Jews of Yemen faced the kind of discrimination and prejudice they now had to suffer inside Israel.[18]

So much for the 'light-skinned' Mizrahim. As for the 'black' Fallashmura Jews from Ethiopia, totalling nearly 100,000, their plight is almost inhuman. Having been lured into the country under false pretences, with promises of privileges and benefits, most of them are treated as criminals. Thousands of them are housed in transit and absorption centres, in the peripheries of cities like Jerusalem, with severe restrictions on their right to movement, employment and even education. An approximate 25,000 Fallashmuras, after being displaced from their traditional homes in Ethiopia under the Zionist migration drives, have been languishing in 'displacement' or 'transit' camps inside Ethiopia's Gondar province. They are waiting there like refugees or asylum seekers because the Zionist enthusiasm for these coloured Jews has suddenly waned with the emergence of white Jewish immigrants from the former USSR. So there are now new quota restrictions on the permissible number of Fallashmura immigrants per annum, and the processing of their aliya applications may take years.

How can Hizbullah, or, for that matter, anyone endowed with human sensitivity, compromise with a state which coldly disrupts human bonds and tramples on the local cultures, traditions and institutions for the sake of a chimerical concept of Zionism that has no roots in verifiable history, carries a chillingly alien spirit, and has the effect of unsettling or destroying everything it touches? Any decent man must recoil from this monstrous invasion that seeks

244 *Martyred but Not Tamed*

*to erase human associations, rooted organically in local histories and replace them with an order that is not merely alien and artificial but feeds on the basest and ugliest of emotions.*

I requested Abdo Saad to be a bit more specific about the 'base and ugly emotions', which according to him sustain the Zionist project and shape human relations in Israel. He looked at his watch once again and, mumbling something about the approaching hour for breaking the day-long fast, said he would close the discussion with two illustrations which ought to satisfy me.

*Many would find it hard to believe that after Iraq's invasion of Kuwait, Israel manipulated the United States into intervening militarily in the region so that it (Israel) might quietly move a million Russian-speaking Jews not only into its 'own' territory but also into the West Bank, while pretending to be pursuing a negotiated settlement with the PLO. This must sound too far-fetched to be true, yet I am convinced that this is exactly what took place. I can see that you have your doubts, and so let me adduce two more examples, on a more modest scale, but well-documented and quite incontrovertible.*

We talked about the airlifting of Yemenite and Ethiopian Jews and their subsequent plight inside Israel. Ben-Gurion, the founder of Israel, was also, as we have seen, one of the masterminds behind the demographic management of Eretz Israel in its early decades. Back in 1947, Ben-Gurion dispatched a sturdy team of Mossad agents to Iraq, to instigate the exodus of the Iraqi Jewry, about 80,000 strong, which had been living there for centuries. The plan, which was duly carried out, was to set off powerful explosions inside the Jewish quarters in Baghdad and to kill many civilians. The mayhem would be blamed on Arab nationalists, create instant panic among the Baghdadi Jews and drive them en masse into the (yet to be proclaimed) state of Israel. This is more or less what happened,[19] except that one of the Mossad agents, Yahuda Tajar, apparently in a fit of remorse, later owned up to the facts and named a number of senior Mossad agents involved in the operation. Well, do you think that these revelations caused a public outcry? Quite the reverse: it met with brazen appreciation! Here is what Abraham Spadron, a well-known media commentator, wrote in *Davar*[20]:

*If I had the power as I have the will, I would select a score of efficient young men, intelligent, decent, devoted to our ideal and burning with the desire to help redeem Jews... and I would send them to countries where Jews are absorbed in sinful self-satisfaction. The task of these young men would be to disguise themselves as non-Jews and plague Jews with anti-Semitic slogans and similar intimacies. I can vouch that the results in terms of sizeable immigration to Israel from these countries would be 10,000 times larger than the results brought by thousands of emissaries who have been preaching for decades to deaf ears...*

These lines appeared in Davar in July 1952. There were other comments in the same vein.

There were scores of covert operations, carried out under the direct supervision of Ben-Gurion in several Middle East countries, to induce Jewish emigration. One such operation received unwanted publicity after five Israeli commandos were caught red-handed in Syria in December 1954. Pinhas Lavon, the then Israeli Defence Minister, who supervised the operation, authorised the hijacking of a Syrian civilian aircraft to compel the Syrian Government to release the five agents. Most member states of the United Nations knew about the scope of Israel's terrorist activities, but Israel's western patrons, with their veto power in the Security Council, made sure that there were no consequences.

So this 1947 bombing spate in Baghdad by Mossad agents is my first example. It perfectly captures the view which Zionism takes of 'lesser Jews' and its methods for dealing with them: bomb the lot into panic, uproot them from the ancestral soil, and herd them into Israel, where they can fend for themselves and live as degraded citizens.

My second example illustrates what a young, hot-blooded Zionist does to a respected founder figure, an Israeli of the pioneer generation, when the latter shows signs of losing his mettle and softens up to the Palestinians.

Yitzhak Rabin, Israel's Army Chief during the Six-Day War in 1967,[21] was murdered at a public function, on 4 November 2005, weeks after signing the Oslo Accord, by a young fanatic, Yigal Amir. Here you have 'murderous love' at work—the spilling of sacrificial blood to renew the Zionist vision. But there is another side to the gruesome event, namely the reaction of the Israeli public. Alongside the horror, which you would expect, there was also a groundswell of sympathy, which you wouldn't believe! The emblematic figure here is Larissa Trembovler. A talented biologist from Moscow, Larissa Trembovler, an orthodox Jewess, claimed her 'right of return' in 1989. She later earned a PhD in Medieval Jewish (and Islamic) Philosophy at an Israeli university. She also started visiting Yigal Amir in jail. The weird courtship ended with a secret marriage, in 1997. It is not too difficult to guess how Trembovler, who wrote a novel titled A Mirror for a Prince, sees Yigal and herself. Well, this Larissa Trembovler, this new-fangled Zionist from Russia, this biologist and philosopher, daughter *to a well-known physicist mother, who had read all of Dostoyevsky, Kafka and Proust in her school years, divorced her Russian husband to sustain her hero through his years of imprisonment.* Abdo Saad looked at me with a quizzical smile as we shook hands to say goodbye.

A few days later, I went to meet with Amal Saad-Ghorayeb, Abdo Saad's daughter, in her posh office at the Carnegie Middle East Center, on Parliament Street in downtown Beirut. An Associate Professor at the Lebanese American University in Beirut, Amal had taken a sabbatical to work with the Carnegie Center as a specialist on Hizbullah, largely on the strength of her book *Hizbullah: Politics and Religion.*[22]

I was slightly taken aback as I shook hands with her. I was expecting to find her in traditional attire, with a headscarf or something. But Amal was wearing jeans and a sleeveless crop-top. Her head was uncovered, showing a modern, fluffy hairdo. I said I was curious about her upbringing, and asked what had motivated her to study Hizbullah. She obliged with a candid self-account, which I will try to sum up.

Amal was born and raised in England where her parents worked for several decades. Her mother, a Maronite Christian from South Lebanon, encouraged Amal to spend her school holidays with her maternal grandparents, who never left their ancestral land, despite the numerous Israeli incursions and the occupation, which began for good in 1975. So Amal visited Lebanon every year until she was 17, by which time her father decided to return to Beirut.

That was in 1989, the year of the Taif agreement which was supposed to end the civil war. So far, Amal had felt much attached to her Christian grandparents. They would take her along to Sunday mass, and now and then speak disparagingly of Muslims. All in all, Amal in her childhood thought of herself more as a Christian than a Muslim. But she also visited, for shorter durations, her paternal grandparents in Beirut, who would berate Christians. Slowly, Amal would become conscious of the Christian–Muslim divide. But she didn't learn about Lebanon's confessional system and tight communalism, or about the Shia–Sunni fracture, until much later, when she began to attend college.

During her last years in England, under the emotional and intellectual influence of her father, Amal began to feel more and more of a Muslim. School life also affected her sense of self and identity. Though

England-born, Amal never felt British. At the social level, she was made to feel her foreignness, her non-belonging. Amal still remembers bringing Lebanese food to school and her classmates making fun of her because her food was so strange and un-British. Such little things contributed as much to her drift towards Islam and Arabism as the political discussions which her father and his friends were continuously having at home. Very early in life, she heard about the Palestinian *catastrophe,* the creation of Israel and what it entailed for the Palestinians.

Amal was at school when the first Palestinian Intifada broke out. She began to wear the Palestinian *keffiyeh* and visit a London mosque regularly. She found attending Friday prayers at the mosque to be an uplifting experience. During *Id,* she would go to the mosque and pray, in silent communion with Muslims from all over the world, immersed in a sense of global Muslim solidarity. Amal also attended the *Ashura* commemoration,[23] a high point in the Shia calendar, which is observed with an abundance of ritual and attendant mourning. Amal remembers how during the celebrations women were segregated from men. There were many Shia widows and mothers there, from Iran and Iraq, whose husbands or sons had been killed in the decade-long war between the two countries. Yet they would weep together, beat their breasts and flagellate themselves in unison, to mourn the loss of their loved ones. It was an extraordinary experience, political no less than religious, whose full significance she would grasp only later.

Thus it was that Amal became a 'political Muslim' in the UK. Even socially, the choice made life simpler: while recognising that she did not belong, she now felt equal, and was no longer intimidated by the British and their ways.

Amal came back to Lebanon fairly politicised. She remembers her first days at Beirut University, where she now teaches. It was very unfashionable then for middle class Muslims to openly pray and fast. Apart from a few hijab wearers, Amal was the only modern young woman at the university who prayed five times a day and fasted during Ramadan. Many made fun of her.

Fashions have changed. Praying and fasting are now the 'in thing', almost a craze. All her students at the Lebanese American University, boys and girls, even the most modern and secular, pray and fast; even those without real religious commitment. It has almost become a fad. She had once felt ostracised for flaunting her religiousness. But everything changed after 9/11.

Back in Lebanon, Amal became engrossed in understanding Hizbullah. Her fascination for the organisation, in a sense, grew out of her disenchantment with the PLO after the Oslo Accords. But the surrender implicit in the Oslo Accord was only the last straw. For years, the PLO had failed the Palestinian refugees, completely ignoring their plight and making no plans for their future rehabilitation. In many ways, the Palestinian refugees in Lebanon were the ones who had catapulted the PLO and Yasser Arafat into their position of uncontested leadership after the Black September purges in Jordan and the Lebanese Civil War. Prior to 1982, in the years before Israel's full-blown invasion of Lebanon, the PLO and Arafat were busy playing hollow power politics, as a state within the state, rather than training to fight Israel. Even after the 1982 rout, most Palestinians continued to support the PLO and Arafat, from a conviction that they would never betray the founding charter. They were taught better when Arafat and the PLO made their triumphal move from Tunisia to the West Bank and Gaza, abandoning the Palestinian refugees in Lebanon and Syria to their stateless, homeless condition, while they themselves were chasing the fireball of political power, only to be consumed by it.

By the time she returned to Lebanon, Amal was also thoroughly disillusioned with the rhetoric of Arab nationalism. What power there had been in Arab nationalism now seemed to have flowed into Islamism. In concrete terms, for Lebanon's Shia Muslims, the real motives of hope were these: first the Islamic Revolution in Iran; then the rise of Hizbullah in Lebanon; and lastly the two Palestinian *intifadas*. To Amal, as indeed to many of her generation, political Islam had replaced Arab nationalism, not only as the defender of Muslim rights but also as the more effective carrier of national aspirations. To her, Hizbullah and Hamas were living proof of this passing of the sceptre. She saw signs of the new Islamic-nationalistic synthesis taking deep roots everywhere in the region, especially after the 2003 American invasion of Iraq. To Amal, in short, Islam was less of an essentialist religion and more of a vehicle for political upliftment—a source of strength and a fount of inspiration to fight injustice, within and without.

I spoke with Amal for many hours, with intermittent phone calls interrupting our conversation. Amal sounded particularly excited after one such phone call, from an Iranian television channel that wanted to interview her. She had to go home and 'change' for the interview because, as she pointed out, it would be unbecoming for a Lebanese woman scholar to talk about Hizbullah on Iranian TV without at least wearing a headscarf.

I did not query Amal about her findings on Hizbullah, as she was pressed for time, but also because, having read her book, I thought it preferable to direct those interested to *Hizbullah: Politics and Religion*[24] and let them judge for themselves. Amal has dedicated her book to her father, acknowledging his intellectual inspiration and also 'his extensive contacts with Hizbullah officials' which gave her 'unparalleled access to many leading figures in the party, without whom this work would not have borne fruition'. From this meeting with Amal, I took away the image of a youthful political enthusiasm, not free perhaps of naivety and immaturity, but quite serious in its commitment.

The last comprehensive conversation I had in Beirut was with a real insider, Rashid W.[25] Now well in his 60s and semi-retired, he still contributes to various magazines like the weekly *Al-Intiqad* and makes occasional appearances on *Al-Manar,* the Hizbullah television channel that emits from a secret, ever-changing location. In his active years, Rashid W. was also a senior Hizbullah functionary, who used to work closely with the organisation's top leadership, including its current Secretary-General Al-Sayyid Hassan Nasrallah.

Like Amal Saad-Ghorayeb, Rashid W. holds a PhD from a British university. Unlike Amal, Rashid learnt his politics at first hand, when he joined the armed struggle against the Israeli military occupation of South Lebanon, which Hizbullah had been waging since 1982. Rashid felt he had to join the resistance after Israel bombed a UN-run refugee shelter in Qana, on 18 April 1996, killing 106 civilians. By that time he was already too old to engage in direct combat action, but worked as a political cadre, also dealing with intelligence gathering. Rashid said that he felt the same irresistible surge of anger four years later, in May 2000, when Israel destroyed an unofficial prison it had been maintaining at Al-Khiyam, in South Lebanon. That was just before Israel was forced to withdraw its troops, practically back to its own borders. Throughout the occupation, it had used its surrogate South Lebanese Army to hold hundreds of Lebanese civilians, without charge, at this informal, inaccessible detention centre. The idea was to use them as hostages, to secure the release of Israeli prisoners or the return of their body parts. Then, on the eve of its humiliating retreat and in a fit of anger against Hizbullah, Israel had all the prisoners at Al-Khiyam murdered. I was keen to take the conversation back to the political. Despite its redoubtable reputation as an armed organisation which forced the withdrawal of the American and French troops in 1982 and finally, through sheer attrition, the roll-back of the Israeli occupation in May 2000, Hizbullah entered politics within a decade of its creation. It already took part in the 1992 parliamentary elections, winning, together with its allies, 12 seats (from a total of 128). Since then, Hizbullah has been going from strength to strength on the domestic political scene. Together with its allies across all sects, it may even, in not so distant a future, form a coalition government. But Hizbullah continues to claim that its primary raison d'être lies in resisting Israeli aggression. It has successfully defied all attempts, internal and external, to have it disarmed.

At the same time, Hizbullah has been respecting the rules of war. It has negotiated conditions for a ceasefire with its 'evil enemy' (even accepting an international monitoring group) while denying it recognition as a legitimate state. In July and August 2006, Hizbullah fought back the aerial offensive which Israel launched not only against the guerrilla bases in Southern Lebanon and in Beirut, but also against Lebanon's civilian infrastructure. The aim was to wreak colossal damage, so as to demoralise the population and estrange it from the resistance movement. The aerial bombing wiped out several villages in South Lebanon and flattened entire districts of southern and western Beirut. Highways, flyovers and bridges, power plants and water tanks, telephone, television and radio towers, petroleum stores and medical supplies were deliberately targeted and destroyed. Approximately 800 Lebanese, mostly civilians, died and more than 2,000 were wounded. More than 700,000 were made homeless.

Faced with this firewall, Hizbullah was not cowed. The Israeli action failed to instigate a mutiny against Hizbullah. On the contrary, people across all sections and sects broadly—some would say, overwhelmingly—hailed the bold resistance of the organisation, which fought back a few tentative incursions by the Israeli ground troops and kept up its rocket attacks into Israeli territory. A total of 35 Israeli soldiers died and Israel felt pressed enough to accept a UN Security Council-sponsored ceasefire (under the resolution 1701) 34 weeks after launching in fanfare its version of *awe and shock*. Israel also shied from mounting a massive ground invasion, though it had threatened one. Hizbullah claimed that the outcome of the war was a triumph. All Arabs, and even outside observers, agreed that Israel had done poorly in military terms and failed in its strategic objectives.

Israel and its allies accused Hizbullah of provoking the war by attacking an Israeli army convoy and capturing two of its soldiers. Hizbullah had carried out the operation to negotiate the release of Lebanese prisoners languishing in Israeli jails without due process. They had launched similar operations before. Nasrallah later pointed out that he had failed to anticipate the scale of Israeli retaliation; otherwise, he would have disallowed the operation. Israel clearly pounced on the cross-border attack as a pretext for doing what it had been itching to do for some time: launching a devastating aerial assault to isolate Hizbullah politically and impress upon all Lebanese the costs of sheltering the militia. Israel also hoped to push the international community and the pro-western government, then in power in Beirut, to disarm Hizbullah. It may well have been encouraged in its strategic (mis)calculations by the Syrian troop withdrawal from Lebanon in 2005.[26]

Hizbullah foiled all these calculations. It emerged from the war politically and militarily stronger. Al-Sayyid Hassan Nasrallah was acclaimed as a hero throughout the Arab world. Despite the military losses, Hizbullah did not give up its defiant stance and continued to oppose the Lebanese formations aligned with the oil enclaves in the Gulf and their western patrons. The broad mobilisation led by Saad Rafiqi, which culminated in the so-called *Cedar Revolution*, was perhaps its most serious challenge but here again Hizbullah weathered the storm. At the same time, Hizbullah seems prepared to deal with its overseas antagonists, chiefly the United States and France, to secure its vital interests. Nor is it above parleying with Israel, even if tersely and indirectly, to resolve humanitarian problems or negotiate the exchange of prisoners. In July 2008, Hizbullah handed over coffins with the corpses of Ehud Goldwasser and Eldad Regev, two Israeli soldiers captured before the start of July 2006 war, in exchange for five Lebanese prisoners and the mortal remains of 200 other Lebanese who had died in Israeli captivity.

But for all its flexibility and readiness for dialogue, there are no signs of Hizbullah shedding the fundamental principles which inform its agenda: the primacy of armed resistance against Israel; the democratisation of

Lebanese politics through an awakening of 'the downtrodden and the oppressed'; developing effective public services; ending the pervasive corruption and the regime of patronage; transcending the sectarian stratification through inter-communal partnerships; and, last though not least, maintaining the ideological comradeship and solidarity of resistance with Hamas, Syria and Iran.

Clearly, there was something very solid, but also sophisticated, refined almost, about this combination of political resilience, ideological stamina, and undaunted resistance against prepotent enemies. Yet, despite hearing repeatedly about Hizbullah's ultimate ambition of bringing peace—a just, principled, lasting peace, a peace with honour—not only to Lebanon but to the entire region, I was still unclear whether there were real chances of the movement ever reaching a comprehensive understanding with Israel, on terms that didn't contradict its core principles. Abdo Saad had been very forthcoming on other questions. He had waxed eloquent when discussing the merits of compromise, negotiations and gradual reform with reference to the Islamic world. But on this one issue—peace with Israel—he seemed to suggest that the Zionist state was beyond the pale, fundamentally *unreformable*, irresponsive to all attempts at humanisation.

I was keen, therefore, to hear Rashid's view. I recapitulated the main points Abdo Saad had made and invited him to comment, from his own perspective as a Hizbullah insider. I said, in particular, that I was curious to know what view he and his comrades were taking of the tribulations of the Jewish diaspora: the desperate urgency felt by the Holocaust survivors; their attempt to turn the page of exile forever; then Israel's violent birth; and as the culmination of it all, the unrelenting, pitiless suppression, Nazi-like in all but scale, of the hapless Palestinians. Then there were the other Arabs. They too seemed helpless, as if bereft of agency, mere play-things of foreign powers. Was it not possible then to view Jews, Palestinians, all Arabs, as fellow victims of history? Was it not possible to draw them all into a common, equitable, human space, where the horrors of history might be recognised and exorcised at last, through conscience, deliberation, dialogue?

Rashid was all patience as I rambled on about my impressions, doubts and queries. He never balked at my points and, when I fell silent, instructed his secretary not to let anyone interrupt our discussion. I was all ears.

*Hizbullah is not against Jews. It does not criticise them on the basis of race or religion. To qualify for respect as human beings, we must extend that respect to others, irrespective of race, religion and politics. That is the ground rule, the basis of our morality as human beings. We cannot call ourselves Muslims if we condone racist or religious exclusivism. You talked about a common space for dialogue. We need more than that. We have to accept the pluralism of human existence as our starting point. We have to accept and respect all groups as worthy constituents of the human tapestry. We, and they, have no choice but to live together.*

Rashid picked up the receiver to answer a telephone call and apologised for the interruption.

*Having clarified our attitude towards Jews as Jews, which is invariably misrepresented, I must now explain our position on Zionist Israel and our idea of a just peace. To do that, however, we must first understand the principles that guide Hizbullah's mission.*

*The historical circumstances responsible for the birth of Hizbullah are fairly well known. What is not so well known is the manner in which Hizbullah dichotomises the power relations which obtain in the world and which call for redress through reform or revolution. The dichotomy that matters to us is the one between the politically subjugated, disenfranchised, disentitled masses, and the oppressors and appropriators of human and material resources. This worldview is clearly articulated in Hizbullah's open letter of 1985 as well as in the political manifesto it released before the elections in 1992. Our detractors of course dismiss this dualism as a narrow sectarian thing, a mere reflection of the age-old Shia love affair with victimhood, reinforced by the all too real griev- ances of Lebanon's Shias. Yet others view this as a variation of the Islamic binary between Dar al-Islam and Dar al-Harb—the 'abode of faith' and the 'domain of the infidels' (literally, 'arena of war')—destined to clash in an apocalyptic battle before the millennial triumph.*

*These interpretations are uninformed and tainted by common misconceptions about Islamic movements. The truth is that Hizbullah belongs to an old histori- cal tradition in Islam which takes pride in championing the oppressed and the dispossessed against the arrogance and vanity of power, the greed, hoarding, and ostentation—all negative tendencies which crept into the Muslim state system very early on, at the beginning of the Umayyad Caliphate. As you must know, this tradition of struggle, of pious courage and self-sacrificing heroism on behalf of the suppressed and the downtrodden, goes back to a series of 'foundational martyrdoms'—the death of Imam Ali, the son-in-law and cousin of Prophet Mohammed; that of Imam Hussein, the grandson of the Prophet; and then of Hussein's two sons, all within a few decades of the Prophet's passing away. They gave up their lives resisting the exactions and oppressive rule of Caliph Yazid on behalf of his victims, the diligent and exploited people of Kufa.*[27] *The population of Kufa consisted mostly of small entrepreneurs, craftsmen, former prisoners of war and new converts to Islam. They invited Iman Ali to lead their struggle for justice, causing him to shift his capital from Medina to Kufa.*

*Although our history of struggle against oppression in the Middle East, in the past and also in the present, would seem to be putting the Shia population in the forefront, the spirit of our struggle is broader than that. It carries universal lessons. The Quran talks about the obligation of all true believers to defend and succour 'all the oppressed on earth'. Period. It doesn't say 'all the oppressed Muslims'. You might even say that this broad Islamic concept of 'the oppressed', as understood by us, has a modern echo in Frantz Fanon's notion of the 'wretched of the earth'.*

*Hizbullah has long been fighting for the Palestinians in Lebanon, although the vast majority are Sunni Muslims. It sympathises with Hamas, which is, likewise, predominantly Sunni. Having stood by the PLO in its darkest hours, at the height of the Lebanese Civil War and during the Israeli invasion, Hizbullah didn't hesitate to categorically denounce the PLO leadership when the latter went down the slippery road of the Oslo process and ended up recognising Israel as a legitimate state, even agreeing to police Gaza on its behalf! Hizbullah was from the start allied with Syria because, even though not an Islamic state, Syria offers its unwavering support to the dispossessed Arab groups in the region and remains constant in its opposition to Zionist hegemony. Hizbullah recognises the de facto reality of Saudi Arabia and the other client regimes of the West throughout the Gulf. However, it doesn't acknowledge their moral legitimacy. It sympathises with the emancipatory struggles all over the world and, within its means, actively coordinates with some of them. Hizbullah is all admiration for those Third World leaders who stand up to imperialist exploitation. It celebrates men like Nelson Mandela, Desmond Tutu, Fidel Castro, the Irish Bobby Sands who died on a hunger strike in prison, or even Venezuela's Hugo Chavez, as exponents of the indomitable spirit of man in his pursuit of freedom and dignity. It opposed the Afghan mujahideen when they accepted America's aid to fight the Soviet occupation of their country, and later unequivocally condemned the Taliban regime for its abusive governance. It denounces the sectarian* terrorism and indiscriminate violence of the sort practised by Al-Qaida and sundry Wahhabi groups.

Sheikh Mohammed Hussein Fadlallah of Lebanon,[28] the highly esteemed philosopher and seer who inspires the political thinking and practice of Hizbullah, has been insisting time and again, whether in public or in his capacity as spiritual counsellor, that for a Muslim to do injustice to a non-Muslim, on the basis of his 'otherness', no matter what the context or provocation, is an unforgivable act, on a par almost with apostasy. He has also made it absolutely plain that it would be dead wrong for anyone, no matter how serious their grievances with the Government of United States, to target individual Americans who are not cognizant of, let alone responsible for, the deviousness of America's foreign policies. Specifically, he condemned the hijacking of civilian planes which were crashed into the Twin Towers of the World Trade Center, killing all passengers and two thousand office workers. These 9/11 attacks, for which Al-Qaida took responsibility, Sheikh Fadlallah said, were an act of terrorism, not feats of martyrdom.

These being the fundamental principles that guide Hizbullah's mission, let us now examine how they shape our attitude towards Israel.

As we all know, Hizbullah does not recognise Israel as a legitimate state. The reasons, too, are well known, so let us not repeat them all over. Hizbullah does not say, mind you, that Jews have no right to live in Palestine. All those Jews whose forebears used to live there can stay on, and even those few outsiders who can establish a bona fide association with Palestinian Jewry may join. But what Hizbullah cannot, and will not, accept is that people who have for generations been living in Palestine, and still keep the keys to their old dwellings must forever remain rootless refugees, so that Jews from Poland, Russia, and all places and corners of the globe, brainwashed into embracing the notion of Eretz Israel, may come and build their sprawling settlements on the land of evicted Palestinians.

Hizbullah's approach to peace in the Middle East is simple: peace without justice is not worth having, and there can be no justice until Israel surrenders the land, and the overlordship on the land, which it stole from the Palestinians through murder and mayhem, and allows all the people who have an existential stake in the Palestinian homeland to select a political system after their heart, and freely elect the government they wish to live under. That is Hizbullah's principled position. Hizbullah cannot recognise the legitimacy of the Zionist State and will oppose any Palestinian leadership or Arab state which does recognise it, for the *simple reason that accepting Israel means denying the history of Palestine and making light of the suffering of its people. For us Arabs, recognising Israel could only mean one thing: surrender to racist aggression and acquiescence in serfdom to power-intoxicated aliens. That's how things look from* an Arab point of view. *But remember what I said a moment ago about Hizbullah trying to rise above parochialism, and so let me add this; from a* human point of view, *to make one's peace with Israel means concurring in the day-to-day denial by Israelis of the nobler side of the Jewish spirit and tradition. More to the point, it means debasing—and in a way negating—the Jewish experience of the Holocaust as a sacred lesson for mankind to ponder and learn from.*

Rashid W. was trying to make an important point here, and I would have liked him to elaborate. But he seemed absorbed in his own thought process, and I refrained from interrupting.

*The state of Israel is an immoral entity, because it has institutionalised (not so much in its laws, but in its practice; that is to say, in the most hypocritical of ways) racism, discrimination and systemic injustice against the Palestinians, that 'lesser breed'. For example, an approximate 1.4 million Muslim Israelis, about 20 per cent of the total population, are compelled to live at the rock bottom of society, without basic rights. Blatantly racist regulations and arbitrary rulings by the authorities responsible for land development ensure that they are not able to build new houses, or often repair existing ones, even on the land they own. In fact, Israel's municipal authorities thrive on demolishing houses, symbolically shattering the Palestinians' dreams for a settled, secure existence. These housing policies are typical of the relationship between Israel and its Muslim subjects.*

I requested Rashid to illustrate his point.

He paused for a while and then asked me to look up Kenize Mourad, a French journalist and writer born of an Indian father and a Turkish mother, known for documenting hundreds of such cases. He mentioned her book *Our Sacred Land: Voices of the Palestine-Israeli Conflict*,[29] suggesting that I get hold of a copy and read it. He then cited from memory two examples, which he said were recorded in the book.

*The first case was that of Salim Shawamreh, a construction engineer from a suburb of East Jerusalem. His parents were from a village which had been torched by the Haganah in 1948. The family then moved to East Jerusalem and opened a coffee shop, which the Israeli army impounded along with the house in 1967 when it took over East Jerusalem after the Six Day war. Salim's family*—*his parents, four brothers and five sisters, and Salim himself*—*shifted to a two-room shelter in a refugee camp. He then trained as a construction engineer, married, and went to work in Saudi Arabia for ten years. Having saved some money, Salim then decided to return home along with his wife and three children. He bought a piece of land in a village not far from his birthplace in East Jerusalem. He wanted to build a house and applied for permission, paying a substantial fee in the process. The application was rejected 18 months later, on grounds that his land fell outside the building area. In reality, there was no building plan for the village. Jews had been putting up structures where and when they wanted. The authorities thwarted Salim's application by simply drawing a line on the land-map which excluded everything outside the existing houses as non-edificandi zone! And that was that.*

*Salim talked to some of his friends who worked for the housing rights of Arab Muslim citizens. With their counsel, he made a second application, again depositing a hefty submission fee. The second application said that he wanted to build an agricultural house to do some farming. The application was again turned down, 18 months later, on grounds that the land was too close to a road used by Jewish commuters. After making a third, fruitless application and losing more money, Salim decided to build his house without the required permit. He lived there for four years.*

*One evening in July 1998, a demolition squad, equipped with a bulldozer and led by soldiers, turned up at the house when Salim and his family were having dinner. The soldiers ordered Salim to move out within 15 minutes with whatever belongings he and his family members could physically carry. Salim tried to raise an alarm but was beaten up, handcuffed, and pinned to the ground. The soldiers then broke windows to lob in tear gas shells to smoke out his wife and children, who had locked themselves in. As Arab Muslim neighbours, startled by the pandemonium, began to gather, the soldiers opened fire, killing seven of them. The house was swiftly demolished. The squad went away, leaving behind a $1,500 bill (the cost of demolition) for Salim to pick up.*

*The family then went to live in a shelter provided by the Committee against House Demolition. Salim's youngest daughter developed a high fever and a form of paralysis, but there was no money for specialised medical examinations or treatment. Salim could not get a job as an engineer and finally settled for working as a truck driver for a newspaper company. To supplement the family income, his 16-year-old son had to give up school to find work as a labourer.*

*That's Salim's story, as documented by Kenize Mourad. It reflects the life ordeals of hundreds and thousands of Israeli Palestinians.*

*Let me tell you about another case of house demolition. Kenize Mourad wrote it down from Ahmed Fayad, a resident of the Jenin refugee camp in the northern West Bank. One of Fayad's brothers was a policeman who worked with the Israeli authorities to keep peace in the area. He had a second brother who was seriously ill and stayed bedridden in the house. The demolition squad first threw a fire bomb and the house started burning. Ahmed Fayad stepped out of the house and saw the bulldozers closing in. His mother and sister were also with him. They started screaming, asking the bulldozers to stop, but they kept moving. Fayad's policeman brother could not control himself and picked up his gun. He was shot dead instantly. Fayad's mother went up to the leading bulldozer to plead with the soldier behind the steer to stop until she evacuated her ailing son. The bulldozer stopped. But as Fayad's mother and sister rushed into the house, the bulldozers started moving again, squashing the front wall. The mother and sister scarcely managed to get out. The bulldozers flattened the house, burying Fayad's ailing brother alive under the rubble.*

*These incidents, and there are myriads of them, show the inhumanity that goes with the Israeli occupation.*

Rashid continued:

*Let us for a moment leave aside Israel's record of malevolence and war crimes, which has few parallels in modern history. Let us merely take a passing look at the organisational structure of the state, and we will see that inhumanity is built into every aspect of its governance, its citizenship laws and its racist regulations.*

*The Zionist understanding of Judaism does not recognise the separation of religion and governance.[30] It also regards the Jews as a chosen people,[31] who at the advent of the Messiah shall be redeemed on a collective basis, irrespective of whether this or that individual Jew keeps or breaks his religious pledges. The Messiah is conceived of as a spiritual-cum-political redeemer of the Jewish collective, and his coming must be preceded by the return of all exiles and their in-gathering in the land of Zion. So much for the foundational myths! At the practical level, Israel incorporated a great amount of Judaic religious law (a mishmash of tenets from the Halacha, the Nevim and Ketuvim—the Torah's prophetic sections—and the Talmud) into its legal corpus, which inevitably infringes on the rights and freedoms—personal, familiar, customary, and religious—of the non-Jewish communities. It is for this reason that Israel* has to this day deferred the adoption of a constitution spelling out universal rights. Instead, it chose to embrace what it calls 'basic laws', which primarily cater to the religious obligations of the 'chosen people'. Israel's declaration of independence says that the state will follow the ideals of 'freedom, justice and peace as envisaged by the prophets of Israel'. It also describes Israel as a 'Jewish State'.

In Israel, a person cannot marry or divorce without making a declaration of religious affiliation. There is no law for civil marriage, which means there can be no inter-religious weddings. An Arab Israeli woman who weds a Palestinian man from the occupied territories immediately loses her right to live in Jerusalem, her social security, health insurance, even her pension. Her children become illegitimate.

All persons, Jewish or otherwise, are tied to their respective religious courts and there is no independent jurisdiction for them to turn to. This corseting of all citizens according to religious affiliations goes hand in hand with the assumption by the state of the power to define, for Jews and non-Jews alike, the exact sphere of rights and freedoms granted under each religion. For example, the Law and Administration Ordinance of 1948 forbids polygamy, which is expressly permitted under Muslim Law. When that Israeli law was challenged by a Muslim citizen, the Supreme Court upheld it by arguing that 'freedom of religion cannot be interpreted as freedom to do what the religion permits'. It held that 'religious freedom' must be construed to mean that the adherent of a given religion is free to fulfil the commandments it imposes, but not to avail himself of all the freedoms his religion permits. This is what the Supreme Court ruled in Muldem vs Qadi of Acco, but the implications go way beyond the issue of Islamic marriage laws.

This usurpation by Israel of the right to interpret the 'sphere of freedom' of other religions received legislative authority when the Knesset passed the Basic Law on Human Dignity and Liberty in 1992. The law was later amended to clarify its purpose, which was 'to protect human dignity in order to anchor in a Basic Law the values of the State of Israel as a Jewish and democratic State'. The law does not mention 'freedom of religion'. Already in 1985, a law passed by the Knesset banned anyone who does not subscribe to the existing structure of the Israeli state from entering the legislative process.

Israeli citizenship is governed by the Law of Return of 1950 and the Nationality Law of 1952, which privilege the 13 million diaspora Jews scattered across the globe over the true sons of the soil—the Palestinians. Diaspora

*Jews are invited, even strongly encouraged, to acquire Israeli citizenship simply by stating that they wish to 'return' to the land, or by 'doing aliya' ('ascent'), as the smug Hebrew phrase goes. Arabs, on the other hand, must establish their birth to Israeli parents, or paramount residence or naturalisation, which is not easy.*

*Israel is also the only country in the world that, for all practical purposes, outlaws the ownership of land and property by the true 'sons of the soil'.*

*All green and fertile swathes of land with irrigation facilities are reserved for Jewish settlements. Arabs are squeezed into scanty, mostly barren land allocations, with no right to build on their properties. Yet, these same Arabs are registered as 'land-owning', and on that ground disqualified from receiving unemployment benefit. All Israeli Arabs between themselves own a miserly 3 per cent of the land, and they are forbidden from building, expanding or even repairing their dwellings without receiving prior official permission, which is habitually denied. Jews, meanwhile, receive their land on long-term lease from the Custodian of Absentee Property and the Jewish National Fund, which own 93 per cent of all immovable property in the name of the state. All Jews on the settlements are, therefore, categorised as 'landless', and as such they qualify for the full spectrum of unemployment and social benefits.*

*The Custodian of Absentee Property is a statutory authority which acquired all its assets by confiscating the land, agricultural equipment, houses, business establishments, jewellery, bank accounts and business investments of the Palestinians who were expelled during the 1948 war, including some 250,000 internal refugees who were displaced from their original homes but continue to live within Israel's borders. There are also approximately 100,000 Palestinians living in what the state refers to as 'unrecognised villages'. The political meaning of this designation is not clear, by the implications are: these 'unrecognised villages' are barred from receiving municipal services like water, sanitation, roads, electricity and telephone. For all practical purposes, these villages and their inhabitants simply do not exist and their properties belong to the state and its guardian agencies like the Custodian of Absentee Property and the Jewish National Fund.*

*The Custodian of Absentee Property doles out its immovable property (mainly land) to Jewish settlements and individuals, and it uses its movable assets (Palestinian money from confiscated bank accounts and investments, said to be worth billions of dollars at current value index) to finance the immigration, naturalisation and settlement of diaspora Jews.*

*The Israeli authorities bulldozed and flattened some 500 villages previously inhabited by Palestinian refugees with the sole objective of preventing their return. The Jewish National Fund acquired the agricultural land of these destroyed villages to lease it out to Zionist communities or for its reforestation programmes. Some 250,000 'internal refugees' are also designated as 'present absentees', an odd official term which applies to those who have forsaken their properties, no matter how briefly, and have therefore forfeited all ownership rights. This is perhaps the most glaring example of how Israel goes about its task of dispossessing and dehumanising the Palestinians, by systematically hacking into all their cultural, communal and religious rights.*

*The Arab schools are controlled by the Shin Bet, Israel's internal security service. They are housed in dilapidated structures without basic facilities and are run by specially selected teachers, scant in numbers, who may deviate from the imposed curricula and ideological guidelines only at the risk of losing their jobs. Arabic is proscribed as a medium of instruction at all higher institutions and universities. More than 95 per cent of the instructors and professors there are Jewish, and many of them are attached to the security services or the military. Speaking in Arabic in public or at work is strongly discouraged, even in informal settings like hotels or restaurants.*

*All important and sensitive positions in government, business, industry, the scientific and security establishments are closed to Arab Israelis. Not a single Arab is on the payroll of the Central Bank of Israel, which has a total staff of approximately 1,000. Both Muslim and Christian Arabs are barred from joining the army, which means they are also excluded from the numberless advantages that go with military service, such as housing, self-employment financing, bank loans, educational quotas and scholarships, etcetera.*

I interrupted Rashid's moving indictment of Israel's racial oppression to take the discussion back to the plight of the Palestinian, and Arab, resistance. The Arabs have been losing war after war. The Palestinian resistance, never very cohesive, is now perhaps more divided than ever. The Arab states keep quarrelling and fighting among themselves and seem more intent on bleeding each other than on facing the challenges of Israeli aggression and western interference. It makes little sense to blame everything on the imperialist powers. Wahhabi fundamentalism, sectarian violence, the authoritarian disposition of the Arab states—all these phenomena look distinctly 'indigenous'. Aren't these home-grown traits largely responsible for the triumphs which Zionism has scored throughout its century-long career, and for the easy ride which the imperialist powers have been having in the region, and are still having? Hizbullah and Hamas talk about resistance. They talk about protracting the struggle until the objective conditions are there for a radical re-modelling of the region. This is a brave stance to take when the enemy is so strong, and the war risks being so long. But let us assume that the resistance survives, endures, and prevails. What then? What is there at the end of the road, whenever that end may appear? Where is the vision of an alternative society? Where is the imagination that can shape a better, fairer and more humane order? Where are the political traditions, the civic habits, the institutionalisation of practice, which alone can sustain such a project?

Rashid listened to my queries patiently, contemplatively, now and then nodding in approval. When he began to reply, his speech was slow and hesitant at first, with pauses between words.

*My answer will be twofold. Firstly, most Arab regimes are imposed, not self-chosen ones. They are imperialist creations, foisted on the people against their will and actually working against their people. Of course, all of them claim legitimacy, but the historical evidence speaks against them, and so does their government practice. Some of them hold rigged elections and claim to receive 99 per cent of the votes. We have kingdoms, sheikhdoms, emirates, authoritarian regimes and dictatorships. But where are the democracies? Public opinion is gagged by the police states—which is another way of saying that there is no public opinion. People are not allowed to speak out, to freely vent their disagreement, to raise their political consciousness through open, plural discourse. The media is monitored and controlled by the governments. The intelligence agencies (mukhabarat) spy on dissidents, arrest them, torture and 'disappear' them. Teachers are kept on a tight leash. Our whole education system is controlled, stifled rather, by the state. Billions are spent on arms that gather dust and rust in the military depots. So, you see, we are not in any sense a free people. We are still under occupation, still under the European mandate. The physical occupation is real enough—the foreign troops in Iraq, Palestine, the Golan heights are real enough. But the indirect occupation—through police states like Egypt, which do the bidding of the West and cosy up to Israel— that 'occupation at one remove', less visible but all the more pervasive, that occupation is still there and keeps us down.*

*Look at our oil resources. They could have been harnessed to transform and reform the entire Middle East. But what happened? Our oil fuelled the industrialisation, modernisation and technological advancement of the western world, which saw to it that every aspect of oil production, whether processing, marketing or revenue collection, remained under its direct control or the control of its own puppets—those scores of petty tyrants bereft of honour, vision, without any sense of responsibility to their own people. Thus, under foreign extraction and control, our oil has turned into a curse. Its revenues sustain our mean dictatorships, which return most of what they earn in the form of arms purchases.*

*What we need is a revolution, not a false one, which starts and ends in bloodshed, but a social revolution, which develops slowly and steadily, draws on the right inspiration and sets the right examples. Hizbullah, in its own modest way, has been trying to initiate such a process. It is a two-pronged experiment: on the one hand it leads an uncompromising armed struggle against outside aggression and occupation, and on the other hand it tries to challenge and redress the deep, systemic corruption of Lebanese politics with democratic means.*

*It is true that we Arabs have lost many wars. Israel routed the PLO in Lebanon in 1982 and marched on to Beirut within 12 hours of launching its invasion. It is also true that the PLO and Fatah, by signing the Oslo deal, have let down the Palestinians who had stood by them through thick and thin and sacrificed their all for the ideals of self-determination, freedom and right of return. Arafat and the PLO leadership went for a mirage: the bait of personal power being dangled before them was hollow and illusory. Oslo did not even determine the status of Gaza and the West Bank, it left the question of their borders open, but it exacted the abandonment of resistance as a precondition. The PLO went back to the occupied territories with pomp and ceremony, and Arafat acted as if he headed a sovereign state. But Israel had given out no more than a set of disconnected enclaves, subcontracted to the PLO for the purpose of cheap policing, and which could at any time, under any pretext, be cut off from each other and instantaneously brought under military rule. Then the decorum of office, which 'President' Arafat so much liked, would show what it was worth. Arafat found out as much on the day when Israel chose to hold him a prisoner inside his own Ramallah headquarters. But disillusionment came too late; he was already dying. We cannot change history, but we can try to reclaim our future, and this is what Hizbullah is attempting.*

*In July 2006, Israel possessed military power greatly superior to what it had in 1982. Yet it was unable to make any serious forays into Lebanese territory. Hizbullah fights with faith in God and faith in the people, and look: the people return that faith.* They believe that Hizbullah is serious about resisting aggression, and serious too in its commitment to the people and their basic needs, such as housing, education, health, livelihood, dignity and social justice. By standing firm in this war, Hizbullah has been able to send out a very eloquent message of power and hope.

Hizbullah is not a state. We know our place, we know our limits, and we want to continue our struggle without raising jealousies or resentments. Hizbullah is a resistance organisation and a political party in Lebanon, one of the smallest countries in the Arab world with a bare 10,000 square kilometres, and Hizbullah leads but one out of Lebanon's 18 confessional communities. So we are small and our role is modest.

At the same time, Lebanon, as Sheikh Fadlallah once put it, is the lung of the Middle East. Lebanon is a laboratory for political experiments; a listening post for monitoring the political trends at work in the Arab world, perhaps even in the entire Islamic world.

We are trying to be an example worthy of emulation. We are still in the phase of fighting for our formal existence. Recall that Israel launched its July 2006 war with the express purpose of annihilating Hizbullah. A large part of the Arab world was behind Israel. They counted on Israel to get rid of us. Most of the Arab states feel challenged by our very existence. Indeed, people have started asking: what do these states have all these armies for; these officers with epaulettes and shining brass and high lifestyles; all these aircrafts, tanks and artillery—what use are they when they cannot fight and win a single war against Israel, even on the smallest scale? How come Hizbullah, with its bunch of armed volunteers, is able to take on Israel's war machine, fight it for thirty-three days on end, and push it back? How come Hizbullah is able to assert its political agenda by democratic means, survive, and prevail over its far more powerful and resourceful adversaries within Lebanon?

While asking such questions, the people are looking at us for inspiration and hope. We want to retain a modest but exemplary profile. Even if we sometimes feel like the harbingers of a new era, the forerunners of a new dawn, we do not want to look like the foolish cock that starts croaking in the morning as if he were pulling the sun out into the world. But let's put it like this: when the sun is on its way, and the hour draws near, we wish to be the watchful lark that anticipates the coming dawn. We know our place is within Lebanon, and it is fine that way. But we hope that our conduct, our discourse, our spirit of active solidarity, may inspire emulation way beyond Lebanon's borders.

# Appendix

## Israel's Treatment of Oriental Jews

Abdo Saad makes much of the ill-treatment of 'oriental Jews'[32] at the hands of the Ashkenazi settlers and their offspring, who still rule the roost in Israeli society. The discrimination and condescension are there, but should be seen in perspective, and not blown out of proportion. These Ashkenazim from Russia and Eastern Europe had just freed themselves from the shackles of 'medieval Judaism' only two or three generations back, and embraced modern European culture. Many leaned towards Marxism, and had little patience with tradition. They were looking with disgust on the culturally static 'Arab Jews' as an image of something they had just turned their back on. Add to that the difference in instruction, energy, ideological drive, and we have all the ingredients for racist condescension. But that never was the whole story. The Ashkenazim may have welcomed the oriental Jews as menials, cheap farm labour, potential cannon fodder etcetera, but they were also looking farther than that: they mostly valued the oriental Jews as prime Jewish material, capable one day of being moulded into full-value Israelis. And this is, roughly, what happened and keeps happening. The melting pot is functioning. There is today a large mass of Israelis of mixed parentage who, behind the uniformity of their Hebrew names and hebraicised surnames, cannot be assigned to any group in particular. And of oriental 'backwardness' there is also little trace at present.

This is hardly surprising. Historically, the cultural edge of Ashkenazim was a fairly recent development. Until the end of the 19th century, in places like France, Holland or Britain, where Ashkenazim and Sephardim rubbed shoulders, the Sephardim were definitely the patronising ones: they were the real Jewish upper crust, the cultured ones, the well-mannered ones, the ones with the long pedigrees going back to their Spanish golden age. And nowadays, when Ashkenazi and Sephardic or even Arab Jews compete on an equal footing in Europe, there isn't much of a difference between them in point of energy, drive, scholarly achievements, or upward mobility.

Returning to Israel, the former power equations there are shifting. The collapse of the Labour party, and the Left in general, largely reflects the waning power of the old Ashkenazi elite. The new migrants from Russia, instead of replenishing the ranks of that elite, went on to constitute, socially and politically, a bloc of their own. Tensions persist, of course, between left-behind oriental Jews and the rest of Israeli society, but the vision, entertained by Abdo Saad, of some sort of alliance—deliberate or merely 'objective'—between the Palestinians and the destitute sections of oriental Jews, seems rather delusional. Oriental Jews may be more familiar with the Arab mind, but they are also the ones most fiercely antagonistic to the Palestinian demands.[33] Thus, they have been conspicuous, all along, by their near-total absence from the Israeli peace movement. Which again is not so surprising: the early Ashkenazi elite had a near monopoly on 'ideology' and 'idealism'. At one end of the spectrum, it could manifest as racial conceit. At the other end, it could turn them into committed peaceniks. Once again, this notion of a common front between Palestinians and Arab Jews looks chimerical. Oriental Jews who feel victimised will much rather jockey for position within the Israeli political system, which offers much scope for that, with its innumerable parties, factions, and unstable coalitions ever in need of propping up. A Marxist analyst might decide that they should shed their 'false consciousness' and join forces with the Palestinians, since 'objectively' they fall into the same category of the economically deprived. But this is not how people function.

# Notes

1. In the course of their history, the Druze often had to pass themselves off as Muslims simply to survive, but internally they are fiercely, irreconcilably anti-Muslim—a fact that was not lost on the Israelis. *E.N.*
2. In the event, the Hariri-led alliance won 71 seats against 56 to the Aoun-led front, despite bagging a much smaller share of the popular vote: 44.5 to 55.5 per cent. There followed five months of political wrangling, after which a coalition cabinet was formed, led by Saad Hariri but with the participation of Hizbullah. *E.N.*
3. London: Pluto Press, 2007, p. 40.

4. Here is another real-life Druze–Maronite anecdote; less maudlin, and with a rather different symbolism. During a Moslem-led pogrom, in the late 19th century, a Christian sheltered a Druze, thereby saving his life. Out of gratitude, the Druze then stabbed the Christian to death, after a hasty ritual to ensure his rebirth as a Druze and spare him the gloomy after-life fate reserved for infidels in the Druze scheme of things. (Reincarnation, we are told, was no part of the early belief system of the Druze. It crept in at a later stage, but became firmly entrenched.) Unfortunately, I cannot source this anecdote. I read it in the French translation, which I no longer possess, of a largely sympathetic history of the Druze, in Arabic, by a Lebanese author, published in the 1950s, if I remember correctly. The point is simply that it is disingenuous to blame the West for the deep, bitter, age-old enmities that tear apart Lebanese society, many of which go back to a time when Europe's nation states didn't even exist. Let us stick with the Druze and their two or three or four layers of scriptures. On the outside, they would pass themselves off as 'special' Muslims, which was a necessity of survival. On the inside, in the esoteric core of their scriptures, they were and are fiercely, irreconcilably anti-Muslim: Mohammed is described there as a bastard, a monkey, a snake. Now Traboulsi would blame all this congealed hatred, these century-old, ineradicable habits of double-talk, pretending and dissembling, on western meddling! *E.N.*

5. Sounds like a lecture on Marxism for slow learners! *E.N.*

6. In contradiction to the unwritten rule that the Prime Minister should be a Sunni! *E.N.*

7. *Hizbu'llah: Politics, Religion,* published by Pluto Press, London in 2002.

8. In fact, Detlev Mehlis resigned owing to threats of assassination. As of now (August 2010) the international tribunal in charge of the inquiry is still withholding its findings, but ought to release them soon. Although the tribunal's report is rumoured to indict 'elements close to Hizbullah', all parties to the affair (including Nasrallah and Rafiq Hariri's son Saad) and their foreign patrons (Syria and Saudi Arabia respectively) seem determined to calm tempers and prevent a clash. *E.N.*

9. All four generals were released on 29 April 2009 by the Hague-based tribunal established by the UN to try suspects connected to the killing of Hariri, even as I was writing the account of my conversations in Beirut. *A.N.*

10. A more charitable explanation would be that Tocqueville scholars have long ago come to the view that their author and his thinking 'soured with age' and that consequently only the writings of his first, wholesome phase deserved publication. *E.N.*

11. *Edited by Roger Boesche and published by the* University of California Press *at Berkeley in 1985.*

12. See *Tocqueville's Oeuvres Complétes, Volume 3, "L'Inde"*, Gallimard, Paris, 1951.
13. The writer Jack London, America's quintessential 'revolutionary socialist', is another case in point. After being abandoned by his parents, he was brought up by his black wet nurse (a freed slave), but this did not prevent him from turning into a rabid racist. 'I am first of all a white man, and only then a socialist.' His socialism was for 'whites only', for he believed that Blacks and other ethnic groups 'should be subjugated or exterminated [....] The history of civilisation is a history of wandering—a wandering, sword in hand, of strong breeds, clearing away and hewing down the weak and less fit.' He even wrote a short story, *The Unparalleled Invasion*, in which he has the United States—with his plain approval—wage biological warfare on China to decimate its population. (See Johann Hari's *Guardian* article of 23-08-2010). As for Charles Dickens, the great empathiser with the downtrodden, he wrote about India's 1857 Mutiny that if he had the power, he would use all 'merciful swiftness of execution to exterminate [these people from] the face of the Earth'. *E.N.*
14. Benjamin Constant was a Swiss-born nobleman, writer and politician, who became involved in French politics in the latter phase of the French Revolution.
15. From Benjamin Constant's pamphlet against Napoleon, *On the Spirit of Conquest and on Usurpation*, 1815.
16. Here, Abdo Saad carefully glosses over the huge range of interpretations to which *wilayat al-faqih* lends itself, both in points of doctrine and political praxis, with Khomeini and Fadlallah respectively exemplifying the 'strict' and 'liberal' extremes. In the past, this tension often would put Hizbullah in an uncomfortable position: the militia had to keep on the right side of its Iranian patrons, while paying obeisance to its spiritual mentor in Lebanon.
17. The figure applies of course to the total Jewish population in the West Bank *and* Israel proper. *E.N.*
18. One suspects some distortion here. These manuscripts were clearly not destroyed: Jews are maniacal about preserving that sort of things. They were probably being jealously guarded as family heirlooms by Yemeni rabbis, who maybe weren't doing much with them. Then, after the transfer, they were requisitioned (with characteristic insensitiveness, likely) by the Israeli authorities, so as to be investigated by suitably trained historians, and made accessible to all. This is akin to a private person stumbling on archaeological remains of great value while digging in his back-garden: the authorities will step in as a matter of course, and take over the operations. The Israeli state has done worse things than that. For Rabbi Shlomo Korah's version, see Arthur Nelsen, *Occupied Minds: A Journey through the Israeli Psyche. E.N.*

19. This at any rate is Uri Avnery's firm conviction. According to Wikipedia, the case is murky and still a matter of dispute. Assuming the real involvement of Jewish agents in this one incident, these bombings must have been rather unique in the annals of the *Yishuv*. The Zionists were ruthless and cynical in their recruiting methods, but bombing their own kind was not their method of choice. *E.N.*

20. *Davar* was a Hebrew daily, which at some point was edited by Zalman Shazar, a one-time President of Israel.

21. Actually, in the tense week that preceded the outbreak of hostilities, Yitzhak Rabin buckled under the pressure, suffered a nervous breakdown, and had to be locked up. After the war started for good, his spirits revived. *E.N.*

22. Pluto Press. 2002, London.

23. Ashura marks the martyrdom of Ali at the battle of Karbala, on the 10th of Moharram, in AD 680.

24. Pluto Press, 2002, London.

25. Rashid W. requested us not to disclose his full name. *E.N.*

26. In actual fact, the 2006 conflict might well be the *only war* that Israel launched under strict American instigation. Israel's Winograd Commission, which inquired into the background and conduct of the war, apportioned blame fairly evenly among Israel's politicians and military chiefs, but it had whole sections of its official report censured, leading to speculation that these sections detailed the 'encouragements' and 'assurances' given to Israel by the US. Recall that US diplomacy, at the time, was desperate to draw attention away from the Iraq fiasco. *E.N.*

27. A city on the banks of the Euphrates river, 170 km south of Baghdad, in present-day Iraq, Kufa was a frontier garrison during the Arab war against Sassanid Persia, between 637 and 651.

28. Born in 1935 in Najaf, Iraq, and educated there, but of Lebanese descent. Fadlallah returned to Lebanon in 1952, and passed away in July 2010. He contributed as an 'inspirer' to the general Shia awakening in Lebanon and to the rise of Hizbullah, without there being any formal affiliation. *E.N.*

29. The English version appeared in Oxford's *Oneworld Publications*, 2004.

30. Neither does Islam, although many Muslim states do. Muslims are on rather shaky ground here, and the fact is that there is considerable secular space in Israeli life. Religion played almost no part in public life in the *Yishuv* phase, and very little during the first twenty years of Israel's existence, the ideological baggage of the founders being Marxism and the labour tradition of the *Bund*. It is true that even then Israel had no laws for civil marriage, but that was because of the tricky question of deciding who is Jewish or not, who is entitled to immigration and citizenship. The only practical solution was to

entrust the matter to the patented specialists in Jewishness—the Rabbis. For the founders of Israel, giving some perks to the Rabbis (in matters of legislation etcetera) also had the advantage of defusing the then general hostility of orthodox Jewishdom to the Zionist project. After the Six Day war, things changed. There was a dramatic resurgence of religion (in 'mutated' forms that strongly departed from exile Judaism, shedding most of its universal values and regressing to Old Testament tribal exclusivism) but even so the secular strand is still dominant in Israeli life and likely to remain so, despite the runaway fertility of the *Haredim* or orthodox Jews. Incidentally, of all past and present Israeli prime ministers, only Menahem Begin was a believing Jew. *E.N.*

31. Again, this does not apply to the founders, most of whom were irreligious. What these folks had in ample measure was a restless sense of 'mission' and zeal for world-transformation—this being what, under the conditions of 19th century Central and Eastern Europe, Judaic messianism had ended up morphing into. *E.N.*

32. We should distinguish the *Sephardim* and the *Mizrahim* proper, though of course there was much intermingling between the two after the 1492 Expulsion Edict, when Sephardic Jews had to leave Spain and resettle in the Maghreb, Turkey, or farther east.

33. Lately, the chief rabbi of Safed, a government employee, decreed that selling or letting apartments to Arabs is a sin. Before 1948, Safed was a mixed town with an Arab majority. Rabbi Ovadia Yosef, the unquestioned leader of the Oriental Jewish community, also decreed that selling land to foreigners—meaning the Arabs who have been living here for more than a thousand years before the venerable rabbi himself was brought to Israel from Iraq—is expressly forbidden by the Jewish religion (from *Gush Shalom* material).

# Afterword

*To have humility is to experience reality, not in relation to ourselves, but in its sacred independence. It is to see, judge, and act from the point of rest in ourselves.*
—Dag Hammarskjöld

*Force is as pitiless to the man who possesses it, or thinks he does, as it is to its victims; the second it crushes, the first it intoxicates. The truth is nobody really possesses it.*
—Simone Weil

## The Root Conflict

Of all the struggles which tear apart the Middle East and are the meat of this book, we shall discuss here but one—the Israeli–Palestinian conflict. To begin with, this is perhaps the only 'Levantine issue' of acute concern to world opinion, the one for which it feels a clear responsibility, and on which it has some significant leverage. Then, it is the oldest of the region's on-going conflicts, the most intractable, as well as the demonstrable cause or aggravating factor of practically all the others. Lastly, it is the matter which the author of the present book had closest at heart, and around which he hoped to mobilise a phalanx of Indo–Arab solidarity.

The media punditry keeps dinning into our ears that the Palestine problem is 'endlessly complex'. Complex it may be in its details, but not in its outline: *an entire people was savagely dispossessed of its land in the wake of a far-away cataclysm of which it was completely innocent, with the culprits behind the cataclysm and their victims quickly reconciling on the backs of the despoiled.* Like it or not, there is a solid thread of simplicity running through the whole sorry chapter, a clear arc of rights and wrongs. The problem is rather with those who revel in the complexities to obfuscate the simplicity. The present book was meant as a frontal attack against such types.

## The Unweighable

If we look at the historic milieu that incubated Zionism—late 19th century central-eastern Europe—we see a strong Jewish urge to *fit and belong* struggling with an equally stubborn reluctance to *dissolve*. There was, from the start, the very natural quest for individual safety, individual adjustment, and individual fulfilment. But another motive, subterranean at first, was making itself heard with increasing insistence: how to ensure the Jews' collective survival as a spirit community, when the cement of religion, endogamy, Yiddish, and life from cradle to grave in close-knit communities—when all these bonds were fraying at the edges? One may, without undue schematism, reduce to four the options that crystalised as attempts to resolve this tension.

1.  To go for more or less complete assimilation into European society—a path already well-trodden by the Jews of Britain, France, Italy and Austro-Germany, and increasingly attractive to those farther east; a path for which the Jews were remarkably well-equipped; which, for some time, looked like being that of least resistance; but on which they were soon to meet with fiercer and fiercer rejection.

2.  To remould the ambient world in a way congruous with (some of) their basic Jewish instincts; for example, under the banner of Socialism or Marxism, but without claiming a special niche for themselves in the striven-after Utopia. Despite being much more ambitious than the first formula, this project of 'active assimilation' (assimilation *of* the other as much as *into* him) also had self-abolition as its logical terminus.

3.  To reach out for untried formulas; for new, fluid patterns of transnational association; for ways of maintaining a measure of cohesion and yet embracing the world, by privileging the 'open', 'outgoing' strands within the Judaic tradition—in a word, becoming a leaven to the nations rather than remaining a ghetto in their midst.

4.  To try to preserve the Jewish identity (*minus* the scars of exile) by converting it into the prosaic currency of the age, that is, by casting it into the mould of the nation-state—complete with language, territory, state apparatus, military. Conceptually, that was a less

imaginative project than formula 3, but with its sharper contours, and because of the sheer obstacles that stood in its way, it was better at catching the imagination and at firing enthusiasm.

Then history went wild; chaos descended; and for the hapless Jews caught in the eye of the storm, the four above options suddenly reduced to: where to hide? whither to flee? where to emigrate? to some safe destination such as America? or to Palestine?

When trying to make sense of the historical sequence, we are of course permitted to retreat, for poise, clarity and perspective, into what Hammarskjöld termed the silent 'point of rest in us', but any fleeting lights gleaned during the visit are better kept to ourselves. Only an innocent or a madman could attempt to pass a final, authoritative, Olympian sentence on the four 'options', let alone comment on the life choices of individuals struggling in the eddies of war and persecution. Only an innocent or a madman could presume to possess the scales on which to weigh the mountains of facts that would need weighing, or to understand the true 'avocation' of so elusive as thing as the 'Jewish race', or to discern the 'sane' from the 'expendable' parts of its tradition, or to know the 'proper path' for its future to take.

The people caught up in the vortex of these events, and forced to make decisions, had no such scales either. They were trying to make the best of the hand that life had dealt them. They were not outsiders sitting in idle judgment, but actors with their all at stake: *their answer was what they did; their answer was them.*

Just two brief observations, before leaving these questions without answers.

First, most of the Jews who chose emigration to Palestine in the first half of the 20th century had no clear picture of what lay in wait for them. They were lured by promises of an Eden in the making—rather, of an Eden which would be theirs to construct, and in that the Zionist propaganda was truthful—but with the indigenous population completely factored out of the equation. Once on the spot, they knew better, but by then, for most of them, whether approving or disapproving, there was no going back.

Second, one probably shouldn't make too much of the initial rejection of Zionism by large sections of Jews, nor view it in too idealised a light.[1] Whether coming from secular Jews who felt comfortable in 'exile', or from orthodox elements who clung to their own notions of how the exile had to end, this Jewish anti-Zionism cannot have been very principled, for it began to crumble after the creation of Israel (and the many concessions made by the new state to the rabbinical establishment) and it completely evaporated after the 1967 war.

## The Role of Outsiders

But let us not get fixated on the pre-history of Zionism, about which no full clarity is to be had, and which distorts our vision by keeping our gaze glued to a time when Jews were persecuted, helpless, and deserving of sympathy. Things have changed a lot since, however much the likes of Elie Wiesel[2] would have us believe otherwise. Jews nowadays are no longer victims. They are one of the most energetic, successful and influential communities on earth, and to the extent that they support Israel's hardline policies, they make themselves fully eligible for criticism, which should not be withheld nor softened.

So, back to the present and *the evil thereof*, which is more than *sufficient unto it.* Outsiders to the Palestinian struggle should of course know their place, which is that of bystanders—no more, no less—and they should mind their business, which is most emphatically not that of prejudging the hard choices and sacrifices which only the belligerent parties are entitled to make. But outsiders have their responsibilities, too, which they cannot evade—as citizens co-responsible for the doings of their governments; as co-shapers of international standards; and, above all, as co-bearers of world opinion, that embryonic voice of world conscience. In the exercise of these minimal, non-abdicable responsibilities, however, they are bound to clash with the full might of the tentacular Israel lobby. So let us take a closer look at the beast, and identify some of its tentacles.

## America Held to Ransom by the Israel Lobby

'We control America', Ariel Sharon once boasted.[3] Add to that the obvious qualification, '*in all matters of concern to us, and quite a few others*' and what you have here is no longer a boast, but a sobre statement of fact. Such is indeed the position, and he who insists on seeing nuance where starkest simplicity reigns is being neither perceptive nor discerning nor subtle, but plain dumb. Let us review a few recent examples, picked almost at random, to show just how right Sharon was.

In 2006–2007 two American academics, John Mearsheimer and Stephen Walt, published their study on *The Israel Lobby and American Foreign Policy*.[4] They define the lobby[5] as a 'loose coalition of individuals and organisations who actively work to steer US foreign policy in a pro-Israel direction: Israel's enemies get weakened or overthrown, Israel gets a free hand with the Palestinians, and the US does most of the fighting, dying, rebuilding, and paying'. The lobby's centrepiece is AIPAC.[6] It concentrates on influencing Congress and the Executive Branch, coordinating pro-Israeli propaganda in the media, orchestrating public campaigns, intimidating US politicians and writers into compliance, and destroying the reputations or careers of recalcitrant elements. The Walt and Mearsheimer book got an entirely predictable, that is, frosty reception from the American critique. It would probably have been denied publication in the US, had it not begun to circulate abroad, in a dozen or so translations.

In 2006, former President Jimmy Carter released his *Palestine, Peace Not Apartheid*, based on his own fact-finding visits in the area. Despite favourable reactions from the American public, the book unleashed a storm of protest in academia and in the media. Carter himself later chose to apologise for rubbing American Jews the wrong way, though of course he did not put it in quite that way.

Throughout his presidential campaign Obama jettisoned all aides who incurred AIPAC's displeasure and backtracked on all statements upon which AIPAC so much as frowned. His advisor Rob Malley,[7] for example, had met with Hamas officials on behalf of the International Crisis Group. Obama forced him to resign at the first whiff of controversy.

Once elected, Obama considered appointing Charles W. Freeman as chair of the National Intelligence Council.[8] This senior diplomat, scholar and author, however, had been openly critical of Israeli violence against the Palestinians. A campaign of character assassination orchestrated by AIPAC and picked up by its ubiquitous relays swiftly put paid to Freeman's candidacy.

In March 2010, General Petraeus, then head of the US Central Command, described the 'perceived US favouritism for Israel as a source of anti-American sentiment among Moslems'. He was immediately taken to task, not for stating the obvious, but for uttering the modern equivalent of a blasphemy. The general, who is rumored to nurse presidential ambitions, promptly back-pedalled, saying his words had been 'picked apart' and 'spun'.

After Israel's murderous air and ground offensive against Gaza during the winter of 2007–2008, the UN appointed a respected international lawyer from South Africa, Richard Goldstone, to head a fact finding mission and investigate possible human rights violation by the warring parties. The Hamas Government in Gaza accepted to cooperate, while Israel refused. The detailed report, *The Goldstone Report*, released in September 2009, accused the Israeli armed forces of war crimes, possibly amounting to crimes against humanity. It also pointed fingers, to a lesser extent, at the Palestinian militants. The US House of Representatives overwhelmingly passed a resolution denouncing the report as 'irredeemably biased and unworthy of further consideration or legitimacy'. Even before the vote, the White House had let it be known that it would ensure the rejection of the report at the UN; and so it did.[9]

In 2010, in an interview with the *Sunday Times*, the politically committed film-maker Oliver Stone (famous for his films on the Vietnam war and, more recently, his documentaries on the 'Bolivarian' movement across South America) complained about Iran's demonisation in the US media and the Jewish influence on US foreign policy. After the predictable outcry from the predictable quarters, Oliver Stone chose, shamefully, to 'apologise for [his] thoughtless, ill-considered remarks'.

But enough of this litany of cravenness and self-abasement. How do we explain so perverse a state of affairs? One reason why America has not managed, thus far, to free itself from the shackles of the Israel lobby is that the country is governed by institutions rather than by its leaders. This builds directional inertia and resistance to change into the system. There are strict limits to what a courageous and clear-eyed president might achieve, even if he were prepared to stake his all for the sake of principle—like putting his presidency on the line to shock the American public into self-examination. That scenario itself is far-fetched, for the system would automatically weed out such an individual long before he could reach the White House. He would be spewed out during the primaries or even further upstream. Conversely, any candidate who survives the process is *ipso facto* tainted. This is a lesson which Obama enthusiasts had to learn the bitter way.

Yet even if the mechanisms at work here are more or less clear, there remains something mystifying, eerie almost, about this spectacle of giant America marching in unbreakable lockstep with Israel and being dragged down a road that can only end in defeat, humiliation and self-diminution. This extraordinary alliance becomes even more puzzling if we pause to consider what are its two main pillars; or at any rate *were* throughout the eight years of the George W. Bush administration. On the one hand we had the so-called neo-conservatives, an assortment of defectors, mostly Jewish, from the far-left (Trotskyites, Maoists, anarchists, libertarians and suchlike) who in mid-life suddenly reversed gear and put their zealotry and doctrinaire energy in the service of far-right ideals, which they slightly tweaked and re-packaged for Israel-compatibility. On the other hand, we had fringe groups (but with mass support) of evangelicals with their own home-grown eschatological expectations, in which Israel happens to play a pivotal role—though not a very flattering one, on closer examination. One could hardly imagine more incongruous bedfellows, people more naturally disposed to mutual loathing, or coming from more incompatible intellectual horizons.[10]

There is no dearth of theories to explain why Americans so readily identify with Israelis. The spontaneous psychological convergence, we are told, flows naturally from the fact that both nations cherish similar self-images: both think of themselves as pioneer nations, trailblazers in democracy, successful melting-pots. There is also, of course, the shared conceit of 'chosenness'—*God's own nation* here, the *chosen race* there. But to really get to the root of this extraordinary bond, it seems we must dig deeper and probe into the recesses of their national unconscious. What binds both nations, above all else, might well be the shared pride that they take in their parallel genocidal pasts. Before they could come into their rightful inheritance, and settle unhampered in the lands so manifestly cut out for them, both nations had to decontaminate the place and cleanse it of the swarthy aboriginals.[11] In the American psyche, the national epic—cleansing the wild east, then the wild plains, then the wild west, and then celebrating the grand finale in countless 'westerns'—cannot fail to resonate with the Israeli epic being played out, live, before their nostalgic eyes, in a crescendo of ever more thrilling episodes.[12] With *Munich*, America's star producer Steven Spielberg even shot what might be properly called an *Israeli western*—a film that interweaves the darkest motives beloved of both nations.[13]

However, it is time now to leave the quicksand of collective psychology for the firm ground of facts. Let us turn to Charles W. Freeman ('Chas' Freeman) for an informed assessment of the Israel lobby,[14] its might and nuisance value. Freeman, we recall, is one of the lobby's most noted critics—and victims:

American taxpayers fund between 20 and 25 per cent of Israel's defense budget, depending on how you calculate this. Twenty-six per cent of the $3 billion in military aid we grant to the Jewish state each year is spent in Israel on Israeli defence products. Uniquely, Israeli companies are treated like American companies for purposes of US defence procurement. Thanks to congressional earmarks, we also often pay half the costs of special Israeli research and development projects [...] Israel gets pretty much whatever it wants in terms of our top-of-the-line weapons systems, and we pick up the tab.

Identifiable US Government subsidies to Israel total over $140 billion since 1949. This makes Israel by far the largest recipient of American giveaways since World War II. The total would be much higher if aid to Egypt, Jordan, Lebanon, and support for Palestinians in refugee camps and the occupied territories were included. These programmes [...] are justified in large measure in terms of their contribution to the security of the Jewish state.

Per capita income in Israel is now about $37,000—on a par with the UK. Israel is nonetheless the largest recipient of US foreign assistance, accounting for well over a fifth of it. Annual US Government transfers run at well over $500 per Israeli, not counting the costs of tax breaks for private donations and loans that aren't available to any other foreign country.

These military and economic benefits are not the end of the story. The American government also works hard to shield Israel from the international political and legal consequences of its policies and actions in the occupied territories, against its neighbours, or—most recently—on the high seas. The nearly 40 vetoes the United States has cast to protect Israel in the UN Security Council are only the tip of an iceberg. We have blocked a vastly larger number of potentially damaging reactions to Israeli behaviour by the international community. The political costs to the United States internationally of having to spend our political capital in this way are huge [....] The US government has been a consistent promoter and often the funder of various forms of Israeli programmes of cooperation with other countries [...] Clearly, Israel gets a great deal from us. Yet it is pretty much taboo in the United States to ask what's in it for Americans. I can't imagine why [....] We need to begin by recognising that our relationship with Israel has never been driven by strategic reasoning. It began with President Truman overruling his strategic and military advisers in deference to personal sentiment and political expediency. We had an arms embargo on Israel until Lyndon Johnson dropped it in 1964 in explicit return for Jewish financial support for his campaign against Barry Goldwater. In 1973, for reasons peculiar to the Cold War, we had to come to the rescue of Israel as it battled Egypt. The resulting Arab oil embargo cost us dearly. And then there is all the time we have put into the perpetually ineffectual and now long defunct 'peace process'.

Still the US-Israel relationship has had strategic consequences. There is no reason to doubt the consistent testimony of the architects of major acts of anti- American terrorism about what motivates them to attack us. In the words of Khalid Sheikh Mohammed, who is credited with masterminding the 9/11 attacks, their purpose was to focus 'the American people [...] on the atrocities that America is committing by supporting Israel against the Palestinian people'. As Osama bin Laden, purporting to speak for the world's Muslims, has said again and again: 'We have [...]stated many times, for more than two-and-a-half-decades, that the cause of our disagreement with you is your support to your Israeli allies who occupy our land of Palestine.' Some substantial portion of the many lives and the trillions of dollars we have so far expended in our escalating conflict with the Islamic world must be apportioned to the costs of our relationship with Israel [...] The truth is that Al-Qaida has played us with the finesse of a matador exhausting a great bull by guiding it into unproductive lunges [....] Meanwhile, Israel has become accustomed to living on the American military dole [....] The [neo-con lobby] is now urging an American military assault on Iran explicitly to protect Israel and to preserve its nuclear monopoly in the Middle East. Their advocacy is fully coordinated with the Government of Israel. No one in the region wants a nuclear-armed Iran, but Israel is the only country pressing Americans to go to war over this.

Against this background, it is remarkable that something as fatuous as the notion of Israel as a strategic asset could have become the unchallenge-able conventional wisdom in the United States.[15]

How long will America's thraldom to Israel last? Attitudes appear to be slowly changing at the moment, especially among students and the educated public. There is even a growing number of US Jews who refuse to let AIPAC speak for them: they have recently founded a rival pressure group, the liberal *J-Street*, dedicated to the cause of peace in the Middle East. These movements, however, are still maidenly timid and babyishly toothless.[16] They have yet to gather momentum. For now, Israel's strangle-hold on US Middle East policies continues unbroken.

## Europe's Degenerate Subservience to the Jewish Opinion Makers

The position in Europe is different. There is not the same degree of self-identification with Israel; only a sense of cultural closeness to what is rightly seen as a European offshoot, plus, all too often, alas, the cement of a shared aversion against Muslims. On the whole, Europe's subservience to Israel is probably no less than America's, but unlike America's, it results from one of those irresistible, all-engulfing tidal reversals of which history offers no few examples—huge swings of the pendulum, which take entire societies from a position of moral disequilibrium to a symmetric, opposed disequilibrium. The reversal is usually slow in the making and long in coming but, when close to tipping point, it is often precipitated by the shock waves of a seismic event. What form and shape the cataclysm took in the present instance needs no recalling. In the event, centuries of European contempt for the Jews were transmuted, in a matter of a few decades,[17] into a fixed pattern of admiration, deference and subservience in most matters intellectual, moral and cultural. A combination of mental debilitation and entrenched feelings of collective guilt (reinforced year in year out by relentless reminders in the form of films, books, commemorations, items on the school curricula—the whole flourishing 'holocaust industry'[18]); the strength of public censure paired with the habit of individual self-censure; the panic fear of incurring the charge of anti-Semitism (that 'absolute evil'—a quaint verbal relict in our modern culture with little sense for 'evil' and none for the 'absolute'); all these have rendered the common run of Europeans incapable not only of assessing and filtering Jewish influences with a free, unconstrained spirit, which is serious enough, but also of standing up to Israel's demands and seeing through its existential lies, which as consequences go is more serious still.

To gauge the extent of this brainwashing, we need only compare current acceptable discourse with the essays, apologias and pamphlets that Europe's pre-War philo-Semites, as a rule men of free and fearless spirit, used to devote to the 'Jewish question' (an expression they rejected). In the present climate, most of their generous prose would not pass muster; it would be condemned as politically incorrect or borderline—for its freedom of tone, for not fully conforming with the Jews' self-image, for not being framed in purely Jewish terms. The only analogy capable of shedding light on Europe's present supine condition is that of the 'colonised mind': at the peak of European power and overseas expansion, even pre-eminent representatives of the subject races, when they made bold to criticise their colonial masters, would often tread with abject caution. They would cushion every timid criticism with protestations of loyalty, begin their argument with praise, lace it with more praise, and end it on one last thick note of praise. Today, when revisiting these monuments to human self-abasement, we struggle with a mixture of embarrassment, pity and disgust. We wince. When shall the people of Europe, looking back on their present condition of moral abdication, wince? Not any time soon, probably. There is a huge inertia in these movements. The present attitude is no passing mood, but the obverse of centuries of Jew-loathing and Jew-baiting. Or you might just as well say: their continuation, if you adopt the logic of the unconscious, which hardly understands negation and knows only obsession.

We might even see this reversal of positions as fair retribution, as a sort of corrective justice, except that the correction here is sadly misapplied and the justice feeds a larger injustice. It blinds Europeans to the rights and wrongs in the Palestine conflict, distorts their views of the Muslim world, and embroils them into supporting misguided policies and into joining open-ended military adventures fraught with calamitous consequences.

Not content with exploiting European compliance and all-excusing sympathies, Israel is trying to institutionalise its grip on the EU's foreign policy. Largely unnoticed, it has developed such strong political, economic and scientific links with the Union and gained such a foothold in its decision-making bodies that it has becomes a EU member in all but name.[19]

One of Israel's latest tools in this strategy of sneaking infiltration is the recently founded (2006) Brussels-based EFI ('European Friends of Israel'), a lobby avowedly modelled on AIPAC. Its present head, Michel Gur Avi, hopes to turn EFI into 'an organisation that will one day enjoy the same influence as AIPAC does in Washington'.[20] Anticipating as it were on this auspicious outcome, the EU is already vying with the US in picking up the slate for Israel's vandalism. It funds projects worth millions of Euros in Palestine,[21] which are regularly destroyed by Israel's US- or EU-made weaponry, in a self-sustaining cycle of re-construction and fresh destruction. It is a measure of EFI's effectiveness that Israeli arms companies such as Motorola Israel (a producer of surveillance sensors and radar systems used to monitor the surroundings of the West Bank settlements) and Israel Aerospace Industries (a manufacturer of warplanes used to terrorise Palestinian civilians) have become eligible for EU funding. Israel's science establishment is already the second-largest recipient of EU grants. A sweeping cooperation agreement between Europol, the EU's police office, and Israel has also been reached and is awaiting ratification.

Parallel with its infiltration of the EU, Israel is also sneaking its way into NATO. In the spring of 2010, Israel's military boss Gabi Ashkenazi paid an official visit to the organisation's headquarters in Brussels to argue for closer ties. Mostly, though, Israel pursues its aims through opaque programmes of 'individual cooperation', which attract little scrutiny but have already resulted in locking Israel into NATO's computer network. Britain has repeatedly admitted to training members of the Israeli military. Most joint programmes, though, are kept secret and come to light only by accident, as was the case in July 2010, when five Israeli servicemen died in a helicopter crash in Romania. It was revealed, after the event, that they had been taking part in a NATO–Israeli exercise.

So much for the *substance* of Israeli–European relations! Let us now reel off a few snapshots from real life, to illustrate the human *tenor* of these same relations, in all their blunt suzerain-over-vassal asymmetry.

In December 2006, the Italian Premier Romano Prodi, to his (slight) embarrassment, was caught on radio-camera preparing for a joint press conference with his Israeli counterpart Ehud Olmert: the Israeli was standing at Prodi's side, instructing him what to say to the pressmen!

The last time I met with Kumar was in Paris, on 27 December 2008 to be precise. Israel was then one week into its land and air offensive against Gaza. The aptly named 'Operation Molten Lead' was meant to avenge the Lebanon fiasco of July 2006. Israel also hoped that by pounding the civilian population hard enough it might make it turn against the Hamas Government and topple it. The offensive lasted a full three weeks and left about 1,400 Gazans dead (against 14 Israeli casualties, many of them from friendly fire). The Israeli public overwhelmingly supported the operation. Psychologically, a threshold was crossed. As Yael Ben Yefet wrote: 'Something snapped. The Gaza assault released Israel from its last humanitarian restraints.'[22] White phosphorus was used to minimise their casualties. Israeli ground troops advanced behind a wall of fire, crushing everything and everyone that stood in their way. Schools and public premises were razed along with those sheltering there. Civilians leaving buildings and waving white flags were shot in cold blood. Throughout, there was hardly a murmur of official protest from Europe, only timid calls for 'restraint' and 'proportionality' addressed to 'both sides'. Even that was too much for Tony Blair in his new incarnation as 'Middle East peace envoy'.[23] Israel's then Prime Minister Ehud Olmert (then grappling with a long string of corruption charges that would eventually cause his downfall), Defence Minister Ehud Barak and Foreign Minister Tzipi Livni continued to interact with their European counterparts on terms of perfect civility, receiving assurances of support, sympathy, comprehension. On my way to Kumar's hotel, on that late Saturday evening, I crossed the path of a large protest demonstration by French Muslims, mostly of Maghrebi origin. Apart from two to three burnt cars and some smashed windows, the affair on the whole was restrained. The riot police was out in force. I tarried to talk to a few demonstrators, just enough to gauge their mood and hear their view of President Sarkozy's 'indefectible commitment to Israel's security'.

Are Europeans more touchy when Israel directly provokes them? Judge for yourself. This is January 2010. A senior Hamas commander, Mahmoud al-Mabhouh has just been assassinated in a Dubai hotel room. The Israeli killer commando, 18-men strong, has been caught on surveillance video cameras. It quickly transpires that they were travelling on forged or fraudulently obtained passports of European nationals—six of them Britons. Britain demands explanations. Israel belly-laughs and says there will be no explanations. Britain takes no as an answer. Still, egged on by the left-wing press, the British Foreign Office goes lamely through the motions of protesting. It summons Israel's ambassador. The Israeli Embassy in London responds by thumbing its nose at Britain. They post on their official website: 'You heard it here first: Israel scored a hit in Dubai.' This is a masterstroke of double entendre and insolence: an Israeli tennis player has just won a tournament in Dubai. The British take the affront lying down. A few days later David Milliband, Foreign Secretary in the outgoing Labour Government,[24] can be seen smiling at a house-warming reception thrown by Israel's ambassador to Britain. Not a single Israeli diplomat is expelled from Britain or any of the European countries which had passports of their nationals copied or stolen by Mossad.

Now, fast-forward six months. This is July 2010. A new Conservative–Liberal coalition is in power in Britain, led by David Cameron and Nick Clegg. In Lebanon Ayatollah Fadlallah, a widely respected figure, has just passed away. The British ambassador in Beirut, Frances Guy, who knew Fadlallah personally and had come to respect him, reminisces about him on her personal blog, which is hosted by the Embassy's official website. The Israelis whistle their displeasure. The Cameron–Clegg cabinet springs to attention and immediately orders the blog be removed, 'after mature'— but expeditious!—'consideration'.

Europeans often complain that the Muslim migrants living in their midst make insufficient efforts to adjust and show scant respect for the values of the host countries. These are indeed grave, totally legitimate concerns, but methinks that the complainers should take a long look at themselves and ponder the question: *who respects people who have fungus on their brains and termites in their spine?*

## Germany's Very Own Predicament

After setting in motion, under Hitler, the train of events that was to lead to the creation of Israel, Germany, after World War II, has probably done more than any other European country to vitiate the debate on Palestine by its slavish support of Israel. The tacit rule became and still remains: *Israel, right or wrong.* It all sprang, of course, from a ground-swell of remorse on the part of Germany's post-war generations; from their desire to expiate, make amends, and relieve, as far as in them lay, the burden of shame and guilt that was crushing the noblest elements among them. The result, however, was dismal, in that it reinforced Israel's already robust sense of impunity and its imperviousness to criticism.

That Germany has forfeited any right to admonish or berate the Jews is self- evident, and to none more so than the Jews, who are taking full advantage. But Arabs also, especially Palestinians, cannot endure being lectured by a country that, albeit at one remove, bears such responsibility for their present misfortune,[25] and continues to extend robot-like support to Israel in all international forums.

Now, what is someone to do who cannot pipe up without getting it wrong? He should keep quiet. Rather than compound its former crimes by abetting fresh iniquities, the decent thing to do for Germany would be to solemnly declare its decision to abstain, on principle, from taking sides in the Palestinian–Israel conflict, and to refrain from making any pronouncement of any sort or from taking part in any international vote, decision or initiative regarding the Middle East.

There would be dignity in such self-curtailment. Having to shut up would also be a wholesome cure by abstinence, and a not inadequate form of penance, for a people who, in their less gracious moods, are second only to the Jews in their zest for lecturing the world.[26] But since there is not the slightest indication that Germany is prepared to do the decent thing, the remedy is for the world to studiously ignore anything that official German voices may choose to say about the Palestinian problem.

One thing which Arabs cannot stand is hearing Germans going on about their 'sacred commitment to Israel's survival'. When provoked beyond endurance by these slimy pontifications, Arabs are apt to point out that if the Germans want to assuage their newfound love of Jews, they can at any time take up the recommendation that the celebrated historian Arnold Toynbee made at the end of World War II: carve a choice piece of their national territory, for example Rhenania, and offer it to on a platter to the landless Jews—or now to the land-challenged Israelis, whose 'survival' has become such a premium German concern. Instead of shrugging off the idea as demented, Germans should turn inward and realise that there was, and there still is, nothing insane about Toynbee's plan. It is just that implementing it would have been then, and would be now, rather bothersome. And unless compelled, why bother? Displacing the Palestinians, on the other hand, was pre-eminently sensible, the proof being that it was done with success, to Israel's and Germany's equal satisfaction. No insanity there, no 'political impossibility', no bother.

## Official India and Israel

Indo–Israeli relations have come a long way since their frosty beginnings in the post-Independence years. Jawaharlal Nehru, who had privately opposed the plan for partitioning Palestine, reluctantly 'endorsed' the creation of Israel in May 1948, but a year later voted against Israel's admission to the UN. In fact, India did not recognise Israel as a nation until 1950 and, as long as members of the Nehru dynasty remained in power, the two countries refrained from exchanging ambassadors. Full diplomatic relations were not established until 1992, under the Congress-led government of P. V. Narasimha Rao, and the real blossoming of Indo–Israeli relations had to wait until the first BJP-dominated coalitions in the late 1990s.

India's initial coolness towards Israel was mainly due to Nehru's sympathies with the Palestinian cause. As Harsh V. Pant writes:

> India was a founder member of the Non-Aligned Movement that was supportive of anti-colonial struggles around the world and this also meant strong support for the Palestine Liberation Organisation (PLO). India became one of the first non-Arab states to recognise Palestinian independence and also one of the first to allow an embassy of the PLO in its capital [….] India's anti-Israel stance was also part of the larger Indian diplomatic strategy of trying to counter Pakistan's influence in the Arab world and of safeguarding its oil supplies from Arab countries. It also ensured jobs for thousands of Indians in the Gulf, helping India to keep its foreign exchange reserves afloat.[27]

India's official position, however, did not prevent it from pursuing discreet contacts with Israel. Thus, during its 1971 war with Pakistan, India secretly approached Israel for a massive purchase of highly effective 160mm mortars. Israel eagerly obliged. The secret cooperation between the intelligence services of the two countries—India's RAW and Israel's Mossad—began at about the same time. The establishment of full diplomatic relations in 1992 led to a steady strengthening of bilateral exchanges. India at first remained coy about this flourishing relationship and did all it could to keep it out of public view. But Indian diplomats began to space out—and tone down—their perfunctory denunciations of Israel's ill-treatment of the Palestinians.

During the Kargil War which lasted from May till July 1999 (along the Line of Control between Indian and Pakistan administered Kashmir), the hard-pressed Indian side approached Israel for help, which was swiftly granted. Israel supplied UAVs ('unmanned aerial vehicles' or 'drones') for high altitude surveillance, laser-guided systems, and many other items— much of it within 24 hours of the requests being made.

The next high-point was L. K. Advani's (then Home Minister) visit to Israel in mid-2000, quickly followed by that of Jaswant Singh (External Affairs Minister). In late 2001 unconfirmed reports began doing the rounds in the Indian press to the effect that a special branch of Mossad, known as Metsada and specialising in assassinations and sabotage, had been invited to India to train RAW operatives. The reports added that Israeli agents were active in many sensitive parts of the Indian territory, especially in Indian-held Kashmir. Over the next years, in close coordination with the Israelis, India also stepped up its presence in Afghanistan.

The full extent of the Indo–Israeli rapprochement came out into the open in September 2003, when Israel's Likud Prime Minister Ariel Sharon visited India and was given a red carpet welcome. There was no need to feign cordiality: the chemistry between India's BJP leadership and the right-wing Sharon could not have been better—it was a real meeting of hearts and minds. The then Israeli ambassador to India Dr Yehoyada Haim, interviewed shortly before leaving his post, gushed about the architects of the Indo–Israeli rapprochement.

> Mr Advani is a quite unique man. I like him very much. Ideologically and personally, he reminds me of some Israelis from an earlier generation. He was very happy as he could personally see the methods we have developed to fight terrorism. He also met Mossad's head. Now, we're going to examine what counter-terrorism methods are appropriate for India.

On the Indian side, BJP apologists like Dr Subhash Kapila could not disguise their glee that 'India, at the turn of the millennium, [has at last] broken out of the straitjacket of moral histrionics of the last 50 years in terms of its foreign policies and approaches to strategic cooperation.'

At its heart, the relationship is obviously driven by a desire for close defence ties and a common obsession with Islamist extremism. The fall-out, as Kapila notes, in economic terms is impressive.

Israel is reported to have emerged as India's number two defence supplier after Russia, and with costs of Russian spare parts for replacement escalating by 300–500 per cent, Israel may soon emerge as India's number one arms supplier. India is presently faced with the daunting prospect of buying immediately $200 million worth of ammunition and further $1.5 billion later to make up for losses in recent fires at Indian Army Ammunition Depots.27. Israel may well be the only source for immediate replacement.[28]

In December 2009, Gabi Ashkenazi, head of Israel's Defence Forces, made a highly publicised visit to India to 'cement the defence ties between the two countries'. He pledged India 'every help in fighting terrorism'. In another significant move, Israel has chosen India to launch its satellites. The latest Israeli spy satellite, TecSAR, was launched by India on 22 January 2008. In March 2009, India launched the RISAT-2 satellite which is based on the technology employed in Israel's TecSAR. The cooperation also extends to crucial areas of scientific research: nanotechnologies, information technologies, water management, and biotechnology. It even includes, as a public front, some projects in agriculture such as the introduction of new crops (olives, dates, grapes) in Rajasthan and the drier parts of Maharashtra.

Relations that *close* are hard to untie and should give the Indian side pause for thought. That India morally defiles itself by consorting with the leper state Israel and mortgages its soul by adopting Israel-like policies, is clearly lost on the likes of L. K. Advani. But even the realpolitik cohorts ought to understand what sort of enduring dependence they are buying into by making Israel their second largest arms suppliers,[29] privileged intelligence partner, and major development adviser. They are unwittingly manoeuvring themselves into a position where they may someday be forced, at Israel's insistence, to break with such natural commercial and political partners as Iran. They would be well inspired to look at Turkey as a cautionary tale. For all the public outrage over the flotilla attacks of May 2010,[30] and the indignant posturing of Turkey's politicians, the incident registered as a mere blip in the trade links between Turkey and Israel, and did hardly any damage to the military cooperation between the two countries: the mutual imbrication was simply too old and too strong to undo or even relax. India's apprentice Machiavellians might also learn from Europe's history of caving in to all Israeli dictates, and its pathetic habit of taking all of Mossad's provocations lying down, be they abductions or assassinations carried out on European soil, or the theft and forgery of European passports. Europe's cowardice is only part of the explanation; the other part must be sought in Europe's strong semi-institutional links with Israel, notably the close collaboration between their secret services—an arrangement which, given the asymmetry of the power equation, obligates Europe while leaving Israel free to do as it pleases.

## The Israelis: Violence on the Mind, Fear in the Heart

These days, Iran has become the latest target in Israel's sights. The hysteria about Iran's nuclear ambitions and the danger it supposedly represents for Israel is, of course, completely overblown. No one in their right mind can for a second believe that the Tehran regime—a clerical oligarchy with a disconcerting mix of dictatorial and democratic aspects, but an essentially rational and risk-weighing player on the international scene—would launch a first strike to court annihilation. According to many observers, it is not even all that clear whether the Iran leadership aspires to full nuclear capability.[31] It might simply want to stay close to the nuclear threshold. The Israeli decision makers are obviously aware of this,[32] but their calculations are different. A nuclear or pro-nuclear Iran would create some minor, but from their perspective, intolerable inconvenience. It might restrict Israel's outreach and freedom of operation in the area, its capacity to carry out with impunity targeted killings, sabotage raids etcetera. It might cause Israel's Arab allies like Egypt to hedge their bets. It might generate in the Israeli population a vague sense of insecurity, and, more to the point, encourage Jewish emigration out of Israel to the greener pastures of America and Europe—that is, an *aliya* ('ascent') in reverse, or *yerida* ('descent')—an annoying trend with which Israel always had to cope.[33] To ward off this 'intolerable' outcome, a huge propaganda drive is now underway, to sell the world the notion that the Iran bomb is a universal menace and that the US should do something about it—that is, bomb all the known nuclear installations in Iran; then try to bring about regime change in Tehran; and, should that fail, pick up the pieces.

It says something about the Israeli leaders that they should, in cold blood, in pursuit of marginal—if not completely imaginary—advantages, try to bully the US into such an invidious course. And it says something about the US political establishment that they are taking the bait or pretending to, for fear of facing the wrath of the Israel lobby.

Yet, at the same time, for all the fraudulence behind this fear-Iran stop-Iran pantomime, for all the tongue-in-cheek cynicism of Israel's propagandists and their army of hirelings, and despite the absence of any objective danger in the near term, the fact remains that there is palpable, unfeigned anxiety in Israel. For heavens' sake, don't conjure the ghosts of the 'Jewish past' or the tropes of 'Jewish angst' for an explanation. Israeli anxiety is one hundred per cent rooted in repressed guilt. It flows from a foreboding that the country may be gliding down the road to ruin; from the anticipation of a coming—or at least deserved—retribution.

## Role and Responsibility of World Opinion

The Palestinians seem to have only bleak options before them, with right, justice, national honour all pointing one way, and political feasibility another. Yet, all the choices are theirs to make. For outsiders, who do not have to shoulder any of the sacrifices attendant on these choices, to admonish or advise the Palestinians from afar (whether to prod them into indefinite resistance or to recommend that they be content with a moth-caten state or statelet) would be equally impertinent and risible. Yet the outside world could make an enormous difference, simply by adopting a less biased approach. We are not speaking here of the foreign powers with influence in the region and their whole farce about 'brokering peace'. These most dishonest of brokers were never serious about putting pressure on Israel, and still aren't. We are speaking of public opinion and those who shape it on a daily basis. For a start, journalists and columnists should drop their odious double standards. They should pause to consider the constraints which asymmetric warfare puts on the weaker side. They should quit reviling as 'terrorism' actions which are often feats of great daring and sacrifice,[34] while routinely excusing Israel's open recourse to state terrorism and collective punishment. They should revise their views of Hamas and Hizbullah based on how these movements actually think and function, instead of parroting the Israeli line about their being 'terrorist outfits'. And if that is too much of a revision for them, they should at least stop demonising Iran for financing and arming Hamas and Hizbullah, while the thuggish West Bank settlers are drenched in American money,[35] and Israel itself is awash with American arms (gifts rather than sales!) and receives donations from the American state to the tune of $8 billion a year—for no reason in particular; simply for being Israel.

This—more honest news reporting and less blinkered news commenting—would only be the first step. It would create a less miasmal atmosphere, in which it would become easier for committed groups or individuals to build up public pressure and get the governments in the West and in Asia to cast their vote according to the justice of the case, at the UN and other international forums, in all issues to do with the Middle East. It might also become possible to agitate for international sanctions against Israel (though unachievable at the moment, it would be worth the effort, for the symbolic value) or, more realistically, to push for volunteer boycotts—commercial, cultural, academic. In anticipation of *a possible unilateral declaration of independence by the Palestinians,* it would also make sense to prepare a ground-wave of opinion that might force the hands of governments worldwide and get them to recognise the self-proclaimed Palestinian state and restrain Israel. Again, in the equally possible event of *a forcible annexation by Israel of the whole of historical Palestine,* the conditions would be ripe for the type of international campaign that ostracised the apartheid regime in South Africa and brought its eventual downfall. In the shorter term, the main priority is probably to counteract the huge propaganda effort by Israel to pressure the US into bombing Iran. As for the South Asian public, which Kumar was primarily targeting while writing this book, it should spare no efforts to foil the fast consolidating Indo–Israeli alliance and the less publicised Sri Lanka–Israel rapprochement.

All these are momentous issues, where a resolute show of public defiance can force the hand of craven governments which, left to themselves, would follow their pro-Israeli instincts.

## The Position at the Time of Kumar's Visit in 2007

The one-state/two-state alternative is a recurrent theme in the current Middle East debate, and one which Kumar's book addresses repeatedly, if obliquely. It is usually presented as a choice between a single bi-national Arab–Jewish state within the limits of historical Palestine (with or without chunks of Jordan), or a Palestinian state (on the West Bank and the Gaza strip) to coexist alongside a pared down Israel, reduced to its pre-1967 borders (possibly with minor, mutually agreeable land swaps).

Privately, Kumar leaned towards the one-state formula. This had, I suspect, much to do with his experience of India's separatist movements, especially in the North East provinces (between Bangladesh and Burma), an area he had travelled and researched extensively. Dozens of armed insurgencies and semi-peaceful campaigns—agitating or fighting either for full independence from India, or a re-drawing of interstate borders within the Indian Union, or the creation of smaller state units—are poisoning life in the seven federal states of the North East by pursuing goals which are impossible to reconcile,[36] and which, even if met halfway, could only generate more unrest, displacements of populations, and a spiral of never-ending fragmentation. Kumar also followed the convulsive break-up of former Yugoslavia in the 1990s and the decade-long horror that ensued in the Balkans. His considered view was that the key to respecting local identities of whatever nature—linguistic, ethnic, ethno-religious etcetera—does not lie in the indefinite multiplication of nation-states, but in the imaginative quest for more flexible autonomy arrangements *within* and, if need be, *across* the existing demarcations, no matter how flawed or whimsical these may appear.

Returning to Palestine: Kumar's book fleetingly mentions two prominent advocates of the one-state solution: the Israeli peace activist Ilan Pappé and the late Palestinian author Edward Said.[37] It also features two Arab interviewees (Abdo Saad and Rashid W.) who at first sight seem to endorse that 'same' solution but outline what are in fact two completely different visions. The first would deny citizenship of the future state to all 'imported' Israeli Jews and restrict it to the minuscule minority that can establish *bona fina* ancestry in Palestine. The other would accept practically every Israeli citizen barring a few unreformed Arab-haters. In the second scenario, such 'details' as the control of the police and armed forces; the question of who would hold the demographic and parliamentary majority; the possibility that the majority might change and the ways of ensuring that the change be smooth—none of these are even discussed. Nor are we told how the one-state arrangement might come about in the first place.

The reason no one makes the slightest effort to flesh out these 'details' is that the whole thing is simply too hard to envision. No one takes it as a serious proposition.

Why then is the idea being bandied about? That is not difficult to understand either. Since the collapse of the Oslo Accord, many Arabs and Palestinians have come to the conclusion that even if a Palestinian state were to come into being, it would be so small, so unviable, so fragmented and pock-marked by Israeli settlement zones, so dependent on the whims and dictates of the all-powerful neighbour to the West, that it would not be worth having. So they have taken to speaking about one common democratic, fraternal state for both Palestinians and Jews to avoid admitting that they see no hope at all, and also because they know that it sounds good as a talking point.

Kumar, however, as is apparent from the dialogues of Chapter 5, was of the view that the one-State formula was being taken seriously by its proponents and that it might after all be a viable option. He was also putting great store by the solemn declarations, by such movements as Hamas and Islamic Jihad, never ever to reconcile themselves to the presence of a Zionist state on Palestine's soil. He was visibly unconvinced when we represented to him that in the view of most Middle East watchers, these organisations, especially Hamas, might eventually accept a two-State solution (and be it through the face-saving ploy of proclaiming a *hudna* or *long-lasting truce* with Israel—a move entirely unexceptionable under Islamic doctrine, and conveniently extendable), though not of course under the derisory conditions of the Oslo Accords.

Since Kumar's 2007 visit, however, the diplomatic and ideological front-lines have shifted somewhat. A new democratic administration is in power in Washington, which (despite a short-lived initial display of firmness by Obama) shows no sign of exerting real pressure on Israel. So there has not been much of a change here. Hamas, however, has toned down its opposition to the two-state solution, while Israel remains hell-bent on creating such 'facts on the ground' (that is, more and more settlements) as would render that solution practically impossible. The most ominous shift, however, has occurred on the question of the 'bi-national state', an idea that seems to be slowly gaining in support both among Palestinians and Israelis, albeit on radically different premises—thus foreshadowing, not a peaceful solution, but a radical exacerbation of the conflict.

## The Two-state Solution

Over the last two years, Hamas has been hinting ever more broadly that, if offered an honourable settlement, it might indeed accept Israel's pre-1967 borders. The organisation's political head, Khaled Meshal, in a recent interview with US journalist David Pollock, confirmed that in so many words. He also clarified where Hamas differed from the PLO, and what sort of mistakes it was keen not to repeat: 'We have learnt from the experience of past PLO negotiations. We are different from the PLO. First, we don't give in to threats, we are not afraid. And second, we are patient.' The position could not be clearer: 'We won't accept crumbs from Israel's table. We won't sell out for a token of sovereignty. To revise our Charter,[38] without a *quid pro quo,* would make no sense.'

Thus, at the level of principle, there would seem to be no insurmountable obstacle in the way of the two-state solution, at least from the Palestinian side. Most opinion polls, for what they are worth, indicate that two in three Palestinians favour this solution, on the basis of the pre-1967 borders. Israeli public opinion also, in its majority, has come to regard the eventual establishment of a Palestinian state as inevitable. Even the present Israeli Premier Netanyahu pays lip service to the formula, as did his predecessor Olmert. So too does the 'international community'. But all successive Israeli governments keep piling new obstacles, mainly by multiplying or enlarging the Jewish settlements on the West Bank and in East Jerusalem, despite feeble attempts by the Obama administration to impose a freeze. Thus, while the one-state solution remains a distinct possibility, the prospects for it look bleaker with every month that passes.

The outlines of a stable, politically feasible two-state solution are more or less clear to all parties. There is no need to go into details here. Any of the formulas being mooted[39] would involve a wrenching renunciation on the part of the Palestinians. They would have to be content with a bare 25 per cent of pre-Partition Palestine (if we count out the al-Nakab desert[40] the proportion would be slightly larger). Their territory would not be of one piece—with the Gaza strip separated from the West Bank by 60 kilometres, and connected by (ground, underground, or fly-over) corridors through Israeli territory. (The Oslo Accord made provisions for four such corridors, none of which were ever opened.) The Palestinian refugees from families driven out of Israel in 1958 would have to waive their right of return into Israel, save perhaps for a token minority. The rest would receive financial assistance to resettle in the Palestinian state-to-be, or in neighbouring countries, or farther afield, according to their wishes and the possibilities on offer. On the other hand, Al-Quds (Jerusalem) would have to be partitioned, with both halves serving as capitals for their respective states. Lastly, the Palestinians would have to be rid of the West Bank colonists. The forceful dismantling of nearly all West Bank colonies, according to most observers, would be fiercely resisted by the settlers, but it would not trigger a civil war in Israel, and if perchance it did, the pro-settler faction would not win that war, despite its rampant infiltration of the IDF.[41]

Normally, a stable two-state arrangement could only result from a negotiated settlement. This, however, would presuppose a huge amount of American arm-twisting, which at the moment is most unlikely. There could also be another, bumpier road to 'two states'—namely through a unilateral proclamation, by the Palestinian Authority, of a Palestinian state within the 1967 borders, with an immediate request for international recognition. In that scenario, the attitude of foreign governments, and their willingness to rein in Israel, would be crucial, and so would the pressure put on these governments by their domestic opinion.

## No Negotiated Road to a Democratic Bi-national State

As an orderly negotiated solution, capable of bringing lasting peace, the 'bi-national state', as already pointed out, has impossibility writ large all across it. Barring completely unforeseeable developments (similar in magnitude to those which made the creation of Israel possible) one cannot even remotely visualise a chain of events that would deliver it into existence.[42] The Palestinians do not want it. Above all, there is not the slightest chance that the Israelis, with their present mindset, sitting as they do on their conventional,[43] nuclear,[44] biological,[45] and chemical[46] arsenal, with their octopus grip on US foreign policy and their effective veto power on all Middle East initiatives of their European *vassals*, would agree to an equitable merger. From the Zionist perspective, which still informs

Israeli mentality, the whole, the sole point of Israel is to provide a place where Jews are in a clear, secure majority, and in no danger of being out-bred.

## Two Perilous Roads to a Unitary State

Though still-born as a coherent vision, the idea of the 'bi-national state' is currently being revived as a cover for two distinct and equally unavowable designs. On the Palestinian side, the plan would amount to telling the Israelis 'annex us' while adding in petto 'so that we may stifle you'. Concretely, 'the Palestinian authority would announce its own dissolution, and the Palestinians would demand Israeli citizenship', knowing well that they would not receive it in full, 'but still hoping to effectively implement the idea of a bi-national state, in which they would soon have a demographic majority'.[47] At the moment, in the total area between the Jordan river and the Mediterranean sea, Jews outnumber Palestinians 59 per cent to 41 per cent. With their much higher fertility, however, the 'annexed' Palestinians, if only they manage to avoid eviction (that's a big if ), could reasonably expect to constitute a majority within twelve to fifteen years. At which point the rough ride would start. The Palestinians prepared to countenance this 'option' (one cannot bring oneself to calling it a 'solution') are still a small minority, but an increasingly vocal one, with recent recruits of note like Nusseibeh.[48]

On the Israeli side, the 'bi-national state', long a pet project of a tiny, Utopian fringe of the left, is in the process of being hijacked by the right and far-right. Six notorious Israeli hawks[49] have recently come out in favour of annexing the entire West Bank,[50] while promising the Palestinians full rights (on certain conditions...) including citizenship and voting rights (although not immediately...). A mere look at these new votaries of bi-nationalism, at their track-record, and at the small print of their proposals, instantly reveals their true intentions: to get a free hand to expand Jewish settlements at a frantic pace all over the West Bank, and then to rely on the well-tried methods of 'soft ethnic cleansing'—perfected over the last 40 years, notably in East Jerusalem—to take care of the surplus Palestinian population.

With the peace process virtually dead, one cannot completely dismiss the possibility that history will actually pick one of these two scenarios, or some weird combination of both. However, given the diametrically opposed game plans of the two partner populations, this could only be a recipe for perpetuating the stalemate, without any resolution in sight, and every chance of a major conflagration not too far down the road.

## The Taboo Option: The Dismantling of Israel

If nothing works and nothing changes, there will be no going around one last, yet unconjured scenario. This last option is the one that would see the total dismantling of the Israeli state, with its citizens returning to Europe, America, or wherever they want to betake themselves. At its mere enunciation, most Westerners howl, shake, or swoon in dismay: they dismiss the idea as politically impossible and morally monstrous. They are, of course, perfectly right on the first count: there is as yet no force on earth with both the means *and* the will to impose it on the Israelis. But let us for a second suspend realism, even reality, and examine the second point: the justice or otherwise of *Rolling back Israel*.

It would uproot a great many Jews who are Israel-born (about 67 per cent), have no obvious place to 'return to', and in some cases speak no other language than modern Hebrew. It would cause an almighty exodus, and produce distress, misery and trauma on an almighty scale. It would in a word compare to the fate that was meted out to the Palestinians, albeit with many mitigating circumstances.[51] Things such as these are not quantifiable, and yet to reach decisions—even if only in imagination—one must do as if they were, and decide which catastrophe weighs heavier. Even honest, sincere people will inevitably hold different views there, according to the information at their disposal, the values they prioritise in life, the culture that shaped them—and of course depending in which *yonis* they were born. What is not permissible, though, is to have eyes only for the misery on one side. Yet commentators who have not the least difficulty in envisioning permanent exile for the true sons of the soil, the Palestinians, and who calmly recommend their resettlement far from home, suddenly find the same idea hair-raising when applied to the Israeli squatters or sons-of-squatters.

So it is high time for the public discourse to change. In the face of Israel's brazen practice of expulsions and land-grabbing, of its relentless harassment and grinding down of the subject race, of its cynical confidence that time will reward its obstinacy and that the world will forever stand by in silence, it is high time to voice the unvoiced.

'Delegitimising Israel', 'dismantling Israel', 'resettling the Israelis'— these are expressions that have got to enter the mainstream. The very fact that they still remain anathema whilst the propriety of discussing the symmetric options for the Palestinians is always taken for granted is in itself an outrage. These expressions, as well as the possibilities they stand for, should be uttered and discussed exactly as the mirror options of *resettling the Palestinians* have been discussed all along, with exactly the same thoughtful and hate-free gravitas. They may not correspond to any short- or even long-term possibility—although we would do well to remember that history has a way of confounding our expectations and of mocking the certainties of the *nashtadrisha*,[52] the *visionless*—but in the ideal space of moral options they are exactly on the same footing. Simply stating these elementary truths quietly and persuasively, and repeating them until they percolate into the thickest heads—heads that respond only to repetition, and minds so timid that they dare think only thoughts that already enjoy some acceptance—would in itself be a progress. It would help move the sign-posts, create clarity, concentrate minds, instil a sense of urgency, and rob the Israelis of the feeling that the world will forever underwrite their sweet right to flout all international laws, and applaud them into the bargain.

## Towards a Worldwide Boycott of Israel

Let us review the objections most commonly levelled against the idea of a boycott.

*Embargoes and boycotts are wrong in principle, and doubly wrong in matters of culture. Our duty as humans is to engage with our dissenters, to convince them by reasoned argument, to appeal to the best in them.*

To imagine that polite entreaties *unsupported by action* can mollify Israel's opinion in its present state of hardening, or sway the blind momentum of Israel's policies, is to be grievously deluded. It is to misjudge the depths of arrogance, self-righteousness and stiff-neckedness in the Israeli psyche; the cold contempt for the Gentile busybodies; also, with a sizable minority of Israelis, the pent-up resentment against an obnoxious outside world that prevents them from making short shrift of the Palestinians, either directly à la Joshua—see *Numbers*—or in some creative adaptation of the canonical model.

*Any boycott of Israel would hurt the Palestinians hardest.*

The rebuttal here is that nearly all Palestinian organisations are clamouring for a boycott, apparently with near-unanimous backing from the population. In the dwindling ranks of Israeli peaceniks, too, there is wide support for the idea, with disagreement limited to the *scope* of the boycott.

*Any trade boycott should be limited to the sole settlers, and any cultural-academic boycott should target only those Israeli institutions that have proven links with the military establishment and the settler movement.*

This has all along been the view of Uri Avnery, a veteran of the Israeli peace camp and a figure of extraordinary integrity.[53] But for all the respect that Avnery's views command, a selective boycott of the sort he envisions might be extremely cumbersome for the outside world to implement (how to disentangle tainted from untainted products? 'untouchable' from 'touchable' institutions?) and correspondingly easy for Israel to circumvent.

*What is there so unique about Israeli malevolence to justify such unique ostracism? What moral right has the West with its loaded past; India with Kashmir; China with Tibet; Russia with Chechnya, etcetera, to condemn the Israeli version of barbarism which, for all its rude health and promise of growth, is still very much in the medium league? Who can afford to be righteous? Where are the nations that arose through immaculate conception? Were they not all born in violence, and consolidated in their youth through force, repression and exclusion?*

The flourishing of five million Israelis comes at the price of the ruin of roughly as many Palestinians, and stands in rather direct causal relation to US policies that visit affliction on uncounted tens of millions in the Arab and Muslim world. To come close to Israel's level of 'per head malevolence', India would have to oppress not just Kashmir but six or seven Pakistans; induce by its machinations disorder on all six continents;

and keep enough conflicts simmering there to threaten the planet with a general conflagration. This should dispose of the objection.

That said, who would dispute that no Indian group could credibly take up the Palestinian cause without in the same breath denouncing official Indian policies in Kashmir? But scores of Indian NGOs are doing just that—denouncing the repression in Kashmir—and they are by and large the ones that have joined the call for sanctions against Israel. No contradiction or hypocrisy there.

The last argument—that Israel is not alone in owing its birth to the successful application of violence—is harder to counter. The main consideration here would be that the time is past, or ought to be past, when wars were part of the natural order; when 'victory' was an apotheosis to be celebrated and defeat a shame to hide; when the title of 'conqueror' (*conquistador, mansour,* and so on) was the highest badge of honour; and when states came in and out of existence with the regularity of the inevitable. The conditions of the modern world and the evolution of mentalities make that materially impossible and morally unacceptable. Israel, admittedly, was born before the complete breakup of the 'northern empires', when things were still in a state of flux, and dozens of today's nations were either newly-born are yet to be born. But these nations, however violent the circumstances of their creation, did not arise in as artificial and contrived a manner as did Israel. The process involved—with a few notable exceptions—no large population transfers. It was often a simple case of a people reclaiming ownership of its ancestral, never-vacated land and re-assuming stewardship of its destiny after a trifling interruption of 'a few momentary centuries' (to use a phrase beloved of Aurobindo). Israel's birth doesn't fit that pattern—hence the stigma that clings to it like the mark on Cain.

Withal, we should not deceive ourselves into believing that matters as grave as these yield to readymade precepts or universal rules; and rather than hiding behind moral or legalistic casuistry, we should frankly acknowledge the irreducible margin of subjectivity involved in reaching any judgment. Israel itself, for all the social and political determinants that paved its way into existence, was born out of the free exercise of human will, out of the fiat of a historical Subject. It is but meet, therefore, that the world, seeing the trend of events sixty years on, and judging the tree by its fruit, should respond with a subjective fiat of its own, and shout: ENOUGH!

So there we are: if the Israeli state decides to continue in its tracks, as it shows every intention of doing; if it persists with its implacable policy of attrition against the Palestinians, harassing the life out of them, restricting their every movement, curtailing their most basic rights, squeezing them into smaller and smaller enclaves to break their spirit and drive them into exile; if it keeps multiplying its brazen 'facts on the ground' in the hope of earning them legitimacy before world opinion, then world opinion should respond in the only fitting way: it should drop all pretence of believing in a peaceful resolution and begin instead to work hard at *delegitimising Israel.*

## South Asia, West Asia and the Global South

Although the emancipation struggles of the Middle East can do with support from all quarters, and deserve sympathy from all reservoirs of human good will, their most desirable allies, in Kumar's estimation, should be the people of the Indian subcontinent, and that too for a host of reasons. For a start, there are deep natural affinities between the Middle East and South Asia, resulting from a long legacy of cultural contact and mongrelisation. Then there are the dovetailing experiences of their peoples as subjects of the same colonial masters, and now their rather analogous positions and commonalty of interests in a globalising world. Lastly, a revival of neighbourliness might act as a welcome corrective against many worrisome trends and artificial enmities currently developing in both places.

Before discussing the modalities of a possible Indo–Arab linkage, and simply to remind ourselves of how *natural* such a rapprochement would be—of how *natural* it would be for South Asia to reach out to West Asia and seek its future in the global South rather than in a link-up with the United States—we can do no better than harken back to India's post-independence days and the then prevalent spirit of Third World brotherhood. Let us quote extensively from the Bengali writer Amitav Ghosh, who was both a witness to, and exponent of, that spirit.[54]

> Broadly speaking, [the dominant mood of those days] could be described as the spirit of decolonisation that held sway over much of the world in the decades after the Second World War; this was the political ethos that found its institutional representation in the Non-Aligned Movement. We are at a

very different moment in history now, when the words 'non-aligned' seem somehow empty and discredited; today the movement is often dismissed not just as a political failure, but as a minor footnote to the great power rivalries of the Cold War. It is true, of course, that the movement had many shortcomings and met with many failures. Yet it is also worth remembering that the Non-Aligned Movement as such was merely the institutional aspect of something that was much broader, wider and more powerful: this, as I said before, was the post-war ethos of decolonisation, which was a political impulse that had deep historical roots and powerful cultural resonances. In the field of culture, among other things, it represented an attempt to restore and recommence the exchanges and conversations that had been interrupted by the long centuries of European imperial dominance. It was, in this sense, the necessary and vital counterpart of the nationalist idiom of anti-colonial resistance. In the West, Third World nationalism is often presented as an ideology of xenophobia and parochialism. But the truth is that many of these movements of resistance tried very hard, within their limited means, to create an universalism of their own. Those of us who grew up in that period will recall how powerfully we were animated by an emotion that is rarely named: this is *xenophilia,* the love of the other, the affinity for strangers—a feeling that lives very deep in the human heart, but whose very existence is rarely acknowledged. People of my generation will recall the pride we once took in the transnational friendships of such figures as Nehru, Nasser, Sukarno, Zhou Enlai and others. Nor were friendships of this kind anything new. I have referred above to the cross-cultural conversations that were interrupted by imperialism. These interruptions were precisely that—-temporary breakages—the conversations never really ceased. Even in the 19th century, the high noon of Empire, people from Africa, Asia and elsewhere, sought each other out, wrote letters to each other, and stayed in each other's homes while traveling. Lately, a great number of memoirs and autobiographies have been published that attest to the depth and strength of these ties. It was no accident therefore that Mahatma Gandhi chose to stop in Egypt, in order to see Saad Zaghloul before proceeding to the Round Table Conference in London. This was integral to the ethos of the time. Similarly, it is no accident that capitals like New Delhi, Abuja and Tunis have many roads that are named after leaders from other continents. Sometimes these names are unpronounceable to local tongues and then they cause annoyance or laughter, and invite dismissal as empty gestures. But the fact that such gestures are not without value becomes apparent when we reflect that we would search in vain for roads that are named in this fashion in such supposedly global cities as London, New York and Berlin. These gestures, in other words, may be imbued with both pomposity and pathos, but they are not empty: they represent a yearning to reclaim an interrupted cosmopolitanism.

The world today is very different from that of 1980, when I came to Egypt. The conversations and exchanges that re-commenced in the post-war period are now in danger of being broken off again. Today, especially in the Anglo–American world, capitalism and empire are once again being packaged together, in a bundle that is scarcely distinguishable from the old 'civilising mission'. Indeed, one of the outcomes of the horrifying attacks of 9/11 was that it led to an extraordinary rehabilitation of imperialism, not merely as a political and military force, but also as an ideology — one that has led to the unfolding catastrophe in Iraq.

Empires are not the sole threat to the continuation of our conversations: over the last fifteen years, in many parts of Asia and Africa, we have seen a dramatic rise in violent and destructive kinds of fundamentalism, some religious, and some linguistic. These movements are profoundly hostile to any notion of dialogue between cultures, faiths and civilisations. They are movements of intolerance and bigotry and they mirror the ideology of imperialism in that they seek to remake the world—or at least their corners of it—in their own images.

Against this background it is tempting to look back on the days of non-alignment with some nostalgia: and indeed there was much that was valuable in that period. Yet it would be idle to pretend that solutions could be found by looking backwards in time. That was a certain historical moment and it has passed [....] Except that this time we must correct the mistake that lay at the heart of that older anti-colonial impulse—which is that we must not only include the West within this spectrum of desire, we must also acknowledge that both the West and we ourselves have been irreversibly changed by our encounter with each other. We must recognise that in the West, as in Asia, Africa and elsewhere, there are great numbers of people who, by force of circumstance, have become xenophiles.[55]

If, emerging from this pleasant jacuzzi of nostalgia and casting off the spell of Amitav Ghosh's emollient prose, we now try to assess the *present* possibilities for South–South solidarity, and more particularly the type of Indo–Arab initiatives on the Middle East that Kumar was trying to initiate, we are immediately struck by a series of daunting obstacles, none of which existed in the 1950s, at least not to the same degree. For one thing, in the present political climate, such initiatives should expect next to zero institutional support. Then they would have to contend with powerful countervailing trends:

- the self-centredness and egoism of Indian and Arab 'elites';
- their obsession with the American way of life;

- their inclination to look down on, rather than embrace, the global South;
- the festering sore of Kashmir, which in turn leads to India's perpetual enmity with Pakistan;
- and, by extension, its estrangement from much of the Moslem world;
- the parallel rise of inward-looking strains of Hindu and Moslem fundamentalism and bigotry in the ideological space vacated by Marxism and socialism.

To take off amidst such forbidding constraints, any Indo–Arab initiative would clearly have to start on a very modest scale; be largely self-supporting; operate mostly at volunteer level; remain sobre, focused, issue-oriented; and guard against the usual distractions and illusory projections that so often derail the most promising undertakings. If, on the other hand, a movement takes shape and survives in the teeth of all these obstacles, it might emerge tempered by adversity (instead of dissolving into vapour, like the non-aligned movement of yesteryears) and turn into a force capable, where it matters, of shaping public opinion and inflecting government policies for the better. That, at any rate, was Kumar's ambition in writing this book. It is to this ambition that, as his friends and survivors, we should now attempt to give shape.

**Jean Ecalle**
10 October 2010

## Notes

1. As Dr Jabbour does. See Chapter 3, towards the middle.
2. A New York based author writing in French, Elie Wiesel is 'Mr Holocaust'. With his eternally tormented mien, tormented voice, and tormented demeanour, he is an inescapable fixture of all remembrance ceremonies. As a writer, he specialises in Judaic religious kitsch, for which he was awarded the Nobel prize for literature. As a public voice, his pronouncements are noticeable for their insensitivity towards non-Jews in general, and Palestinians in particular. He showed special callousness towards the *Roms* or Gypsies, who were, no

less than the Jews, victims of Hitler's extermination drive. Wiesel successfully lobbied to get them excluded from the New York Holocaust museum.

3. If a mere *goy* (non-Jew) had said this, he would immediately have been shouted down and shamed into recanting. Obviously, *quod licet Iovi non licet bovi,* or if you prefer: *double standards are okay with the Israelis.* This puts me in mind of a recent Israeli TV serial which, I am told, dwells complacently, admiringly, lovingly on the vulgar success of the Russian oligarchs-kleptocrats, nearly all of whom are Jews. For the unadorned truth about Jews, one must often go to Israel.

4. It began as a paper commissioned in 2002 by the *Atlantic Monthly* which, seeing the finished product with its title, dropped it like a hot potato. The paper was then rejected by all US journals and publishers and was accessible only on the Internet until a condensed version got published in Britain by the *London Review of Books.* In 2007, it was eventually published as a book by Farrar, Strauss and Giraux in New York.

5. They reject the label 'Jewish Lobby', on the ground that a sizeable section of American Jews have no truck with it and that, conversely, much of its support and funding comes from fringe sections of the Evangelical movement and 'Christian Zionists'.

6. American Israel Public Affairs Committee.

7. Former peace negotiator under the Clinton administration.

8. This is a highly sensitive position, for it is the chair of the NIC that sifts through the intelligence from all US agencies and presents a 'digest' to the President.

9. When discussed at the General Assembly, in November 2009, the Goldstone report was rejected by seven EU governments. Switzerland, Ireland and Portugal voted for it. The UK, France and Spain abstained. Worldwide, there were 114 votes for, 18 against, and 44 abstentions. In all, 22 of the 27 EU countries refused to endorse it.

10. Under normal circumstances, there is nothing that infuriates Jews more than having Christian interpretations foisted on their collective destinies, especially when these interpretations are concocted with the intellectual resources of folksy American evangelism.

11. As regards the Jews, their 'genocidal past' is of course *double* –in biblical and modern times—but also and above all doubly problematic. The modern treatment of Palestinians at the hand of Israelis, barbarous though it is, does not qualify as genocide under any sensible definition (although there is no denying that significant numbers of Israelis harbour explicit genocidal intentions and freely vent them). As for the ancient conquest of Canaan under Joshua and Co. and the attendant, proudly assumed extermination of the indigenous population, it is recounted in texts (the *Book of Numbers* of the Bible) that were

probably written down ca. 600 BC. The events themselves, whether mythical or not, are supposed to have taken place ca. 1200 BC. Mores then were different, and so was the very definition of good and evil. Is it not therefore an unseemly irrelevance to mention the Bible's celebration of genocide in a work on contemporary history? It is not, for the simple reason that these texts are still a living inspiration to hundreds of thousands of Israelis (the Meir Kahane gang; the sort that lay flowers on the tomb of Baruch Goldstein) and continue to inform their attitude towards Arabs or, for that matter, all non-Jews.

12. When reading about the two 'conquests', one is struck time and again by the similarity of outlook and tone, with the recurrence of nearly identical expressions. White Americans never thought of themselves as land thieves; on the contrary, they spoke without irony about 'giving land' to the Amerindians. Similarly, Israelis complaining about Palestinian ingratitude will say: 'We gave them everything, and see...'

13. The thriller shows how a squad of Mossad killers eliminate a list of Palestinians supposedly responsible for the death of eleven Israeli athletes during the hostage drama of the 1972 Summer Olympics in Munich. In actual fact, the Mossad victims had nothing to do with the affair. Mossad simply looked for easy targets and picked PLO diplomats posted in European capitals, who lived quite unprotected. As for the 11 Israeli athletes, the post-mortem reports revealed that nine of them were killed by German policemen in the course of a bungled rescue attempt. For details, see Uri Avnery' column online at http://www.gush-shalom.org/(published on 4 February 2006).

14. American life, of course, is plagued by many other obnoxious lobbies (the Saudi lobby, the oil lobby, the arms lobby) which wield enormous power, 'own' politicians, dictate vote outcomes, and so on, but none enjoys the same sort of immunity from criticism as the Israel lobby does.

15. Charles W. Freeman, 'Israel: Asset or Liability?', presented at the Nixon Center debate that took place on 20 July 2010.

16. *J-Street*, for example, supports sanctions against Iran. It also condemned the Goldstone report for slamming Israel 'too severely', and it denounced a decision by British courts to try the former Israeli premier Tzipi Livni for war crimes during the 2006 Gaza offensive.

17. There was a one-generation interval between the Holocaust, which took place during the later phases of World War II, and the epochal re-calibration of Jewish–Gentile relations, which matured throughout the 1950s and finally crystallised in the late 1960s.

18. From the similarly titled book by Norman Finkelstein, *The Holocaust Industry: Reflections on the Exploitation of Jewish Suffering* (Verso, 2000).

19. The EU General Secretary Javier Solana himself admitted as much during his farewell visit to Israel in the autumn 2009, after meeting Israel's Foreign

Minister, the thuggishly right-wing Avigdor Lieberman. See also *Europes Alliance with Israel: Aiding the Occupation* by David Cronin. Israel's fresh agricultural produce and its processed foods can already be exported to the EU free of customs duties, while Gaza's horticulturists are prohibited from exporting their tomatoes, flowers etcetera.

20. Like its American model AIPAC, the EFI is an umbrella structure devoted to coordinating the lobbying and propaganda activities of dozens of existing Jewish organisations such as the European Jewish Congress, the European branch of Bnai Brith etcetera.

21. The EU concentrates on Gaza while the US, which wants nothing to do with Hamas, pours its heavily string-attached aid into the West bank.

22. Yael Ben Yefet, a Tel Aviv Council member and Israeli peace activist, was the target of a deluge of hate mail.

23. During the 2006 Lebanon war, while still Prime Minister, he had strenuously opposed any call for a 'premature ceasefire', thereby echoing Condoleezza Rice's glee over the 'birth pangs of the new Middle East'. In his memoirs, released in the summer 2010, Tony Blair admitted: 'If I had condemned Israel, it would have been more than dishonest; it would have undermined the world view I had come to hold passionately. I saw the conflict as part of a wider struggle between the strains of religious extremism in Islam and the rest of us'.

24. A Jew and ardent supporter of the Iraq war. At the time of writing, he is the chief contender for the Labour leadership.

25. I remember talking to two colleague-mathematicians from Lebanon during the summer 2006, while Israel was carpet-bombing south Lebanon and the sprawling Shia suburbs of Beirut. They were incandescent with rage at being informed over the airwaves by the German chancellor Angela Merkel that 'Israel had every right to defend its existence!' To soothe them, I ventured that the gracious lady was simply angling for praise from the *Zentralrat der Juden*, Germany's Jewish Council with seat in Frankfurt. The council is beholden to Israel's right-wing Likud party and routinely distributes good or bad marks to Germany's intellectuals and politicians. In the event, Frau Merkel got her top marks from the *Zentralrat* and could be seen purring in meek contentment.

26. *Die Welt soll am deutschen Wesen genesen* or *The German spirit shall heal the world*. The poet Friedrich Schiller said it first, innocently enough, and then the philosopher J. G. Fichte took it up, injecting a whole new meaning into the phrase; then came worse...

27. Harsh V. Pant, 'India-Israel Partnership: Convergence and Constraints', *The Middle East Review of International Affairs*, December 2004.

28. Subhash Kapila, 'India–Israel Relations : The Imperative for Enhanced Strategic Cooperation,' South Asia Analysis Group (1 August 2000). Available online at: www.southasiaanalysis.org\papers2\paper131.html.

29. This is a pattern. It was recently announced (September 2010) that Israel had offered to assist Russia in modernising its armed forces. A long-term agreement has just been reached.

30. On 30 May 2010, Israeli troops boarded, in international waters, an international flotilla of six ships carrying humanitarian aid for the blockade-starved Palestinians of the Gaza strip. On the main ship, *Mavi Marmara,* they met with some resistance and opened fire, resulting in the death of nine activists, mostly Turkish.

31. That would not sit well with the Iranian clerics' repeated condemnations of atomic weapons as 'immoral and un-Islamic'—a position that would be more embarrassing to reverse than all of Iran's diplomatic denials.

32. As even the pathetically disingenuous Jeffrey Goldberg is obliged to concede—to retain some credibility—in his latest plea to the American nation for an attack on Iran. See his cringe-inducing piece 'The point of No Return: War with Iran', in the *Atlantic Monthly,* September 2010.

33. Emigration out of Israel was specially brisk in the years preceding the Six Day war.

34. These acts would probably be commemorated by public statues, monument names, street plaques and the like, if only they had been committed by the resistance movements in German-occupied Europe. That said, one should of course distinguish between spontaneous, despair-driven suicide attacks, of which there have been not a few, and commandeered ones, which again can be of all sorts, with clear instances of revolting manipulation of impressionable teenagers at the lowest end of the spectrum.

35. According to Uri Avnery, a lot of it comes from Jewish-American 'casino kings, brothel moguls, money launderers and tax evaders'.

36. Though many, like the Naga agitation, can, on their own, make a convincing case.

37. Noam Chomsky and Tony Judt are also known to favour it. But the late Tony Judt at least was honest in presenting it as a utopia.

38. In particular the clause calling for the removal of Israel.

39. Like the detailed Nusseibeh–Ayalon plan, prepared by peace activists from both sides and released in 2003. Its outline can be found on http//www. peacelobby.org.

40. Meaning 'the dry place'. This is the rocky desert to the south of Israel, renamed as 'Negev' by the Israelis.

41. The evacuation of the Gaza settlers, in August 2005, was much smoother than anticipated. The West Bank settlers are much more numerous, of course, but comprise only a minority of committed fanatics. The rest were lured to the

settlements by attractive loans and benefits. The general assumption is that, if compensated, they would not mind resettling in Israel.

42. See, on the *Gush Shalom* website, the minutes of the historical debate between Uri Avnery and Ilan Pappé on the merits of the bi-national option.
43. Some $2 billion of America's latest weapons (gifted, not sold): drones, bunker-blasting bombs, etcetera.
44. An estimated 150 to 200 atom bombs.
45. The difficulty here is to find pathogen germs that can target Arabs but not 'Arab' Jews. Israeli ingenuity is hard at work to solve the problem.
46. Its existence is strenuously denied by Israel, but the crash, on 4 October 1992, at Amsterdam's Schipol airport, of an Israeli cargo plane with 114 tons of freight, suggests otherwise. After the accident—the worst air disaster in Dutch history—the affair was hushed-up to assist in the Israeli cover-up. Dutch officials lied to the public, saying the plane was transporting 'flowers and perfumes' (just figure: 114 tons of them!). It took six years before the Dutch newspaper *NRC Handelsblad* revealed, in October 1998, the true contents of the crashed plane and their destination: 'The cargo documents show that the aircraft carried dimethyl methylphosphonate (DMMP) and two other substances needed to make the deadly nerve gas Sarin. The DMPP was destined for the Israeli Institute for Biological Research (IIBR)'.
47. Carlo Stenger, 'After the Middle East Peace Talks Fail', in *Guardian*, 25 August 2010. C, Stenger is a Tel Aviv based Israeli academic.
48. Nusseibeh matters, because he had for many years been a vocal advocate of the two-state solution (see *supra note 41*).
49. Their names and declarations were reported in mid-July 2010 in a long piece in the Israeli daily *Haaretz* and then commented upon by Uri Avnery in his *Gush Shalom* column of 24 July 2010. They are:

   1. Moshe Arens, a former Defence Minister known for his hawkish views;
   2. Reuven Rivin, Speaker of the *Knesset* (the Israeli Parliament);
   3. Tzipi Hutubeli, an MP belonging to the extreme fringe of the right-wing Likud;
   4. Hanan Porat, admirer of Baruch Goldstein and founder of *Gush Emunim*, a messianic movement committed to the colonisation of the entire West Bank; and
   5. Emily Amrussi and Uri Elitsur, two leaders of settler associations.

50. But *not* the Gaza strip, which would be dumped on Egypt. Regarding the West Bank, it may be noted that, for all intents and purposes, the Israeli authorities

have already made up their mind to annex the Jordan valley, for 'strategic depth', and are multiplying settlements there.

51. The Palestinians were treated like dogs in many of their places of exile. The ex-Israelis would be feted and embraced in both hemispheres.

52. This fancy word, for the source-curious, is taken from *Shrimad-Bhagavatam, Canto 1, Ch.3, shl.43.* Irrelevant though it may seem (but isn't a piece of pure pointlessness forgivable once in a while), here is the full *shloka* in the hoary language:

*kṛṣṇe svadhāmopagate dharmajnānādibhiḥ saha
kalau naṣṭadṛśām eṣa purāṇārko 'dhunoditaḥ.*

Freely rendered:

*No sooner had Krishna departed to his own abode, taking along with him righteousness, wisdom, and all joy of life, than there arose this radiant Purana (the Shrimad Bhagavatam) for the guidance of the forlorn, dim-visioned beings trapped and immured in the darkness of the age of Kali.*

These haunting lines with their central jewel of a word—*nashtadrisha*—irresistibly come to mind when one muses over the chaos that is history, and pre-eminently the chunk of history under review in this book. Are we not, all to a man, creatures of impaired vision, groping in the dark and condemned to achieve destiny in a mental muddle?

53. Unlike the doctrinaire US libertarian Noam Chomsky, whose denunciations of Zionism always have a half-hearted, insincere ring about them—almost as if they were a reluctant concession to his general political line. Typically, Chomsky rejects any form of sanctions against Israel on the very specious grounds that 'any boycott should start with the US, which has been and remains directly responsible for most of Israel's crimes'.

54. Amitav Ghosh (born 1954 in Kolkata; now based in New York) spent three years, as a young student of anthropology, in a rural village of Upper Egypt, and confessed to falling under the spell of the place. Egypt, in a sense, made him as a writer, by giving him the material for his first novel, *In an Antique Land* (1992), which interweaves his musings about contemporary Egypt with the semi-fictional adventures of a 12th century Jewish trader between Egypt and India (to decipher the trader's correspondence, Ghosh had to teach himself a long-extinct Judeo-Arabic dialect).

55. From Amitav Ghosh, 'Confessions of a Xenophile'. For the full piece, see http://www.outlookindia.com/article.aspx?239275. The text is adapted from an address given by A. G. to the Arab Writers' League Conference in Cairo, March 2008.

# Select bibliography

T he following list of bibliographical references is based mostly on the author's posthumous papers and manuscripts, but also includes later publications. It does not claim to be exhaustive—no bibliography on the subject could be.

## GENERAL

Aburish, Said K. 1997. *A Brutal Friendship: The West and the Arab Elite*. London: Bloomsbury.

Akhavi, Sharouf. 2009. *The Politics of the Sacred and Secular*. London: Zed Books.

Anderson, Irvine H. 1981. *Aramco, the United States and Saudi Arabia, 1933–1950*. Princeton: Princeton University Press.

Antonius, George. 1969. *The Arab Awakening: The Story of the Arab National Movement*. London: Hamish Hamilton.

Armstrong, Karen. 1991. *Holy War: The Crusades and their Impact on Today's World*. London: Macmillan.

Barnhardt, Michael A. 1987. *Japan Prepares for Total War: The Search for Economic Security, 1919–1941*. Ithaca: Cornell University Press.

Blum, William. 1985. *Killing Hope: US Military and CIA Interventions since World War II*. Common Courage Press.

Chomsky, Noam. 1999. *The Fateful Triangle: The United States, Israel and the Palestinians* With a foreword by Edward Said. MA Cambridge: South End Press.

———. 2000. *Rogue States: The Rule of Force in World Affairs*. London: Pluto Press.

———. 2001. *9/11*. New York: Seven Stories Press.

———. 2003a. *Hegemony or Survival*. New York: Owl Books.

Cordovez, Diego and Selig S. Harrison. 1995. *Out of Afghanistan: The Inside Story of the Soviet Withdrawal*. New York: Oxford University Press.

Feis, Herbert. 1963. *The Road to Pearl Harbor: The Coming of War between the United States and Japan*. New York: Atheneum.

Fisk, Robert. 2005. *The Great War for Civilization*. London: Fourth Estate.

Gates, Robert M. 1996. *From the Shadows: The Ultimate Insider's Story of Five Presidents and How They Won the Cold War*. New York: Simon and Schuster.

Green, Stephen. 1988. *Living by the Sword: America and Israel in the Middle East 1968–1987*. London: Faber & Faber.

Hanson, Victor D. 2002. *Carnage and Culture*. New York: Anchor Books.

Hardt, D. and A. NEGRI. 2000. *Empire*. Cambridge, MA: Harvard University Press.

Heikal, Mohamed. 1978. *Sphinx and Commissar: The Rise and Fall of Soviet Influence in the Middle East*. London: Collins.

Hirst, David. 1977. *The Gun and the Olive Branch*. London: Futura Publications.

Hirst, David and Irene Beeson. 1982. *Sadat,* London: Faber & Faber.

Hourani, Albert. 1983. *Arabic Thought in the Liberal Age, 1798–1939*. Cambridge: Cambridge University Press.

Kedourie, Elie. 1956. *England and the Middle East: The Destruction of the Ottoman Empire, 1914–1921*. London: Bowes and Bowes.

Keen, D. 2006. 'War Without End? Magic, Propaganda and the Hidden Functions of Counterterror', *Journal of International Development*, 18(1), pp. 87–104.

Lapping, Brian. 1985. *End of Empire*. London: Granada.

Lawrence, T.E. *The Seven Pillars of Wisdom*. First published in 1922 (Oxford), now available online (Gutenberg Project).

Louis, William R. 1984. *The British Empire in the Middle East, 1945–1951: Arab Nationalism, The United States and Postwar Imperialism*. Oxford: Clarendon Press.

Love, Kenneth. 1969. *Suez: The Twice-Fought War*. New York: McGraw-Hill.

Maalouf, Amin. 1984. *The Crusades through Arab Eyes*. New York: Schocken Books.

Makiya, Kanan. 1993. *Cruelty and Silence: War, Tyranny, Uprising and the Arab World*. London: Jonathan Cape.

Mansfield, Peter. 1992. *The Arabs*. New York: Penguin. (First published, 1977 under the title *The Arab World: A Comprehensive History*.)

Monroe, Elisabeth. 1963. *Britain's Moment in the Middle East: 1914–1956,* Baltimore: John Hopkins Press.

———. 1973. *Philby of Arabia*. London: Faber and Faber.

Prange, Gordon W., Donald M. Goldstein, and Katherine V. Dillon. 1991. *Pearl Harbor: The Verdict of History*. New York: Penguin.

Putzel, J. 2006. 'Crack in the US Empire: Unilateralism, the "War on Terror", and the Developing World', *Journal of International Development*, 18(1), pp. 69–85.

Pryce-Jones, David. 1995. *The Strange Death of the Soviet Empire*. New York: Metropolitan Books.

Said, Edward. 1979. *Orientalism,* NY: Vintage Books.

Sen, K. and T. Morris. 2008. *Civil Society and the War on Terror.* Oxford: INTRAC.

Simons, Geoff. 1998. *Saudi Arabia: The Shape of Client Feudalism.* Palgrave Macmillan.

Spector, Ronald H. 1985. *Eagle against the Sun: The American War with Japan.* New York: Vintage.

Speer, Albert. 1985. *Inside the Third Reich.* Translated by R. Winston and C. Winston. NY: Macmillan.

Steiner, Zara S. 1977. *Britain and the Origin of the First World War.* New York: St Martin's Press.

Walzer, Michael. 1977. *Just and Unjust Wars: A Moral Argument with Historical Illustrations.* New York: Harper Collins.

Williamson, Samuel. 1969. *The Politics of Grand Strategy: Britain and France Prepare for War, 1904–1914.* Cambridge: Harvard University Press.

Zunes, Stephen. 2003. *Tinderbox: US Middle East Policy and the Roots of Terrorism.* Monroe, ME: Common Courage Press.

# WAR AND INTERNATIONAL LAW

Arend, Anthony C., and Robert J. Beck. 1993. *International Law and the Use of Force: Beyond the UN Charter Paradigm.* New York: Routledge.

Bes, Geoffrey. 1994. *War and Law since 1945.* Oxford: Clarendon Press.

Dinstein, Yoram. 1994. *War, Aggression and Self-defence.* Cambridge: Cambridge University Press.

Hayner, Priscilla B. 2001. *Unspeakable Truths: Confronting State Terror and Atrocity.* New York: Routledge.

Howell, J., and J. Lind. 2009. *Counter-Terrorism, Aid and Civil Society: Before and After the War on Terror.* Basingstoke: Palgrave.

Kalshoven, Frits and Liesbeth Zegveld. 2000. *Constraints in the Waging of War: An Introduction to International Humanitarian Law.* Geneva: ICRC.

Normand, Roger and Chris A. F. Jochnick. 1994. 'The Legitimation of Violence: A Critical Analysis of the Gulf War', *Harvard International Law Journal,* Vol. 35 (Spring).

Shawcross, William. 2000. *Deliver us from Evil: Warlords and Peacekeepers in a World of Endless Conflict.* London: Bloomsbury.

———. 2002. 'The Impact on International Law of a Decade of Measures Against Iraq, (A US–EU dialogue co-sponsored by the University of Michigan)', *European Journal of International Law,* vol. 13 (1).

# THE GULF, CENTRAL ASIA AND OIL POLITICS

Abukhalil, Assad. 2004. *The Battle for Saudi Arabia: Fundamentalism and Global Power.* New York: Seven Stories Press.

Aburish, Said K. 1988. *A Brutal Friendship: The West and the Arab Elite.* London: Indigo.

Anderson, Irvine H. 1981. *Aramco, the United States and Saudi Arabia, 1933–1950.* Princeton: Princeton University Press.

Holden, David and Richard Johns. 1981. *The House of Saud.* London: Sidgwick & Jackson.

Ferrier, R.W. 1982. *The History of the British Petroleum Company* (Vol. 1 & 2). Cambridge: Cambridge University Press.

Hayes, Peter. 1987. *Industry and Ideology: I. G. Farben in the Nazi Era,* Cambridge: Cambridge University Press.

Heikal, Mohamed. 1992. *Illusions of Triumph: Arab View of the Gulf War.* London: Harper Collins.

Giddens, Paul H. 1938. *The Birth of Oil Industry.* New York: MacMillan.

Gulbekian, Nurbar. 1965. *Portrait in Oil.* New York: Simon and Schuster.

Jones, Geoffrey. 1981. *The State and the Emergence of the British Oil Industry.* London: MacMillan.

Kent, Marian. 1976. *Oil and Empire: British Policy and Mesopotamian Oil, 1900–1920.* London: Macmillan.

Longhurst, Henry. 1959. *Adventures in Oil: The Story of British Petroleum.* London: Sidgwick and Jackson.

———. 1968. *Oil in the Middle East: Its Discovery and Development.* Oxford: Oxford University Press.

Mejcher, Helmut. 1976. *Imperial Quest for Oil: Iraq, 1910–1928.* London: Ithaca Press.

Painter, David. 1990. *Oil and the American Century: The Political Economy of US Foreign Oil Policy, 1941–1954.* Baltimore: John Hopkins University Press.

Rashid, Ahmed. 2001. *Taliban: Islam, Oil and the New Great Game in Central Asia.* London: I.B. Tauris.

Salinger, Pierre and Eric Laurent. 1991. *Secret Dossier: The Hidden Agenda Behind the Gulf War.* New York: Penguin Books.

Sifry, Micah L., and Christopher Cerf (eds.). 1991. *The Gulf War Reader: History, Documents, Opinions.* London: Times Books/Random House.

Skogstad, Anne. 1950. *Petroleum Industry of Germany during the War.* Santa Monica: Rand Corporation.

Stivers, William. 1982. *Supremacy and Oil: Iraq, Turkey, and the Anglo-American World Order, 1918–1930.* Ithaca: Cornell University Press.

Yergin, Daniel. 1992. *The Prize: The Epic Quest for Oil, Money and Power.* New York: Free Press.

# LEBANON

Ajami, Fouad. 1986. *The Vanished Imam: Musa al-Sadr and the Shia of Lebanon.* Ithaca, NY and London: Cornell University Press.

Blanford, Nicholas. 2006. *Killing Mr Lebanon: The Assassination of Rafiq Hariri and its Impact on the Middle East.* London: I.B. Tauris.

Fisk, Robert. 1991. *Pity the Nation.* Oxford: Oxford University Press.

Ghorayeb, Amal S. 2001. *Hizbullah, Politics and Religion.* London: Pluto Press.

Hanf, Theodor. 1996. *Coexistence in Wartime Lebanon: Decline of a State and Rise of a Nation.* London and New York: Center for Lebanese Studies and I.B. Tauris.

Kapeliouk, Ammon. *1982.* Sabra et Chatila: Enquete sur un Massacre. *Paris: Seuil.*

Khoury, Gérard D. 1993. *La France et L'Orient Arabe: Naissance du Liban Moderne 1914–1920.* Paris: Armand Colin.

Randall, Jonathan. 1984. *Going All the Way: Christian Warlords, Israeli Adventurers and the War in Lebanon.* New York: Random House.

Salibi, Kamal. 1988. *A House of Many Mansions: The History of Lebanon Reconsidered.* Berkeley: University of California Press.

Traboulsi, Fawwaz. 2007. *A History of Modern Lebanon.* London: Pluto Press.

# IRAQ

Ali, Tariq. 2003. *Bush in Babylon: The Recolonization of Iraq.* London: Verso.

Bullock John and Morris Harvey. 1989. *The Gulf War: Its Origin, History, and Consequences.* London: Methuen.

Cockburn, Andrew and Patrick Cockburn. 2000. *Out of the Ashes: The Resurrection of Saddam Hussein.* New York: HarperCollins. (UK titled, *Saddam Hussein: An American Obsession*).

Cockburn, Patrick. 2006. *The Occupation: War and Resistance in Iraq.* London, New York: Verso.

Heikal, Mohamed. 1992. *Illusions of Triumph: An Arab View of the Gulf War.* London: Harper Collins.

Hiro, Dilip. 2000. *Iraq in the Eye of the Storm.* New York: Nation Books.

Jacob, Satish. 2003. *From Hotel Palestine Baghdad: Pages from a War Diary.* New Delhi: Roli Books.

Khadduri, M., and E. Ghareeb. 1997. *War in the Gulf, 1990–1991: The Iraq–Kuwait Conflict and its Implications.* Oxford: Oxford University Press.

Normand, Roger and Chris A. Jocknick. 1994. 'The Legitimation of Violence: A Critical Analysis of the Gulf War', *Harvard International Law Journal*, Vol. 35.

Middle East Watch. 1990. *Human Rights in Iraq*. Yale University Press.

Putter, Scott and William R. Pitt. 2002. *War on Iraq: What Team Bush Doesn't Want You to Know*. London: Profile Books.

Rampton, Sheldon and John Stauber. 2003. *Weapons of Mass Deception: The Uses of Propaganda in Bush's War on Iraq*. London: Constable Robinson.

Simons, Geoff. 1998. *The Scourging of Iraq: Sanctions, Law and Natural Justice*. London: Macmillan Press.

Winstone, H.V.F. 2004. *Gertrude Bell*. London: Barzan Publishing.

UNICEF, *Child Mortality: Iraq, Current Estimates, 1999*, available online at https://docs.google.com/document/d/1aIOqVuWirC-hXO2e9F0gSXCbJckD-WYCYqFHix6eHDs/edit?pli=1

# IRAN

Abrahamian, Ervand. 1982. *Iran Between Two Revolutions*. Princeton: Princeton University Press.

Bill, J.A., and W.R. Louis (eds). 1988. *Mosadiq, Iranian Nationalism, and Oil*. London: I.B. Tauris.

Roosevelt, Kermit. 1979. *Countercoup: The Struggle for the Control of Iran*. New York: McGraw-Hill.

Rubin, Barry. 1984. *Paved with Good Intentions: The American Experience in Iran*. New York: Penguin.

Zabih, Sepehr. 1982. *The Mossadegh Era: Roots of the Iranian Revolution*. Chicago: Lake View Press.

# SYRIA

Dam, Nikolaos Van. 1996. *The Struggle for Power in Syria: Politics and Society under Assad and the Baath Party*. London: I.B. Tauris.

Little, Douglas. 1990. 'Cold War and Covert Action: The US and Syria, 1945–1958', *Middle East Journal*, vol. 44, (1, Winter).

Longrigg, Stephen H. 1958. *Syria and Lebanon under French Mandate*. London: Royal Institute of International Affairs. Reprinted in Beirut: Librairie du Liban, 1968.

# PALESTINE

Aburish, Said K. 1998. *Arafat: from Defender to Dictator.* London: Bloomsbury.

Aruri, Nasser (ed.). 2001. *Palestinian Refugees: The Right of Return.* London: Pluto Press.

Ashrawi, Hanan. 1995. *This Side of Peace: A Personal Account.* New York: Simon & Schuster.

B'TSELEM (The Israeli Information Center for Human Rights in the Occupied Territories). 1992. 'Activity of the Undercover Units in the Occupied Territories'. Available online at http://www.btselem.org/publications/summaries/199205_undercover_units

Cook, Jonathan. 2008. *Disappearing Palestine: Israel's Experiments in Human Despair.* London: Zed Books.

Said, Edward. 1994. *The Politics of Dispossession: The Struggle for Palestinian Self-Determination 1969–1994.* London: Chatto & Windus.

Schlaim, Avi. 1990. *The Politics of Partition: King Abdullah, The Zionists and Palestine 1921–1951.* Oxford: Oxford University Press.

Zureik, Elia. 1978. *The Palestinians in Israel.* London: Routledge.

# ISRAEL

Biemann, Asher D. (ed.). 2002. *The Martin Buber Reader.* Palgrave, Macmillan.

Charney, Israel. 1999. *Encyclopaedia of Genocide* (2 vols). Santa Barbara: ABC–Clio.

Hersh, Seymour. 1991. *The Samson Option: Israel, America and the Bomb.* London: Faber & Faber.

Herzl, Theodor. 1956. *The Jewish State.* Tel Aviv: Newman.

Kalmar, Ivan D., and Derek J. Penslar. 2004. *Orientalism and the Jews.* Waltham: Brandeis University Press.

Khalidi, Walid. 1988. 'Plan Dalet: Master Plan for the Conquest of Palestine', *Journal of Palestine Studies,* Vol. 69 (Autumn).

Lustick, Ian. 1980. *Arabs in the Jewish State: Israeli Control of a National Minority.* University of Texas Press.

Mari, Sami. 1978. *Arab Education in Israel.* Syracuse University Press.

Morris, Benny. 1989. *The Birth of the Palestinian Refugee Problem.* Cambridge: Cambridge University Press.

Neslen, Arthur. 2006. *Occupied Minds: A Journey through the Israeli Psyche.* London: Pluto Press.

318    *Martyred but Not Tamed*

Orr, Akiva. 1982. *The Unjewish State*. London: Ithaca Press.
Sachar, Howard M. 1996. *A History of Israel*. New York: Knopf.
Segev, Tom and Arlen N. WEINSTEIN. 1998. *1949: The First Israelis*. New York: Owl Books.
Shahak, Israel. 1994. *Jewish History, Jewish Religion: The Weight of Three Thousand Years*. London: Pluto Press.

# Name Index

Full consistency being impossible to achieve in the transliteration of Arabic names, we have opted for simplicity and conformed with current journalistic usage This meant dropping nearly all **hamza** marks (glottal stop), conflating the two **h** sounds, leaving vowel length unmarked etc. In all cases when the spelling fluctuates, preference was given to the vowels **i/u** over e/o, which are absent from the Arabic phoneme system (thus *Hafiz, Umar* rather than *Hafez, Omar*). However, when a spelling was well-established, we respected it (thus *sheikh* rather than *shaykh, G. abdel Nasser* rather than *G. abd al-Nassir*) Lastly, all Arabic names of the form **al/ibn/bin/bint/abu-XYZ** and all Western names of the form **de/O'/Mc/Mac-XYZ** are systematically listed under **XYZ**.

# Subject Index

# About the Author

The late **Ram Narayan Kumar** (1956–2009) was an independent political activist and thinker, based out of Delhi and Kathmandu.

He authored half a dozen books: three major works on Punjab (mainly 'The Sikh Struggle' and 'Reduced to Ashes'), a mid-life political autobiography ('Confronting the Hindu Sphinx'), and a volume on human rights studies. He also wrote numerous pamphlets, situation reports, and newspaper columns. He also led courses on Human Rights at SAFHR (an NGO with headquarters in Delhi and Kathmandu) for participants from all over South Asia.

Kumar's work was close to completion when he succumbed to a sudden heart attack, in June 2009, in Kathmandu. His relatives and closest collaborators then decided to entrust Professor Jean Ecalle, a long-time friend of Kumar's (who had closely followed the book project and regularly discussed Middle Eastern politics with the author) with the task of putting the final touches to the manuscript.

Professor Ecalle has written the foreword to the book and also has provided a much-needed Afterword.